UNITED NATIONS CONFERENCE ON TRADE AND DEVELOPMENT
GENEVA

TRADE AND DEVELOPMENT REPORT, 2011

Report by the secretariat of the
United Nations Conference on Trade and Development

UNITED NATIONS
New York and Geneva, 2011

Note

- Symbols of United Nations documents are composed of capital letters combined with figures. Mention of such a symbol indicates a reference to a United Nations document.

- The designations employed and the presentation of the material in this publication do not imply the expression of any opinion whatsoever on the part of the Secretariat of the United Nations concerning the legal status of any country, territory, city or area, or of its authorities, or concerning the delimitation of its frontiers or boundaries.

- Material in this publication may be freely quoted or reprinted, but acknowledgement is requested, together with a reference to the document number. A copy of the publication containing the quotation or reprint should be sent to the UNCTAD secretariat.

UNCTAD/TDR/2011

UNITED NATIONS PUBLICATION

Sales No. E.11.II.D.3

ISBN 978-92-1-112822-2
eISBN 978-92-1-054816-8
ISSN 0255-4607

Contents

List of tables

List of boxes

List of charts

Classification by country or commodity group

The classification of countries in this *Report* has been adopted solely for the purposes of statistical or analytical convenience and does not necessarily imply any judgement concerning the stage of development of a particular country or area.

The major country groupings used in this *Report* follow the classification by the United Nations Statistical Office (UNSO). They are distinguished as:

» Developed or industrial(ized) countries: the countries members of the OECD (other than Mexico, the Republic of Korea and Turkey) plus the new EU member countries and Israel.

» Transition economies refers to South-East Europe and the Commonwealth of Independent States (CIS).

» Developing countries: all countries, territories or areas not specified above.

The terms "country" / "economy" refer, as appropriate, also to territories or areas.

References to "Latin America" in the text or tables include the Caribbean countries unless otherwise indicated.

References to "sub-Saharan Africa" in the text or tables include South Africa unless otherwise indicated.

For statistical purposes, regional groupings and classifications by commodity group used in this *Report* follow generally those employed in the *UNCTAD Handbook of Statistics 2010* (United Nations publication, sales no. B.10.II.D.1) unless otherwise stated. The data for China do not include those for Hong Kong Special Administrative Region (Hong Kong SAR), Macao Special Administrative Region (Macao SAR) and Taiwan Province of China.

Other notes

References in the text to *TDR* are to the *Trade and Development Report* (of a particular year). For example, *TDR 2010* refers to *Trade and Development Report, 2010* (United Nations publication, sales no. E.10.II.D.3).

The term "dollar" ($) refers to United States dollars, unless otherwise stated.

The term "billion" signifies 1,000 million.

The term "tons" refers to metric tons.

Annual rates of growth and change refer to compound rates.

Exports are valued FOB and imports CIF, unless otherwise specified.

Use of a dash (–) between dates representing years, e.g. 1988–1990, signifies the full period involved, including the initial and final years.

An oblique stroke (/) between two years, e.g. 2000/01, signifies a fiscal or crop year.

A dot (.) indicates that the item is not applicable.

Two dots (..) indicate that the data are not available, or are not separately reported.

A dash (-) or a zero (0) indicates that the amount is nil or negligible.

Decimals and percentages do not necessarily add up to totals because of rounding.

Abbreviations

BIS	Bank for International Settlements
CAC	collective action clause
CFTC	Commodity Futures Trading Commission
CIT	commodity index trader
CIS	Commonwealth of Independent States
CPI	consumer price index
DJ-UBSCI	Dow Jones-UBS Commodity Index
EC-AMECO	European Commission Annual Macro-economic database
EMH	efficient market hypothesis
EMS	European Monetary System
EMU	Economic and Monetary Union
ERM	European Exchange Rate Mechanism
ETF	exchange traded fund
ETN	exchange traded note
EU	European Union
FAO	Food and Agriculture Organization of the United Nations
FDIC	Federal Deposit Insurance Corporation
FSB	Financial Stability Board
GATS	General Agreement on Trade in Services
GDP	gross domestic product
HFT	high frequency trading
IEA	International Energy Agency
IMF	International Monetary Fund
IOSCO	International Organization of Securities Commissions
LLR	lender of last resort
OECD	Organisation for Economic Co-operation and Development
OPEC	Organization of the Petroleum Exporting Countries
OTC	over the counter
PMPU	producers, merchants, processors, users
PPP	purchasing power parity
REER	real effective exchange rate
S&P GSCI	Standard and Poor's Goldman Sachs Commodity Index
SDRM	sovereign debt restructuring mechanism
SIFI	systemically important financial institution
TDR	Trade and Development Report
UIP	uncovered interest rate parity
ULC	unit labour cost
UNCTAD	United Nations Conference on Trade and Development
USDA	United States Department of Agriculture
WTO	World Trade Organization

OVERVIEW

Economic integration and interdependence in the world today have reached an unprecedented level. As a result, the globalized economy cannot function for the benefit of all without international solidarity and cooperation. This was highlighted by the global financial and economic crisis that followed the collapse of big financial institutions, and it has underlined the need for developing approaches to new forms of global collaboration. The G-20, which has become a leading forum for international economic cooperation, successfully coordinated an immediate policy response to the crisis, or "Great Recession" as it is now called. Coordinated monetary policy easing by leading central banks marked the first step, with most members of the G-20 launching large fiscal stimulus packages as well as emergency support programmes to restore financial stability. The aggregate impact of these measures stopped the economic freefall and won policymakers an important first round in battling the crisis. However, despite intense discussions, little progress, if any, has been achieved in major areas that were also of concern to the G-20. These include financial regulation, inter alia for tackling problems related to the "financialization" of markets for many primary commodities, and, even more importantly, reform of the international monetary system for curbing volatile short-term capital flows that are driven mainly by currency speculation.

Meanwhile, global economic recovery has entered a renewed phase of fragility because a process of self-sustaining growth through private spending and employment is not assured, especially in developed countries. Many of these countries have shifted their fiscal policy stance from stimulus to retrenchment, which risks leading to prolonged stagnation, or even to a contraction of their economies. Given the lack of growth in employment and wages in Europe, Japan and the United States, their policies should aim at continued stimulation of their economies instead of trying to "regain the confidence of the financial markets" by prematurely cutting government spending. The main global risk is that wages and mass incomes might not increase sufficiently to feed a sustainable and globally balanced process of growth based on domestic demand. This indicates that the risk of higher inflation resulting from rising commodity prices is very small. Only very few countries that have strong growth and overshooting wage dynamics face inflation risks.

The recovery of commodity prices has helped developing countries maintain their growth momentum, but these prices are prone to considerable volatility as they are strongly influenced by the speculative activities of market participants motivated by purely financial considerations. And although growth in a number of large developing countries has come to rely more on domestic drivers than on exports, it remains vulnerable to adverse developments in the international financial system. In particular, these countries are exposed to short-term capital flows, which tend to exert an upward pressure on their currencies and damage their export industries. Thus developing countries are also facing considerable downside risks, and should aim at maintaining stable macroeconomic conditions domestically and containing external disruptions. As they progress along successful development paths, they need to make their voices better heard in the global debate on a new design of the international monetary and financial system.

The world economy is still struggling to recover from the worst recession since the Great Depression. Courageous, globally coordinated countercyclical policies succeeded in rescuing economies from the brink of collapse. Nevertheless, policymakers cannot afford to waste the opportunity for a more fundamental reorientation of policies and institutions. Strict regulation of the financial sector, orienting it more towards investment in fixed capital, is key to greater stability of the global economy and to its return to a sustainable growth path. This requires increased coherence between the multilateral trading system and the international monetary system. At the national and regional levels, there is a strong case for a reorientation of fiscal policy that takes into account the requirements of the overall macroeconomic situation rather than focusing exclusively on balancing budgets or on achieving rigid public deficit targets. However, unless there is a reversal of the current trend of diminished income expectations of the average household and a return to policies that emphasize the importance of mass income growth as the basis for sustainable and balanced development in rich and poor countries alike, all other attempts to regain growth momentum will be in vain.

Recovery of the world economy is slowing down, with strong downside risks

The pace of global recovery has been slowing down in 2011. Global GDP is expected to grow by 3.1 per cent, following an increase of 3.9 per cent in 2010. In many developed countries, the slowdown may even be accentuated in the course of the year as a result of government policies aimed at reducing public budget deficits or current-account deficits. In most developing countries, growth dynamics are still much stronger, driven mainly by domestic demand.

As the initial impulses from inventory cycles and fiscal stimulus programmes have gradually disappeared since mid-2010, they have revealed a fundamental weakness in the recovery process in developed economies. Private demand alone is not strong enough to maintain the momentum of recovery; domestic consumption remains weak owing to persistently high unemployment and slow or stagnant wage growth. Moreover, household indebtedness in several countries continues to be high, and banks are reluctant to provide new financing. In this situation, the shift towards fiscal and monetary tightening risks creating a prolonged period of mediocre growth, if not outright contraction, in developed economies.

In the United States, recovery has been stalling, with the pace of growth well below what is needed to make a significant dent in unemployment. Even the second round of quantitative easing has failed to translate into increased credit for domestic economic activities, as domestic demand has remained subdued due to stagnating wages and employment. With little scope to lower interest rates further – as they are already at historically low levels – and fiscal stimulus waning, a quick return to a satisfactory growth trajectory is highly unlikely. In Japan, recovery has been delayed by the impact of unprecedented supply-chain and energy disruptions due to the massive earthquake and tsunami in March. In the European Union, growth is set to remain below 2 per cent in 2011, although with significant variations among member countries. In Germany a revival of exports (particularly to Asia) and investment, together with rising public expenditures, resulted in a strong increase in economic activity in 2010 and early 2011, but, as in other developed economies, mass income remains very weak, as does domestic demand.

With the unresolved euro crisis, the reappearance of severe debt market stress in the second quarter of 2011 and the prospect of austerity measures spreading across Europe, there is a high risk that the eurozone will continue to act as a significant drag on global recovery. Austerity measures, as the main means of tackling the euro crisis without regard for regional domestic demand growth, may backfire badly. Crisis-hit countries in the euro area are labouring under extremely adverse conditions. They need low interest rates and a revival of growth, but instead, their growth dynamics are weak and market interest rates on public debt are prohibitively high.

Relatively fast growth in developing countries has relied more on domestic demand

Growth rates in developing countries are likely to remain much higher – at almost 6.5 per cent – than in the developed countries. In many developing countries, growth has been driven more by domestic demand than by exports. Emerging market economies (e.g. Brazil, India, South Africa and Turkey, among the G-20 members) have had to deal with the major challenge of short-term capital inflows, attracted by higher interest rates that reflect higher inflation rates or tight monetary policies. These inflows have been exerting enormous appreciation pressure on their domestic currencies, and tend to weaken their export sectors and widen their current-account deficits. In Brazil, the central bank intervened heavily in the currency market, but at the same time it also increased its policy interest rate further, even though it was already at a very high level in real terms, and the fiscal stance was tightened. The central bank of the Russian Federation had a similar response.

Expansion has remained strong in all developing regions, with the exception of North Africa and some countries in West Asia, where political unrest has adversely affected investment and tourism, and thus also growth. East, South and South-East Asia continue to record the highest GDP growth rates, although there is a tendency towards some slowdown, reflecting supply-chain effects from Japan, tighter monetary conditions and weak demand in some major export markets, notably Japan and the United States. In China, the contribution of net exports to GDP growth has declined, and fixed investment and private consumption are now the two major growth factors. Wage growth in China is an important element in reducing the reliance of the Chinese economy on exports, and thus the full participation of labour in the country's productivity gains is contributing effectively to a rebalancing of global demand.

In Latin America and the Caribbean, expansion continues to be robust. While the Brazilian economy is slowing down, Argentina and most Andean countries are set to record another year of rapid growth. In Mexico and most of the small Central American and Caribbean economies, growth will be much more modest, mainly owing to their dependence on exports to the United States. Sub-Saharan Africa is likely to keep growing at the same rapid pace as in 2010. As a result of terms-of-trade gains, investment in infrastructure and expansionary fiscal policies should promote economic growth in the subregion, and rapid development of the services sector will provide further impetus. However, GDP growth rates in sub-Saharan Africa are unlikely to contribute to significant poverty reduction in the near future, as economic improvements often fail to trickle down to the entire population.

In the transition economies, although growth rates are unlikely to equal that of the developing-country average, they have returned to their pre-crisis trend, and should increase considerably faster than those of developed countries.

Recovery of international trade and price volatility in commodity markets

International trade in both goods and services rebounded sharply in 2010, after having registered its steepest fall since the Second World War. The volume of international trade is expected to return to a single-digit growth rate in 2011, from 14 per cent in 2010, particularly in developed economies. Commodity prices recovered very early in the cycle and have been exhibiting high volatility, owing largely to the greater presence of financial investors in commodity markets.

Although the UNCTAD index for food prices in February 2011 exceeded the levels reached during the food crisis of 2007–2008, the food security situation appears to be less critical than at that time, owing to the relatively low prices of rice and a good harvest for grain crops in Africa in 2010. Moreover, most food-exporting countries refrained from imposing export restrictions, which had been a significant factor in the food crisis of 2007–2008. Nevertheless, the rise in food prices in 2010–2011 could have a serious impact on food security, made worse by the threat of famine in East Africa. It is again adding to extreme poverty, as the food import bill of the low-income, food-deficit countries is expected to increase by 27 per cent in 2011. Therefore, government measures to alleviate the impact on the poorest are needed.

To some extent, rising commodity prices are already contributing to the slowdown of overall activity in the consumer countries, because high prices are reducing purchasing power at a time when household incomes are being hit by high unemployment, slow wage growth and the debt deleveraging process, particularly in developed countries. If higher commodity prices lead to a widespread tightening of monetary policy worldwide, this could become a major threat to the recovery. The European Central Bank, for example, continues to take its cue from headline inflation, and has embarked on monetary tightening since April 2011. However, in view of the enormous labour market slack in the United States and Europe, where even nominal wages are barely growing, the risk of higher commodity prices triggering an inflationary spiral are negligible. Thus a restrictive monetary policy is not an appropriate measure against high commodity prices, which are primarily the result of external factors, mostly related to supply-side shocks and to the impact of financial markets.

Similarly, in emerging market economies, headline inflation is related less to overheating than to the fact that food and energy prices have a much greater weight in the consumer price indices of poorer countries compared with the developed countries. Under these circumstances, monetary tightening in the absence of overheating would appear to be largely misplaced, since second-round effects in most cases have been limited.

Slow wage growth is endangering the recovery

Wage income is the main driver of domestic demand in developed and emerging market economies. Therefore, wage growth is essential to recovery and sustainable growth. However, in most developed countries, the chances of wage growth contributing significantly to, or leading, the recovery are slim. Worse still, in addition to the risks inherent in premature fiscal consolidation, there is a heightened threat in many countries that downward pressure on wages may be accentuated, which would further dampen private consumption expenditure. In many developing and emerging market economies, particularly China, the recovery has been driven by rising wages and social transfers, with a concomitant expansion of domestic demand. However, as developed countries remain important export destinations, subdued growth in those markets, combined with upward pressures on developing countries' currencies, poses the risk of pressures for relative wage compression in developing countries as well.

Wage growth that is falling short of productivity growth implies that domestic demand is growing at a slower rate than potential supply. The emerging gap can be temporarily filled by relying on external demand or by stimulating domestic demand through credit easing and raising of asset prices. The global crisis has shown that neither solution is sustainable. The simultaneous pursuit of export-led growth strategies by many countries implies a race to the bottom with regard to wages, and has a deflationary bias. Moreover, if one country succeeds in generating a trade surplus, this implies that there will be trade deficits in other countries, causing trade imbalances and foreign indebtedness. If, on the other hand, overspending is enticed by easy credit and higher asset prices, as in the United States before the crisis, the bubble will burst at some point, with serious consequences for both the financial and real economy. Therefore, it is important that measures be taken to halt and reverse the unsustainable trends in income distribution.

The case for an incomes policy

Given the importance of consumption for boosting global demand, incomes policies in the biggest economies could contribute significantly to a balanced expansion, especially when the global recovery is still fragile. An essential element of such a policy is the adjustment of real wages in line with productivity, so that domestic consumption can rise in line with supply. This would also help prevent an increase in unit labour costs, and thus keep the main domestic source of inflation under control. Monetary policy could then reduce its focus on price stability and pay greater attention to securing low-cost finance for investment in real productive capacity, which in turn would create new employment opportunities. Wages rising at a rate that corresponds approximately to the rate of productivity growth, augmented by a target rate of inflation, is the best anchor for inflation expectations.

The current problems in the eurozone are largely the result of diverging wage increases in the member States. Since the creation of the eurozone, wages have risen faster than productivity and the official inflation target of the European Central Bank in some member States, and much less in others, causing considerable shifts in competitiveness. Unlike the emerging market economies in similar crisis situations in the past, the countries in the eurozone that have lost competitiveness and now face serious debt problems do not have the option of devaluing their currencies. Therefore, in addition to income transfers, an explicit policy of increasing wages in the surplus countries, particularly in Germany, to reduce the problems of falling competitiveness in the more crisis-hit countries is a crucial part of the solution.

A brief "Keynesian moment"

After many years of calls for a reduced role of the State in economic management, many governments in both developed and emerging market economies launched large stabilization packages to restore aggregate demand, and intervened in the rescue of the financial sector. Before the crisis, expansionary fiscal policies were often considered ineffective, on the grounds that any increase in the public sector deficit would be compensated by a concomitant downward adjustment in private expenditure. But as the impact of monetary policy was limited during the crisis, the orthodox concern with balanced budgets or short-term fiscal targets came to be ignored, and governments were again viewed as "buyers and borrowers of last resort".

However, recent developments in fiscal and monetary policy in many economies, and the recommendations of major international institutions such as the International Monetary Fund (IMF) and the Organisation for Economic Co-operation and Development (OECD), suggest that recognition of the need for fiscal stimulus during the crisis has not been followed up by a more profound rethinking of the principles of macroeconomic policy. In 2011, many governments have again reversed their policy orientation from one of fiscal expansion to fiscal tightening, and others are planning to do so. This is of particular concern since, in most developed economies that were severely hit by the financial crisis, the private sector has not yet completed the deleveraging process whereby non-financial agents try to reduce their indebtedness and banks try to restore their capital ratios. In such a debt-deflation process, even if monetary easing and low interest rates were to be continued, they could not be expected to have a major stimulating effect.

Those who support fiscal tightening argue that it is indispensable for restoring the confidence of financial markets, which is perceived as key to economic recovery. This is despite the almost universal recognition that the crisis was the result of financial market failure in the first place. It suggests that little has been learned about placing too much confidence in the judgement of financial market participants, including rating agencies, concerning the macroeconomic situation and the appropriateness of macroeconomic policies. In light of the irresponsible behaviour of many private financial market actors in the run-up to the crisis, and costly government intervention to prevent the collapse of the financial system, it is surprising that a large segment of public opinion and many policymakers are once again putting their trust in those same institutions to judge what constitutes correct macroeconomic management and sound public finances.

The strong fiscal impact of the crisis

The growing public debt has not been the result of imprudent fiscal policies. Before the crisis, between 2002 and 2007–2008, on a global scale fiscal balances had improved significantly, mainly as a result of strong increases in public revenues both in absolute terms and as a percentage of GDP. This was a by-product of a broad-based acceleration of output growth, and, in many primary-commodity-exporting countries, it was also a result of the price boom in international commodity markets. In addition, there was a widespread decline in the share of interest payments in public expenditure, largely due to lower real interest rates. Hence, many countries had substantial fiscal space when the crisis occurred.

The crisis caused a significant deterioration in public sector accounts as automatic stabilizers operated, which reduced revenues and increased expenditure, and fiscal stimulus packages were launched, many of them unprecedented in size. In many developing countries, fiscal accounts were also strongly affected by a sharp drop in commodity prices and higher interest rate spreads on the public debt. In several developed countries the deterioration of fiscal balances reflected public bailouts of ailing financial institutions, which to a large extent implied a conversion of private into public debt. In 2008 and 2009, government expenditure as a share of GDP increased in all regions, while government revenues declined. This decline was particularly steep in the African, West Asian and transition economies that rely heavily on the proceeds of primary commodity exports for their fiscal revenues, and it was more moderate in most economies of East and South Asia, and Latin America.

In developed countries, strong fiscal stimulus measures were particularly critical to counterbalance sharply shrinking private demand, since even extremely expansionary monetary measures were not particularly effective in an environment of massive private deleveraging. The United States implemented the largest stimulus package, both in nominal terms and as a percentage of GDP, followed by Japan and Germany. In the developed countries, about 40 per cent of the announced fiscal stimulus took the form of tax cuts. In several developing and transition economies, the size of the stimulus packages as a share of GDP exceeded that of developed economies, and there was a much greater emphasis on increased spending than on tax cuts.

The countercyclical policies and the recession led to a sudden jump in the public-debt-to-GDP ratio in developed countries. By the end of 2010 that ratio had risen to well above 60 per cent, surpassing the previous peak of 1998. In developing and emerging market economies, the ratio increased only moderately following a steep reduction in the previous years, so that it is now much lower than that of developed countries. However, there are substantial variations among the developing countries, and a number of low-income countries are still in debt distress.

Fiscal space is not a static variable

As current budget deficits and the stock of public debt have risen sharply in several countries, there is a widespread perception that the space for continued fiscal stimulus is already – or will soon be – exhausted, especially in developed countries. There is also a perception that in a number of countries debt ratios have reached, or are approaching, a level beyond which fiscal solvency is at risk.

However, fiscal space is a largely endogenous variable. A proactive fiscal policy will affect the fiscal balance by altering the macroeconomic situation through its impact on private sector incomes and the taxes perceived from those incomes. From a dynamic macroeconomic perspective, an appropriate expansionary fiscal policy can boost demand when private demand has been paralysed due to uncertainty about future income prospects and an unwillingness or inability on the part of private consumers and investors to incur debt.

In such a situation, a restrictive fiscal policy aimed at budget consolidation or reducing the public debt is unlikely to succeed, because a national economy does not function in the same way as an individual firm or household. The latter may be able to increase savings by cutting back spending because such a cutback does not affect its revenues. However, fiscal retrenchment, owing to its negative impact on aggregate demand and the tax base, will lead to lower fiscal revenues and therefore hamper fiscal consolidation. Since current expenditure can be difficult to adjust (because it is composed mainly of wages and entitlement programmes), fiscal retrenchment usually entails large cuts in public investment. This reduction in growth-promoting public expenditure may lead to a fall in the present value of future government revenues that is larger than the fiscal savings obtained by the retrenchment. The outcome could be an improvement in the immediate cash flow of the government, but with negative consequences for long-term fiscal and debt sustainability. Moreover, making balanced budgets or low public debt an end in itself can be detrimental to achieving other goals of economic policy, namely high employment and socially acceptable income distribution.

The failure to consider these dynamic effects was what led to disappointing outcomes for many countries that implemented fiscal tightening as part of IMF-supported programmes during the 1990s and 2000s. In countries where fiscal tightening was expected to reduce the budget deficit, that deficit actually became worse, often sizeably, due to falling GDP. In Indonesia in the late 1990s, for example, a GDP growth rate of 5 per cent was forecast, but in fact output shrunk by 13 per cent; in Thailand, instead of the expected 3.5 per cent GDP growth there was a 10.5 per cent contraction. Other countries shared similar experiences. The reason for what appears to have been a systematic miscalculation, leading "inevitably to fiscal under-performance", as the IMF's Independent Evaluation Office put it, was overoptimistic assumptions about the "crowding in" of private investment.

Another often neglected aspect of fiscal space is that the way in which the public sector spends and taxes is not neutral; changes in different types of revenue or expenditure generate different macroeconomic outcomes. In principle, an increase in spending on infrastructure, social transfers or targeted subsidies for private investors tends to be more effective for stimulating the economy than tax cuts, because it leads directly to increased purchases and demand. On the other hand, disposable incomes from reduced tax payments are likely to be spent only partially. This is particularly true when the private sector is highly indebted, since it would then use part of the tax proceeds for repaying outstanding debts rather than for consumption and investment. Increased social spending to support low-income groups seems to be a rational way to promote recovery, as it prevents their consumption from falling during a crisis and poverty from rising. If tax cuts are the preferred instrument, reductions of sales and value added taxes as well as income tax cuts for the lower income groups that have a higher propensity to spend are generally more effective in raising demand and national income than tax cuts for the higher income groups.

Determinants of public debt

High and rising public debt ratios are clearly a legitimate political concern, but like fiscal space, public deficit and debt limits are difficult to define, since they have strong interrelationships with other macroeconomic variables. Therefore, any attempt to identify a critical level of "sustainable" debt is a difficult task. Governments' economic policies and debt strategies have to take into account their specific circumstances and social needs as well as their external relationships.

Empirical evidence shows that, even though fiscal deficits and public debt constitute a relatively high proportion of GDP in some parts of the world today – especially in some developed countries – in many countries they are not large by historical standards. Moreover, it is not only the absolute stock of debt that matters for the sustainability of the public debt, but the relationship between that stock and some other key variables. These variables include, in addition to the primary fiscal balance, the average interest rate to be paid on the outstanding debt, the growth rate of the economy and the exchange rate. The latter strongly influences not only the domestic value of the foreign-currency-denominated debt, but also the demand for domestically produced goods.

Therefore, unsustainable public debt positions are not always the outcome of expansionary – or irresponsible – fiscal policies. Primary deficits caused by discretionary fiscal policies have even been found to contribute less to higher debt ratios than slower (or negative) GDP growth and banking and currency crises. Conversely, even if government budgets are in primary deficit, the public-debt-to-GDP ratio can be reduced, provided the nominal interest rate on public debt is lower than the growth rate of GDP. Thus, monetary policy plays an important role in determining the sustainability of the public debt. However, countries that have foreign-currency-denominated debt, or that do not have control over their own monetary policy, may experience sudden surges in borrowing costs during economic crises precisely when their ability to pay is limited. In developing countries, empirical evidence shows that contractionary efforts have not been particularly successful, and that, normally, debt sustainability has been achieved by promoting higher rates of economic growth.

The response to a crisis should depend on its cause. If a crisis originates from the bursting of an asset bubble, a more rational response would be financial reform, and even quite the opposite of fiscal retrenchment, namely countercyclical policies to absorb private sector deleveraging so as to reduce the macroeconomic slump created by asset deflation. If the crisis originates from overexposure to foreign creditors and excessive appreciation of the domestic currency, the appropriate response at the national level might be to improve the debt structure, as well as introduce policies aimed at avoiding misalignments of the real exchange rate and imposing controls on capital inflows.

Financial deregulation opened the door to excessive risk taking

The recent sharp increase in public sector deficits and public indebtedness is the result of a grave crisis in the financial system following a wave of financial liberalization, led by the so-called "Anglo-Saxon" economies. It is, therefore, somewhat ironic that the financial agents that caused the crisis should have become the judges of the suitability of public policies adopted to contain its damage. Financial liberalization and deregulation was based on a widespread belief in the greater efficiency of market forces, and it led to the creation of increasingly sophisticated financial instruments. Deregulation was in part a response to pressure from competitive forces in the financial sector, but it was also part of a generalized trend towards less government intervention in the economy. New financial instruments and continued liberalization in the financial system allowed speculative activities to expand significantly, so that gambling became an important and, at times dominant, feature of financial activities. This became a source of instability in many economies, and indeed, in the entire international economic system. By contrast, it is difficult to find any new financial instruments that have contributed to increasing the efficiency of financial intermediation for the benefit of long-term investment in real productive capacity.

Even when financial deregulation and current-account liberalization resulted in an increasing number of financial crises in both developed and developing countries, the strong belief that markets are the best judges of efficient factor allocation led policymakers to continue with financial deregulation. It took the global financial crisis to finally force a serious debate about the necessity for fundamental reforms to prevent similar crises in the future. Widespread consensus that deregulation was one of the main factors leading to the global financial and economic crisis led to calls for strengthening financial regulation and supervision.

Markets are important, but financial markets work differently

Financial markets do not function in the same way as typical markets for goods and services. While entrepreneurs participating in goods markets are concerned with the creation of new real assets that have the potential to improve productivity and increase all incomes in the future, financial market participants are primarily concerned with the effective use of information advantages concerning existing assets. In goods markets, price discovery is based on information from a multitude of independent agents who act according to their own individual preferences, and opportunities for profit arise from individual pioneering actions based on the private, circumstantial information of the market participants. By contrast, in financial markets, especially those for assets which fall in the same broad risk category (such as equities, emerging-market currencies, and more recently, commodities and their derivatives), price discovery is based on information related to a few, commonly observable events, or even on mathematical models that mainly use past – rather than only current – information for making price forecasts.

The fatal flaw in the functioning of financial markets lies in the fact that the most profitable activities are often derived from herd behaviour (i.e. following the trend for some time and disinvesting just before the rest of the crowd does). Acting against the majority, even if justified by accurate information about fundamentals, may result in large losses. Thus, whenever market participants "discover" that price trends in different markets provide an opportunity for "dynamic arbitrage" (i.e. investment in the probability of a continuation of the existing trend), and all bet on the same outcome, such as rising prices of real estate, equities or other assets, since the same information is available to all market participants, there is a strong tendency for herd behaviour. As a result, the herd acquires the market power to move those prices in the desired direction.

This is why prices in financial and "financialized" markets sometimes tend to overshoot, which gives rise to wrong prices for extended periods of time. As herding dominates the scene, no single participant questions whether the underlying information is correct or can be rationally related to events and developments in the real economy. This phenomenon has been observed not only in securities markets and markets for financial derivatives, but also in currency and commodity futures markets. Thus financial markets themselves have created most of the "fat tail" risks that have led to their collapse in financial crises. Uncertainty about the appropriate values of bank assets during such bubbles can become so high that no capital requirement or liquidity buffer can absorb the subsequent shock, so that governments have to step in with rescue packages.

Re-regulation of financial markets is indispensable

Over some 150 years of banking history, an implicit accord had emerged that in times of crises, governments, or central banks serving as "lender of last resort", would provide the necessary support to prevent the collapse of individual financial institutions and of the overall system. In return these institutions were subject to government regulation and supervision. There had always been a risk that events in the real economy, such as failure of a large debtor or a generalized recession, could generate difficulties in the financial sector. This became particularly evident during the Great Depression of the 1930s, as a consequence of which lender-of-last-resort functions were institutionalized, together with deposit insurance aimed at preventing bank runs.

However, with the trend towards deregulation of the financial system over the past three decades, the situation has been reversed: today, the financial sector has increasingly become a source of instability for the real sector. At the same time, official support for this sector has become more frequent and involves ever larger injections of public money. Financial markets were deregulated, despite frequent failures of those markets. Therefore, to protect the real sector of the economy from the negative spillover effects that are endogenously generated in the financial market itself, a considerable degree of official re-regulation is needed which would re-establish a proper balance between government protection of the financial sector and government regulation of financial institutions.

Because financial markets are so little understood, an unresolved issue is the systematic underestimation of risks that arise when all participants in a certain segment of the financial market move in the same direction through herd behaviour. This can result in so-called "tail risks", which, although occurring very rarely, when they do occur, the consequences can be catastrophic. The markets can only be stabilized if they no longer have the power to move prices in the wrong direction or to overshoot the fair value by a wide margin. Thus, systematic intervention by governments should become a legitimate tool to correct market failures.

The deregulation of financial markets has also allowed an increased concentration of banking activities in a small number of very big institutions, as well as a shift in bank funding, from a reliance on deposits to a greater reliance on capital markets, and from lending to trading. Moreover, it has paved the way for the development of a largely unregulated "shadow financial system", particularly in developed economies. By early 2008, the liabilities of that system were almost twice those of the traditional banking sector. By absorbing many of the newly created finance companies or money market funds, or by creating their own ones under the umbrella of bank holding companies, banks outsourced a large segment of their credit intermediation functions to associated companies in the shadow system. Some parts of this system (e.g. money market funds) played the same role as that of banks but with virtually no regulation, and the volume of activities of such groups has always been backed by too little capital.

Much of the systemic risk in the financial system has derived from the systemically important financial institutions. Proposals to address this "too-big-to-fail" problem have concentrated, so far, on additional capital requirements and improved supervision rather than on restructuring. A more comprehensive approach should also include a special resolution procedure in case of crises, which should not place a burden on government resources, and the introduction of size caps, which may be absolute or relative to GDP.

Towards a restructuring of the banking system

As the problem of mispricing is a systemic feature of financial markets, regulation should focus on the system, rather than on behaviour inside the system, with a view to ensuring that the system as a whole better serves real productive investment and growth in the real economy. A clear separation of deposit-taking institutions from those that are engaged in investment banking activities could help prevent gambling by commercial banks. This would also reduce the size and increase the diversity of banking institutions. Publicly owned banks could play a more important role, not only for development finance purposes, but also as an element of diversity and stability. These kinds of banks have turned out to be more resilient during crises, and they have partly compensated for the credit crunch in the private system caused by the recent crisis. They may also help promote competition in situations of oligopolistic private banking structures.

As the latest financial crisis was generated in the private financial sector, many of the arguments repeatedly advanced over the past few decades against publicly owned banks have further lost credibility. When the crisis struck, large banks in Europe and the United States were able to survive only because they benefited from public funds and guarantees. While during the boom period private institutions and individuals enjoyed large profits and bonuses, governments – or the taxpayers – have had to bear the downside risk during slumps. Therefore the point that only publicly owned banks enjoy an advantage through their access to public resources has been proven wrong. Moreover, the fact that these institutions are public entities reduces their incentive to engage in herd behaviour, exaggerated risk exposure and maximization of returns.

Growing financial speculation in primary commodity markets

Commodity prices have displayed considerable volatility over the past decade. The commodity price boom between 2002 and 2008 was the most pronounced in several decades – in magnitude, duration and breadth. The subsequent price decline following the eruption of the current global crisis in mid-2008 was notable both for its sharpness and for the number of commodities affected. Since mid-2009, and especially since the summer of 2010, global commodity prices have been rising again, though there was some flattening out in the first half of 2011.

Some observers consider broad-based changes in fundamental supply and demand relationships as the sole drivers of recent commodity price development. However, analyses are increasingly supporting the view that these fluctuations have also been influenced by the growing participation of financial investors in commodity trading for purely financial motives – a phenomenon often referred to as the "financialization of commodity trading".

While participation of financial actors in commodity markets is generally recognized as a normal feature of the market, a crucial question is the size of the financial flows and that they drive prices away from fundamentals and/or increase their volatility. In general, their participation could be economically beneficial by making markets deeper and helping to accommodate the hedging needs of commercial users and reduce their hedging costs, but their herd behaviour destroys these benefits. Financial investors such as index funds do not promote liquidity in markets, which would bring diversity to those markets; most of them follow the same strategy by going long in the strong belief that prices on those markets will continue to rise in the foreseeable future. Such financialization of commodity markets has caused those markets to follow less the logic of a typical goods market and more that of financial markets where herd behaviour often dominates.

Herding in commodity markets can be irrational, based on what may be called "pseudo-signals" such as information related to other asset markets and the use of inflexible trading strategies, including momentum investment or positive feedback strategies. Such strategies assume that price developments of the past carry information on future price movements, giving rise, for example to trend chasing. This results in buying after prices rise and selling after prices fall, independently of any changes in fundamentals.

But herd behaviour can also be fully rational. Information-based herding, for example, refers to imitation when traders believe that they can glean information by observing the behaviour of other agents. In other words, investors converge in their behaviour because they ignore their private information signals. Position-taking based only on other peoples' previous actions will lead to price changes without any new information being introduced to the market. A sequence of such actions causes a snowball effect, which will eventually lead to self-sustaining asset price bubbles. Informational herding is most likely to occur in relatively opaque markets, such as in commodity trading.

Correlated movements on equity, commodity and currency markets

Identifying the extent to which financial investment has affected the level and volatility of commodity prices is challenging due to the limited transparency and level of disaggregation of existing data. However, there is evidence to support the view that financial investors have affected price dynamics in the short term. One such piece of evidence concerns the role of dramatic changes in financial positions in the oil market between February and May 2011. Another relates to strong correlations between commodity price movements and developments on equity and currency markets, which are known to have been exposed to speculation.

A comparison of commodity and equity price developments over various business cycles shows that those prices used to move in opposite directions during the early upswings of previous cycles. In contrast, there has been a remarkable synchronization of those price movements in the most recent cycle. This increased synchronization is surprising because of the very low level of capacity utilization in the wake of the "Great Recession" of 2008 and 2009, which meant very low demand for commodities. Despite this, commodity prices increased even before the recovery began in the second quarter of 2009 and kept growing in the two subsequent years, partly due to rising demand in emerging economies but also to a large extent because of purely financial operations. Consequently, two years later monetary policy has reacted, even though there is still a very low level of capacity utilization in developed economies. This points to another worrying aspect of the impact of financialization that has so far been underestimated, namely its capacity to inflict damage on the real economy as a result of sending the wrong signals for macroeconomic management.

Measures in response to commodity price instability

Short-term emergency measures are needed to prevent or mitigate the negative impact of adverse commodity price developments. At the same time it is necessary to devise ways of improving the functioning of commodity derivatives markets to enable those trading venues to better fulfil their role of providing reliable price signals to commodity producers and consumers, or at least prevent them from sending the wrong signals.

In light of the vital role of information in commodity price developments, a set of four policy responses to improve the functioning of those markets should be considered, especially for food and energy commodities. First, there should be greater transparency in physical markets through the provision of more timely and accurate information about commodities, such as spare capacity and global stock holdings for oil, and for agricultural commodities, areas under plantation, expected harvests, stocks and short-term demand forecast. This would allow commercial market participants to more easily assess current and future fundamental supply and demand relationships. Second, there needs to be a better flow of and access to information in commodity derivatives markets, especially regarding position-taking by different categories of market participants. This would further improve market transparency. In particular, measures designed to ensure reporting requirements for trading on European exchanges, similar to those enforced in United States exchanges, would considerably improve transparency of trading and discourage regulatory migration. Third, tighter regulation of financial market participants, such as setting position limits, could reduce financial investors' impacts on commodity markets. Proprietary trading by financial institutions that are involved in hedging transactions of their clients could be prohibited because of conflicts of interest. This requires finding the right balance between adopting overly restrictive regulation, which would impair the risk-transfer functions of commodity exchanges, and overly lax regulation, which would equally impair the basic functions of the exchanges.

Fourth, market surveillance authorities could be mandated to intervene directly in exchange trading on an *occasional* basis by buying or selling derivatives contracts with a view to averting price collapses or to deflating price bubbles. Such intervention could be considered a measure of last resort to address the occurrence of speculative bubbles if reforms aimed at achieving greater market transparency and tighter market regulation were either not in place or proved ineffective. While most of the trigger mechanism could be rules-based, and therefore predictable, such intervention would necessarily have some judgemental components. However, doubts have sometimes been raised about the ability of market authorities or government agencies to understand and follow the market. These are unfounded, because there is no reason why their understanding should be any different from that of other market participants; in markets that are prone to herd behaviour, they all have access to similar information. Moreover, contrary to the other market participants, an intervening authority would have no incentive to engage in any form of herd behaviour. Rather, it could break the informational cascades that underlie herd behaviour by announcing when it considers prices to be far out of line with fundamentals.

Exchange rates have become disconnected from macroeconomic fundamentals

The current debate on reform of the international monetary system has been dealing mainly with symptoms rather than with the main problems. The strong increase in foreign exchange reserves, the still hegemonic role of the dollar and destabilizing short-term capital inflows are mainly due to serious defects in the global exchange rate regime. Foreign exchange markets are under the dominant influence of financial market behaviour that is disconnected from macroeconomic fundamentals. This is a source of current-account imbalances, distortions in international factor allocation and additional uncertainty for all participants in international trade.

Even after the breakdown of the Bretton Woods system and the adoption of widespread exchange rate floating in 1973, international economic policy-making has often assumed that it is mainly real shocks, rather than monetary shocks, that need to be tackled by the international system. However, after several decades of experience it has become clear that monetary shocks, particularly in a system of flexible exchange rates, are much more significant and harmful. Whereas the international exchange of goods and services is subject to the rules and disciplines of the multilateral trading system, the absence of an international monetary system allows individual countries autonomy in their exchange rate policies, even when such policies have adverse impacts on the global economy by creating financial booms and busts and distortions in international trade.

Exchange rate developments that diverge from those that would be warranted on the basis of fundamentals can be attributed to two major factors: either significant cross-country differences in the evolution of unit labour costs in the context of a regime where nominal exchange rates are not flexible enough, or excessive short-term capital inflows that lead to an appreciation of an overly flexible nominal exchange rate. In a situation where unit labour costs vary among countries, because of differences in the growth of wages relative to productivity, exchange rate adjustments are necessary to prevent the build-up of trade imbalances arising from a shift in competitiveness among countries. Not all current-account disequilibria are due to misaligned exchange rates. However, deviations of the real exchange rate from fundamentals, especially if persisting over long periods, have a major impact on the international competitiveness of producers, particularly of manufacturers of any country, and thus on the pattern of international trade and trade balances.

On the other hand, deviations of exchange rates from what would be warranted by economic fundamentals can also arise from the impact of private short-term capital flows that are attracted by positive interest rate differentials. In such cases, the exchange rate of a country with higher interest rates – reflecting a higher rate of inflation or tight monetary policy – appreciates, although the macroeconomic conditions would require a depreciation. Once the underlying interest rate differential narrows or disappears completely, or in a situation of crisis, the earlier appreciation is typically followed by an overshooting currency depreciation that is again out of line with fundamentals.

Redesigning the exchange rate system

In the current non-system, individual countries have tried to find temporary and pragmatic solutions to the problems of over- or undervaluation. One solution is unilateral intervention in the currency markets, even on a daily basis; another is capital controls or the taxation of inflows of hot money. All of these measures are justified in an environment where there is still a belief that, in principle, "the market" is able to find the right exchange rates. However, they do not solve the most urgent problem, that of applying the "categorical imperative" of international exchange by finding the international value of the currency of one country which all its trading partners can accept.

A better design of the global exchange rate system has to ensure that private financial actors, whose behaviour is often driven by purely speculative considerations and herding, do not exert excessive influence on the determination of exchange rates, and thus on the competitiveness of producers of different countries in international trade. Governments and central banks need to take the initiative by targeting exchange rates and ensuring that deviations from those targets are minimal and temporary.

A system of exchange rate management that helps prevent trade distortions and serves as a source of stability in international financial relations would need to include rules that provide: (a) sufficient stability of the real exchange rate (the most comprehensive measure of competitiveness) to enhance international trade and facilitate decision-making on fixed investment in the tradable sector, and (b) sufficient flexibility of the exchange rate to accommodate differences in the development of interest rates across countries.

Rules-based managed floating to curb speculation

Greater stability of the real exchange rate could be achieved by a system of rules-based managed floating. In principle, such a regime may be regarded as a dynamic version of the Bretton Woods system, which was based on the rule of fixed but adjustable nominal exchange rates. Like the Bretton Woods system, it would aim at avoiding fundamental balance-of-payments disequilibria; but unlike that system, it would rely on continuous adjustments of the nominal exchange rate along a path based on purchasing power parity (PPP) or uncovered interest rate parity (UIP). In order to achieve greater stability of the real exchange rate, the nominal exchange rate would be adjusted according to divergences in the evolution of consumer prices or unit labour costs in the first case, or to differences in short-term interest rates in the second.

Exchange rate management based on such a system would remove the incentives for speculation of the carry-trade type. Thus, short-term capital movements that have no linkages with trade or real investment, but are entirely motivated by expectations of profits from interest rate arbitrage across currencies and subsequent exchange rate appreciation of the target currency, would disappear.

Over the medium term, a strategy of managed floating based on a UIP rule is not very different from a strategy that targets the exchange rate based on a PPP path. In a UIP-based system, the nominal exchange rate would depreciate whenever a positive interest rate differential arose, and would thus cancel any gain that could be had from the interest rate differential. It has the advantage of directly dealing with financial markets. These markets are more sensitive to UIP deviations than goods markets, which react to PPP deviations. The UIP rule also has the advantage that UIP can be identified at very short notice, and on the basis of official interest rates rather than statistical measurements. However, it may be difficult to apply in situations of very large interest rate differentials, because the required adjustments of the nominal exchange rate would cause significant increases in import prices and a sharp rise in the domestic currency value of the external private and public debt. In this case, applying the PPP rule based on unit labour cost might be the more appropriate solution. Under this rule, the nominal exchange rate would be depreciated by an amount determined by the differential in unit labour costs, thereby neutralizing its impact on international competitiveness.

The concrete terms of a system of rules-based exchange rate management would need to be discussed and elaborated further. The problem of how to determine the level and allowable range of nominal exchange rate changes at the outset would have to be resolved. This would require a detailed investigation into the purchasing power of all currencies. Countries could also approach the starting exchange rate of such a system by making discrete parity adjustments before engaging in the rules-based managed floating strategy.

The need for symmetric intervention

In a system of rules-based managed floating along these lines, central banks would gain a degree of freedom in setting domestic short-term interest rates in line with domestic macroeconomic objectives. At the same time, its implementation would be considerably facilitated if the policy to control inflation were to rely mainly on an incomes policy that aims to check inflationary pressures instead of on a monetary policy.

To some extent, rules-based managed floating can be practiced as a unilateral exchange rate strategy. If a country is faced with the problem of short-term capital inflows generating appreciation pressure on its currency, this strategy could be applied without quantitative limitations, and without entailing operating costs for its central bank. However, when faced with the problem of capital outflows, there are limits to the extent of central bank intervention, which, in the absence of appropriate support from international financial institutions, are determined by the amount of its foreign exchange reserves. In this case, symmetric intervention by one or more countries whose currencies tend to appreciate as a counterpart to the first country's currency depreciation pressure will be necessary to make the system work. Therefore, the next best solution would be the application of the system through bilateral agreements or as a key element of regional monetary cooperation. The greatest benefit for international financial stability would result from the rules for managed floating being applied multilaterally as part of global financial governance.

Towards greater efficiency of international goods markets

The principle of rules-based managed floating should not be contentious, although the concrete terms and details need to be worked out. It would make the international markets for goods and services more efficient by preventing international financial markets from creating serious distortions in international trade relations. It acknowledges that financial markets do not function in the same way as goods markets, and are therefore more prone to herd behaviour that can lead to over- and undershooting of the fair value of currencies. The frequent argument that governments cannot know the correct value of a currency better than markets has been refuted by the performance of financial markets, which have consistently failed to find the right values.

In any case, if currency appreciation as a result of speculative capital flows could be avoided by the system in the first place, the risk of a speculative attack that could subsequently lead to depreciation pressure would be much smaller. This would also reduce the need for central banks to accumulate foreign exchange reserves for precautionary reasons, and therefore the need for symmetrical intervention altogether. Nevertheless, should such a situation arise, the use of capital controls as a supplementary measure should be welcomed by the international community as another line of defence, since predictable exchange rates are at least as important for the functioning of the international trading system as multilaterally agreed trade rules.

The reform agenda in the wake of the global financial crisis is far from being completed. It has advanced slowly, and much of the enthusiasm for reform has waned. There is a very real risk of new crises erupting, and, in a highly integrated and excessively financialized world economy, such crises would not be limited to specific segments of the financial system or to specific countries or regions. Even if a crisis has its origin in developed countries and their complex financial markets, developing countries and emerging market economies will also be affected, as evidenced by the latest crisis. The G-20 has recognized this fact, but actions by the G-20 alone are not enough. The world economy as a whole is faced with serious and fundamental challenges, such as eliminating poverty and the transition to more climate-friendly patterns of production and consumption. To tackle these challenges successfully, all the other countries in the world need to participate, sooner or later, in the process of finding solutions. These include creating a stable macroeconomic environment that encourages an appropriate level of investment in fixed capital, which is needed for supporting the necessary structural change. Therefore it remains imperative for the international community and its institutions to address the unfinished elements in the global reform agenda more vigorously than has been done so far.

Supachai Panitchpakdi
Secretary-General of UNCTAD

Chapter I

CURRENT TRENDS AND ISSUES IN THE WORLD ECONOMY

A. Recent trends in the world economy

1. Global growth

The pace of global economic recovery has been slowing down in 2011, following a rebound from its nosedive worldwide in 2009. This year, world gross domestic product (GDP) is expected to grow by 3.1 per cent, compared with 3.9 per cent in 2010. Although the economic slowdown will affect developed and developing countries alike, growth rates will remain much higher in the developing economies (at close to 6.3 per cent) than in the developed ones (at around 1.8 per cent), while the transition economies of the Commonwealth of Independent States are set to grow at an intermediate rate of close to 4.5 per cent (table 1.1). This continues the "two-speed recovery" witnessed in 2010, and the more rapid growth rates of all developing regions since 2003 compared with that of developed countries. More importantly, it may be indicative of some specific obstacles to an economic revival in the developed countries that are not affecting most developing countries.

As forecast in the *Trade and Development Report 2010*, inventory rebuilding and the fiscal stimulus programmes have been gradually ending since mid-2010. Hence, as the initial impulses from temporary factors are waning, the fundamental weakness of the recovery in developed economies has

become apparent, namely that the growth of private demand is not sufficiently strong to maintain the momentum of the upturn. This is partly due to the persistently high levels of household indebtedness in several countries, and the reluctance on the part of banks to provide new credit. But a major reason is that consumers do not expect their incomes to rise consistently over the medium term. In Europe, Japan and the United States, the current recovery is characterized not only by jobless growth – a feature common to previous recoveries – but also by stagnating wages, which hitherto had been a phenomenon observed mainly in Japan. Unemployment remains high and is dragging down wage growth. This effect is compounded by more flexible labour markets, and could reach a point where negative expectations of wage-earners could hinder the return to normal patterns of consumption, and consequently, of investment in fixed capital. Profits rebounded in the first phase of the recovery, as a result of the positive demand effects from government programmes, but developed economies lack the energy for sustainable expansion due to the continuing weak demand of wage-earners.

Another factor that could delay or endanger economic recovery is the implementation of tighter fiscal and monetary policies based on the questionable diagnosis that private-sector-led economic growth

Table 1.1

WORLD OUTPUT GROWTH, 2003–2011

(Annual percentage change)

Region/country	2003	2004	2005	2006	2007	2008	2009	2010	2011[a]
World	**2.7**	**4.1**	**3.6**	**4.1**	**4.0**	**1.7**	**-2.1**	**3.9**	**3.1**
Developed countries	**1.9**	**3.0**	**2.5**	**2.8**	**2.6**	**0.3**	**-3.6**	**2.5**	**1.8**
of which:									
Japan	1.4	2.7	1.9	2.0	2.4	-1.2	-6.3	4.0	-0.4
United States	2.5	3.6	3.0	2.6	2.1	0.4	-2.6	2.9	2.3
European Union (EU-27)	1.4	2.5	2.0	3.2	3.0	0.5	-4.2	1.8	1.9
of which:									
Euro area	0.8	2.2	1.7	3.1	2.8	0.5	-4.1	1.7	1.8
France	1.1	2.5	1.9	2.2	2.4	0.2	-2.6	1.5	2.1
Germany	-0.2	1.2	0.8	3.4	2.7	1.0	-4.7	3.6	3.0
Italy	0.0	1.5	0.7	2.0	1.5	-1.3	-5.0	1.0	0.9
United Kingdom	2.8	3.0	2.2	2.8	2.7	-0.1	-4.9	1.3	1.3
European Union (EU-12)[b]	4.3	5.5	4.7	6.5	6.2	4.0	-3.6	2.2	3.2
South-East Europe and CIS	**7.2**	**7.7**	**6.5**	**8.3**	**8.6**	**5.4**	**-6.7**	**4.1**	**4.4**
South-East Europe[c]	4.1	5.6	4.7	5.2	6.1	4.3	-3.7	0.5	2.2
CIS, incl. Georgia	7.6	7.9	6.7	8.7	8.8	5.5	-7.0	4.5	4.5
of which:									
Russian Federation	7.3	7.2	6.4	8.2	8.5	5.6	-7.9	4.0	4.4
Developing countries	**5.4**	**7.5**	**6.9**	**7.6**	**8.0**	**5.4**	**2.5**	**7.4**	**6.3**
Africa	5.2	8.0	5.3	6.0	5.9	5.4	1.8	4.4	3.5
North Africa, excl. Sudan	6.6	4.9	5.1	5.4	4.7	4.8	1.5	4.1	0.2
Sub-Saharan Africa, excl. South Africa	5.5	13.0	5.4	6.8	7.2	6.8	4.2	5.5	5.8
South Africa	2.9	4.6	5.3	5.6	5.5	3.7	-1.8	2.8	4.0
Latin America and the Caribbean	1.8	5.8	4.6	5.5	5.6	4.0	-2.2	5.9	4.7
Caribbean	3.0	3.7	7.5	9.4	5.9	3.0	0.3	3.3	3.4
Central America, excl. Mexico	3.8	4.2	4.8	6.5	7.1	4.3	-0.5	3.6	4.3
Mexico	1.4	4.1	3.3	4.8	3.4	1.5	-6.5	5.5	4.0
South America	1.9	6.9	5.1	5.5	6.7	5.3	-0.4	6.4	5.1
of which:									
Brazil	1.1	5.7	3.2	4.0	6.1	5.2	-0.6	7.5	4.0
Asia	6.9	8.1	8.1	8.7	9.1	5.8	4.2	8.3	7.2
East Asia	7.1	8.3	8.6	10.0	11.1	7.0	5.9	9.4	8.0
of which:									
China	10.0	10.1	11.3	12.7	14.2	9.6	9.1	10.3	9.4
South Asia	7.8	7.5	8.2	8.4	8.9	4.5	5.8	7.2	6.9
of which:									
India	8.4	8.3	9.3	9.4	9.6	5.1	7.0	8.6	8.1
South-East Asia	5.6	6.5	5.8	6.2	6.6	4.2	1.0	7.8	5.0
West Asia	6.3	9.4	7.8	6.7	5.2	4.8	-0.8	6.0	6.4
Oceania	2.4	2.0	2.2	1.4	2.8	2.5	1.4	2.9	3.5

Source: UNCTAD secretariat calculations, based on United Nations, Department of Economic and Social Affairs (UN/DESA), *National Accounts Main Aggregates* database, and *World Economic Situation and Prospects (WESP) 2011: Mid-year Update;* ECLAC, 2011; *OECD.Stat* database; and national sources.

Note: Calculations for country aggregates are based on GDP at constant 2005 dollars.

   a Forecasts.

   b New EU member States after 2004.

   c Albania, Bosnia and Herzegovina, Croatia, Montenegro, Serbia and The former Yugoslav Republic of Macedonia.

is already under way. For example, the International Monetary Fund (IMF) believes fiscal expansion is no longer needed since "private demand has, for the most part, taken the baton" (IMF, 2011a: xv). Moreover, the Bank for International Settlements (BIS) argues that inflation is presently the main risk in an otherwise recovering world economy, and therefore suggests "policy [interest] rates should rise globally" (BIS, 2011: xii). According to these views, economic policy should no longer aim at stimulating growth, but instead should focus on controlling inflation and reducing fiscal deficits and public debt. But with nearly all the governments of the large developed economies trying to curb public expenditure, including cutting or freezing public sector wages, the consequent diminished expectations of private households threaten to derail recovery of the world economy. With weak labour market indicators in the United States, risks of financial contagion in Europe and a deterioration in some leading indicators for global manufacturing (JP Morgan, 2011), the implementation of restrictive macroeconomic policies increases the probability of a prolonged period of mediocre growth, if not of an outright contraction, in developed economies.

Developing economies present a different picture. Rapid recovery from the crisis and the subsequent sustained growth have been the result of various factors, including countercyclical measures, the recovery of commodity prices since mid-2009 and an expansion of real wages. Some analysts suggest that higher commodity prices have been the main cause of recovery in developing countries (IMF, 2011a). However, while the higher prices have been essential for commodity exporters, commodity-importing developing countries have also grown at a rapid pace. A major factor that should not be underestimated is that in many developing countries the Great Recession has not led to cuts in real wages; on the contrary, domestic income and demand have remained on a growth trajectory. In that sense, the recovery in many developing countries, which has been largely wage-led, contrasts with that of developed economies, which is associated with wage stagnation. In addition, since the financial systems in developing countries were largely unaffected by the most recent crisis, their domestic demand is further supported by the availability of domestic credit. Therefore, their growth has become increasingly dependent on the expansion of domestic markets, which may explain the continuing growth and resilience of these economies, despite slow growth in developed countries.

However, economic expansion in developing countries faces several challenges. Paradoxically, some of their problems result from their resistance to financial contagion during the recent crisis. In particular, because emerging market economies appeared to be less risky, they attracted even more short-term capital inflows. Such flows may generate asset bubbles and pressures for exchange rate appreciation, which would erode their competitiveness. Moreover, higher inflation in several of these countries, owing largely to commodity price increases, has led them to tighten monetary policy and raise interest rates, which further attract foreign capital in the form of carry-trade operations. At the same time, volatility in highly financialized commodity markets suggests that a negative shock originating in developed economies might exert a strong downward pressure on the prices of primary commodity exports, as already happened in 2008 (see chapter V of this *Report*). Hence, despite the greater role of domestic markets in driving growth, there are significant external risks to sustained economic expansion in developing countries due to economic weaknesses in developed economies and the lack of significant reforms in international financial markets.

It is therefore evident that the widely varying pace of economic recovery is one of the main characteristics of the post-crisis world economy. While developing and transition economies, as a group, have regained their pre-crisis growth trend following the 2008–2009 slowdown, growth in developed economies remains very sluggish, which suggests that their economic output is currently well below potential (chart 1.1). In the *United States*, economic recovery has been stalling since early 2011, so that growth is too slow to significantly reduce unemployment. Labour indicators deteriorated sharply between the end of 2007 and mid-2009, with steep increases in both unemployment and underemployment rates, and they did not improve with the subsequent economic recovery. In the first quarter of 2011, payroll employment remained below its level of the first quarter of 2009 (at the trough of the economic cycle), and real hourly wages remained stagnant. As a result, wage-earners did not profit at all from the economic recovery; between the second quarter of 2009 and the first quarter of 2011, it was corporate profits that captured 92 per cent of the accumulated growth in national income. Such a recovery, which has been referred to as "jobless and wageless" (Sum et al., 2011), implies little, if any, contribution of consumer

Chart 1.1

REAL GDP AT MARKET PRICES, 2002–2011

(Index numbers, 2002 = 100)

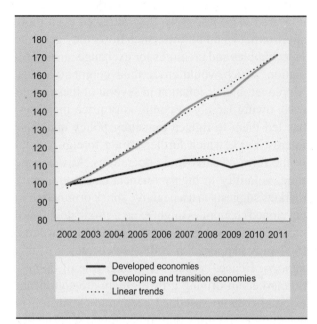

Source: UNCTAD secretariat calculations, based on UN/DESA, *National Accounts Main Aggregates* database, *World Economic Situation and Prospects 2011: Mid-year Update*; ECLAC (2011); *OECD.Stat* database; and national sources.
Note: Linear trends correspond to 2002–2007.

spending to GDP growth. In addition, continued weakness in the housing market will delay recovery in residential investment and personal credit. Despite this lack of dynamism in private demand, macroeconomic policies have shifted to a less supportive stance. Government spending fell in late 2010 and early 2011, and, given the political differences over how to deal with the fiscal deficit and public debt ceiling, there is unlikely to be any further fiscal stimulus. The second round of quantitative easing, which ended in June 2011, failed to translate into increased credit for domestic economic activities: indeed, between the first quarters of 2008 and 2011, bank credit to the private sector fell by 11 per cent in real terms. Monetary policy will remain accommodative overall, with interest rates remaining at historically low levels, but the monetary authorities do not envisage new rounds of quantitative easing.

Natural disasters badly affected *Japan, Australia and New Zealand*. The Japanese economy, which had already been on a downward trajectory since mid-

2010, owing to declining household consumption, government expenditure and net exports, fell officially back into recession in the first quarter of 2011. In March, its manufacturing sector suffered unprecedented supply-chain and energy disruptions due to the massive earthquake and tsunami. Preliminary figures point to a rapid revival of manufacturing, owing to fewer electricity shortages. In addition, strong public and private demand for reconstruction will continue to boost economic activity in the second half of the year and into 2012. While this will not prevent an overall GDP contraction in 2011, it will certainly lead to a significant recovery next year. However, pre-existing obstacles to growth, including shrinking real wages, an appreciating currency and attempts to reduce the huge public debt through fiscal tightening, will need to be addressed in the medium term. By contrast the negative effects of Australia's floods and New Zealand's earthquake are expected to be more short-lived, and are unlikely to push these two countries into recession.

In the *European Union (EU)*, growth is forecast to improve slightly, from 1.8 per cent in 2010 to around 1.9 per cent in 2011, although with significant variations among the different member countries. Germany and France experienced a quarter-on-quarter acceleration in early 2011. In Germany, growth relied on investment and net exports – as in 2010 – while private consumption remained subdued because of stagnating real wages. In France, fixed investment and stocks are still recovering from the crisis, but household consumption appeared relatively weak in the first months of 2011, partly due to rising energy prices and partly to the withdrawal of public incentives to boost consumption. In the United Kingdom, declining domestic demand in the context of rising inflation and slow wage growth, as well as stagnant corporate investment resulted in meagre positive GDP growth during the first quarter of 2011, only just offsetting its previous decline in late 2010. The situation seems even grimmer in peripheral Europe: public debt crises, such as in Greece, Ireland and Portugal, have increased the costs of debt rollovers. These countries have been forced to implement fiscal austerity measures, as a precondition for emergency financing by the IMF and the EU. Other countries that face the risk of contagion (e.g. Italy and Spain) are also implementing fiscal tightening in an attempt to maintain the confidence of financial markets. The restrictive policy stances, combined with the already high levels of unemployment, may cause these countries to remain in recession in 2011 or, at best, record weak positive GDP growth. The policy dilemmas faced by European countries are further discussed in section B below.

In developing countries, growth rates are also expected to slow down in 2011, but this is due to the higher comparison base of 2010 and, in some cases, to slow growth in developed economies rather than to endogenous obstacles to growth. *Asian* economies continue to record the highest GDP growth rates. However, recent high-frequency indicators, such as those relating to industrial production and trade, suggest that economic growth in *East* and *South-East Asia* moderated in the second quarter of 2011, following a strong first quarter. The slowdown reflects a number of short-term factors, including the supply-chain effects of the Japanese earthquake and the impact of tighter monetary policies on domestic economic activity, as well as more long-lasting factors such as weaknesses in some major export markets, notably Japan and the United States. As a result, the contributions of exports – and to some extent investment – to growth are expected to weaken in 2011, affecting a number of export-oriented countries, for example Malaysia, Singapore and Thailand. Countries with large domestic markets and growing household consumption, such as China and Indonesia, will register only a mild, if any, slowdown. In China, net exports have reduced their contribution to GDP growth in comparison with the pre-crisis situation. Fixed investment (in the first place) and private consumption are the two major factors driving growth. The increased role of domestic demand is in line with the Government's aim to rebalance growth, but the relative share of consumption vis-à-vis investment still remains to be adjusted.

In *South Asia*, India continues to pursue rapid economic growth (close to 8 per cent), based mainly on strong domestic consumption and investment, but also on the positive contribution of net exports. A good winter harvest added to domestic activity, which remained solid. Most other countries in this region are also experiencing growth, but at slower rates, largely due to domestic demand. Rising import prices since the last quarter of 2010 have been affecting trade balances and increasing inflationary pressures, which could prompt more restrictive macroeconomic policies in the near future.

West Asia is set to keep growing at a relatively high rate, although with wide differences among the countries of the region. In several countries, political unrest is expected to adversely affect short-term growth prospects because of its impact on investment and tourism. In other, mainly oil-rich countries, however, political risks have led governments to implement expansionary measures, including tax cuts, higher wages in the public sector and new infrastructure programmes, in order to prevent social or political unrest. The resultant massive amounts injected into the economy are likely to boost GDP growth. In Turkey, which has not been affected by political instability, growth will remain high this year. Its current-account deficit is expected to reach 9 per cent of GDP in 2011, as hot money from abroad has fuelled credit growth – which increased by 35 per cent in real terms over the past year – and accentuated currency appreciation. Consequently a capital reversal could adversely affect the entire economy.

Growth in *Africa* is forecast to decline, almost entirely due to political turmoil in a number of *North African* countries. Growth in Egypt and Tunisia will slow down significantly in 2011, owing to plummeting investments and a slowdown in the vital sector of tourism. However, the most serious impact of conflict has been in the Libyan Arab Jamahiriya, where much of the economic activity has ground to a halt, including oil production and exports. This contrasts with *sub-Saharan Africa*, where overall GDP growth rates are projected to continue at their 2010 pace. Investments in infrastructure and expansionary fiscal policies should boost economic growth in the subregion. Rapid development in services such as telecommunications will provide a further impetus. While mineral- and energy-exporting countries have recorded improvements in their terms of trade as a result of strong demand for raw materials from other large developing economies, in many of the countries there are other sectors that have been the main contributors to growth. In Nigeria, for instance, where the sturdy output growth of 7.6 per cent in 2010 continued into early 2011, the non-oil sector grew at about 8.5 per cent, compared with about 3 per cent in the oil sector. In South Africa, GDP growth accelerated during the first quarter of 2011, owing to strong growth of the manufacturing sector. Several service industries have also been expanding, although not as rapidly. Even though open unemployment remains high, at 25 per cent, real wages have been growing significantly, and private consumption remains the most important driver of economic growth.

Latin America and the Caribbean recovered rapidly from the crisis, with a GDP growth of almost 6 per cent in 2010 – one of the highest in decades. Growth in several countries even accelerated in late 2010 and early 2011, on a quarter-to-quarter basis. However, compared with the relatively high benchmark of 2010, growth is likely to slow down in 2011 to below 5 per cent. Growth will be driven mainly by domestic demand, both in terms of consumption and investment, boosted by the significant improvement in labour conditions and the expansion of credit. In general, governments are likely to moderate their economic stimulus programmes, but there may be only a few countries that shift to a restrictive fiscal stance. Economic growth has kept fiscal deficits and public debts in check. The volume of exports will not increase as fast as in 2010, but commodity exporters will continue to benefit from significant terms-of-trade gains. This in turn will enable an expansion of imports, in particular of capital goods. Higher commodity prices are pushing up inflation rates: by May 2011, the regional average reached 7.5 per cent, while core inflation (excluding food and fuels prices) was only 5.5 per cent (ECLAC, 2011). In response, several central banks have tightened their monetary policy stance, although this has further encouraged undesired inflows of short-term capital. Governments thus face a policy dilemma, and some of them have established or strengthened capital controls in order to mitigate macroeconomic disturbances and currency appreciation resulting from such flows.

Growth in Brazil is declining, from 7.5 per cent in 2010 to around 4 per cent this year, as fiscal and monetary policies have been tightened with the aim of increasing the primary budget surplus and curbing inflation. This contrasts with Argentina, where growth is expected to exceed 8 per cent owing to double-digit growth in private consumption and fixed capital investment. The Andean countries, which are important fuel or mineral exporters, are forecast to either improve their growth rate (the Bolivarian Republic of Venezuela, Bolivia, Chile, Colombia and Ecuador) or maintain rapid growth (Peru), owing to significant terms-of-trade gains. On the other hand, most of the small economies of Central America and the Caribbean will likely continue to experience lacklustre growth, due to their dependence on the United States economy and to a deterioration in their terms of trade and competitiveness which hamper their sustained development. However, in Panama, significant infrastructure projects will boost economic

activities and stimulate employment creation. Mexico will experience an estimated growth of about 4 per cent, with a recovery of private consumption and investment, although growth might lose momentum in the second half of the year due the slowdown in the United States economy.

The transition economies of the *Commonwealth of Independent States* (CIS) should continue their economic upturn, with GDP growing by more than 4 per cent, as in 2010. Terms-of-trade gains are expected to continue to improve the scope for fiscal stimulus in the fuel- and mineral-exporting countries, including the largest economies (the Russian Federation, followed by Ukraine and Kazakhstan). In these economies, GDP growth has relied mainly on domestic factors, with the recovery of investment and relatively robust household demand as a result of some improvement in employment. The monetary authorities in the Russian Federation have been facing several challenges related to non-performing loans in a number of large banks, high levels of capital outflows and inflationary pressures due to rising food prices. These have led to several rounds of monetary tightening, which, nevertheless, should not affect growth in the short run. After a strong economic contraction in 2009 and a moderate recovery in 2010, Ukraine is benefiting from steady external demand for its minerals, which account for 40 per cent of its total exports. In Kazakhstan, where the 2009 recession was much milder, economic growth is being bolstered by public and private expenditure, including domestic and foreign investment. Improved economic conditions in the Russian Federation have been supporting most of the energy-importing CIS economies, by providing a market for their exports and through increased workers' remittances. In addition, growth in Central Asia is supported by substantial, officially funded investment, especially in the energy-exporting economies. However, in Belarus, growth is slowing down after the local currency was devalued by 36 per cent in May 2011, which caused product shortages and prices to shoot up in the domestic market.

Growth is slower in the economies of *South-Eastern Europe*, which are unlikely to return to their 2008 GDP level before 2012. Croatia's economy contracted again in 2010. Elsewhere, there was a mild rebound, but recovery is expected to be slow owing to weak domestic demand. Unemployment continues to be a critical problem in the region, with Croatia and Serbia facing a rise in unemployment in early 2011.

2. International trade

International trade rebounded sharply in 2010, after having registered its greatest downturn since the Second World War. The volume of world merchandise trade recorded a 14 per cent year-on-year increase, which roughly offset its decline in 2009 (table 1.2). The upturn in global trade started in the second half of 2009 and was particularly strong until the end of the first half of 2010, as firms refilled their inventories. Thereafter, it lost some traction as inventory cycles moved to a new phase and economic activities ran out of steam in several developed countries. In 2011, the growth of international trade is expected to return to a single-digit figure, in the range of 7–8 per cent.

Although the World Trade Organization (WTO) has identified new restrictive measures on imports taken by G-20 countries, these remain modest, and they only affect 0.6 per cent of total G-20 imports (WTO, 2011a). So far, they do not represent any significant increase in trade barriers, but they are fuelling fears that, at a time of high unemployment and fiscal belt-tightening in developed economies, and complaints of "currency wars" by developing economies, governments may impose more import controls.

Mirroring the differences in strength of domestic aggregate demand, the revival of trade has also been uneven among countries and income groups of countries. In developed countries, trade (in terms of volume) has yet to bounce back to a level above its

Table 1.2

EXPORT AND IMPORT VOLUMES OF GOODS, SELECTED REGIONS AND COUNTRIES, 2007–2010

(Annual percentage change)

Region/country	Volume of exports				Volume of imports			
	2007	2008	2009	2010	2007	2008	2009	2010
World	**6.0**	**2.4**	**-13.3**	**14.0**	**6.6**	**2.6**	**-13.4**	**13.6**
Developed countries	**4.1**	**2.5**	**-15.1**	**12.6**	**3.8**	**-0.1**	**-14.5**	**10.3**
of which:								
Japan	8.9	2.3	-24.9	27.9	0.8	-0.6	-12.4	10.3
United States	6.8	5.5	-14.9	15.3	1.1	-3.7	-16.4	14.7
European Union	3.2	2.4	-14.3	11.2	4.9	0.8	-14.3	9.0
South-East Europe and CIS	**9.3**	**-0.2**	**-14.3**	**11.7**	**26.7**	**15.5**	**-28.1**	**15.6**
South-East Europe	17.9	-13.5	-20.6	11.5	23.7	-9.4	-20.7	-5.3
CIS	8.8	0.5	-13.9	11.8	27.3	18.4	-28.9	18.3
Developing countries	**8.8**	**3.2**	**-10.3**	**16.7**	**10.4**	**6.7**	**-9.9**	**18.9**
Africa	6.6	-2.1	-10.7	9.0	12.6	10.2	-2.5	1.3
Sub-Saharan Africa	6.9	-2.2	-9.6	10.4	11.5	2.8	-2.6	0.4
Latin America and the Caribbean	2.4	-0.5	-11.2	11.0	11.5	8.8	-18.4	25.0
East Asia	15.6	7.2	-10.5	24.1	10.2	0.4	-5.3	24.6
of which:								
China	21.8	10.5	-13.6	29.4	14.1	2.3	-1.7	30.0
South Asia	5.6	7.0	-5.6	10.3	9.7	20.8	-2.9	6.9
of which:								
India	6.9	16.8	-6.6	12.7	14.7	29.7	-0.8	4.2
South-East Asia	7.1	1.6	-10.7	18.6	7.0	8.2	-16.5	22.2
West Asia	1.8	4.3	-4.7	7.3	14.1	13.3	-13.8	10.6

Source: UNCTAD secretariat calculations, based on *UNCTADstat*.

Chart 1.2

WORLD TRADE VOLUME, JANUARY 2000–APRIL 2011

(Index numbers, 2000 = 100)

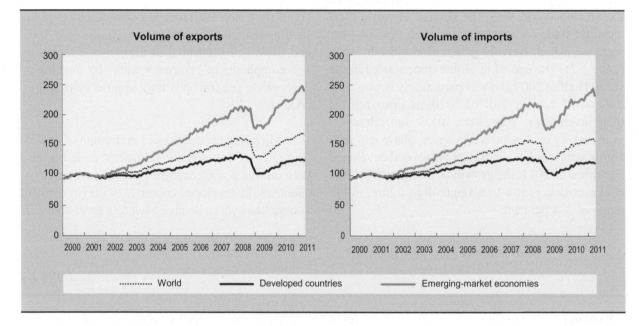

Source: UNCTAD secretariat calculations, based on the CPB Netherlands Bureau of Economic Policy Analysis, *World Trade* database.

pre-crisis levels. These countries recovered part of their previous trade losses between mid-2009 and mid-2010, but there has been no growth since then (chart 1.2). Similarly, transition economies' trade also failed to reach its pre-crisis level by the end of 2010. The situation was even worse in South-Eastern Europe, where imports contracted even further in 2010, in the context of weaker aggregate demand and rising overall unemployment in the region. In sharp contrast, the volume of both imports and exports in most groups of developing countries already exceeded their 2008 peak in the course of 2010, with East Asia leading the upturn.

On the export side, differences arise mostly from the composition of countries' exports. In countries that produce durable and capital goods (demand for which is typically postponed during crises), such as China and Japan, exports increased in volume by almost 30 per cent as their industrial production recovered from the crisis. On the other hand, in developing economies that export mainly primary commodities, the volume of exports has

been relatively stable. Unlike durable manufactured goods whose markets adjust mostly through quantity, primary commodity markets adjust more through prices, while their volume is frequently determined by supply-side conditions. Therefore, as their trade flows generally contracted less in 2009, they also experienced a milder expansion the year after, with percentage changes of only one digit in both cases. For some products (e.g. food products), this was related to the low elasticity of demand, while for other products changes in inventories followed a countercyclical pattern, as some leading importers took advantage of the lower prices of commodities in 2009.

Import volumes normally change in parallel with those of exports in countries or regions that trade mainly manufactures, and where the industrial system is highly integrated in global trade and exports incorporate a large share of imported inputs (e.g. in the EU and South-East Asia). However, in other cases, export and import volumes may evolve at quite different rates, in particular when countries use previously accumulated international reserves or

Chart 1.3

NET BARTER TERMS OF TRADE, 2000–2010

(Index numbers, 2000 = 100)

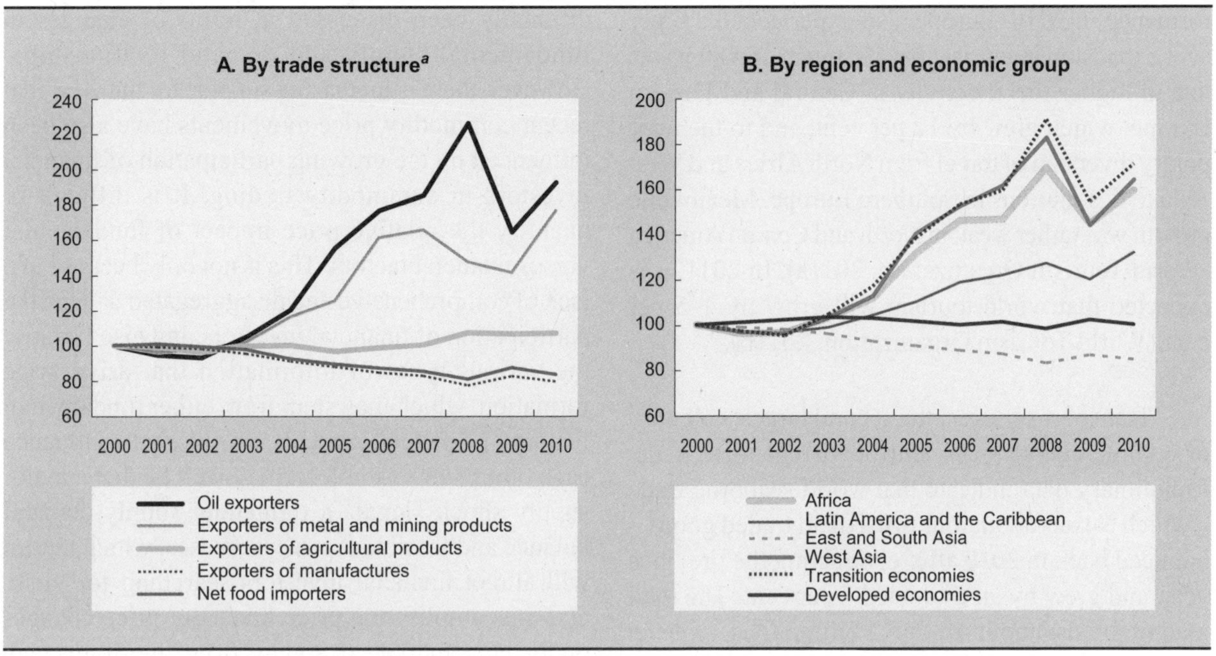

A. By trade structure[a]

B. By region and economic group

Legend A:
- Oil exporters
- Exporters of metal and mining products
- Exporters of agricultural products
- Exporters of manufactures
- Net food importers

Legend B:
- Africa
- Latin America and the Caribbean
- East and South Asia
- West Asia
- Transition economies
- Developed economies

Source: UNCTAD, secretariat calculations, based on *UNCTADstat*.

Note Net food importers are low-income food-deficit countries, excluding exporters of fuels, metal and mining products.

a Developing and transition economies.

international aid to finance imports of final goods, or when gains or losses from the terms of trade significantly affect the purchasing power of exports. African countries, China and Japan are examples of the first case, as their imports in 2009 fell at a much lower rate than their exports, and consequently tended to recover at a slower pace in 2010. Latin America is a good example of how terms-of-trade losses and gains accentuated import contraction in 2009 and expansion in 2010 (table 1.2).

In 2010, the evolution terms of trade mostly returned to its pre-crisis pattern (chart 1.3). Among developing countries, oil and mineral exporters experienced significant gains; in the latter, terms-of-trade indices even exceeded their previous 2007 peak. In contrast, exporters of manufactures lost part of their 2009 gains. Examining terms of trade by geographical region, they improved markedly in Africa, West Asia and the transition economies in 2010, owing to higher prices for fuel and minerals. The terms of trade in countries in Latin America and the Caribbean

reached unprecedented high levels, owing to gains in South American countries. On the other hand, in East and South Asian countries the terms of trade declined by some 2 per cent in 2010. However, this did not significantly affect the purchasing power of their exports, which increased by nearly 20 per cent.

Trade in services has followed a similar pattern to trade in goods, although with smaller fluctuations. With regard to travel and tourism services – which accounts for approximately 25 per cent of trade in services and for 6 per cent of all trade in goods and services – international tourist arrivals grew by nearly 7 per cent in 2010 to reach 940 million, compared with 882 million in 2009 and 917 million in 2008. In the first few months of 2011, tourism continued to grow at an annual rate of nearly 5 per cent. Indeed, growth was positive in all subregions of the world during January and February 2011, except in West Asia and North Africa, where it fell by about 10 per cent. Similar to overall economic activities, growth rates in international tourism arrivals were, on average, the highest in developing countries. They increased by 15 per cent in South America and South Asia, and by 13 per cent in sub-Saharan Africa. In the Asia-Pacific region, growth in tourist arrivals slowed down to 6 per cent, although from a very strong performance in 2010. Europe also experienced a 6 per cent expansion in tourist arrivals, much of which was due to higher travel activity in Central and Eastern Europe, which grew by 12 per cent, and to the temporary diversion of travel from North Africa and West Asia to destinations in Southern Europe. Meanwhile growth was rather weak in North and Central America (World Tourism Organization, 2011a). In 2011, it is expected that world tourism will grow by 4–5 per cent (World Tourism Organization, 2011b).

Transport services, the second largest category of commercial services, mirror merchandise trade. Preliminary data indicate that world seaborne trade – which carries about four fifths of all traded goods – bounced back in 2010 after contracting the previous year, and grew by an estimated 7 per cent. The total load of goods amounted to 8.4 billion tons – a level that exceeds the peak reached in 2008 (UNCTAD, 2011). However, these aggregate figures hide substantial variations in types of cargo. Container shipping followed a V-shape recovery, expanding by 13 per cent in 2010 after plummeting by 10 per cent in 2009, whereas the volume of tanker trade expanded by 4.2 per cent in 2010, which slightly more than offset its decline in 2009. Growth in the volume of major dry bulk shipments remained positive in 2009 and strongly accelerated in 2010 with an increase of 11.3 per cent. This diversity highlights the responsiveness of trade in manufactures to changes in the global economic situation, and particularly to manufacturing growth in countries of the Organisation for Economic Co-operation and Development (OECD). Interestingly, it also reflects the resilience of trade in some primary commodities, even during the global crisis, with demand from China playing an important role.

Maritime freight prices – unlike oil prices – declined steadily throughout 2010. The strong positive correlation observed from early 2008 until mid-2009 between the two price aggregates started to reverse in 2010 owing to an oversupply of vessels. In 2011, maritime freight prices are expected to stay low in comparison with their historically high levels of the previous decade.

3. Recent developments in commodity markets

Commodity price developments have traditionally been discussed in terms of changes in fundamental supply and demand relationships. However, there is increasing support for the view that recent commodity price movements have also been influenced by the growing participation of financial investors in commodity trading. It is difficult to quantify the relative price impact of fundamental versus financial factors. This is not only because of a lack of comprehensive and disaggregated data on the participation of financial investors, but also because the various types of information that drive price formation, which may stem from either fundamental factors or financial markets, are likely to influence each other. For example, it may well be that a major supply shock signals a tightening supply-demand balance and imminent price increases, which in turn will attract financial investors searching for yield, and thus amplify the price hike. But price changes on financial markets or signals from algorithms may also prompt financial investors to adjust their commodity portfolios, which may be misinterpreted by producers and consumers as signalling fundamental changes. This may cause them to adjust their activities in line with market fundamentals and reinforce price movements. Chapter V of this *Report* provides a detailed analysis of the role of information in this context. This section focuses on price developments, as well as on shifts in fundamental supply-demand balances.

Uncertainty and instability have been the major distinguishing features of commodity markets in 2010 and the first half of 2011. This is reflected in greater volatility of commodity prices than in the past, similar to the period of the commodity boom prior to the eruption of the global financial and economic crisis in 2008. The increase in commodity price volatility over the past decade can be illustrated by comparing the standard deviation of the monthly commodity price data in chart 1.4 between 2002–2005 and 2006–2011 for different commodity groups. Between these two periods, this simple measure of volatility multiplied by a factor of 3.8 for food commodities and vegetable oilseeds and oils, by 2.7 for agricultural raw materials and tropical beverages, and by 1.6 for minerals and metals and crude petroleum.[1]

Chart 1.4

MONTHLY EVOLUTION OF COMMODITY PRICES, EXCHANGE RATE AND WORLD INDUSTRIAL PRODUCTION, JANUARY 2002–MAY 2011

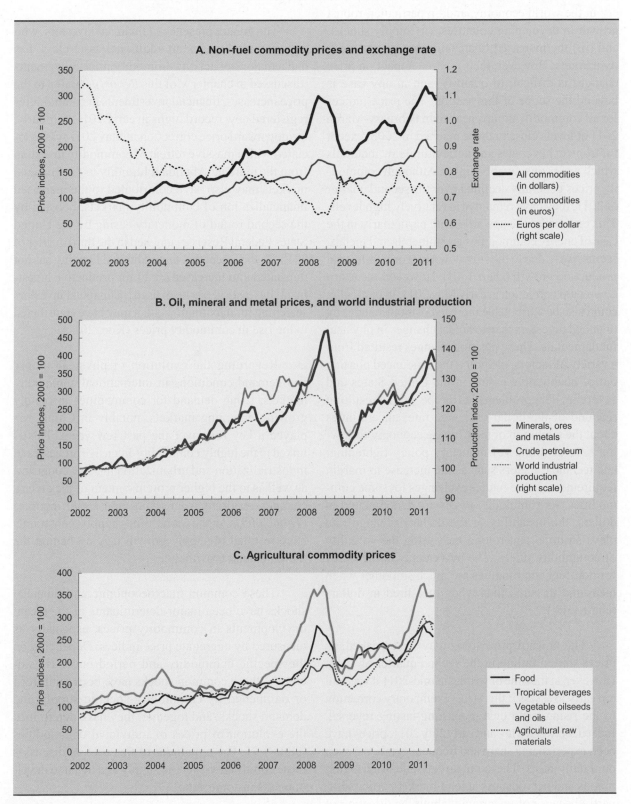

Source: UNCTAD secretariat calculations, based on UNCTAD, *Commodity Price Statistics Online*; World Bank, *Commodity Prices* (Pink Sheet) database; *UNCTADstat*; and CPB Netherlands Bureau of Economic Policy Analysis, *World Trade* database.

Note: Price indices are in current values and world industrial production is in constant values.

After declining in the second quarter of 2010, commodity prices generally surged until early 2011. Price increases were associated with three broad tendencies: (i) rising demand that reflected the recovery in the world economy, and, in particular, robust growth in developing countries; (ii) supply shocks; and (iii) the increased financialization of commodity markets. However, their relative impact on price changes is difficult to quantify, and in any case is beyond the scope of this section. The price indices for all commodity groups peaked in February-March 2011 at levels close to those reached in 2008, except for tropical beverages and agricultural raw materials which were considerably higher. Although commodity prices generally declined over the second quarter of 2011, they have remained at relatively high levels. This reversal of the upward trend, particularly in the case of energy commodities and minerals and metals, seems partly due to the slowdown in world industrial production growth (chart 1.4B). However, the sharp downward correction in early May 2011, in particular, could also be attributable more to position changes by financial investors than to actual changes in physical fundamentals. These position changes resulted from a variety of factors, including the announced phasing out of quantitative easing in the United States and sovereign debt problems in Europe, with a resulting rebound of the dollar exchange rate; uncertainties about the evolution of the Chinese economy following several rounds of monetary policy tightening; and technical factors such as the increase in margin requirements in the futures exchanges for some commodities. As commodity prices are denominated in dollars, the instability of the dollar exchange rate plays an important role in measuring the volatility of commodity prices. The movements in the index for non-fuel commodities are much smoother when measured in euros than when measured in dollars (chart 1.4A).

The upward price trend may have peaked, as prices started falling in the second quarter of 2011. However, at the time of writing in mid-2011 it was still too early to assess if this is just a temporary correction in the rising trend or a more long-lasting reversal. Indeed, between May and early July 2011, prices have been experiencing sharp and frequent gyrations, even on a daily basis. These are largely due to changing moods and nervousness among market participants, partly because of uncertainty about the direction of financial market developments. In the particular case of oil, as discussed below, policy decisions of the

Organization of the Petroleum Exporting Countries (OPEC) and, especially, the International Energy Agency (IEA), which took market participants by surprise, have also played a role.

The greater presence of financial investors, who treat commodities as an additional asset class, has had a major impact on commodity price movements (discussed in chapter V of this *Report*). Parallel to the price increases, financial investments in commodities registered new record highs in early 2011. Similarly, the downward price correction in May 2011 was associated with a massive retreat of commodity investors from the market.[2] Abundant liquidity in the financial markets may also have contributed to the increased financialization of commodity markets, boosted by the second round of monetary easing by the United States Federal Reserve launched in the third quarter of 2010. To the extent that this additional liquidity has not translated into increased credit for productive investment, but instead has been used by financial investors searching for maximum yield, it may have contributed to the rise in commodity prices (Koo, 2011).

Regarding the evolution of physical supply and demand conditions in international commodity markets, rising demand for commodities in rapidly growing emerging markets, notably in China, has played a key role over the past few years. This is linked to the highly commodity-intensive processes of industrialization and urbanization in these countries, as well as to the higher protein content of the dietary changes resulting from rising household incomes (*TDR 2005*). At the same time, supply constraints have resulted in supply growth lagging behind the rapid demand growth.

These common macroeconomic and financial shocks have been major determinants of the recent developments in commodity prices, especially as measured by aggregate price indices. Depending on the specific commodity and period under consideration, these common shocks have been reinforced or dampened by commodity-specific supply and demand shocks, and together, they have determined the evolution of prices of individual commodities (table 1.3). The remainder of this section discusses these commodity-specific supply and demand developments in some detail.

In the *crude oil* market, prices were fluctuating within a $70–$80 band during the first three quarters

Table 1.3

WORLD PRIMARY COMMODITY PRICES, 2005–2011

(Percentage change over previous year, unless otherwise indicated)

Commodity groups	2005	2006	2007	2008	2009	2010	2011[a]	2009–2011[b]
All commodities[c]	**11.6**	**30.2**	**13.0**	**24.0**	**-16.9**	**17.7**	**21.8**	**62.1**
All food	**6.3**	**16.3**	**13.3**	**39.2**	**-8.5**	**7.4**	**20.7**	**39.6**
Food and tropical beverages	**8.8**	**17.8**	**8.6**	**40.4**	**-5.4**	**5.6**	**18.5**	**33.9**
Tropical beverages	25.5	6.7	10.4	20.2	1.9	17.5	32.1	71.5
Coffee	43.8	7.1	12.5	15.4	-6.9	27.3	49.0	104.5
Cocoa	-0.7	3.5	22.6	32.2	11.9	8.5	3.6	25.1
Tea	9.1	11.7	-12.3	27.2	16.5	-1.0	9.5	28.4
Food	7.2	19.0	8.5	42.5	-6.0	4.4	17.1	30.5
Sugar	37.9	49.4	-31.7	26.9	41.8	17.3	23.7	101.2
Beef	4.1	-2.4	1.9	2.6	-1.2	27.5	22.4	68.3
Maize	-12.0	24.4	38.2	34.0	-24.4	13.2	52.8	74.5
Wheat	-1.4	26.6	34.3	27.5	-31.4	3.3	44.5	42.3
Rice	17.1	5.5	9.5	110.7	-15.8	-11.5	-1.2	-17.6
Bananas	9.9	18.5	-0.9	24.6	0.7	3.7	13.3	13.5
Vegetable oilseeds and oils	**-9.5**	**5.0**	**52.9**	**31.9**	**-28.4**	**22.7**	**36.4**	**89.8**
Soybeans	-10.4	-2.2	43.0	36.1	-16.6	3.1	24.8	42.5
Agricultural raw materials	**3.2**	**13.3**	**12.0**	**20.5**	**-17.5**	**34.0**	**31.5**	**97.1**
Hides and skins	-2.1	5.1	4.5	-11.3	-30.0	60.5	14.5	142.3
Cotton	-11.6	5.9	10.2	12.8	-12.2	65.3	93.7	266.4
Tobacco	1.8	6.4	11.6	8.3	18.1	-23.3	-75.7	-80.5
Rubber	16.7	40.6	9.5	16.9	-27.0	90.3	54.1	285.7
Tropical logs	0.3	-4.7	19.5	39.3	-20.6	1.8	8.8	9.2
Minerals, ores and metals	**26.2**	**60.3**	**12.8**	**6.2**	**-30.3**	**33.7**	**20.2**	**104.2**
Aluminium	10.6	35.4	2.7	-2.5	-35.3	30.5	17.4	87.7
Phosphate rock	2.5	5.3	60.5	387.2	-64.8	1.1	36.6	-13.1
Iron ore	..	..	77.4	26.8	-48.7	82.4	22.3	152.3
Tin	-13.2	18.9	65.6	27.3	-26.7	50.4	47.9	173.9
Copper	28.4	82.7	5.9	-2.3	-26.3	47.0	25.7	183.6
Nickel	6.6	64.5	53.5	-43.3	-30.6	48.9	20.4	150.8
Lead	10.2	32.0	100.2	-19.0	-17.7	25.0	20.8	124.3
Zinc	31.9	137.0	-1.0	-42.2	-11.7	30.5	8.5	99.9
Gold	8.7	35.9	15.3	25.1	11.6	26.1	16.3	57.1
Crude petroleum[d]	**41.3**	**20.4**	**10.7**	**36.4**	**-36.3**	**28.0**	**32.4**	**136.7**
Memo item:								
Manufactures[e]	**2.5**	**3.4**	**7.5**	**4.9**	**-5.6**	**1.1**	..	..

Source: UNCTAD secretariat calculations, based on UNCTAD, *Commodity Price Statistics Online*; and United Nations Statistics Division (UNSD), *Monthly Bulletin of Statistics*, various issues.

Note: In current dollars.

   a Percentage change between the average of January to May 2011 and the average for 2010.

   b Percentage change between the average of January to May 2011 and the average of January to March for 2009 (period of trough in commodity prices due to the global financial crisis).

   c Excluding crude petroleum.

   d Average of Brent, Dubai and West Texas Intermediate, equally weighted.

   e Unit value of exports of manufactured goods of developed countries.

of 2010. They then surged in the last quarter of the year, to reach a monthly average of $116.3 in April 2011 (UNCTADstat). Global oil demand rose by 3.2 per cent in 2010, after having declined by 0.8 per cent and 1.3 per cent in 2008 and 2009 respectively. Oil demand in OECD countries increased by a meagre 1.1 per cent, while that of non-OECD countries grew by 5.5 per cent, with Chinese oil demand growing at 12.3 per cent in 2010.[3] Therefore, non-OECD countries were responsible for over 80 per cent of the increase in oil demand. At the same time, oil supply increased by only 2.1 per cent in 2010 (IEA, 2011a). One of the main reasons for oil production growth lagging behind that of demand, and for the surging oil prices in late 2010 and the first months of 2011, is the tensions in West Asia and North Africa. These affected oil production, reducing global oil supply and providing an incentive for financial investors to bet on rising oil prices.

Oil production in the Libyan Arab Jamahiriya, which accounts for about two per cent of global production, with 1.6 million barrels per day, virtually stopped. Although Saudi Arabia stepped in and increased its production, this does not seem to have completely made up for the shortage of supply. This is mainly due to the difference in the quality of crude oil produced in the Libyan Arab Jamahiriya and that of the spare capacity oil in Saudi Arabia. By May 2011, amidst growing worldwide concerns that high oil prices were posing a major threat to the global economic recovery, the IEA observed a dent in oil demand, particularly in developed countries (IEA, 2011b). In this context of high prices, there were repeated calls for OPEC to increase production quotas. However, at its meeting on 8 June 2011 OPEC failed to reach an agreement to change the production quotas. While prices increased following the OPEC meeting, Saudi Arabia, which has by far the largest spare capacity among the OPEC members, announced that it would unilaterally increase production beyond the quota. Furthermore, two weeks later the IEA surprised the market with a release of emergency stocks, an extraordinary measure that had been taken only twice before.[4]

The prices of *food commodities* also surged during the second half of 2010 and early 2011, mainly due to weather-related events which affected harvests, thereby signalling an imminent deterioration in supply-demand balances. Markets for grains, excluding rice, generally remained tight by mid-

2011. The immediate trigger of the sharp increase in wheat prices was droughts and related fires in the Russian Federation and Ukraine, compounded by export bans in these countries. Global demand for maize has been rising fast, because of increased use as animal feed and also because its use for biofuel production expanded, especially as the profitability of biofuel production increases with rising oil prices. Data from the United States Department of Agriculture (USDA) show that in 2010/11 about 40 per cent of maize harvested in the United States went to biofuel production, up from 20 per cent in 2006/07. This would explain why growth in global demand for maize has exceeded that of production: while global demand growth was 3.6 per cent in 2010/11, production growth was only 0.9 per cent. As a result, there has been a significant depletion of maize inventories.[5]

In this context, prices have varied recently in line with changing expectations of harvests for 2011/12, again closely related to evolving weather conditions. In May 2011, delays in the planting season in the United States due to heavy rains and floods, together with dry weather in Europe which threatened cereal harvests, led to tighter supply-demand balances. Climatic conditions have also been affecting agricultural production in China. However, by early July 2011, those pressures appeared to have eased as a result of the lifting of grain export restrictions in the Russian Federation and Ukraine, as well as better-than-expected data from the USDA regarding stocks and plantings.

Even though in February 2011 the UNCTAD index for food prices surpassed the alarming levels of the food crisis of 2007-2008, a number of factors limited their impact on food security, which was therefore less critical than it had been previously. First, the price of rice, which is a major staple food and strongly affects food security, has remained relatively low in comparison with the levels reached in 2008. Second, grain inventories had been built up in 2009, which initially provided some buffer against the pressure to increase prices, although vulnerabilities had become more evident in this respect by mid-2011. Third, a number of countries in Africa also had good grain harvests in 2010. And finally, apart from some exceptions like the Russian Federation and Ukraine, most countries refrained from imposing export restrictions which had exacerbated the food crisis of 2007-2008. Nevertheless, the rise in food prices in 2010-2011 could have a serious impact on food security, made worse by the threat of famine in East Africa. Overall, the World Bank has estimated that the increase in food prices between June and December 2010 drove 44 million people into extreme poverty (Ivanic, Martin and Zaman, 2011). Furthermore, the food import bill of the low-income, food-deficit countries is expected to increase by 27 per cent in 2011 (FAO, 2011). Therefore, high food prices remain a worrying threat to food security in poor countries, and many of the structural causes that were behind the crisis in 2008 still need to be adequately addressed (see also *TDR 2008*, chapter II). In 2008 it was generally agreed that to tackle this problem, increased official development assistance would be needed to boost investment in agriculture in developing countries.

Climatic conditions have also been a major factor influencing market developments relating to other agricultural commodities. The price of sugar hit a 30-year high in early 2011. The supply-demand balance in world sugar markets had been expected to tighten strongly due to concerns about supply shortages in major producing countries, high consumption growth and low inventories, but these expectations were reversed by the anticipation of more favourable harvests. In the *tropical beverages* group, reduced harvests of coffee in major producing countries, notably Colombia and Viet Nam, combined with buoyant consumption, particularly in emerging markets, led to sharply tightening supply-demand balances and resulted in very low inventory levels. As in the case of sugar, cocoa prices were in a boom and bust situation in 2010-2011: following a steep rise up to February 2011 as a result of political tensions and a related export ban in the major producing country, Côte d'Ivoire, they declined sharply once these tensions were resolved and an increased supply became available.

Prices of *agricultural raw materials* also soared in 2010. Strong demand, especially from China, together with poor harvests in countries like China and Pakistan, led to lower levels of cotton inventories[6] and contributed to record price hikes in February 2011. Falling prices in the second quarter of 2011 are partly due to slowing demand as a reaction to the higher prices. Similarly, record highs in natural rubber prices in early 2011 were a result of strong demand for tyres for vehicle production in emerging markets and of higher oil prices, which made synthetic rubber more expensive. Moreover, supplies

were tight due to unfavourable weather conditions in South-East Asia, the major natural rubber producing region, which accounts for more than 70 per cent of global supply. However, in the second quarter of 2011, some easing of the supply situation, along with monetary tightening in China and the impact of the earthquake in Japan on automobile production, contributed to a decline in rubber prices.

In the markets for *metals and minerals*, prices rose steeply in the second half of 2010, and peaked in February-March 2011. Movements in metal and mineral prices tend to be highly correlated with changes in industrial production. Thus the price increase in 2010 was linked to global economic activity. In the case of copper, the tightness in the market is also due to supply shortfalls. The fall in prices since March 2011 appears to be partly associated with slower growth in global industrial production. Regarding nickel, recent price declines are also related to an increase in supplies. Moreover, it appears that the recent evolution of prices in mineral and metal markets has been influenced by unrecorded warehousing by financial institutions as well as by inventory dynamics in China, particularly for copper. However, these trends are hard to track owing to lack of information (see chapter V). It could well be that the lower growth in Chinese imports reflects a drawing down of inventories which had been previously built up, and would not necessarily be signalling reduced use of the metal. Consequently, as stocks should eventually be refilled, there are growing expectations of Chinese import demand picking up later in the year.

The prices of *precious metals*, particularly gold and silver, have been benefiting from uncertainties about the global economy. Demand for these metals has increased because investors have turned to them as a safe haven. In fact, it has been widely acknowledged that the soaring prices of silver were evidence of a speculative bubble which burst in early May 2011. And the increase in margins for silver futures contracts was considered one of the major triggers of the retreat of commodity investors at that time.

To a certain extent, rising commodity prices were the result of an acceleration of the global economic recovery in 2010, but they may in turn contribute to its slowdown in 2011. This is partly because high prices act like a tax on consumers and reduce purchasing power at a time when household incomes are already being adversely affected by high unemployment, slowly rising (or stagnating) wages and the debt deleveraging process, particularly in developed countries. Most importantly, the recovery may stall if high commodity prices lead to monetary policy tightening worldwide. A reaction to high commodity prices, which are primarily the result of external factors (mostly related to supply shocks or to conditions in the financial markets), through monetary policy measures that reduce domestic demand does not seem to be the most appropriate solution.

Given the prevailing uncertainties and high level of instability in commodity markets, and in the world economy in general, commodity prices are set to remain highly volatile in the short term, particularly if financial investors continue to exert a significant influence on these markets. Demand for commodities will depend on the pace of the recovery, which in turn will be shaped by economic policies.

In the longer term, demand for commodities in emerging developing countries is expected to remain robust in view of their lower per capita commodity consumption in comparison with developed countries. At the same time, supply of energy commodities, as well as minerals and metals, is likely to increase as a result of stepped up investments in exploration and extraction driven by high commodity prices. Indeed, worldwide, spending on non-ferrous exploration increased by 45 per cent in 2010 to reach the second highest amount on record (Metals Economics Group, 2011). However, given the existing supply constraints in the extractive industries, related for example to more costly extraction in remote areas or to the lack of skilled workers in the sector, it is not certain that the expected additional supply will be sufficient to meet higher demand. In the agricultural sector, OECD-FAO (2011) expects prices to remain on a higher plateau in 2011–2020 compared with the previous decade. This is because higher costs could dampen yield growth and limit production, while demand is likely to increase rapidly due to growing population and rising incomes in large emerging developing countries, and to the increasing non-food use of grains for feedstock and biofuels. The latter are expected to be driven by high oil prices and policy mandates on the use of biofuels.

An additional issue to consider is how the earthquake, tsunami and subsequent nuclear problems in Japan in March 2011 have affected commodity markets. In particular, rethinking of the role of nuclear energy in the energy mix may affect the markets of other energy commodities, creating additional price pressures in the oil market.

B. Incomes policies and the challenges ahead

Over the past year, the instruments available to policymakers for supporting economic recovery seem to have been limited, especially in developed economies. On the one hand, there was little scope for monetary policy to provide additional stimulus, as interest rates were already at historic lows. The only possible monetary stimulus seemed to be quantitative easing, which several central banks were reluctant to implement, and which, given the ongoing deleveraging process, proved to be of little help in reviving credit to boost domestic demand. On the other hand, higher public-debt-to-GDP ratios have convinced many governments that they should shift to fiscal tightening.

However, there is much larger space for macroeconomic policies, especially for proactive fiscal policies, than is perceived by policymakers (as discussed in chapter III). Moreover, there are other policy tools that have been largely overlooked, but which could play a strategic role in dealing with the present challenges, such as incomes policies.

1. The role of wages in economic growth

In the period of intensified globalization from the early 1980s until the global crisis, the share of national income accruing to labour declined in most developed and developing countries. If real wage growth fails to keep pace with productivity growth, there is a lasting and insurmountable constraint on the expansion of domestic demand and employment creation (*TDR 2010*, chapter V). To offset insufficient domestic demand, one kind of national response has been an overreliance on external demand. Another kind of response has taken the form of compensatory stimulation of domestic demand through credit easing and increasing asset prices. However, neither of these responses offers sustainable outcomes. These are important lessons to be learned from the global crisis. Over and above the risks inherent in premature fiscal consolidation, there is a heightened threat that deflationary policies may accentuate downward pressures on labour incomes as a result of the slump in the labour market. Such policies ignore the vital role of consumer spending in contributing to a sustainable global recovery.

From the perspective of a single country, strengthening the international competitiveness of producers may seem to justify relative wage compression. However, the simultaneous pursuit of export-led growth strategies by many countries has systemic implications: a race to the bottom with regard to wages will produce no winners and will only cause deflationary pressures. With widespread weakness in consumer demand, fixed investment will not increase either, despite lower labour costs. Global deflationary tendencies and the drag on global demand resulting from wage compression in many developed countries would need to be countered by some form of policy-engineered higher spending somewhere in the world economy. In the pre-crisis era, widespread resort to export-led growth strategies was made possible mainly by fast-growing imports in the United States, leading to increasing external deficits and financial fragility in that economy. Subsequent crises, with private sector deleveraging and increasing public debt, clearly showed the deficiencies of this approach. Rethinking fiscal policy and avoiding premature consolidation is one issue; halting and reversing unsustainable distributional trends is another.

Trends in income distribution since the 1980s confirm that inequalities within many developed economies have increased as globalization has accelerated (European Commission, 2007; IMF, 2007a and b; OECD, 2008). In particular, wage shares have declined slowly but steadily over the past 30 years, with short reversals during periods of recession (particularly in 2008-2009), when profits tend to fall more than wages. After such episodes, however, the declining trend has resumed (chart 1.5A). This trend is creating hazardous headwinds in the current recovery. As wages have decoupled from productivity growth, wage-earners can no longer afford to purchase the growing output, and the resultant stagnating domestic demand is causing further downward pressure on prices and wages, thus threatening a deflationary spiral.

In most developing and transition economies, the share of wages has behaved differently. That share is generally between 35 and 50 per cent of GDP[7] – compared with approximately 60 per cent of GDP in developed economies – and it tends to oscillate significantly, owing mainly to sudden changes in real wages. In many of these economies, the share of wages in national income tended to fall between the 1980s and early 2000s, but has started to recover since the mid-2000s, though it has not yet reached the levels of the 1990s (chart 1.5B). The positive evolution of wages and the role played by incomes policies, particularly transfer programmes to the poor, may be the main factors behind the present "two speed recovery".

In developed countries, real wages grew on average at less than 1 per cent per annum before the crisis, which is below the rate of productivity gains; they then declined during the crisis, and tended to recover very slowly in 2010. Arguably, the early move to a more contractionary fiscal policy and the relatively high levels of idle capacity and unemployment imply that the pressures for higher wages could remain subdued, thereby reducing the chances of a wage-led recovery. In contrast, since the early 2000s, in all developing regions and in the CIS, real wages have been growing, in some instances quite rapidly (table 1.4). In some countries, this may represent a recovery from the steep reductions in the 1990s or early 2000s, and in others it is more than a mere recovery, as wages follow the same path as productivity gains. Even during the difficult years of 2008 and 2009, real wages did not fall in most developing countries, as had generally been the case in previous crises. This suggests that to some extent recovery in

Chart 1.5

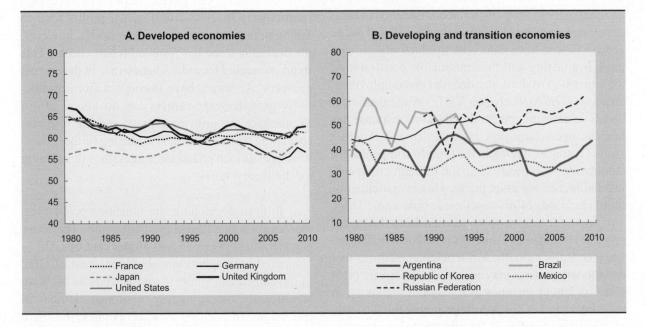

SHARE OF WAGES IN NATIONAL INCOME, SELECTED ECONOMIES, 1980–2010

(Per cent)

Source: UNCTAD secretariat calculations, based on OECD, *Main Economic Indicators* database; and Lindenboim, Kennedy and Graña, 2011.

developing countries was driven by an increase in domestic demand, and that real wage growth has been an integral part of the economic revival.

Examining the evolution of total wage income, which depends on employment and real wages, is essential for understanding the risks of wage deflation. A fall in real wages, rather than leading to an increase in the demand for labour, will affect demand by inducing a fall in consumption (Keynes, 1936). Generally, there is a very close relationship between the rate of change of total wage income and that of final consumer spending. In this respect, Japan's "lost decades" provide a stark warning of the growing challenge at the global level today. Failure to halt downward pressures on prices and domestic demand left the Japanese economy excessively dependent on exports, resulting in persistent deflation and stagnation for two decades. As wage-earners' real income stopped growing, so did private consumption (chart 1.6). Germany seems to be going the way of Japan owing to deliberate wage compression since the mid-1990s, with vastly destabilizing consequences in the euro area. In the United States, even though

consumption was mainly driven by a credit and property boom until the inevitable bursting of the bubble, there is also a strong relationship between the wage bill and private consumption. Wage compression in that country was magnified by regressive tax policies and a strong tendency for households in the upper 1 per cent of the income distribution to appropriate more and more of the total income (Piketty and Saez, 2007).

At the current juncture, in view of the unemployment legacies of the crisis, downward pressures on wages in developed economies risk strangling any incipient recovery of private consumption, which is the necessary basis for a sustainable and balanced recovery. The widely shared agenda of structural reform that aims at improving labour market flexibility would only reinforce the bargaining power of employers in labour markets in developed economies.

In contrast, the rise of the wage bill after periods of decline in several developing and transition economies in the 1980s and 1990s boosted private consumption. For instance, the decline in wages in

Table 1.4

REAL WAGE GROWTH, SELECTED REGIONS AND ECONOMIES, 2001–2010

(Annual change, in per cent)

	2001–2005	2006	2007	2008	2009	2010[a]
Developed economies	**0.5**	**0.9**	**0.8**	**-0.5**	**0.6**	**0.1**
Germany	-0.9	0.0	1.1	1.2	-0.5	1.7
Japan	-0.4	1.6	-1.0	-1.1	-2.9	1.4
United Kingdom	2.8	2.6	3.9	-1.5	-2.2	-1.8
Unites States	-0.3	-0.1	0.5	0.1	2.8	-0.7
Developing and transition economies						
Africa	**1.3**	**2.8**	**1.4**	**0.5**	**2.4**	**..**
South Africa	0.3	5.1	0.2	2.3	3.2	5.2
Asia	**7.8**	**7.6**	**7.2**	**7.1**	**8.0**	**..**
China	12.6	12.9	13.1	11.7	12.8	..
India	2.6	0.4	-0.6	8.3	..	..
Republic of Korea	4.4	3.4	-1.8	-1.5	-3.3	1.2
Latin America and the Caribbean	**0.4**	**4.2**	**3.3**	**1.9**	**2.2**	**2.5**
Brazil	-2.6	3.5	1.5	2.1	1.3	2.4
Chile	1.6	1.9	2.8	-0.2	4.8	2.1
Mexico	0.9	1.4	1.0	2.2	0.8	-0.6
Eastern Europe and Central Asia	**15.1**	**13.4**	**17.0**	**10.6**	**-2.2**	**..**
Russian Federation	15.1	13.3	17.3	11.5	-3.5	2.6

Source: UNCTAD secretariat calculations, based on ILO, 2011; *EC-AMECO* database; ECLAC, 2010; Economist Intelligence Unit; and national sources.

a Preliminary.

the Republic of Korea and the Russian Federation after the crises of the late 1990s was followed by a significant upturn, which was not reversed by the Great Recession. Similarly, in Mexico wages recovered to some extent, but the economic influence of the United States may explain the negative rate of growth of the wage bill during the latest crisis.

The rise in real wages and the wage bill in developing countries, in addition to the real appreciation of exchange rates, indicate that the recovery in those countries depends increasingly on the expansion of domestic markets rather than on exports to developed countries. Nevertheless, developed countries remain important export destinations, and subdued growth in those countries, combined with upward pressures on developing countries' currencies, risks reigniting or reinforcing pressures for relative wage compression in developing countries as well. So far, this has not occurred, but the slowdown in global industrial production in the second quarter of 2011 increases that risk. Indeed, a macroeconomic policy

mix in developed economies featuring fiscal austerity, tighter monetary policies and wage compression could create new global vulnerabilities, which may also affect developing countries. The global recovery would be ill-served by merely shifting fragility from the North to the South instead of directly addressing the fragilities at their source.

2. Incomes policy and inflation control

Growth-friendly macroeconomic policies, of which a proactive incomes policy is a key element, can also help to contain inflation, since investment and productivity growth create the capacities needed to meet the desired steady expansion of domestic demand. An incomes policy based on clear rules for determining wage income in a growing economy can greatly facilitate policymakers' task, and support capital formation and sustainable development. Such

Chart 1.6

TOTAL WAGE BILL AND PRIVATE CONSUMPTION AT CONSTANT PRICES, SELECTED COUNTRIES, 1996–2010

(Annual percentage changes)

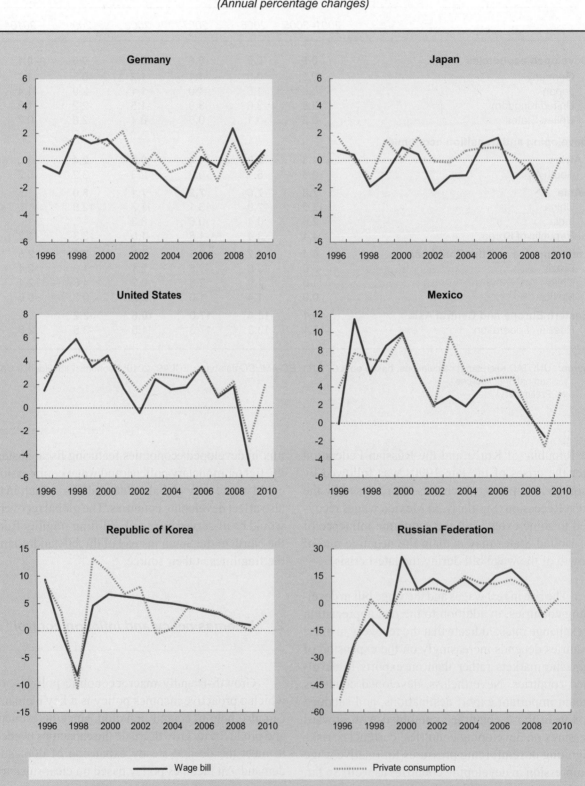

Source: UNCTAD secretariat calculations, based on IMF, *World Economic Outlook* database; and *International Financial Statistics* database; and Lindenboim, Kennedy and Graña, 2011.

a policy, which aims at achieving wage growth in line with productivity growth (plus an inflation target), paves the way for a steady expansion of domestic demand as a basis for expanding investment while containing cost-push risks to price stability.

Wages are the most important determinant of the overall cost of production in a modern, vertically integrated market economy. An incomes policy is therefore also an instrument of inflation control. Wage growth based on the above-mentioned principle would contribute to keeping inflation within the government's target by preventing an overshooting of unit labour costs and maintaining a steady increase in demand. While incomes policy could focus on inflation control, monetary policy could concentrate on securing low-cost finance for investment in real productive capacity, which would create new employment opportunities. In several countries where real wages and the wage share fell due to prolonged economic stagnation and deteriorating labour conditions – as in Latin America and Africa in the 1980s and 1990s – real wages could be allowed to rise faster than productivity for some time in order to restore the desired income distribution pattern. Such a change in income distribution would probably need negotiations among the social partners and the government in order to avoid a wage-price spiral, and it is likely to be facilitated by economic recovery and subsequent improvements in the labour market.

By achieving a rate of wage growth that corresponds approximately to the rate of productivity growth, augmented by a target rate of inflation, it would be possible to control inflation expectations. The problem in the euro area is that these macroeconomic considerations have not been taken into account in some of the member countries (as discussed in chapter VI).

In view of the slow recovery in developed countries (as indicated in chart 1.1), the risk of demand inflation in these countries is minimal. The United States and Europe are experiencing enormous labour market slack, despite the fact that real wages are barely growing. Weak employment growth and stagnant wages, resulting in slow growth of disposable income, are hindering a sustainable domestic-demand-led recovery and are increasing the risk of an excessive reliance on exports for growth. In certain peripheral euro-area countries in particular, debt deflation is an additional acute threat. Fears that the increase in the monetary base in major economies will lead to an acceleration of inflation fail to take into account the context of deflationary forces in which these developments have been occurring. These forces include the ongoing deleveraging processes under way in the still weak financial systems and households of the respective developed economies.[8]

In this context, increases in food and energy prices may cause higher headline inflation in the short run. However, this should not pose a threat of sustained inflation, because the increase in the overall price level is only temporary, and a "second round" of price increases triggered by a wage-price spiral that could make the inflation hike permanent is highly improbable. Furthermore, anti-inflationary policies involving monetary tightening would also be ineffective, to the extent to which the increase in food and energy prices did not result mainly from higher demand for these goods, but rather from the speculative activities of financial investors (see chapter V). Even if restrictive monetary policies could trigger a severe world recession, causing commodity prices to plunge, as they did in the second half of 2008, the remedy would be worse than the illness.

In spite of that, the European Central Bank (ECB) has continued to take its cue from headline inflation, embarking on monetary tightening in April 2011. The Italian central bank governor and recently appointed head of the ECB, Mario Draghi, warned, as early as November 2010, that a "clear and present danger" of overheating justified a "greater need to proceed with monetary policy normalisation" to prevent inflation from being imported from emerging market economies (cited in Wiesmann, 2011). However, faster wage growth in China does not pose any imminent threat of global inflation;[9] rather, it is an important element in rebalancing the Chinese economy towards increasing private consumption. And rebalancing the Chinese economy not only pre-empts the deflationary threat potentially posed by an unravelling of China's fast-track catching up; it also contributes positively to the rebalancing of global demand. Indeed, rising wages amount to a real appreciation of the yuan. Moreover, inflation in China is being driven by rising prices of food, energy and industrial raw materials. However, more generally, rising headline inflation in developing economies is less an issue of overheating than a reflection of the fact that food and energy prices have a much greater weight in the consumer price indices of poorer countries than of developed countries (*TDR 2008*, and chapter V of this *Report*).

More serious concerns arise from asset price inflation, strong credit growth and the widening of current-account deficits observed in some developing countries (e.g. Brazil, India, South Africa and Turkey, among the G-20 members). In the case of Brazil, the central bank raised the interest rate, which was already high in real terms, and the fiscal stance was also tightened. The Russian central bank took similar action. In both cases, it seems that core inflation beyond food and energy prices had also increased. However, that does not necessarily mean that contractionary monetary policy should be the instrument of choice to curb the rise in domestic prices. Price management and supply-side policies that increase the provision of goods and services, along with social pacts that link the rise of real wages to a rise in productivity, might be used to contain cost pressures when an economy still has spare capacity.

3. The European crisis and the need for proactive incomes policies

The lack of proactive and coordinated incomes policies is one of the main causes of present tensions in Europe, particularly within the euro area. Since the launching of the Economic and Monetary Union (EMU), serious imbalances have been building up as a result of diverging national wage trends. In a monetary union, national wage trends are the main determinant of the real exchange rate among its member economies. To avoid dislocations in intraregional competitiveness positions, national wage trends need to follow an implicit norm that is the sum of national productivity growth and the agreed unionwide inflation rate (defined by the ECB as "below but close to 2 per cent"). Countries in the periphery that are experiencing severe public-debt crises today departed from this norm somewhat in the upward direction, whereas Germany, the economy with the largest trade surplus within the euro area, also missed that implicit norm, but in a downward direction. As a result, over time Germany experienced cumulative competitiveness gains vis-à-vis its European partners, especially vis-à-vis the countries in the periphery (*TDRs 2006* and *2010*; Flassbeck, 2007; Bibow, 2006). If inflation rates differ among countries with

their own national currencies, they always have the possibility to compensate for inflation differentials by means of exchange rate adjustments. However, this solution is not possible within the EMU, which makes the resolution of the crisis even more difficult than that of comparable crises in a number of emerging market economies over the past 30 years.

Widening current-account imbalances inside the euro area occurred partly as a result of lending flows, which in some cases caused property bubbles. The bursting of those bubbles resulted in private debt overhangs that first triggered banking crises and eventually turned into today's sovereign debt crises. As a result, banks in the surplus countries became heavily exposed to debtors in the deficit countries.

With the reappearance of severe debt market stress in a number of countries in the second quarter of 2011, most governments are convinced that fiscal austerity is needed for debt sustainability, and that wage compression and labour market reform will restore competitiveness. Reflecting a dogmatic rejection of government intervention, the euro-area authorities only reluctantly considered fiscal stimulus measures. Initially slow to act, they were then the first to call for an early exit from global stimulus, even before recovery had properly taken root. In the event, the euro area has proved the laggard in the global recovery and is now a hotspot of economic instability. Today's financial and economic instabilities arise from an unresolved debt crisis that has its origins in private debt, and which the euro area's policy-making mechanism seems ill-equipped to handle. The area's policy response remains single-mindedly focused on fiscal retrenchment and on "strengthening" the socalled Stability and Growth Pact that was established to govern and asymmetrically discipline member countries' fiscal policies.

Apart from a perceived lack of fiscal discipline, today's crisis in the euro area is widely seen as evidence of a lack of labour market flexibility. But neither fiscal profligacy nor insufficiently flexible labour markets can explain the crisis. Rather, the area's policy regime lacks suitable coordinating mechanisms that would assure stable domestic demand growth while preventing intraregional divergences and imbalances. In concrete terms, excessive wage increases in the economies now in crisis, on the one hand, and stagnating unit labour costs in Germany on the other, have allowed the accumulation of current-account surpluses in the latter at the expense of other countries in the area. By further weakening economic growth, the policies proposed by the euro-area authorities may not succeed in improving debt sustainability either (see chapter III).

Austerity measures in the deficit countries may reduce intra-area current-account imbalances through income compression, but they may also worsen the underlying solvency problem through debt deflation (especially if emergency liquidity is provided at penalty rates). If the debtor countries receive sufficient official financing at reasonable rates (as decided by the European Council on 21 July 2011), they may avoid or postpone default, but this will not resolve the underlying problem of their lack of competitiveness and growth. Owing to erroneous regional policy responses, the crisis countries in the euro area are today labouring under extremely difficult conditions: their GDP growth is flat or even negative, while their market interest rates on public debt are prohibitively high. Seen globally, however, these local conditions are highly exceptional. While their budget deficits are generally high and their public debt ratios are rising, inflation remains low. Thus the current predicament in Europe should be resolved by promoting growth and reducing intraregional imbalances. The European experience holds important lessons for the rest of the world, in particular that austerity without regard for regional domestic demand growth may backfire badly. Well-coordinated monetary policies and debt management aimed at keeping borrowing costs in check regionwide is therefore of the utmost importance.

C. Progress towards global rebalancing, growth and development: an assessment of global cooperation

The latest global financial and economic crisis originated in the United States and Western Europe as excessive private debt led their tightly integrated financial systems to the verge of collapse. With the financial meltdown, which had the potential to cause another Great Depression of global dimensions, policymakers realized that dealing with the fallout would require urgent international coordination of economic policies.

At the peak of the global crisis there was a rare display of international solidarity, with coordinated monetary stimulus by major central banks leading the way. At the G-20 summit meetings in November 2008 in Washington and in April 2009 in London, Heads of State and Government committed to providing sizeable fiscal stimulus packages and emergency support programmes for restoring financial stability. The aggregate policy impact of these measures stopped the economic freefall and won global policymakers an important first round in battling the crisis. Today, the G-20 continues to be a leading forum for international economic cooperation. The Framework for Strong, Sustainable and Balanced Growth, launched at the G-20 summit meeting in Pittsburgh in September 2009, has also become the centrepiece of economic policy coordination among members. The framework commits G-20 members to "work together to assess how [their national] policies fit together, to evaluate whether they are collectively consistent with more sustainable and balanced growth, and to act as necessary to meet [our] common objectives" (G-20, 2009). A country-led, consultative "mutual assessment process" (MAP) was initiated to review members' actions for that purpose.

The success of these exercises critically hinges on a certain degree of commonality of policy views among members, which remains problematic. Since mid-2010, there has been a clear shift in the general policy orientation. While the previous position was that fiscal stimulus should be maintained until recovery was assured, the Toronto Summit Declaration established fiscal consolidation as the new policy priority. Accordingly, developed countries announced their commitment to at least halve their fiscal deficits by 2013 and to stabilize or reduce their public-debt-to-GDP ratios by 2016 (G-20, 2010a). The subsequent Seoul Action Plan of November 2010 called for a common effort to safeguard the recovery and achieve strong, sustainable and balanced growth. A range of policies was identified as potentially contributing to reducing excessive imbalances, including a move towards ensuring that exchange rates are determined by "market fundamentals". In addition, members committed to implementing structural reforms "to reduce the reliance on external demand and focus more on domestic sources of growth in surplus countries while promoting higher national savings and enhancing export competitiveness in deficit countries" (G-20, 2011a).

In this context, it was agreed to monitor the implementation of countries' commitments and assess progress towards meeting their shared objectives. It was decided to enhance the MAP by means of "indicative guidelines" to serve as a "mechanism to facilitate timely identification of large imbalances that require preventive and corrective actions to be taken" (G-20, 2010b). Accordingly, it was agreed to establish a set of indicators, including public debt and fiscal deficits; private debt and savings rates; and current-account balances, "taking due consideration of exchange rate, fiscal, monetary and other policies" (G-20, 2011).

The definition of such indicators is neither obvious nor neutral: a lack of official data, different national methodologies, the choice of an appropriate reference period and the production of consistent country forecasts are some of the issues that need to be resolved. Looking at the components of the current account rather than just at the overall balance would add valuable insight to the analysis, especially as changes in the current-account balance can be driven by a variety of factors.[10] Moreover, there are different views as to how global imbalances could be reduced.

Much is at stake in finding a globally coordinated answer to this issue of global imbalances, but there are conflicting policy views. Disagreements pertain to how global imbalances contributed to the global crisis, which policy adjustments may be best suited for reducing excessive imbalances, and which countries should undertake most of those adjustments. One point of view is presented by the IMF, based on a distinction between developed and emerging G-20 economies on the one hand, and deficit and surplus countries on the other. It calls for stronger fiscal consolidation, mainly in the developed countries that have a deficit, and for emerging economies with a surplus to reorient their growth strategy from a reliance on external demand to a reliance on domestic demand. However, the developed surplus economies are not asked to do the same (i.e. to stimulate their domestic markets instead of continuously relying on net exports) (Lipsky, 2011).

On the other hand, a Feasible Policy Coordination Scenario for Global Rebalancing and Sustained Growth produced by the United Nations (UN/DESA, 2011) proposes a stronger role for fiscal policy in the short term (see also chapter III). It forecasts that a policy that postpones fiscal tightening in developed economies, and uses incentives to foster private investment, while also increasing government spending on improvements in infrastructure and on research and development for greater energy efficiency will be more favourable to GDP growth. Fiscal policy could either support or restrain household disposable incomes and spending in both current-account surplus and deficit countries. In this Feasible Policy Coordination Scenario, a general narrowing (or containment) of current-account imbalances to less than 4 per cent of GDP is achievable by 2015, or earlier, with only a moderate further depreciation of the dollar.

Examining the evolution of global current-account imbalances since the global crisis erupted raises doubts about the effectiveness of the existing initiatives. In current dollars terms, global current-account imbalances peaked in 2007–2008, shrank in 2009 – when the volume and value of global trade declined sharply – and are widening again in 2010–2011 as trade and GDP recover. Imports and exports (by volume) generally fall and rise in parallel in both deficit and surplus major economies. They fell and recovered at very similar paces in the EU, the United States and the developing economies as a group (see table 1.2). Among the surplus countries, only in China and Japan did the volume of exports fall more than that of imports in 2009, thereby contributing to global rebalancing. Changes in prices played an even more important role: the decline in commodity prices (especially of oil) in 2009 helped reduce the deficit in the EU (excluding Germany) and the United States in 2009, and their recovery is contributing to a widening of these deficits in 2010 and 2011. An inflated oil import bill is today the largest contributor to the increase in the current-account deficit of the United States, as that country's non-oil merchandise trade balance has improved significantly. The counterpart to these developments is the reduction in 2009 of the current-account surplus of the major oil-exporting countries, and its subsequent renewed rise. In current dollars terms, or as a percentage of world GDP, global imbalances are still below their pre-crisis highs, but they are already approaching the levels of 2006 (chart 1.7).

Current-account imbalances have been reduced if measured in terms of their share in each country's GDP. In 2010, the current-account deficit in countries such as the United States and Spain roughly halved from its pre-crisis levels (falling from 6 per cent to 3.2 per cent and from 10 per cent to 4.5 per cent, respectively); but it did not fall significantly in the United Kingdom. On the other hand, developed economies that had a surplus reduced that surplus rather moderately. In Germany, it remained at almost 6 per cent of GDP in 2010, mainly due to its trade surplus. In Japan, the surplus was around 3.5 per cent of the GDP, owing mainly to net income revenues, which, being a rather stable source of income, are likely to maintain this surplus in the foreseeable future. Among the developing countries with a current-account surplus, China's surplus has fallen sharply from its pre-crisis peak of over 10 per cent of GDP to around 5 per cent in 2010, and it is probably even lower in 2011. This is partly due to a decline in its trade surplus, but also to its continuing GDP growth, which is more rapid in current United States dollars than in constant yuan due to a real appreciation of its currency.

Current-account positions have been affected by the timing and characteristics of countries' recovery from the global crisis. A decomposition of growth into domestic demand and net exports shows that growth in Brazil, China, India and the Russian Federation has been largely driven by an increase in domestic demand. This suggests that these developing and transition economies are honouring their commitment to help reduce global imbalances. In other countries, such as Japan and members of the

Chart 1.7

CURRENT-ACCOUNT BALANCES, SELECTED COUNTRIES AND COUNTRY GROUPS, 2005–2011

(Billions of current dollars)

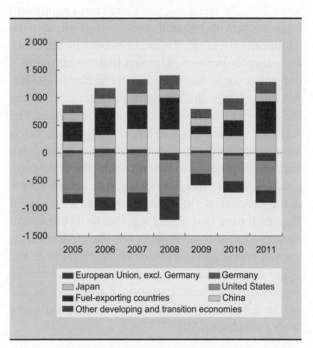

Source: UNCTAD secretariat calculations, based on UN/DESA, *National Accounts Main Aggregates* database, and *WESP 2011: Mid-year Update*; and IMF, *World Economic Outlook* database.
Note: Data for 2011 are forecast.

euro area, it is net exports that have been the major engine of growth. In the United States, net exports have played a near-neutral role in the recovery. While Germany and Japan have greatly benefited from brisk export growth to China, which outpaced their growth in imports, the increase in United States exports was balanced by a similar increase in its imports.

Exchange rates and interest rates are key variables that affect the sustainability of current-account imbalances. Exchange rates determine countries' international competitiveness, and adjustments in those rates may therefore serve to correct imbalances in competitiveness. Interest rates matter because of their influence on countries' net investment income, and also because of their role as drivers of capital flows, thereby indirectly affecting exchange rates and competitiveness. The question is whether global currency markets can be trusted to establish equilibrium in exchange rates on their own.

Since 2007, there has been a sizeable depreciation in the real effective exchange rate (REER) in two large current-account deficit countries, the United Kingdom and the United States (chart 1.8), which seems to be in line with rebalancing requirements.[11] The same holds for the marked rise in China's REER since 2005. In Germany, there has been a significant improvement in competitiveness in the context of the European crisis, which is inconsistent with the country's surplus position. The fact that the euro area's current account has been mostly balanced overall does not change this assessment; rather, it confirms the existence of serious intraregional imbalances. The increase in Germany's external competitiveness is inconsistent with the objective of achieving a global balance. Equally inconsistent with global requirements was the marked depreciation of Japan's REER in the pre-crisis period. The pronounced weakness of the yen during that period was due to its attractiveness as a carry-trade funding currency. Afterwards, the yen appreciated, as policy interest rates in all the major developed economies were cut to near zero in response to the global crisis, and the yen lost its role as the most important funding currency for carry trade (see chapter VI).

Brazil's REER moved sharply in the opposite direction to the Japanese yen, as carry-trade positions unwound at the peak of the crisis, but it has since resumed its sharp appreciation reflecting the Brazilian real's renewed attractiveness as a carry-trade target currency. As a result, Brazil's exports of manufactures have suffered a loss of competitiveness, and the country's trade balance has declined despite the ongoing commodity price boom, although it still remains in surplus. What has dramatically increased is its deficit in investment income, owing mainly to profit remittances by transnational corporations and, to a lesser extent, interest payments on debt. Similar exchange rate trends have been observed in other developing countries, a number of which have meanwhile drifted into sizeable current-account deficit positions – a new form of the "Dutch disease" – which may herald future instabilities of systemic significance (Bresser-Pereira, 2008). The currencies of Chile, India, Mexico, the Republic of Korea, the Russian Federation, South Africa and Turkey, for example, underwent a significant appreciation of their REER following the recovery from the crisis (chart 1.8).

Exchange rate movements that are persistently inconsistent with achieving balanced global competitiveness positions provide strong evidence for the need to coordinate global currency markets. National governments may intervene in currency markets in pursuit of national policy objectives, either to offset market failures and prevent exchange rate misalignment or to attain a competitive advantage. The point is that exchange rates are intrinsically a multilateral issue that requires multilateral management.

The Seoul Action Plan includes a commitment to "move toward more market-determined exchange rate systems, enhancing exchange rate flexibility to reflect underlying economic fundamentals, and refraining from competitive devaluation of currencies." It also states, "Advanced economies, including those with reserve currencies, will be vigilant against excess volatility and disorderly movements in exchange rates" (G-20, 2010b). If these commitments herald a move towards floating exchange rates and withdrawal of government intervention, the action plan will not succeed in achieving global stability. The evidence is overwhelming: left on their own, currency markets are a primary source of instability and systemic risk.[12]

Globalization requires proper global economic governance. However, the existing system of global governance, especially the global monetary and financial system, has major shortcomings, as highlighted by the latest global crisis. This is why continued G-20 efforts to promote international economic cooperation are important. The crisis also highlighted serious flaws in the pre-crisis belief in liberalization and self-regulating markets. Liberalized financial markets have been encouraging excessive speculation (which amounts to gambling) and instability. And financial innovations have been serving their own industry rather than the greater social interest. Ignoring these flaws risks another, possibly even bigger, crisis. The new emphasis on adopting a macroprudential perspective and paying greater attention to cross-border spillovers is laudable, but questions remain as to whether the system's functional efficiency in contributing to growth and stability of the real economy will be assured. So far, policymakers have been merely tinkering with, rather than fundamentally changing, the global economic governance regime.

Globalization has created a fundamental tension between global economic integration and national economic policies aimed at effectively meeting the responsibilities of national governments (Rodrik, 2011). It has also shifted the balance of power in

Chart 1.8

REAL EFFECTIVE EXCHANGE RATE, SELECTED COUNTRIES, JANUARY 2000–MAY 2011

(Index numbers, 2005 = 100, CPI based)

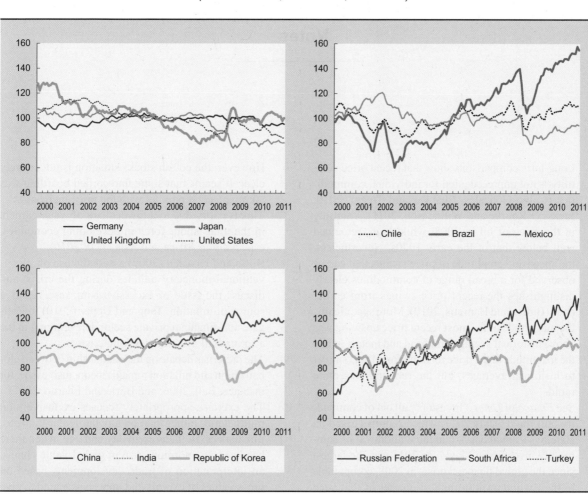

Source: Bank for International Settlements, *Effective Exchange Rate Indices* database.

favour of large, globally active corporations and players, including financial institutions, and left employees more vulnerable to global forces compounded by often weakened (or even absent) national safety nets. In many developed as well as developing countries, the forces unleashed by globalization have produced significant shifts in income distribution resulting in a falling share of wage income and a rising share of profits. But the global crisis has clearly exposed the limitations of this model. Today, more than ever before, there is an urgent need for a shift in the policy paradigm, together with fundamental reform of the global system of governance. The Seoul Development Consensus states that "for prosperity to be sustained it must be shared." This laudable slogan is true not only between countries but also within them. *TDR 2010* proposed productivity-led growth of labour income as the basis for a successful development strategy that gives priority to employment creation and poverty reduction. This strategy is even more important today, when the world is in the midst of a fragile two-speed recovery. ■

Notes

1   Long-term comparisons show that recent price volatility is not unprecedented for individual commodities (Calvo-Gonzales, Shankar and Trezzi, 2010;
Jacks, O'Rourke and Williamson, 2011). Volatility
in the price of oil in 2008, while high, remained
well below that of the early 1970s. Nevertheless,
the speed and amplitude of price swings that can be
observed for a broad range of commodities clearly
distinguishes the recent price swings from earlier
ones (Baffes and Haniotis, 2010). More specifically,
the magnitude of the most recent price upswing was
above historical averages for food and metals, while
the magnitude of the price rebound for oil was similar
to historical averages, but the rebound was more
rapid.

2   See *Financial Times*, "Investors pull out of commodity bull run", 6 July 2011, which reports (based on
Barclays Capital data), that the withdrawal of commodity investors in May-June 2011 was the largest
since the global financial crisis in 2008, comparable
to their withdrawal in the last quarter of that year.
IMF (2011b) also notes that the corrections partly
reflected the unwinding of an earlier build-up of non
commercial derivative positions.

3   In 2010 China surpassed the United States as the
world's largest energy consumer (BP, 2011).

4   On 23 June 2011, IEA member countries agreed
to make 2 million barrels of oil per day available
from emergency stocks over an initial period of 30
days (IEA press release, "IEA makes 60 million
barrels of oil available to market to offset Libyan
disruption", at: http://www.iea.org/press/pressdetail.
asp?PRESS_REL_ID=418).

5   Calculations are based on data from the USDA
Production, Supply and Distribution online database,
as well as the USDA *Feed Grains Data: Yearbook
Tables*.

6   However, the cotton stocks situation is not entirely
clear. It seems that some unrecorded hoarding was
taking place in parallel with the price increases.

7   This is partly due to a lower share of wage-earners
in the total labour force in developing economies,
especially in Africa and Asia (*TDR 2010*).

8   Borio and Disyatat (2009) assess the use of unconventional monetary policies during the crisis, and
discuss the issue of excessive bank reserves as a
source of inflation. Tang and Upper (2010) investi-
gate non-financial private sector deleveraging in the
aftermath of systemic banking crisis.

9   The pre-crisis debate on the relationship between globalization and inflation remains inconclusive (see, for
instance, Ball, 2006; and Borio and Filardo, 2007).

10 The exercise appropriately focuses exclusively on
multilateral, rather than on any particular bilateral,
imbalances. In the present day and age, when there
has been an enormous rise in global value chains,
an interpretation of trade developments based on
gross values of exports and imports is bound to give
a distorted picture of bilateral trade imbalances (for
example, see Xing and Detert, 2010). The Director-
General of the World Trade Organization (WTO)
recently suggested that "trade in value-added" would
serve as a better measurement of world trade (WTO,
2011b; see also WTO, 2011c).

11 In the case of the United States, the sharp appreciation of the dollar at the peak of the global crisis,
owing to a "dollar shortage", interrupted the adjustment (see *TDR 2010*). In the case of the United
Kingdom, the country's aggressive fiscal austerity
programme is taking place in relatively benign conditions, supported by an accommodative monetary
policy and currency depreciation.

12 Chapter VI of this *Report* outlines a proposal for a
multilateral system of managed exchange rates.

References

Baffes J and Haniotis T (2010). Placing the 2006/08 commodity price boom into perspective. Policy Research Working Paper 5371, World Bank, Washington, DC.

Ball LM (2006). Has globalization changed inflation? NBER Working Paper No. 12687. Cambridge, MA, National Bureau of Economic Research.

Bibow J (2006). The euro area drifting apart: Does reform of labor markets deliver competitive stability or competitive divergence? In: *Structural Reforms and Macro-Economic Policy*. Brussels, European Trade Union Confederation: 76–86.

BIS (2011). *81st Annual Report*. Basel, Bank for International Settlements, June.

Borio C and Disyatat P (2009). Unconventional monetary policies: An appraisal. BIS Working Paper no. 292. Bank for International Settlements, Basel, November.

Borio C and Filardo A (2007). Globalization and inflation: New cross-country evidence on the global determinants of domestic inflation. BIS Working Paper no. 227. Bank for International Settlements, Basel.

BP (2011). *Statistical Review of World Energy*. London, British Petroleum, June.

Bresser-Pereira LC (2008). The Dutch disease and its neutralization: a Ricardian approach. *Revista de Economia Politica*, 28(1): 47–71.

Calvo-Gonzales O, Shankar R and Trezzi R (2010). Are Commodity Prices More Volatile Now? A Long-Run Perspective. Policy Research Working Paper 5460, World Bank, Washington, DC.

ECLAC (2010). *Preliminary Overview of the Economies of Latin America and the Caribbean 2010*. Santiago, Chile, Economic Commission for Latin America and the Caribbean, December.

ECLAC (2011). *Economic Survey of Latin America and the Caribbean 2010–2011*. Santiago, Chile, Economic Commission for Latin America and the Caribbean, July.

European Commission (2007): *Employment in Europe*. Brussels.

FAO (2011). *Food Outlook*. Food and Agriculture Organization of the United Nations, Rome, June.

Flassbeck H (2007). Wage divergences in Euroland: Explosive in the making. In: Bibow J and Terzi A, eds. *Euroland and the Global Economy: Global Player or Global Drag?* Basingstoke, Palgrave Macmillan.

G-20 (2009). Leaders' Statement, the Pittsburgh Summit, 24–25 September.

G-20 (2010a). Leaders' Statement, the Toronto Summit, 26–27 June.

G-20 (2010b). Leaders' Statement, the Seoul Summit, 11–12 November.

G-20 (2011). Communiqué of the Meeting of Finance Ministers and Central Bank Governors, Paris, 18–19 February.

IEA (2011a). Oil Market Report. Paris, International Energy Agency, June.

IEA (2011b). Oil Market Report. Paris, International Energy Agency, May.

ILO (2011). *Global Wage Report 2010/11: Wage Policies in Times of Crisis*. Geneva.

IMF (2007a). *World Economic Outlook*. Washington, DC, April.

IMF (2007b). *World Economic Outlook*. Washington, DC, October.

IMF (2011a). *World Economic Outlook*. Washington, DC, April.

IMF (2011b). *World Economic Outlook Update*. Washington, DC, June.

Ivanic M, Martin W and Zaman H (2011). Estimating the short-run poverty impacts of the 2010–11 surge in food prices. Policy Research Working Paper 5633, World Bank, Washington, DC.

Jacks DS, O'Rourke KH and Williamson JG (2011). Commodity Price Volatility and World Market Integration since 1700. *Review of Economics and Statistics* (forthcoming).

JP Morgan (2011). JP Morgan Global Manufacturing PMI. May 2011 Survey, 1 June.

Keynes JM (1936). *The General Theory of Employment, Interest and Money*. London, Macmillan.

Koo R (2011). QE2 has transformed commodity markets into liquidity-driven markets. Nomura Equity Research, Tokyo, May.

Lindenboim J, Kennedy D and Graña JM (2011). Share of labour compensation and aggregate demand: Discussions towards a growth strategy. UNCTAD Discussion Paper (forthcoming). Geneva.

Lipsky J (2011). US Fiscal Policy and the Global Outlook. Speech at the American Economic Association Annual Meeting, Roundtable on The United States in the World Economy Denver, 8 January. Available at: www.imf.org/external/np/speeches/2011/010811.htm.

Metals Economics Group (2011). *World Exploration Trends*. A special report from the Metals Economics Group for the Prospectors and Developers Association of Canada (PDAC) International Convention 2011, Toronto.

OECD (2008). *Growing Unequal? Income Distribution and Poverty in OECD Countries*. Paris.

OECD-FAO (2011). *Agricultural Outlook 2011–2020*. Paris and Rome.

Piketty T and Saez E (2007) Income Inequality in the United States, 1913-2002. In: Atkinson AB and Piketty T, eds. *Top Incomes over the Twentieth Century: A Contrast between Continental European and English-Speaking Countries*. Oxford, Oxford University Press: 141–225.

Rodrik D (2011). The Globalization Paradox: Democracy and the Future of the World Economy. New York, Norton.

Sum A, Khatiwada I, McLaughlin J and Palma S (2011). The "Jobless and Wageless" Recovery from the Great Recession of 2007-2009. Center for Labor Market Studies, Northeastern University, Boston, MA, May.

Tang G and Upper C (2010). Debt reduction after crises. *BIS Quarterly Review*. Basel, Bank for International Settlements, September: 25–38.

UNCTAD (*TDR 2005*). *Trade and Development Report, 2005. New features of global interdependence*. United Nations publications, Sales No. E.05.II.D.13, New York and Geneva.

UNCTAD (*TDR 2006*). *Trade and Development Report, 2006. Global partnership and national policies for development*. United Nations publications, Sales No. E.06.II.D.6, New York and Geneva.

UNCTAD (*TDR 2008*). *Trade and Development Report, 2008. Commodity Prices, Capital Flows and the Financing of Investment*. United Nations publications, Sales No. E.08.II.D.21, New York and Geneva.

UNCTAD (*TDR 2010*). *Trade and Development Report, 2010. Employment, Globalization and Development*. United Nations publications, Sales No. E.10.II.D.3, New York and Geneva.

UNCTAD (2011). *Review of Maritime Transport 2011*. Geneva (forthcoming).

UN/DESA (2011). *World Economic Situation and Prospects 2011* (update as of mid-2011). New York, United Nations.

USDA (2010). Oilseeds: World Markets and Trade. Washington, DC, United States Department of Agriculture, December.

Wiesmann G (2011). Draghi warns on global recovery. *Financial Times*, 25 May.

World Tourism Organization (2011a). *UNWTO World Tourism Barometer,* 9 (interim update), Madrid, April.

World Tourism Organization (2011b). *UNWTO World Tourism Barometer*, 9(1), Madrid, February.

WTO (2011a). Report on G20 trade measures (mid-October 2010 to April 2011). Geneva.

WTO (2011b). Lamy suggests "trade in value-added" as a better measurement of world trade. Press release, Geneva, 6 June.

WTO (2011c). Trade patterns and global value chains in East Asia: From trade in goods to trade in tasks. Geneva.

Xing Y and Detert N (2010). How the iPhone widens the United States trade deficit with the People's Republic of China. ADBI Working Paper No. 257, Asian Development Bank Institute, Tokyo, December.

Chapter II

FISCAL ASPECTS OF THE FINANCIAL CRISIS AND ITS IMPACT ON PUBLIC DEBT

A. Introduction

The global financial crisis once again brought fiscal policies and, more generally, the role of the State to the forefront of the economic policy debate. After many years of neoliberal policies oriented towards reducing the role of the State in economic management, governments in most countries came under pressure to undertake widespread and massive intervention to rescue the financial sector and compensate – at least partly – for the shrinking private demand. Previous obsessions with fiscal targets or balanced budgets were temporarily forgotten. Yet the virtually unanimous calls for public intervention started to subside when most countries returned to positive growth rates and their focus changed to the deterioration of fiscal deficits and public debt. Less than two years after the collapse of the large investment bank, Lehman Brothers, the financial markets came to view governments' fiscal policy more as part of the problem than the solution.

Public sector accounts have been dramatically affected by the global crisis. In addition to policy-driven fiscal stimulus packages, which typically involved a discretionary increase in public spending and/or tax cuts to counter the macroeconomic impact of the crisis in the financial sector, the crisis itself affected fiscal balances and public debt through several channels. One reason for the increasing public deficits and debts was the operation of automatic stabilizers, in particular reduced tax revenues, which reflected the downturn in economic activity, and, in countries with well-developed social security systems, increasing social expenditure, especially higher unemployment allowances.

In many other countries, fiscal accounts were also strongly affected by other crisis-related factors. On the revenue side, an abrupt fall in commodity prices reduced government income in countries where such income is linked to revenues from their exports of primary commodities. On the expenditure side, currency depreciation and higher interest rate spreads increased the burden of public debt, in some cases significantly. And in several developed countries, to a large extent the rise in public debt is a direct result of the crisis, as governments bailed out ailing financial institutions, which amounted to converting former private debt into public debt. All these factors adversely affected the fiscal balance without delivering significant economic stimulus. Clearly, therefore, the crisis was not the outcome of excessive public expenditure or public sector deficits; rather, it was the cause of the high fiscal deficits and/or high public-debt-to-GDP ratios in several countries.

Nevertheless, some governments have already changed their policy orientation from providing fiscal stimulus to fiscal tightening, while others are planning to do so, in an effort to maintain or regain the confidence of financial markets which is viewed as key to economic recovery. This policy reorientation comes at a time when private economic activity is still far from being restored to a self-sustained growth path, as discussed in chapter I. Although it is universally recognized that the crisis was the result of financial market failure, little has been learned about placing too much confidence in the judgement of financial market actors, including rating agencies. Many of the financial institutions that had behaved irresponsibly were bailed out by governments in order to limit the damage to the wider economic system. It is therefore surprising that, now that "the worst appears to be over" for those institutions, a large body of public opinion and many policymakers are once again putting their trust in those same institutions to judge what constitutes correct macroeconomic management and public finance.

In any case, the shift towards fiscal tightening appears to be premature in many countries where private demand has not yet recovered on a self-sustaining basis, and where government stimulus is still needed to avoid a prolonged stagnation. Premature fiscal tightening could be self-defeating if it weakens the recovery process, hampers improvement in public revenues and increases the fiscal costs related to the recession and bailouts. Hence, by hindering economic growth, such a policy would fail to achieve fiscal consolidation.

A clear assessment of the roots of the crisis and the evolution of public debt is of utmost importance for elaborating policy recommendations. Focusing almost exclusively on the current levels of public debt risks treating the symptoms but not the causes of the problem. And a wrong diagnosis would not only leave some fundamental problems unsolved, but would also render economic policy ineffective. This chapter examines the recent evolution of fiscal accounts and public debt, both in developed and developing economies, and discusses their relationship with the crisis. Chapter III then focuses on the related policy challenges.

This chapter argues that the recent global financial and economic crisis was not due to profligate fiscal policies, and that the increase in public debt in a number of developed countries was the result of the Great Recession. Primary deficits caused by discretionary fiscal policies were a much smaller contributory factor to higher debt ratios than the

slower (or negative) GDP growth and the banking and currency crises. Therefore any policy that seeks to reduce public debt should avoid curbing GDP growth; without growth, any fiscal consolidation is highly unlikely to succeed. These findings challenge the influential "Lawson Doctrine", that financial crises are caused by excessive public sector borrowing, and that private sector debt never poses a problem because it is the outcome of optimal saving and investment decisions.[1] Consequently, the usual corollary of that doctrine, which is that debt crises always require fiscal retrenchment, is also debatable.

Section B of this chapter examines the evolution of public revenues and expenditures before, during and after the crisis in different groups of countries. It discusses to what extent government savings (and dissavings) may have contributed to the build-up of the crisis, and assesses how the crisis itself has affected fiscal outcomes. Countries felt the impact of the crisis in different and specific ways, and their ability and willingness to conduct countercyclical policies varied. The section considers the different challenges facing the major developed economies, the most vulnerable European and transition economies – many of which sought financial support from the International Monetary Fund (IMF), the European Union (EU) and other sources – and emerging market and developing economies, in particular those that rely heavily on earnings from commodity exports for their fiscal revenues. It also examines the various countries' responses to those challenges.

Section C reviews the evolution of public debt in developing and developed countries. It shows that, prior to the eruption of the crisis in 2008, developing countries had managed to sharply reduce their average debt-to-GDP ratios and also made progress towards altering the composition of their public debt by borrowing more domestically than from abroad. The crisis stopped this trend but did not completely reverse it. In developed countries, by contrast, the crisis led to a sudden jump in debt ratios. Lower debt ratios in most developing countries generally had not been due to a reduction in the stock of public debt – except for a number of heavily indebted poor countries that obtained debt reductions – but rather to their rapid GDP growth. Over the same period of time, some developing countries started accumulating large external reserves, so that their ratios of net external public debt to GDP fell dramatically, and previous currency mismatches in their aggregate balance sheets were corrected. These buffers provided the fiscal and external space that enabled many of these countries to respond to the global recession with various countercyclical policies, whereas other developing countries, especially the low-income ones, did not have similar fiscal space to conduct

proactive fiscal policies. This section also discusses the different factors that can cause a debt crisis. It shows that in general the primary budget deficit is a fairly small component of debt growth, the most important factors being those related to balance-sheet effects and banking crises. Section D concludes.

B. Fiscal aspects of the global crisis

1. Fiscal balances and global imbalances before the crisis

Economic crises and fiscal accounts are closely interrelated, although the nature of that relationship is controversial. It is clear that fiscal balances deteriorated significantly in all regions with the crisis, but this correlation does not reveal causality. At a time when several governments and international institutions are adopting a policy of fiscal austerity aimed at reducing their public-debt-to-GDP ratios as a priority, it is important to examine whether such a policy tackles the roots of the problem, or whether it is merely treating the symptoms and forgetting the cause of the illness on the assumption that the illness has already been cured (Aglietta, 2011: 47). In other words, there is a need to assess whether fiscal imbalances were a major cause of the crisis, because they led to overindebtedness or widened global imbalances; or if, in general, fiscal deficits were the consequence rather than the cause of the crisis.

A review of a number of systemically important countries (including developed and emerging market economies) shows that the evolution of government savings[2] is not the main factor behind external imbalances. In the United States, the current-account balance fell steadily, from equilibrium in 1991 to a deficit of 6 per cent of GDP in 2006, in the build-up to the crisis (chart 2.1). Government savings can hardly explain this trend: they first increased significantly

between 1992 and 2000, as a result of strong growth of GDP and tax revenues as well as what was then called the "peace dividend"; they subsequently fell due to slower growth and policy shifts that reduced taxes and increased military expenditure, but this shift had no noticeable impact on the current account. The progressive decline of household savings would be a better explanation for the widening current-account deficit, but this alone could not have been sufficient, as discussed below with reference to Japan. Rather, the trade and current-account deficits were more likely the result of a combination of rising consumption – by incurring ever-increasing private debt (which lowers household savings rates) – and the loss of industrial competitiveness. However, the lower household savings were less of a contributory factor than the greater consumption of imported rather than domestically produced goods, which slowed down growth of domestic income, corporate profits and tax revenue for the state and federal governments (*TDR 2006*, chapter I).

Another major developed economy, Japan, has run a current-account surplus every year over the past three decades, with a rising trend from 1.5 per cent of GDP in 1990 to 4.8 per cent in 2007 (chart 2.1). During that period, government savings plunged by 8 percentage points of GDP, and household savings also fell by an equal amount. Thus the country's current-account surplus was clearly not because the Government or households decided to save more. Similarly, in Germany the shift in the early 2000s

Chart 2.1

GROSS CAPITAL FORMATION, CURRENT-ACCOUNT BALANCE AND NATIONAL SAVINGS IN SELECTED COUNTRIES, 1990–2010

(Per cent of current GDP)

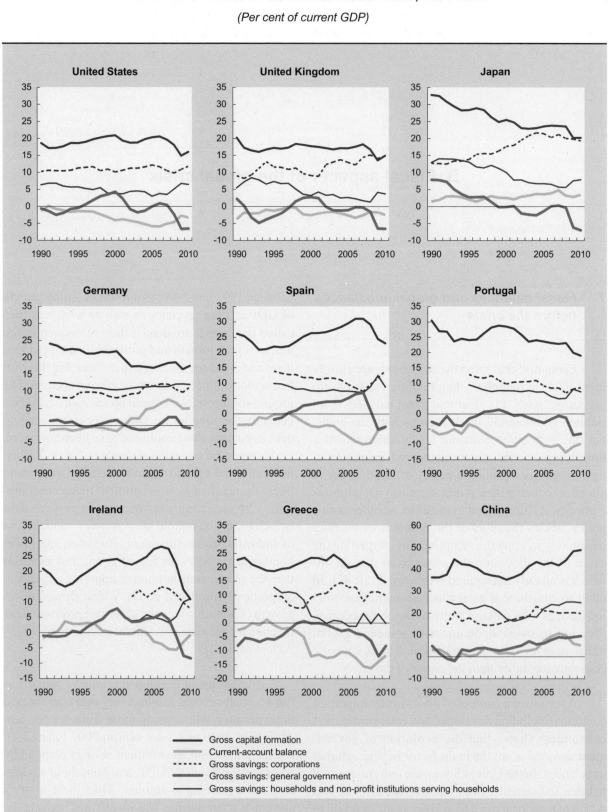

Gross capital formation
Current-account balance
Gross savings: corporations
Gross savings: general government
Gross savings: households and non-profit institutions serving households

Chart 2.1 (concluded)

GROSS CAPITAL FORMATION, CURRENT-ACCOUNT BALANCE AND NATIONAL SAVINGS IN SELECTED COUNTRIES, 1990–2010

(Per cent of current GDP)

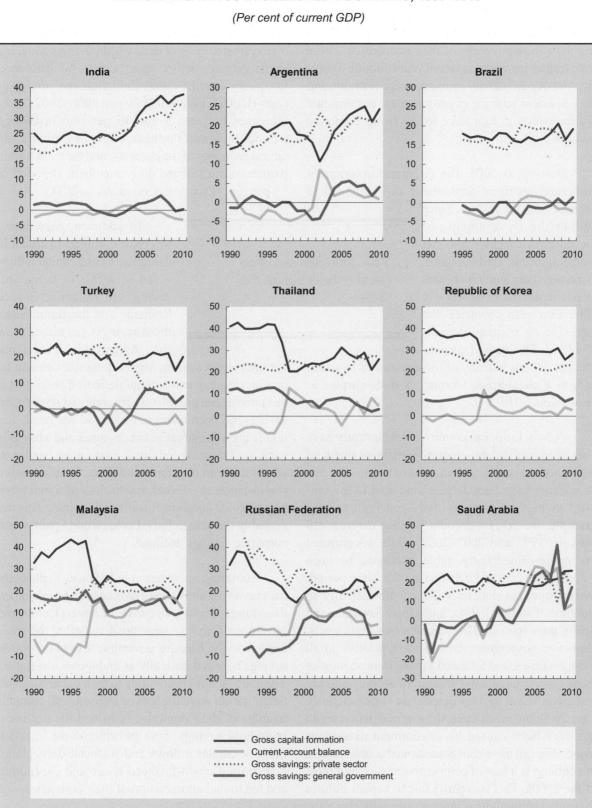

Source: UNCTAD secretariat calculations, based on *EC-AMECO* database; IMF, *World Economic Outlook* database; and national sources.

from a deficit to a large surplus in its external account coincided with a reduction in the government savings rate, while that of households remained stable. The large trade surpluses of these two economies are therefore not the result of *ex ante* household or government savings, but of the strategic specialization and the competitiveness of their economies. These have further increased in recent years through a combination of productivity gains and wage restraint, and are consistent with the *ex post* increase in corporate profits, which in turn have led to rising corporate savings.

Starting in 2005, the German Government embarked on fiscal adjustment and managed to generate positive savings. Since neither the Government nor the corporate sector had net financing needs, German banks increased their lending abroad, in particular to borrowers in other European countries that were facing competitiveness problems. This caused current-account deficits in many of these countries to widen and, as a counterpart, Germany's trade surplus to grow (Koo, 2010).

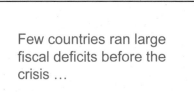

Few countries ran large fiscal deficits before the crisis …

Even in European countries that currently have a sizeable public debt – requiring massive financial assistance to avoid default in some of them – external imbalances have been largely unrelated to government savings. In Hungary, Italy and Portugal, for example, the current-account balance deteriorated between 1995 and 2007–2008, while government savings remained fairly stable, averaging between 0 and -1 per cent of GDP. During the same period, current-account deficits widened dramatically in Bulgaria, Estonia, Latvia, Lithuania, Romania and Spain, their ratio to GDP reaching two-digit levels. However, government savings were positive in all these countries, and followed a rising trend in most of them. Only in Greece did the current-account balance and government savings deteriorate simultaneously after 2000; but, even there, the external deficit could not have been caused by government dissavings alone. What all these above-mentioned countries have in common is a loss of competitiveness during most of the 2000s. This was partly due to capital inflows that were attracted by interest rates differentials, combined with a perception that these countries presented a low exchange-rate risk (in some cases

because of their membership of the Eurosystem) and that their equity and real estate markets offered opportunities for making rapid profits. These capital inflows fuelled speculative bubbles and led to real currency appreciation in the host countries. Since the nominal exchange rate as an instrument of monetary management does not exist within the eurozone, real exchange rates drifted apart, driven by differences in country-specific rates of inflation and unit labour costs (ULCs): between 2000 and 2006–2007, ULCs increased between 5 and 15 per cent in Greece, Ireland, Italy and Portugal, while in Germany, the largest economy of the eurozone and the main trading partner of most of the other members, they fell by 13 per cent (European Commission, 2011).

In addition, easy access to credit – linked to financial deregulation and capital inflows – led to a fall in household savings. In Bulgaria, Greece, Romania and the Baltic States those savings even turned negative. As a result of their real currency appreciation, higher domestic demand led to widening current-account deficits. The impact of this unbalanced growth on corporate and government savings has been ambiguous: on the one hand, economic growth increased the revenues and savings of some governments and firms; on the other hand, easy access to credit may have weakened fiscal discipline (for instance, in Greece), and the loss of competitiveness affected corporate profits and savings. This was probably the case in Italy, Portugal and Spain, where corporate savings declined.

Summing up, external imbalances in the countries reviewed above were not caused by government dissavings, firstly, because in several countries government savings were positive before the crisis, and secondly, because government (and corporate) savings behaved basically as endogenous variables. The main factors contributing to their current-account deterioration were the loss of international competitiveness of their domestic firms and the decline in household savings, both of which were linked to massive capital inflows and financial deregulation that spurred credit-financed household expenditure and led to real appreciation of their currencies.

These experiences replicate, to a large extent, those of many Latin American and Asian countries that suffered from financial crises between 1982 and 2002. In all these countries, changes in the real exchange rate were a major factor contributing to the crises and also to recovery. In Argentina, Brazil, Chile, Mexico and Uruguay, anti-inflation policies relied on exchange-rate anchors, which eventually led to real currency appreciation and a loss of competitiveness, and consequently to lower corporate profits and output growth. As long as capital inflows were attracted by interest rate differentials and benefited from implicit insurance against exchange-rate risk, these countries could finance their resulting current-account deficits. Capital inflows were not used primarily to increase fixed investment, but rather to finance private consumption and public debt service. Foreign savings thus caused a fall in domestic savings of both households and firms (as a result of lower profits). Government savings also tended to decline – even turning negative in Argentina and Brazil – due to slower growth which lowered fiscal revenues, and to the increasing cost of public debt, as monetary authorities tried to preserve their currency pegs by raising domestic interest rates.

The situation changed dramatically with the steep currency devaluations in Mexico in 1994–1995, in Brazil in 1999 and in Argentina in 2002. In Argentina, the current account swung from a deficit to a huge surplus in a single year, due partly to devaluation and partly to severe economic contraction (chart 2.1). The growth of private savings in 2002 was particularly surprising, since almost all conceivable factors for discouraging such savings were in place: freezing of bank deposits, debt default, negative real interest rates and deep depression. Despite these conditions, corporate profits in the tradables sector increased very rapidly, and, as a consequence, so did corporate savings in response to the new relative price structure. In the subsequent recovery of the real economy to very high growth rates, households and the Government generated significant savings from higher revenues and the investment rate more than doubled, with financing from domestic resources. Mexico also rapidly reduced its current-account deficit, although it did not turn this into surplus, and corporate savings also increased as a result of currency devaluation. In subsequent years, private savings of both households and the corporate sector remained high.

> ... such deficits were the consequence rather than the cause of the crisis.

In Brazil, the current-account balance improved after the crisis and devaluation of 1999, but moved back into deficit during the last phase of the 2003–2008 period of boom, when high interest rates and consequent capital inflows led to renewed currency appreciation (chart 2.1). Similarly, but at less spectacular rates, the expansion of output and investment created the conditions for higher private and public savings. However, improvement in the fiscal accounts was limited by the high level of interest payments on the public debt. Indeed, although the Government generated a sizeable primary surplus of close to 3 per cent of GDP between 2005 and 2010, it still ran an overall deficit (e.g. including net interest payments) of a similar magnitude. The fiscal deficit in Brazil is clearly the consequence of high interest rates, and not its cause as suggested by some authors (e.g. Bacha, 2011; Lara Resende, 2011).

Among the Asian countries, China and India witnessed a strong increase in investment rates and national savings in the 2000s. In China, government savings have accounted for about 9 per cent of GDP in recent years, while private savings grew to more than 44 per cent of GDP in 2006–2010 – by far the highest private savings rate among the G-20 countries. Until 2007, the current-account surplus grew significantly, but again it would be a mistake to conclude that these savings have been the cause of China's large current-account surplus. That surplus is more likely to have been the result of an endogenous process whereby fast income growth, fuelled by massive investment and exports, boosted government and private savings.

Distinct from China, India has maintained its current-account balance at close to equilibrium over the past two decades. It has even registered a small deficit close to 2 per cent since 2008. Here, the large increase in the investment rate was the counterpart of higher domestic savings. Hence, India's external imbalances were not caused by domestic dissavings, and, as they were rather small, they did not have major global repercussions.

The performance of several South-East Asian countries differs from these two largest Asian developing countries. In most countries of this region, such as Indonesia, Malaysia, the Philippines, the Republic of Korea and Thailand, the 1997–1998 crisis marked a clear break in their investment pattern. In some of them, the sharp adjustment of current-account balances during the Asian crisis coincided with falling investments (chart 2.1). Even after that crisis, investment rates never returned to their pre-crisis levels. The evolution of government savings prior to that crisis had little to do with its eruption. More recently, between 2008 and 2009, the increased government spending sought to compensate for lower private demand, which increased private savings.

In major oil- and mineral-exporting countries, external and public budget balances are heavily dependent on export revenues. Therefore both variables tend to closely follow the evolution of export prices: high prices lead simultaneously to fiscal and current-account surpluses – or "negative foreign savings" – and vice versa. As a result, in countries such as Algeria, Azerbaijan, Bolivia, Gabon, Kuwait, the Russian Federation and Saudi Arabia, there is a strong negative correlation between government savings and foreign savings. Since private savings are positively influenced by economic activity, which normally accelerates when prices are high and current accounts are in surplus, those savings also tend to be negatively correlated with foreign savings. However, this trade-off between domestic and foreign savings does not indicate any causality between them; for instance, current-account surpluses in recent years have not resulted from residents' decisions to save more. ·

These examples suggest that both public and private savings are largely endogenous variables that are determined by a number of domestic and external factors. The most important factor is the international competitiveness of domestic producers, which derives from productivity and relative prices. It determines to a large extent the current-account balance, or in other words, "foreign savings". While a relationship necessarily exists between national savings, foreign savings and investment – the elements of a national accounting identity – causality may run in different directions. In most of the countries reviewed, current-account imbalances were not the result of changes in government savings. Either the causality ran in the opposite direction, or other factors (i.e. international competitiveness and/or commodity prices) determined both current accounts and fiscal imbalances. In many of these countries, the main counterpart of external deficits was shrinking

household savings, associated with an expansion of credit and the formation of speculative bubbles.

When the crisis erupted, new credit dried up in most developed economies, and households were compelled to adjust their expenditure to pay off debt. From 2007 to 2009, private savings increased by between 2 and 3.5 percentage points of GDP in Japan, Portugal, the United Kingdom, and the United States, and between 5 and 10 percentage points in the Baltic States, Ireland and Spain (chart 2.1). Government savings declined sharply in these countries, due partly to the effects of automatic stabilizers and partly to discretionary increases in public expenditure as governments sought to compensate for lower private demand. Fiscal balances moved substantially into the red, but this was a consequence rather than a cause of the crisis.

2. The evolution of fiscal accounts and the impact of the crisis

While the previous section looked at the record of fiscal balances and their possible linkages with domestic and global imbalances, this section examines the recent evolution of fiscal revenues and expenditure and how they affected countries' room for manoeuvre in their policy response to the crisis. It also discusses the impact of the crisis on fiscal accounts, as a result of "automatic" changes in revenues and expenditures, and how countries responded by means of proactive policy measures such as stimulus packages.

Between 2002 and 2007–2008, fiscal balances improved significantly in many countries, although some governments continued to run relatively large deficits. On the eve of the crisis, fiscal accounts were balanced, on average, in East, South and South-East Asia, and Latin America; and in Africa, the transition economies and West Asia, governments were achieving sizeable surpluses. In developed economies, fiscal deficits had fallen, on average to less than 1.5 per cent of GDP. However, the crisis caused fiscal accounts to turn into deficit in all the regions (chart 2.2).

In general, the improvement of fiscal balances in the years preceding the crisis did not result from fiscal retrenchment and expenditure cuts; in most countries, government revenues and expenditures

Chart 2.2

GOVERNMENT REVENUES AND EXPENDITURE AND FISCAL BALANCE IN SELECTED REGIONS, 1997–2010

(Per cent of current GDP, weighted average)

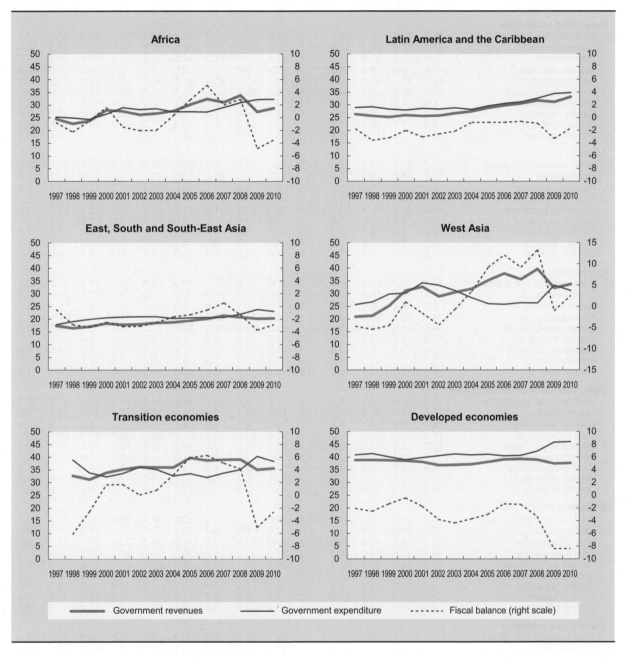

Africa

Latin America and the Caribbean

East, South and South-East Asia

West Asia

Transition economies

Developed economies

Government revenues ——— Government expenditure ------- Fiscal balance (right scale)

Source: UNCTAD secretariat calculations, based on the *EC-AMECO* database; OECD, *Economic Outlook* database; ECLAC, *CEPALSTAT*; IMF, *World Economic Outlook* database; and national sources.

Note: **Africa** excludes: Botswana, Burkina Faso, Cape Verde, Central African Republic, Equatorial Guinea, Lesotho, Liberia, Madagascar, Mauritania, Mayotte, Saint Helena, Seychelles, Somalia, Western Sahara and Zimbabwe. **West Asia** excludes: Iraq, Occupied Palestinian Territory and Yemen. **East, South and South-East Asia** comprises: China, China, Hong Kong SAR, India, Indonesia, the Islamic Republic of Iran, the Republic of Korea, Malaysia, Nepal, the Philippines, Singapore, Sri Lanka, Taiwan Province of China, Thailand and Viet Nam. (Data for China refer to budget revenue and expenditure, they do not include extra-budgetary funds or social security funds.) **Transition economies** exclude: Croatia and Montenegro, but include Mongolia. **Latin America** comprises: Argentina, Bolivia, Bolivarian Republic of Venezuela, Brazil, Chile, Colombia, Costa Rica, Ecuador, El Salvador, Mexico, Nicaragua, Peru and Uruguay. **Developed economies** comprise: Austria, Belgium, Bulgaria, Canada, Cyprus, the Czech Republic, Denmark, Estonia, Finland, France, Germany, Greece, Iceland, Ireland, Italy, Japan, Latvia, Lithuania, Luxembourg, Malta, the Netherlands, Norway, Poland, Portugal, Romania, Slovakia, Spain, Sweden, Switzerland, the United Kingdom and the United States.

Table 2.1

EVOLUTION OF FISCAL INDICATORS, SELECTED REGIONS, 1997–2010

(Per cent of current GDP)[a]

	1997	1998	1999	2000	2001	2002	2003	2004	2005	2006	2007	2008	2009	2010
Developed economies														
Total revenue and grants	38.8	38.9	38.8	38.5	38.1	36.8	36.9	37.2	38.1	39.1	39.3	39.0	37.5	37.7
Current revenue	37.6	37.8	37.7	37.4	36.9	35.6	35.7	35.9	36.9	37.8	38.1	37.7	36.1	36.6
Tax revenues	33.4	33.6	33.5	33.2	32.7	31.4	31.6	31.8	32.6	33.4	33.6	33.1	31.2	31.5
Non-tax revenues[b]	5.4	5.3	5.3	5.3	5.4	5.4	5.3	5.5	5.5	5.8	5.7	6.0	6.3	6.2
Total expenditure	40.9	41.4	40.1	39.0	39.8	40.6	41.3	40.9	41.1	40.5	40.7	42.3	45.9	46.1
Current expenditure	36.4	36.1	35.6	34.8	35.3	36.1	36.9	36.7	36.7	36.5	36.7	37.9	40.9	41.1
Interest payments	4.4	4.2	3.8	3.6	3.4	3.1	2.8	2.7	2.7	2.7	2.8	2.7	2.6	2.7
Capital expenditure	4.4	5.3	4.5	4.2	4.5	4.4	4.4	4.2	4.4	4.0	4.1	4.5	5.0	5.0
Primary balance	2.3	1.7	2.4	3.2	1.7	-0.7	-1.5	-1.0	-0.3	1.3	1.3	-0.6	-5.8	-5.7
Overall balance	-2.1	-2.5	-1.3	-0.4	-1.7	-3.8	-4.3	-3.7	-3.0	-1.4	-1.4	-3.3	-8.4	-8.4
Africa														
Total revenue and grants	24.5	22.6	23.8	28.0	27.5	26.1	26.6	27.7	30.1	32.4	31.1	33.8	27.3	28.8
Tax revenues	17.6	16.6	18.1	19.5	18.9	17.2	17.8	18.3	19.6	19.9	19.8	21.0	19.0	19.0
Non-tax revenues[b]	6.9	6.0	5.6	8.5	8.6	9.0	8.8	9.3	10.6	12.4	11.3	12.8	8.3	9.8
Total expenditure	25.3	24.9	24.3	26.4	29.0	28.2	28.6	27.3	27.4	27.2	29.1	30.9	32.2	32.3
Current expenditure	19.5	19.3	18.8	21.4	22.9	22.3	23.2	21.9	21.7	21.0	21.6	22.5	24.0	24.6
Interest payments	3.0	3.0	3.0	3.8	3.6	3.3	3.5	2.8	2.6	2.2	2.1	1.8	1.9	2.1
Capital expenditure	5.7	5.5	5.4	4.9	6.0	5.5	5.0	5.2	5.6	6.1	7.2	8.2	8.1	7.6
Primary balance	2.1	0.4	2.2	5.3	1.9	1.1	1.3	2.9	5.3	7.2	3.7	4.4	-3.3	-1.7
Overall balance	-0.8	-2.3	-0.5	1.6	-1.5	-2.0	-2.0	0.3	2.8	5.1	2.0	2.9	-4.9	-3.5
Latin America														
Total revenue and grants	26.4	25.7	25.2	26.0	25.6	25.8	26.8	27.5	28.9	29.8	30.6	31.8	31.2	33.2
Tax revenues	18.8	19.1	18.4	18.2	18.1	18.0	18.4	18.9	20.0	20.6	21.3	21.7	21.9	23.5
Non-tax revenues[b]	7.2	6.4	6.7	7.8	7.5	7.8	8.3	8.6	8.8	9.2	9.1	10.0	9.2	9.7
Total expenditure	29.0	29.3	28.4	28.0	28.6	28.4	28.9	28.2	29.6	30.6	31.2	32.7	34.5	34.9
Current expenditure	26.5	25.8	25.3	25.1	25.5	25.0	25.9	24.9	26.2	27.0	27.4	28.5	29.9	29.8
Interest payments	3.2	4.1	4.4	3.9	4.0	4.0	4.6	3.8	4.0	3.7	3.4	3.4	3.4	2.7
Capital expenditure	2.5	3.4	3.1	2.9	3.1	3.3	3.0	3.3	3.4	3.6	3.8	4.2	4.6	5.0
Primary balance	1.3	0.5	1.3	1.9	1.0	1.4	2.4	3.0	3.2	3.0	2.9	2.5	0.1	1.1
Overall balance	-1.8	-3.6	-3.2	-2.0	-3.0	-2.6	-2.1	-0.8	-0.8	-0.8	-0.6	-0.9	-3.3	-1.7
East, South and South-East Asia														
Total revenue and grants	17.3	16.4	17.0	18.2	17.8	17.9	18.5	18.7	19.4	20.1	21.4	20.7	20.2	20.3
Tax revenues	13.0	12.6	12.9	13.7	13.6	13.8	14.1	14.4	14.9	15.4	16.3	16.3	16.0	16.5
Non-tax revenues[b]	4.4	3.8	4.1	4.6	4.2	4.1	4.4	4.3	4.5	4.8	5.1	4.4	4.2	3.8
Total expenditure	17.8	19.0	19.9	20.6	20.8	20.9	21.0	20.3	20.5	20.6	20.7	21.9	23.8	23.0
Current expenditure	13.3	14.5	15.3	16.2	16.5	16.6	16.4	16.1	16.3	16.3	16.3	17.4	18.9	18.3
Interest payments	1.9	2.1	2.4	2.3	2.4	2.3	2.2	2.0	1.8	1.8	1.7	1.6	1.5	1.4
Capital expenditure	4.6	4.7	4.8	4.4	4.4	4.4	4.5	4.2	4.3	4.4	4.4	4.6	5.0	4.8
Primary balance	1.4	-0.4	-0.5	0.0	-0.7	-0.7	-0.3	0.3	0.7	1.3	2.3	0.4	-2.1	-1.2
Overall balance	-0.5	-2.6	-2.9	-2.3	-3.1	-3.0	-2.5	-1.6	-1.1	-0.5	0.7	-1.2	-3.6	-2.7
West Asia														
Total revenue and grants	20.9	21.3	25.2	31.2	32.6	28.9	30.5	31.9	35.2	37.9	35.6	39.6	32.2	33.7
Tax revenues	10.6	11.6	7.9	7.2	7.4	8.0	8.9	8.4	8.2	8.7	9.1	8.6	9.3	9.5
Non-tax revenues[b]	10.3	9.7	17.4	23.9	25.2	20.9	21.6	23.5	27.0	29.2	26.5	31.0	22.9	24.2
Total expenditure	25.7	26.8	29.8	30.1	34.2	33.3	31.2	28.3	26.0	25.8	26.4	26.3	33.3	31.2
Current expenditure	22.8	24.3	27.0	27.3	30.6	29.5	27.7	25.2	22.6	22.1	21.8	21.8	27.0	25.1
Interest payments	5.4	7.7	6.3	7.0	7.8	7.1	6.5	5.2	3.7	3.2	3.0	2.5	2.8	2.3
Capital expenditure	2.8	2.5	2.8	2.8	3.6	3.7	3.5	3.1	3.4	3.6	4.6	4.4	6.3	6.0
Primary balance	0.7	2.3	1.7	8.0	6.2	2.6	5.8	8.7	12.9	15.3	12.1	15.9	1.7	4.8
Overall balance	-4.7	-5.4	-4.6	1.0	-1.6	-4.4	-0.7	3.5	9.2	12.1	9.2	13.3	-1.1	2.5
Transition economies														
Total revenue and grants						36.1	35.9	35.9	39.7	38.7	39.0	39.1	35.0	35.6
Tax revenues						25.1	24.7	25.2	29.8	29.3	29.7	29.4	24.6	26.2
Non-tax revenues[b]						10.9	11.2	10.7	9.9	9.4	9.3	9.7	10.4	9.4
Total expenditure						36.1	35.1	32.6	33.5	32.0	33.7	35.1	40.3	38.3
Current expenditure						28.0	28.5	25.6	28.7	25.9	27.9	28.8	34.1	32.1
Interest payments						1.9	1.5	1.1	0.9	0.7	0.6	0.5	0.7	0.7
Capital expenditure						8.1	6.7	7.1	4.8	6.1	5.9	6.3	6.3	6.2
Primary balance						1.9	2.3	4.4	7.1	7.4	5.8	4.5	-4.7	-2.1
Overall balance						0.0	0.8	3.3	6.3	6.7	5.3	4.0	-5.3	-2.7

Source: UNCTAD secretariat calculations, based on *EC-AMECO* database; OECD, *Economic Outlook* database; ECLAC, *CEPALSTAT*; IMF, *World Economic Outlook* database; and national sources.

Note: For the composition of country groups, see chart 2.2.

    a Corresponds to general government except for Argentina, Bolivia, the Bolivarian Republic of Venezuela, Colombia, Costa Rica, Ecuador, El Salvador, Mexico, Nicaragua and Uruguay, for which indicators refer to the non-financial public sector.

    b Includes capital revenues.

increased together, although at different rates. With the exception of developed countries, where they remained flat as a percentage of GDP, government revenues expanded significantly in all regions from 2002–2003 onwards. This was supported by broad-based acceleration of growth and increased earnings from commodity exports. The latter resulted not only from higher prices, but also from changes in the distribution of natural resource rents, with a larger share going to the governments in several of the producing countries. In Africa, the transition economies, East, South and South-East Asia and Latin America, expenditure ratios also increased, in many cases from relatively low levels (table 2.1).

West Asian countries seem to have followed a different pattern. Between 2001 and 2008, government expenditure as a percentage of GDP fell significantly, especially in Kuwait, Saudi Arabia, Turkey and the United Arab Emirates. However, this does not indicate a reduction of government expenditure in absolute terms; the expenditure ratio decreased mainly because GDP at current prices rose very rapidly in the major oil-exporting countries due to higher oil prices. In addition, lower interest payments on public debt accounted for a large share of the fall in government expenditure: in Turkey, they fell from 22.4 per cent of GDP in 2001 to 4.4 per cent in 2010, owing to a significant decline in public debt ratios and an even more impressive decline in domestic interest rates. The reduction in interest payments was also significant in Jordan, Kuwait, Lebanon, Qatar and Saudi Arabia (where they fell from almost 8 per cent of GDP in the early 2000s to only 2.3 per cent in 2010).

The declining share of interest payments in public expenditure has been a widespread trend (table 2.1). It resulted from the reduction of public debt ratios in most developing and emerging economies (as discussed further in the next section), as well as from lower real interest rates in most countries. In Africa, Latin America and East, South and South-East Asia, interest payments fell by 1 to 2 percentage points

> Many developing economies had improved their fiscal balances before the crisis, with higher public revenues and expenditure, which enlarged their policy space.

> In 2008 and 2009, government expenditure soared in all regions, while government revenues declined, especially in developed economies and commodity exporters.

between the periods 1998–2000 and 2008–2010. In the transition economies there was a similar reduction between 2002 and 2008–2010. In all these regions, the decline in interest payments was even greater in relation to fiscal revenues. During the same period, the share of fiscal revenues that had to be used for interest payments fell from 14 to 7 per cent in Africa, from 16 to 8 per cent in Latin America, from 16 to 12 per cent in East and South Asia, and from 25 to 7 per cent in West Asia. This meant that a significant proportion of fiscal resources could be redirected from debt servicing to more productive uses. Indeed, social transfers and capital expenditure increased significantly in developing regions. Capital expenditure alone gained between 2 and 3 percentage points of GDP between 2000 and 2010 (table 2.1). Hence, not only did the size of public sector finances increase (measured either as the share of government revenue or expenditure in GDP), but also its support for capital formation and improvements in income distribution grew.

Such expansionary adjustments of fiscal balances, with higher revenues and primary expenditure, implied a structural change in many developing and transition economies, and served to enlarge their policy space which they were able to use when hit by the financial crisis. Almost from the onset of the crisis there was wide consensus in the major economies that fiscal measures were necessary for pulling the economies out of recession. In 2008 and 2009, government expenditure as a share of GDP soared in all the regions, while government revenues declined, but in varying degrees: steeply in the regions that rely heavily on primary commodity exports (i.e. Africa, the transition economies and West Asia), significantly but less sharply in developed economies, and very moderately in East, South and South-East Asia and Latin America.

In developed countries with well-established social security systems and a comparatively high share of direct taxes in fiscal revenues, changes in government revenues and expenditure are partly related to automatic stabilizers. Between 2007 and 2010, spending on social security benefits increased by 3 per cent of GDP in Japan and the United States, and by between 1.5 and 4.3 per cent of GDP in most European countries, with the highest increases in those countries where unemployment rose the most, such as Greece and Spain. On the revenue side, the loss of receipts from income, profits and capital gains taxes was particularly severe in the United States: almost 4 per cent of GDP between 2007 and 2009. But not all supplementary social benefits and lower tax revenues were "automatically" triggered by the recession and higher unemployment; in several countries, they were also part of discretionary fiscal stimulus packages, including tax cuts and increased spending, as part of governments' efforts to stimulate domestic demand and counteract the effects of the global economic crisis.

In addition, the monetary authorities lowered interest rates and provided the liquidity necessary to avoid financial collapse. But such policies could not revive credit and restore global demand, as a massive private deleveraging process was under way. Fiscal stimulus was therefore even more critical to counterbalance the shrinking demand of the private sector.

3.   Fiscal responses to the crisis

The fiscal responses to the crisis in the major economies varied considerably across regions and countries, not only in terms of the size of their economic stimulus, but also in terms of its composition and timing. A detailed assessment of fiscal stimulus packages is not straightforward, because it is difficult to distinguish policy measures that were adopted in response to the crisis from others that were already planned or that would have been implemented in any case (e.g. public investments for reconstruction following natural disasters). In addition, official announcements are not always executed at the expected time, and they only provide a general idea of the size and composition of the packages. Among developed countries, the United States implemented the largest stimulus package, in both nominal terms and as a percentage of GDP, followed by Japan and Germany (table 2.2). A relatively large share of the announced fiscal stimulus took the form of tax cuts

(about 40 per cent) in developed countries, compared with only 5 per cent in the developing and transition economies listed in table 2.2. However, in a number of developed countries that announced multiple waves of stimulus packages, the spending component increased compared with tax cuts in the subsequent announcements (Prasad and Sorkin, 2009).

In several developing and transition economies, the relative size of the stimulus packages as a share of GDP actually exceeded that of developed economies. For instance, China and the Republic of Korea announced packages equivalent to 13 and 10 per cent of their respective GDP. In China, three major fiscal packages were announced between November 2008 and March 2009, totalling almost $570 billion. All these resources were allocated to increased spending, 74 per cent of which was capital expenditure, in particular for post-earthquake reconstruction projects and investment in infrastructure. The Government of the Republic of Korea made four major announcements of stimulus between November 2008 and March 2009, involving the equivalent of $95 billion, of which 97 per cent was in the form of increased expenditure. Thereafter, in August 2009 the Government announced a fifth package which consisted exclusively of tax incentives and deductions, but there is no estimation of the cost of this additional component. In Indonesia, the Government announced a fiscal programme that was relatively small in comparison, and mainly comprised tax incentives and deductions. Nevertheless, overall stimulus packages in developing Asia, including Bangladesh, India, Malaysia, the Philippines, Singapore and Thailand emphasized higher spending, particularly for infrastructure investment (Hur et al., 2010).

In Latin America, at the end of 2008 the major economies launched a set of measures to counter the effects of the economic and financial crisis. Argentina announced the largest stimulus package as a percentage of GDP, followed by Brazil, Chile and Mexico. The composition of these packages reflected the view that increased spending, rather than tax cuts, was the most appropriate tool to stimulate domestic demand under the prevailing circumstances. Increased spending provides a direct means of boosting demand, whereas tax cuts increase the private sector's disposable income, a large proportion of which, in a context of uncertainty, is likely to be saved rather than spent. In some countries, the increased expenditure was partly covered by fiscal revenue

Table 2.2

FISCAL STIMULUS PACKAGES, AS ANNOUNCED IN SELECTED ECONOMIES, 2008–2010

(Billions of dollars and percentages)

	Total amount ($ billion)	GDP (Per cent)	Tax cut share	Spending share
Developed economies				
Australia	23	2.4	45.2	54.8
Canada	24	1.8	52.4	47.6
France	21	0.8	6.5	93.5
Germany	47	1.4	68.0	32.0
Italy	6	0.3	33.3	66.7
Japan	117	2.3	30.0	70.0
Spain	35	2.4	58.4	41.6
United Kingdom	35	1.5	56.0	44.0
United States[a]	821	5.7	36.5	63.5
Total	1129	3.3	38.3	61.7
Unweighted average		*2.1*	*42.9*	*57.1*
Developing and transition economies				
Argentina	17	6.0	8.5	91.5
Brazil	45	3.6	15.0	85.0
China	568	13.1	0.0	100.0
Chile	4	2.8	46.0	54.0
India	43	3.4	0.0	100.0
Indonesia	8	1.5	76.9	23.1
Mexico	21	2.4	0.0	100.0
Republic of Korea	95	10.2	2.9	97.1
Russian Federation	80	6.4	31.3	68.7
Saudi Arabia	50	9.4	0.0	100.0
South Africa	8	2.6	0.0	100.0
Total	937	8.0	4.7	95.3
Unweighted average		*5.6*	*16.4*	*83.6*

Source: UNCTAD secretariat calculations, based on European Commission, 2009; ECLAC, 2009; CBO, 2011; OECD, 2009; Hur et al., 2010; Ponomarenko and Vlasov, 2010; Prasad and Sorkin, 2009; and United States Government, 2011.

a The amount reported for the United States refers only to the stimulus package provided under the American Recovery and Reinvestment Act (ARRA) of 2009; it excludes the cost of industry bailouts and capital infusions that were components of the Troubled Asset Relief Program (TARP).

from new sources. For instance, in Argentina this was achieved through social security reform (reverting from a private-dominated capitalization regime to a pay-as-you go public system), whereas in Brazil, higher capital expenditure was financed by selling oil exploration rights.

Governments of many natural-resource-rich countries where public finances had a strongly pro-cyclical bias in the past were generally able to adopt proactive countercyclical policies despite the fall in commodity prices (World Bank, 2009). During the commodity boom in the 2000s, when several of these countries adopted fairly prudent fiscal policies, the resulting reserves they managed to accumulate served

them well when the crisis erupted, by enabling them to increase their spending to moderate its impacts. At the same time, many countries were able to significantly reduce their public debt.

In Latin America, in 2009 Chile used the reserves that the Government had accumulated in its stabilization fund during the years of high copper prices to counter the impact of the crisis (Villafuerte, López-Murphy and Ossowski, 2010; Torre, Sinnott and Nash, 2010). Many oil-producing countries in North Africa and West Asia, as well as in the Commonwealth of Independent States, were also able to implement fiscal stimulus packages (Abdih et al., 2010). In countries such as Kazakhstan and the Russian Federation, where the domestic financial sector was strongly affected by the global financial and economic crisis, a significant proportion of fiscal expenditure was targeted at rescuing that sector (Heuty and Aristi, 2010). A number of governments in sub-Saharan Africa also followed an expansionary stance as a response to the crisis, based on public revenue perceived from their extractive industries (Kasekende, Brixiová and Ndikumana, 2010; Osakwe, 2011; Brixiová, Ndikumana and Abderrahim, 2010).

In a context of rising commodity prices, many of these resource-rich countries recovered rapidly from the crisis, and currently present a better fiscal situation and much lower ratios of public debt to GDP than in the early 2000s. Given that commodity prices in general have rebounded since mid-2009, and have continued to grow strongly, it is difficult to assess whether economic growth in the natural-resource-rich countries in 2010 and 2011 has been due to their fiscal stimulus policies or whether it is a consequence of the rising commodity prices. However, there are indications that in many of these countries GDP growth started to recover when commodity prices were still in a trough, mainly in the first quarter of 2009. This would suggest that the fiscal stimulus succeeded in expanding their economies. Moreover, these countries probably would have been in a much worse situation had the fiscal stimulus not been implemented. In any case, although economic recovery in these countries may imply that the extraordinary fiscal stimulus can be discontinued, they may need to maintain higher levels of expenditure than before the crisis for developmental purposes. Infrastructure investment and social transfers, for example, are fundamental elements of a long-term development strategy. As long as government revenues are healthy as a result of economic growth and high commodity prices, a reduction in these expenditures would not be justified.

Financial crises – such as those that struck many emerging-market economies in the past – typically create fiscal costs through interest rate hikes, currency devaluation that increases the burden of public debt denominated in foreign currencies, and public-funded bailouts. This is in addition to the direct effects of slower growth or recession on current revenues and

> Fiscal stimulus in developing countries consisted of an increase in public spending, while in developed countries it consisted largely of tax cuts.

expenditures, and on discretionary fiscal stimulus measures. In the context of the latest crisis, bail-out operations have been taking place mainly in developed economies. Developing countries were generally able to avoid this kind of fiscal cost, because most of them did not experience banking crises, and therefore did not need to bail out any of their banks. There were a few exceptions, such as Dubai and Trinidad and Tobago, where the governments provided support to investment companies. In addition, a relatively solid external payments position made it possible for most developing-country governments to manage the initial financial turbulence caused by short-term capital fleeing to "safe havens". They used international reserves and controlled currency depreciation, without resorting to monetary "overkill". Although the monetary authorities in several countries initially increased interest rates, they were able to return rapidly to a more accommodative monetary stance. As a result, public finances in developing and emerging market economies were not affected by rising interest rates on the domestic public debt.

In contrast, fiscal accounts in several developed countries were severely affected by the financial crisis. In these countries, the authorities gave top priority to preventing the collapse of the financial system, making available the financial resources necessary to achieve this objective. In 22 EU countries, "approved government aid"[3] to the financial sector between October 2008 and October 2010 exceeded €4.5 trillion, which represents 39 per cent of EU-27 GDP for 2009. The first 25 per cent of this aid was disbursed in 2008 and another equal amount in 2009. These "actually used amounts" are lower than the upper limits of support, since in some countries, such as Denmark and Ireland, a significant share of the approved aid consisted of large blanket-guarantee schemes which covered the entirety of their banks' debts. From the €4.5 trillion of total approved aid, €2.3 trillion was provided through special schemes or particular financial institutions in 2008 and 2009, of which 25 per cent (€237 billion in 2008 and €354 billion in 2009) was finally treated as an "aid element" by the Commission, since the total amount used cannot be treated as a benefit. However, to put them in perspective, the crisis-related aid measures to financial institutions in 2009 represented about five times the overall amount of State aid granted to all other sectors (agriculture, fisheries, industry, other services and transport, excluding railways) in the EU-27. Of the €354 billion aid element in 2009, 40 per cent was used for recapitalization measures, 36 per cent for guarantees, 21 per cent for asset relief interventions, and the remaining 3 per cent was disbursed for liquidity measures other than guarantee schemes (European Commission, 2010a).

In the United States, the Troubled Asset Relief Program (TARP) allowed the United States Treasury to purchase – or insure – up to $700 billion worth of troubled assets, mainly from the financial sector, and to a lesser extent from the automotive industry. In Switzerland, the Government provided $5.6 billion in capital to the largest Swiss bank at the time, to recapitalize it and to help it cope with a liquidity shortage. In several countries, the actual fiscal loss represented only a small fraction of the total amount of resources made available to the financial sector.[4] In some rare instances the Government even made a profit. In other countries, the support programmes nullified all efforts that could be made for reducing

the fiscal deficit: in Ireland, for example, capital transfers from the Government (basically its support to domestic banks) amounted to 20.8 per cent of GDP in 2010 (up from 3.3 per cent the year before), causing a revision of the deficit from 14.3 per cent of GDP to 32.4 per cent. Meanwhile, the Irish Government embarked on a drastic budgetary consolidation programme – weighted significantly in favour of spending cuts – which is forecast to reduce the GDP growth rate by 1.5 to 2 percentage points in 2011 (Government of Ireland, 2010).

Interest payments have remained stable in most developed countries, despite higher public-debt-to-GDP ratios, owing to their accommodative monetary policies that reduced interest rates to historic lows. Only in a handful of countries did the interest payments impose a significant burden on fiscal balances, due to a sudden and sharp increase in their debt ratios (Iceland) and/or a rise in the risk premium (Greece and Ireland). However, the accumulation of substantial public debt means that any normalization of monetary policies (i.e. increasing policy interest rates to pre-crisis levels) could entail significant fiscal costs.

C. The evolution of public debt

1. Recent trends in public debt in developed and developing countries

Over the past 40 years the median ratio of public debt to GDP has changed considerably in both developed and developing countries. Beginning at relatively low levels in 1970 – at 20 and 25 per cent of GDP in developing and developed countries, respectively – that ratio increased significantly until the mid-1990s. It exceeded 60 per cent of GDP in the upper-middle-income developing countries in the second half of the 1980s, when Latin America was strongly affected by a debt crisis, and by the mid-1990s it had reached a peak of 90 per cent of GDP in the low- and lower-

middle-income developing countries (chart 2.3).[5] In developed countries, the median public-debt-to-GDP ratio reached nearly 60 per cent in 1998. At the turn of the new millennium that ratio declined rapidly in both developed and developing countries to a level between 30 and 40 per cent of GDP. However, the Great Recession reversed this trend and led to a sudden jump in the ratio in many developed countries, so that by the end of 2010 the median ratio in those economies was well above 60 per cent and had surpassed the previous peak of 1998.[6]

The low- and lower-middle-income countries did not experience a similar surge in the median public-debt-to-GDP ratio as a result of the crisis,

Chart 2.3

**RATIO OF PUBLIC DEBT TO GDP
IN DEVELOPING COUNTRIES, BY
INCOME GROUP, 1970–2010**

(Median, in per cent)

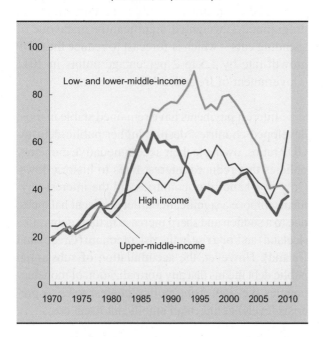

Source: UNCTAD secretariat calculations, based on World Bank,
Global Development Finance; and national sources.
Note: The classification of income groups follows that of the
World Bank.

In 2002, when their median public-debt-to-GDP ratio
peaked at 65 per cent of GDP, about 80 per cent of
their total public debt was external and only 20 per
cent was owed to residents. By 2010, the ratio had
dropped to 35 per cent, and only 44 per cent of it was
owed to non-residents (chart 2.4). Thus, the median
public debt owed to non-residents in developing
countries fell from approximately 50 per cent of
GDP in 2002 to 15 per cent in 2010. In upper-middle-
income countries the median public debt owed to
non-residents had fallen to 12 per cent of GDP and in
low-income countries to 17 per cent. Indeed, it was
this steep decline that explains the overall reduction
in the public debt ratio in developing countries.

The dramatic reduction in the median external
public-debt-to-GDP ratio in developing countries
was due more to their relatively rapid GDP growth
than to a reduction in the stock of their external debt.
Between 1998 and 2009 their stock of external public debt remained more or less constant, at around

Chart 2.4

**RATIO OF TOTAL, DOMESTIC AND
EXTERNAL PUBLIC DEBT TO GDP IN
DEVELOPING COUNTRIES, 1970–2010**

(Median, in per cent)

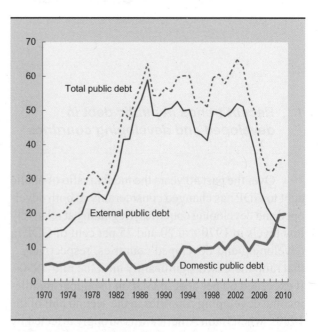

Source: UNCTAD secretariat calculations, based on World Bank,
Global Development Finance; and national sources.

and there was only a small increase in that ratio
in the upper-middle-income countries. As a result,
the median public-debt-to-GDP ratio in developed
countries is now much higher than that of developing
countries. However, there are substantial variations
among the latter group of countries: in 23 countries the debt-to-GDP ratio in 2010 was at least
5 percentage points higher than in 2008, and 14 of
these countries had a debt-to-GDP ratio in 2010 that
was 10 percentage points higher than in 2007. The
cross-country dispersion of the debt-to-GDP ratio
of developing countries remains as high as it was
in the 1990s (*TDR 2008*, chapter VI). Indeed, the
World Bank still classifies about 40 per cent of the
low-income countries as being either in debt distress
or at risk of debt distress.

Not only did developing countries reduce their
public-debt-to-GDP ratios, but they also altered the
composition of their public debt, as their governments borrowed more domestically and less abroad.

Chart 2.5

EXTERNAL DEBT IN DEVELOPING COUNTRIES, BY TYPE OF DEBT, 1970–2009

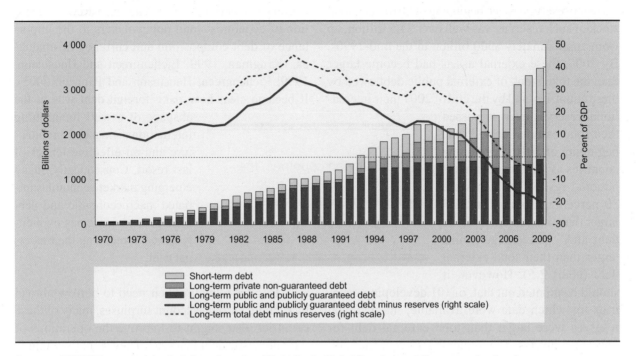

Source: UNCTAD secretariat calculations, based on World Bank, *Global Development Finance*; and national sources.

$1.4 trillion (chart 2.5). However, a debt management strategy in several countries geared towards reducing their reliance on foreign capital and increasing domestic borrowing also contributed to this trend.

The relative weight of a debt denominated in foreign currency also depends on the real exchange rate; for instance, a currency devaluation that is not followed by a similar increase in domestic prices (the GDP deflator) may suddenly increase the external debt ratio. This is what happened in many developing countries during the 1980s, and again between 1997 and 2002. Conversely, a real appreciation makes the GDP increase more rapidly in current dollars, so that the external debt ratio declines more rapidly. After the strong devaluations in the late 1990s and early 2000s, most developing countries' currencies underwent some real appreciation, which contributed to a reduction in their foreign debt ratios.

> In the past decade, despite the crisis, the ratio of public debt to GDP in developing countries declined significantly.

It is worth pointing out that while the external public debt of developing countries remained more or less constant, corporate long-term external debt grew rapidly, almost tripling over the 1998–2009 period (from $450 billion to nearly $1.3 trillion). The same period also saw a net increase in short-term external debt, from $390 billion in 1998 to $750 billion in 2009 (chart 2.5). Even if the increases in short-term and corporate borrowing are factored in, the average external-debt-to-GDP ratio of developing countries as a group fell by nearly 20 percentage points over the period 1998–2009.

Although governments that subscribe to the Lawson Doctrine may ignore external financial fragility related to private debt, policymakers need to keep in check the behaviour of private borrowers, because the inability of the corporate sector to service its debts can lead to a currency and banking crisis, and ultimately to a fiscal crisis.

In addition to reducing their public debt ratios, developing countries as a group also accumulated large amounts of external assets in the form of foreign currency reserves. At the beginning of 2010, their total stock of such reserves was well over $4.5 trillion, up from approximately $500 billion in the mid-1990s. By 2005, these external assets had become larger than the total stock of external public debt owed by these countries, and by the end of 2007 their international reserves even surpassed their total external debt. At the beginning of 2010, developing countries as a group held international reserves which were 20 percentage points of GDP larger than their external public debt and 7 percentage points larger than their total external debt (chart 2.5). However, it should be pointed out that, of 101 developing countries for which data were available, international reserves were larger than total external debt for only 22 countries. The remaining 79 countries still had a net foreign debt. Thus the fact that developing countries, as a group, are no longer net debtors is due to large debt reduction and/or reserve accumulation by some large developing countries and is not representative of the situation of the majority of developing countries.

Even if there are substantial cross-country variations, on average, developing countries have been successful in reducing their external debt ratios. This improvement in debt ratios has been due to a combination of factors. Favourable external conditions and associated rapid GDP growth over the period 2003–2007 certainly played a role in both middle- and low-income countries. Low-income countries also benefited from debt relief under the Heavily Indebted Poor Countries (HIPC) Initiative, even though actual debt relief provided under the Initiative is probably lower than what is reported in official statistics (see *TDR 2008,* chapter VI). In middle-income countries, however, the reduction in external debt was mostly a response to the wave of financial crises that hit many of them, particularly the emerging market economies during the second half of the 1990s.

These crises exposed serious flaws in the current international financial architecture and raised doubts about the ability of the IMF to act as an effective international lender of last resort. They also drew the attention of economists and policymakers to the importance of debt composition and currency mismatches. (Krugman, 1999; Eichengreen and Hausmann, 1999; Eichengreen, Hausmann and Panizza, 2005). It became clear how risky foreign debt was in the absence of a well-functioning international financial architecture and an effective lender of last resort. Consequently, many emerging market economies initiated macroeconomic and debt management strategies explicitly aimed at reducing their external debt.

> In developed countries, the public-debt-to-GDP ratio almost doubled between 2007 and 2010.

Besides reducing their need to borrow abroad by running current-account surpluses, many of these countries also sought to improve the operations of their domestic debt markets.[7] They were thus able to issue more debt at a fixed rate and denominated in domestic currency, and to extend the average maturity of the domestic public debt. A recent survey of the domestic bond market in 23 emerging market economies shows that approximately 70 per cent of their domestic bonds (public and private) are now issued at a fixed rate. Bonds issued on the domestic market are also becoming long-dated. A survey of government bonds in the same 23 emerging and developing countries shows that the average original maturity of these bonds is now 9 years, up from 7 years in 2000 (Hausmann and Panizza, 2011).

Currency mismatches associated with foreign-currency-denominated debt play a major role in limiting a country's macroeconomic policy space. Countries with large mismatches in their aggregate balance sheets tend to have less room for countercyclical fiscal policies and often adopt a monetary policy stance that is geared towards achieving currency stability rather than output growth. In 2008–2009, lower external borrowing and rapid reserve accumulation contributed to a decline in currency mismatches, which in turn enabled many developing countries to implement countercyclical monetary policies.

2. The contribution of non-fiscal factors to debt crises

"Financial crisis" is a broad term that encompasses many types of crises. A *public debt crisis* occurs when a government is unable to fully comply with its debt service obligations vis-à-vis either domestic or external creditors. Such a crisis is thus associated with budgetary imbalances that have become unsustainable. An *external debt crisis* originates from a country's overall inability to service its debt owed to external creditors. It is therefore associated with an external transfer problem (Keynes, 1929). This may reflect either private or public domestic imbalances. A *currency crisis* is characterized by a sudden drop in the value of the domestic currency, well below a level justified by the country's macroeconomic fundamentals. It is usually triggered by perceptions and market expectations that affect capital movements. Finally, a *banking crisis* happens when a significant segment of a country's banking sector is either insolvent or is subject to a generalized panic.[8]

While the focus of this section is on public-debt crises, these different types of crises are closely related to each other: one type of crisis often is the cause of the other. Indeed, the other types of crises may interact with, and actually lead to public debt crises.

Debt crises – including public-debt crises – do not always have a fiscal origin. In order to gain a better understanding of this issue, it is worth reviewing some important, albeit abstruse, accounting definitions. A good starting point for discussing the origin of debt crises and the view that debt crises always originate from excessive budget deficits, is the basic public debt accumulation equation. According to this equation, the change in the stock of public debt is equal to the deficit accumulated during the period under consideration, represented as follows: $Debt_{t+1} - Debt_t = Deficit_t$. Practitioners know that this identity rarely holds, and therefore work with the following equation:

Change in Debt = Deficit + Stock Flow Reconciliation

In this set-up, the stock flow reconciliation is a residual entity which reconciles the change in debt

(a stock variable) with the deficit (a flow variable). Although practitioners know about the stock-flow reconciliation, this residual term rarely appears in textbook descriptions of the evolution of public debt because it is often assumed to be quantitatively small and driven mainly by measurement error. This is an incorrect assumption; the stock-flow reconciliation is, on the contrary, a key driver of debt growth, and therefore deserves much more attention.

Before discussing the nature of the stock-flow reconciliation, it should be emphasized that it is not the stock of debt that really matters for assessing the risk of a debt crisis, but the relationship between the stock of debt and some other variables, such as GDP, which capture a country's ability to service its debt. Changes in the debt-to-GDP ratio (Δd) are determined by the primary (non-interest) deficit (p), the average interest rate to be paid on the outstanding debt ($i \times d$), the growth rate of the economy multiplied by the initial stock of debt ($g \times d$), and the stock-flow reconciliation (sf), as follows:

$$\Delta d = p + (i \times d) - (g \times d) + sf$$

This decomposition separates the primary deficit from the interest bill because policymakers are supposed to have direct control over the former but only an indirect influence on the latter. Through their monetary and exchange rate policies, governments can influence the interest bill related to domestic and foreign public debt, respectively.

This simple decomposition yields several insights. First, policymakers can directly control only one (two, if policies affecting the interest rate are considered) out of four factors that determine the growth rate of a country's debt-to-GDP ratio. Second, the growth rate of the economy is an important driver of the debt-to-GDP ratio. Contractionary fiscal policies that reduce output growth may therefore increase a country's debt-to-GDP ratio, even if they manage to reduce the primary deficit, which is not guaranteed.[9] Third, even the primary deficit cannot be completely controlled by the fiscal authorities. As already discussed in the previous section, primary deficits tend to rise during slumps and fall during booms because of the impact of automatic stabilizers, such as reductions in tax revenues and increases in

> Any policy that seeks to reduce public debt should avoid curbing GDP growth.

transfers (e.g. unemployment benefits). Hence, GDP growth not only affects the denominator but also the numerator of the debt-to-GDP ratio.

Fourth, economies with growth rates that are higher than the nominal interest rate on public debt can reduce their public-debt-to-GDP ratio, even if they run a primary deficit. Under certain conditions, an accommodating monetary policy can improve a country's debt situation by simultaneously reducing the interest bill on domestic debt and increasing GDP growth. However, countries that have foreign-currency-denominated debt, or that do not have control over their own monetary policy, may experience sudden surges in borrowing costs during economic crises, exactly when their ability to pay is limited. Fifth, the stock of debt has only a small effect on debt dynamics, insofar as it does not lead to high interest rates. For instance, in a country with a real interest rate of 3 per cent and a real GDP growth rate of 2 per cent, the initial debt-to-GDP ratio will multiply by 0.01, and even a very large increase in that ratio will have a small effect on fiscal sustainability (i.e. if the debt increases by 50 per cent of GDP, the debt stabilizing primary surplus will increase by 0.5 per cent of GDP). Therefore debt may end up being permanently higher, but it may not necessarily follow a steep growth path. Finally, the decomposition makes it possible to evaluate the importance of the stock-flow reconciliation as a factor contributing to actual debt growth. Indeed, it appears to be a major element in rapid debt increases during times of crisis.

Primary deficits can thus be responsible for a slow accumulation of public debt but they can rarely be blamed for a sudden surge in debt. With respect to the current crisis, for instance, the IMF (2010) estimates that the average debt-to-GDP ratio of developed countries will increase by 35 percentage points over the period 2007–2015. Of this increase, at most 3.5 percentage points will be due to expansionary discretionary fiscal policies. On the other hand, large debt surges frequently result from banking and/or currency crises, which eventually require huge public-funded rescue operations or sudden revaluations of existing foreign-currency-denominated debt. These events usually fall within the stock-flow reconciliation term.

> Primary deficits can cause a slow accumulation of public debt, but sudden surges are generally caused by financial crises, currency devaluations and bank bailouts.

Among recent examples of sudden debt explosions is the Icelandic crisis. At the end of 2007, Iceland had a total government debt of 29 per cent of GDP, which surged to nearly 115 per cent by the end of 2010. This was not caused by irresponsible fiscal policy; budget deficits could explain only one quarter of the total debt increase (22 out of 86 percentage points of GDP), and even these deficits were not due to profligate fiscal policies. Rather, they were a consequence of the economic crisis which followed the collapse of Iceland's largest banks. In the case of Ireland, public debt rose from 25 per cent of GDP in 2007 to 96 per cent by the end of 2010. Of the 71 percentage point difference, 41 points correspond to capital transfers to the financial sector disbursed between 2008 and 2010, 13 points to the remaining public deficit accumulated during this period, and 17 points to stock-flow reconciliation (EC-AMECO database).[10] Hence the bulk of the debt increase cannot be attributed to fiscal policy, and again, the large operating deficits of 2008–2009 were driven by the country's financial collapse and not by explicit fiscal policy decisions.

Similar examples exist for emerging market economies. For instance Brazil's net debt-to-GDP ratio stood at approximately 42 per cent in December 1998 and by January 1999 this ratio exceeded 51 per cent. It seems unlikely that the Brazilian Government could have run a deficit of almost 10 per cent of GDP in just one month. In Argentina, in 2001 public debt was about 50 per cent of GDP and by 2002 it was well above 160 per cent of GDP. Again, it seems unlikely that in just one year the Argentinean Government could have run up a deficit equal to 110 per cent of GDP.

The explanations for the debt explosions documented above are well known. In Iceland and Ireland the increase in public debt was due to the governments of these two countries assuming the debts of their banking systems.[11] In Argentina and Brazil, the sudden increase in debt was mainly due to negative balance sheet effects caused by the impact of currency devaluation on the domestic currency value of their foreign-currency-denominated debt. In 2001, more than 90 per cent of the Argentinean public debt was denominated in foreign currency. When the exchange rate between the Argentinean peso and the dollar changed overnight from 1 peso to 1 dollar to 3 pesos to 1 dollar, Argentina's debt-to-GDP ratio nearly tripled.

Such events have been important factors in the build-up to public-debt crises in many countries. Chart 2.6, which summarizes the main results of a study using data for up to 117 countries for the 1985–2004 period, shows the importance of stock-flow reconciliation as a determinant of debt growth (Campos, Jaimovich and Panizza, 2006). In the chart, the bars below the zero line show the factors that contribute to a decrease of the debt-to-GDP ratio (mostly nominal GDP growth), and the bars above the zero line show the factors that contribute to an increase of that ratio. The value points measure the difference between the two sets of bars, and thus report the average annual debt growth for each region over the period under observation. Thus, the average debt-to-GDP ratio grew by approximately 1 percentage point per year in the developed economies, in South Asia, Latin America, East Asia and the Middle East and North Africa regions. In the countries of Eastern Europe and Central Asia (for which the data start in the early 1990s) it remained more or less constant, and in countries in sub-Saharan Africa it fell by approximately 3 percentage points per year.

The primary deficit plays a relatively small role in debt growth. Only in three regions (South Asia, the Middle East and North Africa, and sub-Saharan Africa) was the average primary deficit greater than 1 per cent of GDP; in East Asia and Pacific the primary balance showed, on average, a small surplus, whereas in the other regions there was a small deficit. South Asia is the only region where the primary deficit has been the main contributor to debt growth. Developed countries, as a group, ran balanced primary budgets and had fairly large interest payments. In the remaining five regions it was the stock-flow reconciliation that was primarily responsible for debt growth. In developing countries, the stock-flow reconciliation has always been more than 1 per cent of GDP and larger than average debt growth. This suggests that, other things being equal, if the stock-flow reconciliation had been zero, all these regions would have exhibited declining debt ratios during this period. Therefore, the stock-flow reconciliation, rather than being a residual of little importance, is actually a key determinant of debt growth in both developing and developed countries.

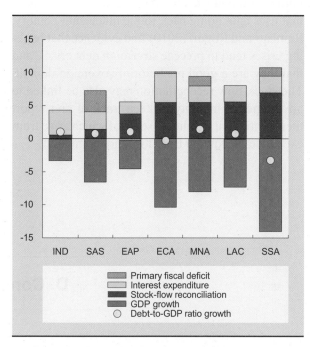

Chart 2.6

**CONTRIBUTIONS TO GROWTH OF
DEBT-TO-GDP RATIO, 1985–2004**

(Per cent)

Source: Campos, Jaimovich and Panizza, 2006.
Note: IND: High-income OECD members; SAS: South Asia; EAP: East Asia and Pacific; ECA: Europe and Central Asia; MNA: Middle East and North Africa; LAC: Latin America and the Caribbean; SSA: sub-Saharan Africa. In most developing countries the period covered is 1985–2003.

What factors are responsible for the stock-flow reconciliation? Measurement error may be one factor, since data on the level and composition of public debt tend to be of poor quality (Panizza, 2008) and assembled from various sources which often differ from those used to gather fiscal data. However, if the difference between deficits and the change in debt were purely due to random measurement error, positive errors would compensate for negative errors and the stock-flow reconciliation would average zero over the long run. The data show that this is not the case. The long-running average of the stock-flow reconciliation tends to be positive and large. Campos, Jaimovich and Panizza (2006) show that in countries with a large stock of debt denominated in foreign currency, a depreciation of the domestic currency is associated with a large increase in the debt-to-GDP ratio. This finding, which is in line with the experiences of

Argentina and Brazil, as mentioned above, confirms that balance-sheet effects associated with currency mismatches can indeed have a dramatic consequence for debt sustainability. The same research also finds that banking crises are often followed by sudden jumps in the stock-flow reconciliation. In a study that uses data going back to the nineteenth century, Reinhart and Rogoff (2010) find evidence that banking crises tend to precede sovereign debt crises, and that they are a good predictor of sovereign default. The stock-flow reconciliation may also be linked to governments' inability to keep track of and report their contingent liabilities (some of which arise from excessive borrowing from local governments).

Increasing the transparency of fiscal accounts would contribute to solving this problem. A partial solution would be for countries to adopt an asset-liability management framework which would allow them to keep track of the overall evolution of the government's balance sheet. More generally, currency mismatches and contingent liabilities caused by the financial sector pose significant fiscal risk for governments, and make them vulnerable to macroeconomic shocks. It would therefore be advisable for them to adopt a macroeconomic and dynamic view of fiscal accounts and public debt in the same way that private financial risks need macroprudential surveillance in addition to microprudential rules.

D. Conclusions

The current obsession with fiscal tightening in many countries is misguided, as it risks tackling the symptoms of the problem while leaving the basic causes unchanged. In virtually all countries, the fiscal deficit has been a consequence of the global financial crisis, and not a cause. Few countries ran large fiscal deficits before the crisis; indeed, some were even in surplus. Today's fiscal deficits are an inevitable outcome of automatic stabilizers and measures aimed at countering the effects of the crisis, including policy-driven stimulus packages that involved increased government spending, lower tax rates and public-funded bailouts of financial institutions. Empirical evidence from different countries and regions shows that the crisis was caused by underlying changes in national competitiveness and private sector imbalances, which were closely related to a malfunctioning financial sector in developed countries. These fundamental causes are not being addressed in the current focus on fiscal tightening in some countries. Worse still, the diversion of attention away from the underlying causes and towards so-called fiscal profligacy in other countries, which in turn could eventually lead to fiscal tightening, increases the risk of stalling, or even reversing, economic recovery.

With regard to today's fiscal deficits and public debt, empirical evidence shows that, even though these constitute a relatively high proportion of GDP in some parts of the world – especially in some developed countries – in many countries they are not large by historical standards. Even more significantly, the data show that in all regions of the world, interest payments on the public debt as a percentage of GDP were lower in 2010 than they have been at any time in the past 13 years. With a few extreme exceptions, interest rates have mostly remained low, even though the size of the public debt has increased. Even in the developed countries that are carrying by far the largest public debt as a ratio of GDP, interest repayments in 2010 were significantly lower than in the late 1990s (at 2.7 per cent of GDP compared with 4.4 per cent).

Policymakers should not focus only on debt stock. They need to consider the relationship between the stock of debt and the flow variables, including interest rates and fiscal revenues that affect a country's ability to support its debt. A major factor that influences changes in the burden of public debt is GDP growth: it is virtually impossible to lower high debt-to-GDP ratios when an economy is stagnant, unless the debtor obtains a significant debt reduction. Hence, the level of a country's fiscal deficit (or surplus) needs to be viewed from a more holistic and dynamic perspective, in the context of its impact on the sustainability of a country's financial position and on its economic stability and growth prospects. From this perspective, the composition of fiscal revenues and expenditures and many other variables that have an impact on a country's fiscal space are also important. These issues are discussed in the next chapter.

Notes

1 The Lawson Doctrine takes its name from a 1988 speech by the then British Chancellor of the Exchequer, Nigel Lawson, when commenting on the current-account deficit of the United Kingdom. He stated that the position of his country was strong because the current-account deficit was driven by private sector, and not public sector, borrowing. The United Kingdom entered into a deep recession soon after that speech. Strictly speaking, the Lawson Doctrine (sometimes referred to as the Lawson-Robichek Doctrine, after Walter Robichek, a senior IMF official in the 1970s, who formulated the doctrine well before Lawson) refers to foreign borrowing and to the accumulation of large external deficits, but similar arguments are often used to justify the large accumulation of private domestic debt.

2 Government savings correspond to the operating balance, which equals current revenues minus current expenditures (including net interest payments).

3 A distinction needs to be made between the *approved aid*, the *actually used amounts* and the *aid element* extended to the financial institutions. According to the Commission, *approved aid* corresponds to the upper limits of support which member States are allowed to grant to the financial institutions. The *actually used amounts* express the actual amount of aid which member States provided through a particular scheme or to a particular financial institution. Finally, the *aid element* expresses the monetary advantage granted to individual banks either through schemes or ad hoc interventions. In most cases the aid element is much lower than the actually used amounts because not the entire amount actually used can be considered as a benefit passed on to a beneficiary. For example, the aid element of a guarantee is the benefit expressed as the difference between a guarantee fee offered by a member State and that offered by the market. However, in some cases it may be difficult to determine the exact amount of the aid element due to lack of information on the prevailing market prices. Therefore, member States and the Commission use particular proxy methods (European Commission, 2010a).

4 Recent estimates suggest that the final cost to the United States Federal Government will amount to $19 billion or less (Congressional Budget Office, 2011). In the EU-27, State aid to the financial sector in 2008 and 2009 represented about 1.7 per cent and 3 per cent, respectively, of EU-27 GDP (European Commission, 2009 and 2010b). In Switzerland, the Government made a $1.1 billion profit by selling its stake in UBS in August 2009 after investing in the bank in the aftermath of the crisis.

5 In this discussion, the classification by income groups follows that of the World Bank, as the data used in this section draw primarily on its databases.

6 Focusing on a simple average of the debt-to-GDP ratio yields a similar result. A weighted average yields even higher debt-to-GDP ratios for the developed countries, mainly because of the large debt-to-GDP ratio of Japan.

7 Some domestically issued debt could be owed to non-residents and thus would count as external debt. Therefore, external debt should not be confused with debt denominated in foreign currency or with debt issued on the international market.

8 To this list, Reinhart and Rogoff (2009) add episodes of high inflation.

9 One way to evaluate how GDP growth affects debt ratios is to compare the actual debt-to-GDP ratio with the debt-to-GDP ratio that would be obtained

by scaling actual debt with trend GDP, estimated by looking at GDP growth over the previous 20 years. Applied to developed economies, this calculation shows that in 2010 the debt-to-trend-GDP ratio was approximately 15 percentage points lower than the actual debt-to-GDP ratio. The difference between the actual debt-to-GDP ratio and debt-to-trend-GDP ratio is even larger (reaching 20 percentage points) if one only considers the European countries that are currently facing some difficulty in the debt market (i.e. Greece, Ireland, Portugal and Spain).

10   Ireland, unlike most other countries, recorded bank bailouts within its fiscal expenditure as capital transfers. Therefore, in this example, most of the costs of the banking crisis are not included in the stock-flow reconciliation.

11   The increase in the net debt of these countries is lower than the increase in gross debt because their governments received some assets (whose real value, however, is probably well below its face value) in exchange for taking over the banks' liabilities.

References

Abdih Y, López-Murphy P, Roitman A and Sahay R (2010). The cyclicality of fiscal policy in the Middle East and Central Asia: Is the current crisis different? IMF Working Paper, no. 10/68. International Monetary Fund, Washington, DC.

Aglietta M (2011). Ne pas confondre symptômes et maladie. In: Lorenzi J-H, ed., *A la Recherche de la Nouvelle Croissance*. Le Cercle des Economistes, Descartes & Cie, Paris, March.

Bacha E (2011). Além da tríade: como reduzir os juros. In: Bacha E and de Bolle M, eds., *Novos Dilemas de Política Econômica: Ensaios em Homenagem a Dionisio Dias Carneiro*. LTC Editora, Rio de Janeiro.

Brixiová Z, Ndikumana L and Abderrahim K (2010). Supporting Africa's post-crisis growth: The role of macroeconomic policies. Working Paper Series No. 117, African Development Bank Group, Tunis, Tunisia.

Campos C, Jaimovich D and Panizza U (2006). The unexplained part of public debt. *Emerging Markets Review*, 7(3): 228–243, Elsevier.

CBO (Congressional Budget Office) (2011). Report on the Troubled Asset Relief Program, March 2011. Washington, DC, The Congress of the United States. Available at: http://www.cbo.gov/ftpdocs/121xx/doc12118/03-29-TARP.pdf.

ECLAC (Economic Commission for Latin America and the Caribbean) (2009). *Economic Survey of Latin America and the Caribbean*. Santiago de Chile.

Eichengreen B and Hausmann R (1999). Exchange rates and financial fragility. Paper presented at the symposium on New Challenges for Monetary Policy, 26–28 August, Jackson Hole, WY.

Eichengreen B, Hausmann R and Panizza U (2005). The Pain of Original Sin. In: Eichengreen B and Hausmann R, eds., *Other People's Money*, Chicago University Press.

European Commission (2009). *Report from the Commission: State Aid Scoreboard – Report on State Aid granted by the EU Member States,* Autumn 2009 update. Brussels. Available at: http://eur-lex.europa.eu/LexUriServ/LexUriServ.do?uri=CELEX:52009DC0661:EN:NOT.

European Commission (2010a). *Report on State Aid Granted by the EU Member States*, Brussels, 1 May 2010.

European Commission (2010b). Facts and figures on State aid in the Member States. Accompanying the *Report from the Commission: State Aid Scoreboard,* Autumn 2010 update. Commission Staff Working Document. Brussels, Belgium. Available at: http://eur-lex.europa.eu/LexUriServ/LexUriServ.do?uri=COM:2010:0701:FIN:EN:PDF Last access: 24/5/2011.

European Commission (2011). *Annual Macro-economic (AMECO) Database*. Economic and Financial Affairs, Economic databases and indicators. Available at: http://ec.europa.eu/economy_finance/db_indicators/ameco/zipped_en.htm.

Government of Ireland (2010). *Budget 2011: Economic and Fiscal Outlook.* Department of Finance, Dublin. Available at: http://budget.gov.ie/budgets/2011/Documents/Economic%20and%20Fiscal%20Outlook.pdf.

Hausmann R and Panizza U (2011). Redemption or abstinence? Original sin, currency mismatches and counter cyclical policies in the new millennium. *Journal of Globalization and Development* (forthcoming).

Heuty A and Aristi J (2010). Fool's gold: Assessing the performance of alternative fiscal instruments during the commodities boom and the global crisis. New York, NY, Revenue Watch Institute.

Hur SK, Jha S, Park D and Quising P (2010). Did fiscal stimulus lift developing Asia out of the global crisis? A preliminary empirical investigation. ADB Economics Working Paper Series, Asian Development Bank, Manila.

IMF (2010). *World Economic Outlook*, Fall. Washington, DC.

Kasekende L, Brixiová Z and Ndikumana L (2010). Africa: Africa's counter-cyclical policy responses to the crisis. *Journal of Globalization and Development*, 1(1).

Keynes JM (1929). The German Transfer Problem: The Reparation Problem: A Discussion; II. A Rejoinder: Views on the Transfer Problem; III. A Reply. *Economic Journal,* 39, March: 1–7; June: 172–178; September: 404-408.

Koo R (2010). Learning wrong lessons from the crisis in Greece. Nomura Securities Co Ltd, Japanese Equity Research – Flash Report, Tokyo, 15 June.

Krugman P (1999). Balance sheets, the transfer problem, and financial crises. *International Tax and Public Finance*, 6(4): 459-472. Springer.

Lara Resende A (2011). Juros: equívoco ou jabuticaba? *Valor Econômico*, 16 June.

OECD (2009). Fiscal packages across OECD countries: Overview and country details. Paris, March.

Osakwe PN (2011). Africa and the global financial and economic crisis: Impacts, responses and opportunities. In: Dullien S, Kotte D, Marquez A and Priewe J, eds., *The Financial and Economic Crisis of 2008-2009 and Developing Countries*. Geneva and Berlin, UNCTAD and Hochschule für Technik und Wirtschaft.

Panizza U (2008). Domestic and external public debt in developing countries. UNCTAD Discussion Paper No. 188, UNCTAD, Geneva.

Ponomarenko AA and Vlasov SA (2010). Russian fiscal policy during the financial crisis. Helsinki, Institute for Economies in Transition, Bank of Finland, July.

Prasad E and Sorkin I (2009). Assessing the G-20 stimulus plans: A deeper look. Washington, DC, Brookings Institution.

Reinhart C and Rogoff K (2009). *This Time is Different.* Princeton, NJ, Princeton University Press.

Reinhart C and Rogoff K (2010). Growth in a time of debt. Paper prepared for the American Economic Review Papers and Proceedings, 7 January. Princeton, NJ, Princeton University.

Torre ADL, Sinnott E and Nash J (2010). Natural Resources in Latin America and the Caribbean: Beyond Booms and Busts? Washington, DC, World Bank.

UNCTAD (*TDR 2006*). *Trade and Development Report, 2006. Global partnership and national policies for development*. United Nations publications, Sales No. E.06.II.D.6, New York and Geneva.

UNCTAD (*TDR 2008*). *Trade and Development Report, 2008. Commodity prices, capital flows and the financing of investment*. United Nations publications, Sales No. E.08.II.D.21, New York and Geneva.

United States Government (2011). Recovery.gov, Track the Money. Available at: www.recovery.gov/Pages/default.aspx.

Villafuerte M, López-Murphy P and Ossowski R (2010). Riding the roller coaster: Fiscal policies of non-renewable resource exporters in Latin America and the Caribbean. IMF Working Paper, no. 10/251, International Monetary Fund, Washington, DC.

World Bank (2009). Global Economic Prospects 2009: Commodities at the Crossroads, Washington, DC.

Chapter III

FISCAL SPACE, DEBT SUSTAINABILITY AND ECONOMIC GROWTH

A. Introduction

The global financial and economic crisis has raised important macroeconomic policy issues concerning the appropriate fiscal response, and its size, composition and duration. After an initial wide consensus on the necessity of proactive macroeconomic policies to support demand, many policymakers have now shifted their focus from fiscal stimulus to fiscal tightening. The policy debate today is about what measures should be taken to achieve the widely agreed objectives of recovery from the crisis and an improvement in fiscal accounts, as well as the sequencing of those measures. The debate reflects, explicitly or implicitly, different views on economic mechanisms and the role of governments. One view is that the impact of fiscal policy tends to be weak or ineffective, based on the assumption that there is a trade-off between public and private expenditure. According to this view, the private sector will adjust its expenditure in a way that counterbalances any change in public sector action. Those who oppose this view maintain that fiscal policy is the most appropriate tool for pulling an economy out of recession.

For a proper assessment of the role of fiscal policy, it has to be considered from a macroeconomic and dynamic perspective, taking into account the impact of that policy on total income and GDP growth, and consequently on fiscal revenues. A restrictive fiscal policy aimed at fiscal consolidation may not succeed for the simple reason that a national economy does not function in the same way as an individual household. Indeed, there is a fallacy of composition

in such an analogy: an isolated agent may be able to increase savings by cutting back spending because such a cutback does not affect its revenues; but this does not hold for governments.

An argument frequently advanced in support of fiscal retrenchment is that there is no more fiscal space available for further fiscal stimulus, even if it is acknowledged that such policies were useful at the initial stages of the crisis. However, this argument overlooks the fact that fiscal space is not a static variable. It would be a mistake to consider this policy space as exogenously determined rather than a largely endogenous variable. An active fiscal policy will affect the fiscal balance by altering the macroeconomic situation through its impact on private sector incomes, as those incomes generate fiscal revenues. In addition, it is possible to increase the economic impact of fiscal policies by changing the composition of public expenditure or public revenues in a way that maximizes their multiplier effects without necessarily modifying the total amount of expenditure or the fiscal balance. Conversely, fiscal adjustment that reduces growth and productive investment can eventually reduce the fiscal space.

Indeed, there is a general misconception in the debate on fiscal policies that confuses policy measures with policy results. Fiscal consolidation (i.e. improvement of the fiscal balance), which is actually a policy result, tends to be equated with fiscal tightening, which is a policy measure. However, fiscal tightening (i.e. increasing taxes and/or cutting expenditures) may improve the fiscal balance, but equally it may lead to its deterioration. On the other hand, fiscal consolidation can also result from an expansionary fiscal policy stance. The final result will depend on the macroeconomic effects of fiscal measures, in particular how they affect economic growth and, in turn, fiscal revenues. Therefore, fiscal consolidation as a result of policies should be clearly distinguished from policies of fiscal tightening or expansion.

Additionally, the case of natural-resource-rich countries deserves special attention. In a majority of these countries, government revenues largely depend on the extractive industries and are therefore vulnerable to volatile international commodity prices. This poses unique policy challenges, owing to the extreme instability of their fiscal resources and the future depletion of the source. Moreover, the insufficiency of compensatory effects (such as automatic stabilizers) in times of fiscal imbalances makes their governments prone to adopting a procyclical fiscal stance. At the same time there is a chronic tendency to currency appreciation, which has negative effects on domestic manufacturing, also known as Dutch disease effects.

Finally, varying interpretations of the meaning of fiscal space and divergent opinions about the adequacy of policies for recovery from the crisis have led to differing views on the risks involved in the accumulation of public debt, and how to deal with fiscal sustainability issues. First, it is worth emphasizing the trivial but often forgotten point that different types of debt crises need different types of policy responses. Reacting to a crisis that originates from excessive private sector borrowing with fiscal tightening does not appear to be an appropriate policy response, particularly if the crisis is associated with asset market deflation that has a contractionary impact on the economy. Even crises that originate from an irresponsible fiscal policy may need a short-term response which might be different from what is needed in the long run.

There are also important differences in the management of debt crises, depending on the currency in which the debt is denominated. When sovereign debt is denominated in domestic currency an outright default is less likely to occur since the government can always monetize the public debt, unless stiff restrictions are imposed on its financing by the central bank. Of course, depending on the overall macroeconomic situation, such a response can have an impact on goods and asset prices (including the exchange rate), with resulting distributional effects, among others. In the case of public debt denominated in foreign currency, there are greater limitations, and it may be necessary to consider the implications of an eventual insolvency. Experiences with different mechanisms for resolving debt crises reveal variations in the distribution of costs and benefits. However, in general they have shown that sovereign defaults are less costly than commonly considered, either for debtors or creditors.

Bailouts of countries facing external constraints and difficulties in servicing their debts have proven to be relatively benign. It is often thought that providing support to a country that lacks access to voluntary credit entails costs for the lending institution (or the taxpayers that sustain the institution when it is a public agency, as it normally is). However, this is rarely the case, because the country in trouble usually pays back.[1] In fact, a strategy that tries to reduce these costs by charging punitive interest rates on emergency loans may backfire, because it will validate markets' expectations and actually increase the probability that the crisis-affected country will not be able to repay.

Most of the understanding about recent sovereign debt crises – before the current one – arises from the experiences of developing countries. Empirical evidence shows that contractionary efforts in those countries were not particularly successful, and that debt sustainability was achieved by promoting higher rates of economic growth, although in several cases some form of debt relief was also required.

In this context, the following section discusses the main challenges to fiscal policy linked to the Great Recession in the form of premature pressures for fiscal tightening in both developed and developing economies. The issue of fiscal space is discussed in section C, with an emphasis on the need for governments to have sufficient room for manoeuvre in realizing their policy objectives without this leading to an unsustainable accumulation of debt. The role of monetary policy in creating fiscal space is also highlighted. Section D analyses the question of public-debt accumulation, including policies aimed at preventing public-debt crises and those needed to resolve such crises.

B. Fiscal policy challenges

For many years, fiscal policies were marginalized as a macroeconomic tool. They were considered ineffective, impractical and redundant. Ineffective, because it was believed that any change in public expenditure would be compensated for by a concomitant change in private expenditure; impractical, because the design and implementation of fiscal policy, as well as its effects, would take more time than any recession itself; and redundant because monetary policies seemed to be adequate for maintaining both low inflation and a stable output gap.

The crisis prompted a rethinking of macroeconomic ideas, as monetary policy showed certain limitations, and governments were once again viewed as buyers and borrowers of last resort (Blanchard, Dell'Ariccia and Mauro, 2010). It seems, however, that the acceptance of short-term fiscal stimulus did not involve a revision of macroeconomic principles, but only agreement that the exceptional circumstances required temporary fiscal action. Influential policymakers have now returned to a traditional vision by once again supporting a policy of fiscal adjustment. In most developed countries, their priority goal is a reduction of what they consider to be overly high public debt levels, even though they acknowledge that the recovery has been moderate and is still fragile. They are also calling for fiscal adjustment in developing countries, which generally display much lower debt ratios than most developed countries and have returned to their pre-crisis growth rates. This is based on the belief that these economies should avoid overheating and should reconstitute the fiscal buffers that could be used if a new crisis episode were to erupt, for example if the conditions that allowed recovery were to disappear. And even countries that did not resort to fiscal stimulus when the crisis broke, because they engaged in early adjustment programmes with the support of the IMF and/or the EU, are being urged to apply further fiscal adjustments (IMF, 2011a). Finally, there are specific fiscal challenges facing the natural-resource-rich developing countries, where fiscal policy tends to be procyclical and associated with changes in commodity prices.

1. Exit strategies and the shift to fiscal tightening

The proposed shift to fiscal restraint raises several interlinked issues – both empirical and conceptual – concerning the need for fiscal adjustment, the ways in which such an adjustment could be achieved and the economic consequences of this strategy. The starting point is the perception that the space for fiscal stimulus is already – or will soon be – exhausted, especially in developed countries. This is based on the belief that debt ratios have already reached or are approaching a level beyond which fiscal solvency is at risk. After that point, the government would not be able to generate a primary balance to cover the growing interest payments. This implies that the public-debt-to-GDP ratio would rise without bound (Ostry et al., 2010). However, it can be argued that such a debt limit is difficult to identify, since it depends on the prevailing interest rate, economic growth and primary fiscal balances. First, the interest rate is itself a macroeconomic policy variable, and this implies that monetary policy might have a significant impact on debt sustainability. Second, both GDP growth and the primary balance could be influenced by debt-financed government spending, as tax revenues rise with the growth of national income. In other words, debt-to-GDP ratios may be increasing only temporarily in the short run, and their growth might be instrumental in boosting GDP growth and reducing the debt burden in the long run.

In a different but complementary approach to that of Ostry et al. (2010), some authors have estimated a threshold for the public-debt-to-GDP ratio that an economy could not exceed without negatively affecting growth rates, which in turn would undermine fiscal solvency. According to these estimates, the critical level is 90 per cent of GDP for developed economies and 60 per cent for emerging market economies (Reinhart and Rogoff, 2010). The finding that developing countries are constrained by a lower debt-to-GDP ratio seems to be associated with their propensity to issue foreign-currency-denominated debt and with foreign ownership of their debt. Nersisyan and Wray (2010) found that out of 216 observations, only five revealed debt-to-GDP ratios that exceeded 90 per cent. This is not a sufficiently large sample to conclude that high debt-to-GDP ratios are correlated with low levels of economic growth. More importantly, correlation does not necessarily imply causation.

The IMF, despite favouring countercyclical policies at the early stage of the crisis, is strongly supporting the austerity programmes now being pursued by many countries. According to conventional wisdom, a given debt ratio that seemed sustainable may become unsustainable if, beyond a tipping point, risk premiums increase interest rates or impede the normal roll-over of the debt that is reaching maturity in a self-fulfilling prophecy. Still, according to the conventional view, given that financial markets have increased their focus on fiscal weaknesses, it is urgent to avoid a widespread loss of confidence in fiscal solvency, which would have huge cost impacts. Therefore, credibility must be regained with a "convincing deficit reduction plan" that would curb any increase in public debt ratios; otherwise, developed countries' debt will reach 115 per cent of GDP by 2015. This is why the IMF believes "fiscal strategies should aim at gradually – but steadily and significantly – reducing public debt ratios" (IMF, 2010a: 4). According to the IMF and

the mainstream view, the risk of a confidence crisis in the financial markets would be more serious than that of a double-dip recession, since it is believed that private demand in the developed economies is recovering on a sustainable basis and replacing public demand (IMF, 2011b). Thus, according to this logic, it should be possible to tighten fiscal policies without jeopardizing global recovery.

Even assuming that the immediate policy goal is to curb the public-debt-to-GDP ratio, this can be done by reducing the numerator (the amount of the debt), increasing the denominator (current GDP), or arriving at a combination of these two options. The preferred strategy of the mainstream position is reducing debt, even if the policies chosen to do this may also negatively affect GDP growth. In fact, even among the advocates of fiscal tightening it is recognized that "fiscal consolidation typically causes short-term contractionary effects" (Bornhorst et al., 2010: 7; see also IMF, 2010b). However, these short-term costs are assumed to be moderate and temporary, and to be much lower than the long-term costs, which allegedly would be avoided as a result of fiscal tightening.

> In developed economies, fiscal policy is shifting from stimulus to restraint in order to tackle high public debts.

The IMF used its Global Integrated Monetary and Fiscal Model to estimate the impact of fiscal adjustment in developed economies, and found that a "fiscal consolidation equal to 1 percent of GDP typically reduces real GDP by about 0.5 percent after two years" (IMF, 2010b: 98). According to the simulation, the type of fiscal adjustment applied influences the final cost: an adjustment through reduced spending would be less contractionary than an adjustment through tax increases.[2] The difference does not result from dissimilar multipliers associated with higher taxes or lower spending, but from the assumption that the latter is typically accompanied by a large dose of monetary stimulus, which lowers the interest rate, causes a depreciation of the currency and generates net exports. On the other hand, the IMF assumes that central banks typically are reluctant to reduce interest rates when fiscal tightening is undertaken by increasing taxes, because indirect tax hikes would raise prices (IMF, 2010b).[3] Hence, IMF calculations that show a relatively low cost of fiscal adjustment in terms of GDP growth do not measure the impact of the adjustment itself; rather, they show the impact of a package composed of a spending-based fiscal adjustment plus monetary expansion, along with a net increase in exports. In addition, it is assumed that trade partners will accept an appreciation of their currencies and a deterioration of their trade balances. This raises the issue of simultaneity of fiscal consolidation, since not all countries can expand their net exports at the same time. Without the above-mentioned compensatory factors, the estimated GDP cost of fiscal contraction would be substantially higher. Thus, if interest rates are not lowered, a spending cut equivalent to 1 per cent of GDP leads to an output loss of 1.1 per cent in the first year and 1 per cent in the second year. If, in addition, the rest of the world undertakes fiscal consolidation at the same time, GDP contraction will double to 2 per cent in the first two years, and the negative effect will last for five years (IMF, 2010b).

Even if it is acknowledged that fiscal tightening has a short-term negative impact on growth, it is assumed that it will have a positive impact in the medium and long term. Lower government debt levels – resulting from fiscal restraint[4] – would reduce the burden of interest payments and increase the supply of savings. This, in turn, would reduce the real interest rates and "crowd in" private investment. Overall, IMF simulations find an ambiguous effect of fiscal adjustment on growth, with short-run temporary costs but also more permanent GDP gains. The losses are expected to be entirely offset by the gains within five years (IMF, 2010b).

Hence the central mechanism that is expected to moderate the short-term costs of fiscal adjustment and deliver long-term gains in developed economies stems basically from the reduction of interest rates that would be associated with lower debt ratios (Bornhorst et al., 2010). However, this negative relationship between real interest rates and the level of public debt is far from evident. Analysis of the data for a set of developed countries shows that either the correlation between the two variables was weak and statistically insignificant or (more frequently) that it moved in the opposite direction than that expected: higher debt was actually associated with lower interest rates and vice versa (chart 3.1). The same results were obtained when real interest rates were compared

with the changes in the public-debt-to-GDP ratio: a reduction in that ratio was associated with higher, not lower, interest rates.

Consequently, it cannot be assumed that successful fiscal consolidation will lead to lower interest rates, since those rates are managed by monetary authorities. But even if it did, this would not necessarily lead to an improvement in demand, investment and growth. Indeed, in the developed economies that were severely hit by the financial crisis, the private sector has not yet completed the deleveraging process through which non-financial agents try to reduce their indebtedness and banks try to restore their capital ratios. In such a "debt-deflation crisis" (Fisher, 1933) or "balance sheet recession" (Koo, 2010), low interest rates and fresh credit cannot be expected to lead the way out of the crisis. In such a situation, monetary policy has asymmetrical outcomes: monetary tightening could make matters worse, but monetary expansion will have little stimulating effect. Thus, relying on monetary or credit expansion is like "pushing on a string", whereas fiscal retrenchment would effectively stall economic recovery. And if it weakens GDP growth and fiscal revenues, fiscal consolidation itself may not be achieved.

> If austerity measures reduce GDP growth and fiscal revenues, fiscal consolidation may not be achieved.

Despite the lack of solid conceptual foundations, most developed economies have embarked on fiscal tightening, concentrating on the expenditure side. Spending cuts on welfare, health care and pensions have been the most frequently used measure in OECD countries, occurring with up to 60 per cent frequency (OECD, 2011). Pension reforms include raising the retirement age, or freezing or reducing pension payments. Other age-related cuts in expenditure include health care and long-term care, with projected cuts accounting for 3 per cent of GDP, on average. Other measures relate to public sector salaries and jobs (e.g. Greece, Ireland, Slovenia and Spain have cut salaries, while France and Italy have frozen them). On the other hand, cuts in government spending on agricultural subsidies have been the least frequently applied in OECD countries, occurring with less than 15 per cent frequency. Further, in the United States, for example, rules requiring state and local governments to maintain a balanced budget are already being revived, bringing to an end the period of grace

Chart 3.1

RELATIONSHIP BETWEEN PUBLIC DEBT AS A PERCENTAGE OF GDP AND REAL LONG-TERM INTEREST RATES IN GERMANY, JAPAN AND THE UNITED STATES, 1981–2010

(Per cent)

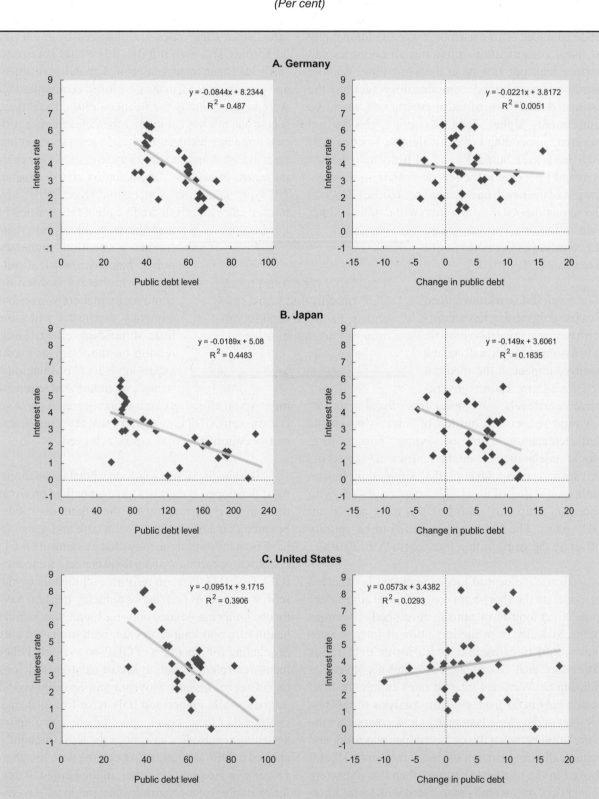

Source: UNCTAD secretariat calculations, based on IMF, *Historical Public Debt Database*, and *World Economic Outlook* database.

that was made possible by subsidized funding from the Federal Government. This means that the clamp down will be felt at all levels of the economy.

Tax hikes accounted for one third of the fiscal tightening policies announced by OECD countries. Consumption taxes are the single most widely adopted tax measure, having been increased in 20 OECD countries. Value added taxes, for instance, have been increased by 4 percentage points in Greece, by 3 points in Portugal and 2 points in Spain, giving rise to concerns about their adverse impacts on the poor, who spend the largest proportion of their income on consumer goods and services. Income tax, on the other hand, has been increased by much fewer countries. Some countries increased income tax imposed on the upper income groups or industry (e.g. in the United Kingdom, the Government's one-off bank payroll tax in 2010 and a number of other measures aimed at high-income earners), but other countries lowered their corporate taxes, and higher taxes imposed on the financial sector occurred with only 25 per cent frequency (OECD, 2011).

Overall, the fiscal measures have tended to cut spending and increase taxes on items that would most likely have a negative impact on income distribution, and as a result they might have a further negative effect on the already feeble recovery, since lower income groups have a higher propensity to spend.

2. *Fiscal tightening without a previous stimulus: the rationale for procyclical fiscal policies*

When the crisis erupted, a number of European and transition economies that were among the most seriously affected turned to the IMF for emergency financing. Although at the time the IMF approved of countercyclical fiscal policies, in most of these countries the programmes it supported entailed fiscal adjustment, as has been typical of its conditionality. Hence fiscal restraint was required without a previous injection of fiscal stimulus aimed at limiting the impact of a crisis that, in general, was not caused by fiscal deficits, as discussed earlier. Given the pressure on financial markets, no fiscal space was assigned to those countries by creditors.

In order to obtain IMF support, countries are expected to adjust their current-account deficits by reducing domestic absorption (including fiscal retrenchment), which normally slows GDP growth. Those eventual impacts are evaluated by IMF staff, and reflected in a letter of intent (LOI) signed by the governments concerned. These LOIs contain economic forecasts and goals to be reached by the countries. It is interesting to compare their short-term forecasts (for the year following the signature of the LOI) with the actual results of the IMF-supported programmes. Chart 3.2 presents these data for countries that resorted to IMF assistance because of a financial crisis in two periods: the late 1990s and early 2000s, and the present crisis. The data show similar patterns. The crisis-recovery packages recommended by policymakers, including the IMF, during both episodes present a systematic overestimation of the private sector's ability to recover, or an underestimation of the time taken for investment and consumption to return to previous levels. There is also a divergence between the estimated GDP growth rate during post-crisis periods on the horizontal axis (calculated by the IMF on the assumption that countries would implement the proposed policies) and the GDP growth that actually occurred (vertical axis). A 45 degree line running through the graph indicates what would be a one-to-one mapping between estimate and experience. All countries are located to the right hand side of that line (or on the line), with the exception of the Russian Federation in the late 1990s and Iceland in the late 2000s (where debt default occurred), indicating that outcomes systematically failed to live up to expectations. In some cases, the gaps are sizeable: in 1998, a GDP growth of 5 per cent was forecast for Indonesia, but in fact it experienced minus 13 per cent growth; Thailand was expected to achieve 3.5 per cent growth, but growth actually contracted by 10.5 per cent; and the Republic of Korea was expected to achieve 2.5 per cent growth but it actually recorded minus 5.7 per cent. In recent years, growth outcomes have been overestimated by more than 5 percentage points in Georgia, Hungary, Latvia, Serbia and Ukraine.

There are also systematic differences between LOI forecasts and actual outcomes with regard to current-account and fiscal balances. There is a clear bias towards underestimating current-account adjustment, while the LOI are overly optimistic in their forecasts for fiscal consolidation. It appears that fiscal adjustments and GDP contraction were excessively

Chart 3.2

COMPARISON BETWEEN FORECASTS OF GDP GROWTH, FISCAL BALANCES AND CURRENT-ACCOUNT BALANCES IN IMF-SPONSORED PROGRAMMES AND ACTUAL VALUES FOR SELECTED COUNTRIES

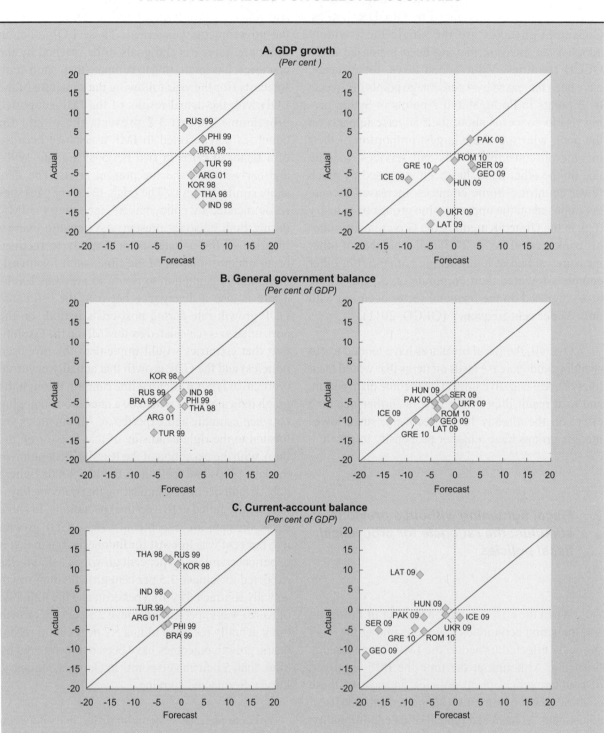

Source: IMF, Letters of Intent, available at: http://www.imf.org/external/np/cpid/default.aspx; and UNCTAD Globstat.

Note: The years refer to the year following the Letter of Intent signature.

ARG 01: Argentina, 2001; BRA 99: Brazil, 1999; GEO 09: Georgia, 2009; GRE 10: Greece, 2010; HUN 09: Hungary, 2009; ICE 09: Iceland, 2009; IND 98: Indonesia, 1998; LAT 09: Latvia, 2009; PAK 09: Pakistan, 2009; PHI 99: the Philippines, 1999; KOR 98: the Republic of Korea, 1998; ROM 10: Romania, 2010; RUS 99: the Russian Federation, 1999; SER 09: Serbia, 2009; THA 98: Thailand, 1998; TUR 99: Turkey, 1999; UKR 09: Ukraine, 2009.

severe in order to achieve the desired adjustment in the current account; or that the architects of the programmes did not expect these costs to be so high in those countries.

Misjudging the effects of fiscal tightening seems to be the rule rather than the exception in IMF-backed programmes. A detailed examination of fiscal adjustment in 133 IMF-supported programmes in 70 countries carried out by the IMF's Independent Evaluation Office (IEO) notes that there was "a tendency to adopt fiscal targets based on over-optimistic assumptions about the pace of economic recovery leading inevitably to fiscal under performances" and "over-optimistic assumptions about the pace of revival of private investment." The report observes that "a more realistic assessment in certain circumstances could have justified the adoption of a more relaxed fiscal stance on contracyclical grounds" (IMF, 2003: vii).

In country after country where fiscal tightening was expected to both reduce the budget deficit and boost investment and economic growth, the opposite happened. Private sector demand and investment, in particular, responded much more sluggishly than the IMF had expected. In addition, fiscal balances, on average, failed to improve during the first two years of the fiscal adjustment programmes, even though this was an explicit goal of those programmes. The main reason for the shortfalls in countries that made large fiscal adjustments was that government revenues fell far below expectations. On the other hand, the spending cuts were on target.

This record of failed IMF-sponsored adjustment programmes suggests that they are based on a fundamental macroeconomic misconception. The conceptual basis is not quite clear. The majority of programmes reviewed by the IMF-IEO did not explain the links between the targeted fiscal adjustment and the envisaged improvement in the external situation, or the assumptions driving the projected recovery of private spending and how it was linked to the fiscal policies recommended. Indeed, there seems to have been "surprisingly little rationale" for

> IMF-sponsored programmes have systematically overestimated economic recovery and fiscal consolidation.

the fiscal tightening policies that were recommended in most of these programmes. One implicit assumption seems to be that "private investment demand is buoyant and fiscal contraction creates room for private investment to be financed" (IMF, 2003: 6), meaning that the public and private sectors are in competition with each other for the use of productive resources – even during severe recessions – and that public sector expenditure crowds out investment by the private sector. Another implicit assumption appears to be that fiscal tightening is the key test of a government's determination to honour its debts, and is therefore necessary for "a quick return of investor confidence and a rapid pickup in growth." In this view, the pace of recovery of private sector demand, and particularly investment, "depends on investor confidence and financial market conditions, which in turn are a function of the perceived degree of commitment of the authorities to adhere to the program" (IMF, 2003: 111).

The conflicting views about whether public spending should be seen as a substitute for, or as a complement to, private sector spending, revolve around the "crowding-out" debate. For those who believe in crowding out effects, increases in government spending reduce private expenditure. In this case, either supplementary spending is financed with borrowing and leads to a higher interest rate which lowers investment and consumption, or the government opts to raise taxes to bridge the fiscal gap, which reduces private disposable income and demand. Hence, public stimulus will be irrelevant at best, and may even be counterproductive if it raises concerns among private investors. Theoretical models supporting this view have been criticized for their unrealistic assumptions – such as perfect foresight, infinite planning horizons, perfect capital markets, and an absence of distribution effects through taxation – which make them unsuitable for policy decisions in the real world. In particular, their starting point usually assumes full employment, when the discussion is precisely how to recover from an economic slump. Even in more normal times, however, the empirical evidence for crowding out is weak at best (see box 3.1).

Box 3.1

FISCAL STIMULUS AND CROWDING OUT

The view that a fiscal stimulus will fail to boost aggregate demand is based on the notion that expansionary public policies will necessarily reduce private expenditure, thus nullifying the stimulus that was intended.

In order to clarify the argument, it is useful to start by defining fiscal stimulus as an increase in public expenditure not matched by an increase in taxes, or a cut in taxes not matched by a fall in public expenditure. Either of these would deteriorate the fiscal balance and could increase the fiscal deficit.

One argument for the ineffectiveness of fiscal policy is that a higher budget deficit will require the issuance of government bonds, which in turn will increase the interest rate and crowd out private investment. The magnitude of this crowding out depends on many factors, and there is a consensus that crowding out is unlikely to occur in periods of slack demand and low global interest rates.

An alternative argument for the inefficiency of fiscal policy is based on the idea that an increase in debt will lead to higher taxes in the future, and that forward-looking individuals may want to increase their savings in order to be able to pay future taxes (Barro, 1974). Thus a higher deficit would lead to a direct reduction of consumption, and it would have no impact on the level of economic activity.

According to these views, even if a fiscal stimulus were to increase public demand or private disposable income, two different factors may counterbalance the expansionary public stance: higher interest rates due to public net borrowing, which will hinder private investment, or higher private savings on the expectation of future tax payments. Both these assumptions are problematic. Regarding the first argument, even a relatively large increase in government borrowing is unlikely to push interest rates up, because this increase would still be marginal compared with the total amount of assets in the capital market, and it would come at a time when private borrowing is falling because of recession. Moreover, even if interest rates were raised, the debt-financed government spending would cause aggregate demand – and thus the willingness to invest – to grow. In that case, there would be two effects working in opposite directions, but whereas the demand effect is certain, the interest effect is not, especially as it can plausibly be assumed that if debt-financed government spending were to increase, the central bank would embark on monetary easing and lower interest rates.

The second assumption supposes that agents, aware of the intertemporal government budget constraint, would expect that an increase in the fiscal deficit financed by debt will lead to future tax increases, and that consequently they will restrain their present spending. This assumption of behaviour is based on the rational expectation hypothesis, market clearing logic and other stringent assumptions, including perfect credit markets, perfect foresight, lump sum taxes and infinitely-lived agents or intergeneration links among all agents. All these unrealistic assumptions should make policymakers cautious about policy recommendations derived from this hypothesis (known as the Ricardian Equivalence Theorem in the literature). In addition, an implicit assumption is that private agents do not expect the government to seek monetary financing from the central bank – instead of raising taxes – for future debt services. If they did so, following the theorem's logic, potential taxpayers would have no reason to increase their savings rate. More fundamentally, the very starting point of Barro's reasoning that public debt must be repaid is far from evident. In general, public debt that is reaching maturity is rolled over or replaced by new debt, since what rentiers seek is to perceive a reasonable return on their capital rather than recovering it.

Furthermore, this theorem completely ignores the dynamic effects of fiscal stimulus policies, especially in an economy with low level of production capacity utilization. In that case, an increase in fiscal expenditure will generate new demand and greater output, which in turn will boost both private income and fiscal revenues. In such a situation, it is more likely to have a crowding-in outcome, as a result of supplementary public expenditure inducing higher private demand, than a crowding-out effect. Even if the stimulus

Box 3.1 (concluded)

package leads to a higher fiscal deficit and public debt in the short run, this is not a sufficient reason for the private sector to curb its spending, since it can rationally expect its income, and thus the tax base, to grow as a result of the expansionary effect of the spending increase. Moreover, the debt-to-GDP ratio will normally tend to fall with economic recovery, and future generations will inherit not only that debt, but also the productive capacity it contributed to financing.

Empirical evidence on the alleged crowding-out effects of deficit spending is weak. Aschauer (1989) indicated for the United States that public investment had an overall crowding-in effect on private investment, and that public and private capital could be seen as complementary. Eisner (1995; 2006) showed that in the United States and all other OECD countries fiscal deficits – cyclically and inflation-adjusted – tend to reduce unemployment and have a positive effect on output and investment. Also, he found no significant effect on prices.

Regarding the effects of fiscal deficits on interest rates, Gale and Orszag (2003) found that in the United States these effects were positive, but economically insignificant. Laubach (2004) showed that for the G-7 countries, except France, the coefficients on the deficit-to-GDP ratio were either insignificant or implied that deficits actually reduced real long-term interest rates, as in Germany and Japan. In reviewing the relevant literature on the issue, IMF economists Hemming, Kell and Mahfouz (2002: 36) concluded that "there is little evidence of direct crowding out or crowding out through interest rates and the exchange rate. Nor does full Ricardian equivalence or a significant partial Ricardian offset get much support from the evidence." Angeriz and Arestis (2009) reached a similar conclusion.

3. The special case of natural-resource-rich countries

The IMF is also pushing for fiscal tightening in fast-growing developing countries with low levels of public debt, on the grounds of avoiding overheating rather than of lowering high debt ratios (IMF, 2011b). In particular, it argues that governments benefiting from sizeable fiscal revenues owing to high commodity prices should refrain from increasing public spending, and instead should reconstitute financial buffers to be used in times of falling or low commodity prices (IMF, 2011a).

Of course, based on the logic presented in the previous section, it is not clear that fiscal adjustments would actually deliver countercyclical effects (i.e. slowing down rapid economic growth), because they could further boost investors' confidence and crowd in more private investment. However, it is true that economic authorities in natural-resource-rich countries face specific challenges in their management of fiscal policy, especially in developing and transition

economies where a significant share of government revenues originate from their extractive industries. This subsection examines these challenges.

One of the challenges relates to the high price volatility of hydrocarbons and mineral resources, which makes government revenues uncertain and unstable, and may lead to boom and bust cycles in expenditure. Another challenge is that, since natural resources are exhaustible and will eventually be depleted, fiscal authorities also need to address issues of long-term fiscal sustainability and intergenerational distribution of the proceeds of the natural resources. In addition, macroeconomic management in these countries may be complicated by Dutch disease problems, as the foreign exchange earnings from extractive industries' exports may lead to an appreciation of the currency, which would result in a loss of competitiveness of other non-resource-based sectors of the economy, such as some agricultural activities and manufacturing.

The dependence of fiscal balances on revenues from natural resources is particularly high in many

West Asian and African oil-exporting countries, where they often exceed 70 per cent of total fiscal revenues.[5] Moreover, the importance of natural resources for fiscal revenues in these countries seems to have been increasing during the years of the commodity boom (Torre, Sinnott and Nash, 2010; OECD, 2010).

Governments of natural-resource-rich countries are confronted with difficult choices in their fiscal policies. First of all, in order to have the fiscal space necessary for pursuing counter-cyclical fiscal policies and meeting their development objectives, they need to secure an adequate share of the rents from their primary resources. Thus, fairness in the distribution of these rents between the government and the private sector (often foreign transnational corporations) should be guaranteed (*TDR 2005*, chapter III and *TDR 2010*, chapter V). During the commodity price boom of 2002–2008 a number of commodity-exporting countries revised their fiscal regimes. This process of changing the taxation of extractive industries may have been interrupted, or even reversed in some cases, when the global financial and economic crisis began, as the bargaining power of governments vis-à-vis the transnational mining and oil corporations was weakened. With the renewed price increases in 2010–2011, some governments are once again attempting to revise those regimes.[6]

Once a government receives the revenues from natural resource exploitation, it has to decide on the respective shares to be spent and saved, either for macroeconomic stabilization purposes for use in bad times, or for future generations. The share earmarked for expenditure can either be used for current consumption or for capital investment. These choices will have different implications for long-term growth and development. For example, capital expenditure may improve infrastructure and expand productive capacity in the country, and thus facilitate diversification and structural change and reduce commodity dependence. Current expenditure on education and health can also make a significant contribution to growth by increasing labour

> Natural-resource-rich countries are vulnerable to price volatility and should create space for countercyclical policies.

> A significant share of the proceeds from natural resource exploitation should finance public infrastructure and social services to achieve diversification and structural change.

productivity. To the extent that all these expenditures increase productive capacity, they will also benefit future generations. Using government revenues from the extractive industries to increase public investment, for instance in infrastructure, would also be a way of increasing the productivity and competitiveness of the non-resource sectors of the economy. Finally, expenditure can be directed to imports or to domestic goods, which may also provide some stimulus to domestic supply. However, expenditure on imports of capital goods and technology may be particularly necessary in the poorest countries to promote long-term development.

Since natural-resource-rich countries are particularly vulnerable to external factors, the countries that do not exercise countercyclical fiscal policies tend to endure strong economic fluctuations. Indeed, in these countries, automatic stabilizers that could help counter external shocks are usually weak or totally missing. When commodity prices fall, government resources diminish, which normally impacts public expenditure and economic activity. In this case, deterioration of the fiscal balance is not due to lower taxes paid by nationals or, for example, to higher transfers to the unemployed; it is simply due to declining public revenue resulting from reduced income from exports. Hence, fiscal deficits lack any significant automatic stimulus element. Similarly, during periods of high commodity prices, increases in public revenues do not have any restrictive effect on domestic demand, because they do not take away income from domestic taxpayers. In other words, these countries cannot rely on automatic stabilizers, and must therefore set policy rules and mechanisms for creating space for countercyclical policies.

The negative impact of instability in government revenues due to the volatility of commodity prices can be alleviated through fiscal rules, conservative assumptions in the budget regarding future prices of the commodities concerned, and commodity stabilization or savings funds. In order to fulfil a countercyclical purpose, the funds would work in such a way that in good times, when prices are high, resources would be deposited in the fund for release during bad times when prices fall. Funds deposited abroad would help avoid an appreciation of the exchange rate, in addition to providing a reserve for macroeconomic stabilization or spending by future generations.

The priorities of fiscal policy in natural-resource-rich countries will differ depending on the level of development. In high-income countries, policies favouring intergenerational equity and stabilization may be of greater importance. In Norway, for example, oil revenues are deposited in the government pension fund, and the returns from the investments in this fund, estimated at 4 per cent, are spent over time (NORAD, 2009). In middle-income developing countries, such as Chile, macroeconomic stabilization may also be a relevant goal; indeed stabilization funds facilitated countercyclical policies during the crisis in that country.

However, in the lower income countries, which have pressing needs in terms of poverty reduction and development, withdrawing most of the funds from the economy to be invested in financial assets abroad does not seem to be the most appropriate option. Rather, using a significant part of the proceeds from natural resource exploitation for public investment in infrastructure, for improvements in education and health and for the provision of basic social services may provide better returns. If successful, this could bring about diversification and structural change, which in turn would lead to an expansion of the tax base and therefore reduce government dependence on revenues from commodities. Nevertheless, these countries would still need to withdraw part of the revenues to provide them with the financial means for implementing countercyclical policies and smoothing expenditure.

The strong impact of the global financial and economic crisis on natural-resource-dependent countries has highlighted the importance for these countries to pursue countercyclical fiscal policies. Moreover, it has become even more evident that they need to diversify their production and export structure in order to reduce their dependence on the revenues obtained from only a small basket of commodities, the prices of which are highly volatile. In this context, it is important to integrate policies relating to the extractive industries into national development strategies aimed at transforming their natural resource base into physical capital, generating new employment opportunities and promoting human development. This in turn will reduce their fiscal vulnerabilities and expand their fiscal space.

C. Qualitative and quantitative aspects of fiscal space

An apt definition of fiscal space is that the public sector's budget provides sufficient financing for a desired purpose without reducing the sustainability of the public accounts (Heller, 2005; Ostry et al., 2010). Heller emphasizes revenue creation and reprioritization of spending and borrowing on a sustainable basis as the main means of creating fiscal space. While these are possible ways, monetary and other aspects of fiscal policy can also make a significant contribution, because both affect the government's revenue stream, and therefore have an impact on sustainability. This is why trying to find a critical level of debt, beyond which solvency would be compromised, without considering the dynamic effects of other macroeconomic policies is a futile endeavour. This section highlights the need for a dynamic definition of fiscal space, while showing that other factors, such as monetary policy and the international financial environment, might also be relevant for creating that space. The section also includes a discussion of the types of fiscal policies that would be more conducive to enlarging fiscal space.

1. A dynamic and comprehensive view of fiscal space

When the global financial crisis began, it seemed relatively clear that governments in both developed and developing countries had sufficient fiscal space to cope with the economic downturn. Although initially there was significant consensus that an expansionary fiscal policy was needed to overcome the crisis (Spilimbergo et al., 2008), the increasing levels of debt have caused a rapid shift of opinion towards favouring fiscal tightening to avoid the perceived risks resulting from higher levels of public debt. This view is in line with conventional wisdom, which tends to suggest that, just as families cannot spend more than they earn, governments too should mind their purses.

However, if every economic agent curbs spending, the flow of income will fall. Unless some other agent is willing to spend, "tightening the belt" becomes counterproductive for the economy as a whole. By definition, income can only be generated if somebody spends. In the context of a deep depression, only the government can increase spending in domestic currency and reverse the downward spiral of less spending and reduced income and employment. Further, since a certain amount of spending takes place on the basis of credit, there is a relationship between expenditure and debt for the economy as a whole, with part of the debt being private (families and firms) and the other part public. If private debt falls and all else remains constant, spending will have to fall. In that case, public debt will have to be increased in order to support spending, and it can only be reduced once the private ability to increase indebtedness has been re-established.

If government spending has an effect on economic activity, which, as a result leads to higher growth rates than increases in indebtedness, the debt-to-GDP ratio will tend to fall (Barba and Pivetti, 2009). Higher fiscal expenditure does not necessarily translate into an equivalent increase in the primary fiscal deficit, because it may also generate some fiscal revenues. However, it is necessary to assess the evolution of interest rates on public debt, which some analysts link to the level or the evolution of that debt.

In other words, the overall impact of fiscal stimulus measures on the fiscal deficit and growth needs to be evaluated. If their impact on growth is greater than their immediate impact on the overall fiscal balance, then the government does not have a solvency problem, even if the deficit is large in the short run. The question of sustainability of public debt is therefore central to any discussion concerning the appropriate fiscal policy, and the variables that determine sustainability, fiscal deficits, GDP growth and interest rates on public debt are central to an understanding of fiscal policy.

Interest rates on public debt are affected by monetary policy, since they tend to fall when the central bank reduces the short-term interest rate. This is to be expected, since government bonds, bills and other low-risk assets still pay a liquidity premium vis-à-vis the basic monetary rate. However, unless there is reason to believe that these assets pose an additional risk, the liquidity premium should not change, and the bond and bill rates should follow approximately the ups and downs of the basic rate.

The central bank can also directly intervene in the bond markets and influence the long-term interest rate. Quantitative easing is used when setting the short-term interest rate is insufficient to affect economic spending, and therefore the central bank directly targets the long-term rate. In that case, the central bank buys government bonds in secondary markets, signalling that interest rates will remain low with the aim of stimulating spending (Bernanke and Reinhart, 2004).

More importantly, lower long-term interest rates imply lower levels of debt service for the public sector, thereby increasing the fiscal space, since resources allocated to interest payments can then be used for other purposes. In this sense, quantitative easing underscores the strong interdependence between monetary and fiscal policy. Fiscal policy is more efficient when short-term nominal interest rates reach their lower zero bound limit (Christiano, Eichenbaum and Rebelo, 2009; Woodford, 2011); but also monetary policy aimed at maintaining lower rates on long-term government debt provides an essential lever for improving the efficiency of fiscal policy.

2. Interest rates and fiscal space

As discussed in chapter II of this *Report*, to a large extent debt-to-GDP ratios respond to the interaction of interest rates and output growth. In this sense, it is possible for economies with persistent fiscal deficits to have a sustainable – and even a declining – debt-to-GDP ratio if the rate of interest is consistently lower than the rate of growth (Pasinetti, 1997; Roubini, 2001). This is the basis for what Keynes referred to as the "euthanasia of the rentier", whereby low rates of interest allow fiscal expansion on a sustainable basis.

During the post-war boom period, low interest rates permitted fiscal expansion for recovery and for the creation of the Welfare State in European and other developed countries, as well as for infrastructure building and a considerable amount of catching up by the developing world. This period is often referred to as the "Golden Age of Capitalism" (Marglin, 1990). The evolution of interest rates dynamics saw two important breaks. In the first break, starting in the late 1970s and early 1980s, there was a sharp increase in interest rates, which led to a reversal of the debt dynamics. The second, which took place in the early 2000s, relates to the lower rates of interest, on average, in developed countries.

After the first break, for the most part real interest rates were higher than the rate of GDP growth in developed countries (e.g. Germany, Japan and the United States), as well as in Latin America (e.g. Mexico), Eastern Europe (e.g. Poland), and sub-Saharan Africa (e.g. South Africa), but not in the Asian economies (e.g. China and the Republic of Korea). In the subsequent phase, between 2001–2003 and the Great Recession, there was a reversal (chart 3.3), with real interest rates lower than growth rates in almost all countries in the chart. And despite the brief fall in GDP, this trend has continued to the present day.

This suggests that, while debt-to-GDP ratios increased in developed countries as a result of high interest rates until the turn of the century, thereafter, despite a significant fall in interest rates, those ratios continued to increase because of the Great Recession. This resulted in reduced growth and increased fiscal deficits. On the other hand, in Asia debt-to-GDP ratios have been under control, even though both the Asian crisis and the Great Recession put pressure on fiscal balances. In other words, the lower rates of interest in Asian countries allowed them greater fiscal space.

In Latin America, sub-Saharan Africa and Eastern Europe, debt sustainability was achieved through a combination of significant expansionary fiscal adjustments (i.e. growth in spending accompanied by rising revenues). These adjustments were made possible by achieving and maintaining primary surpluses for extended periods, by debt renegotiations that reduced the debt overhang, and, in recent years, by relatively rapid economic growth. In that sense, monetary policy was less critical for the creation of fiscal space in those regions.

In part, the problem of higher interest rates in some developing countries is associated with the difficulties of dealing with volatile capital flows and the need to prevent capital flight. Also, in some countries, particularly in Latin America the interest rate is maintained at higher levels as an anti-inflationary policy instrument.

The crisis has created higher levels of public debt in many developed economies. However, it is not clear that these levels are unsustainable, and whether fiscal policy should become contractionary if economic recovery and low real interest rates are sufficient to maintain the debt-to-GDP ratio on a stable path. To a large extent, central banks around the world control the rate of interest, and there is no justifiable reason for raising interest rates when global recovery is still fragile. If inflationary pressures not directly associated with excess demand develop, there are alternative policies that might be used to deal with the problem, such as an incomes policy (*TDR 2010*). Even in countries where a perceived solvency risk has led to a rise in interest rates, efforts should be made to keep the rates down to moderate levels, because very high rates will not induce a return to voluntary lending. In order to limit a rate increase, extraordinary measures that provide credit at lower rates should be sought, as discussed in the next section.

In sum, monetary policy is an essential instrument, not just to promote the level of activity while maintaining stability, but also to create the necessary space for fiscal policy. There are good reasons to believe that monetary policy should continue to create fiscal space by maintaining low interest rates in a two-speed global recovery in which developed countries

Chart 3.3

REAL INTEREST RATE AND REAL GDP GROWTH, SELECTED COUNTRIES, 1991–2010

(Per cent)

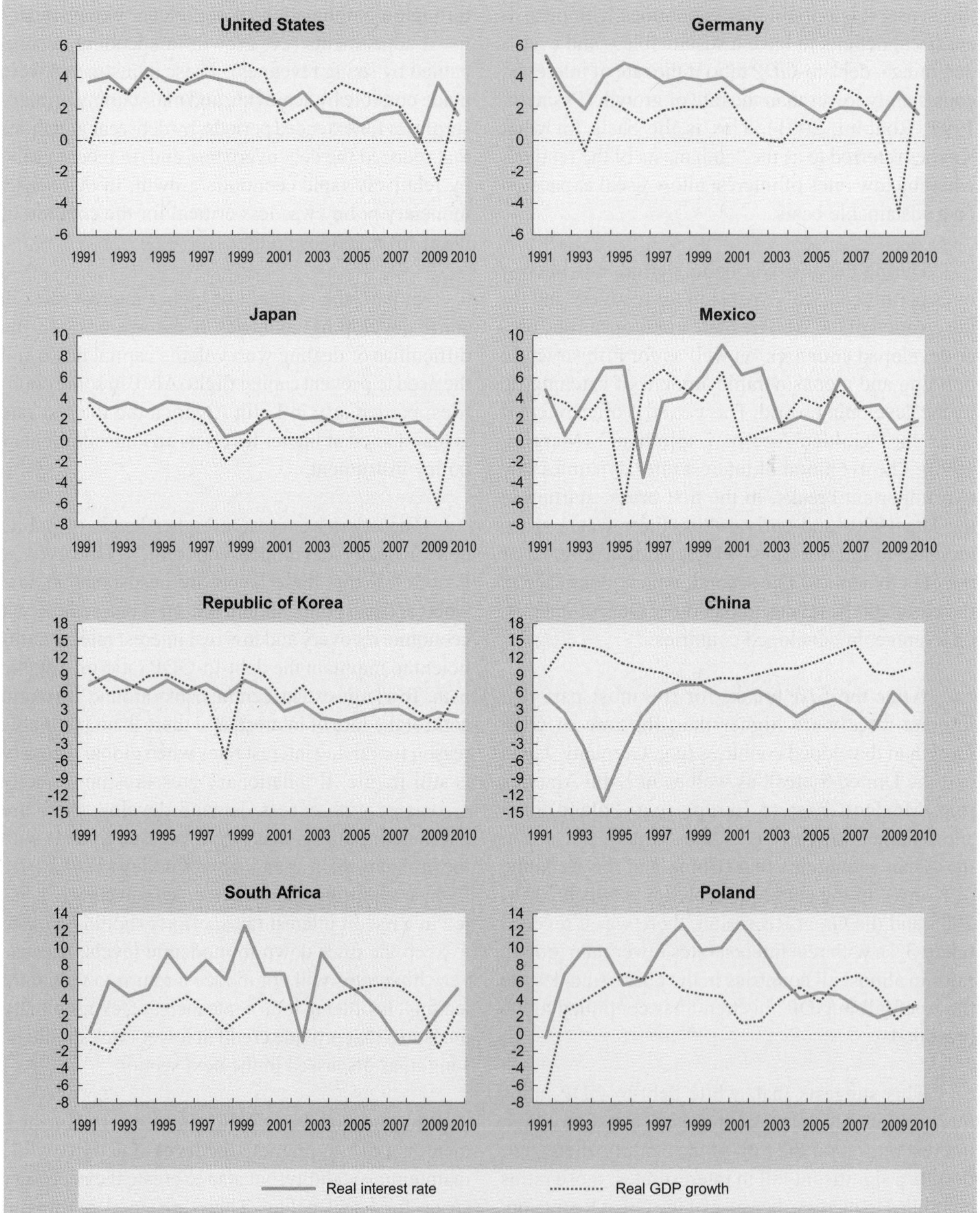

Real interest rate ·············· Real GDP growth

Source: UNCTAD secretariat calculations, based on *UNCTADstat*; IMF, *International Financial Statistics* database; and sources for table 1.1.

such as Japan, several European countries and the United States face a sluggish recovery, and developing countries remain steadfast on their catching up path.[7] However, particularly when interest rates are low, or at the lower zero bound level, and demand for credit remains weak, as is normally the case after a financial crisis (Corsetti, Meier and Müller, 2010), fiscal policy should bear full responsibility for promoting output growth. In that respect, the way the public sector spends and collects revenue becomes an essential ingredient.

3. Functional finance and fiscal multipliers

An important qualitative aspect of fiscal space is that the way in which the public sector spends and taxes is not neutral; different policy choices allow resources to be committed to specific objectives and they generate different macroeconomic outcomes (see box 3.2). This approach has sometimes been referred to as "functional finance", since it concentrates on the functions of spending and taxing in the economy, rather than suggesting, a priori, that all types of fiscal intervention have similar effects (Berglund and Vernengo, 2006).

In principle, as noted by Spilimbergo et al. (2008), spending should have an immediate advantage over tax cuts in stimulating the economy, simply because it directly leads to increased purchases and demand, while tax cuts require that economic agents spend the proceeds of their reduced tax payments. This is particularly true when the private sector is highly indebted, since it would then use part of the tax proceeds for repaying outstanding debts rather than for consumption and investment.[8] Further, it would be expected that in a relatively open economy some of the effects of both government spending and tax cuts would leak to the foreign sector, in which case a concerted global effort would certainly work more efficiently. Indeed, the evidence seems to corroborate this view (Ilzetzki, Mendoza and Vegh, 2010).

Furthermore, some types of expenditure are bound to have not only larger spending multiplier effects (i.e. more additional spending for each dollar spent by the public sector), but also larger employment multiplier effects (i.e. more workers hired for the same amount of money spent). Therefore, spending in sectors with larger employment multiplier effects seems more appropriate for promoting recovery. Besides the obvious social advantages of increasing employment, this type of expenditure, by reducing spending on a safety net for the unemployed, frees up resources for other purposes, thereby increasing fiscal space.

Moreover, social spending in such areas as unemployment benefits, education, health, housing, pensions and other benefits for low-income groups seems to be a rational way to promote recovery as it allows levels of consumption to be maintained during a crisis. In addition, it reduces poverty levels and increases productivity. All of these enable more spending and lead to higher rates of economic growth. Lindert (2004) refers to this kind of social spending that has a positive effect on long-term growth as the "free lunch" paradox. This suggests that income distribution considerations should be part of fiscal policy.

The way taxes are levied can also be an important instrument for dealing with recessions without creating an unsustainable increase in public debt. Lowering social contributions, which tend to have a regressive impact, should, in principle, generate higher income than corporate tax cuts. Zandi (2008) suggests that the evidence for the United States backs this proposition. Reductions of sales and value added taxes, if passed on to prices, would also have a relatively significant effect on the level of activity. Similarly, income tax cuts should be targeted at the lower income groups that have a higher propensity to spend.

> Social spending and public investment have larger multiplier effects on GDP and employment than tax cuts.

Beyond the question of how expenditures and taxes are implemented, which may or may not enhance the fiscal space, the overall economic context in which fiscal policy is implemented is also important in determining the size of the multiplier. Ilzetzki, Mendoza and Vegh (2010) highlight the importance of a managed exchange rate regime that avoids a significant currency appreciation, as such appreciation would weaken the positive effects of

Box 3.2

FISCAL MULTIPLIERS

Fiscal multipliers are hard to measure because of the endogeneity of fiscal variables and the difficulty of obtaining reliable instruments for exogenous spending and tax changes.[a] There are fundamentally two methods for estimating fiscal multipliers: the structural macroeconometric model in the Cowles Commission tradition, which incorporates the main elements of the Keynesian Revolution; and the atheoretical, vector autoregressive (VAR) model, where the specification is determined purely on the basis of available data.

The essential difference is that the old macroeconometric model specifies the estimation on the basis of a theoretical model and is concerned with measuring coefficients, while the VAR does not impose many restrictions on parameters. The VAR is associated with the development of real business cycles theories and has been incorporated in the new Keynesian Dynamic Structural General Equilibrium (DSGE) model, which assumes that the business cycle can be seen as a deviation from the trend. Booms and busts are temporary, and agents with rational expectations know this. There is a strong assumption that the economic system will return to equilibrium after a shock. In other words, the VAR was essentially developed to analyse exogenous shocks to autoregressive mean-reverting series. Not surprisingly, the old structural macroeconometric model tends to predict higher values for policy multipliers.

The table below presents some recent results compiled from the growing literature on the effects of fiscal policy on the level of activity, using both methods. All the studies show a range of multipliers, which depend on several aspects: spending and tax multipliers, the monetary policy stance, the exchange rate regime and the existence of a financial crisis. Hall (2009), Corsetti, Meier and Müller (2010), Ilzetzki, Mendoza and Vegh (2010), and UNCTAD's estimates use a VAR methodology. These VAR estimates for the United States from 1980 to 2010 find a range of multipliers, from 0.71 (for tax cuts) to 1.87 (for spending), which are fundamentally in line with other results in the literature. The only significant difference is that other works using VAR do not differentiate between tax cuts and spending increases.

TAX AND SPENDING MULTIPLIERS

Study	Method	Period	Coverage	Approximate results	
				Tax cut	Spending
Zandi (2008)	Structural model (SM)	Indeterminate	United States	0.3 to 1.26	1.36 to 1.73
Hall (2009)	VAR	1930 to 2008	United States	–	0.5 to 1.7*
OECD (2009)	SM	Indeterminate	OECD countries	0.6 to 1.0	0.9 to 1.3
Corsetti Meier and Müller (2010)	VAR	1975 to 2008	17 developed countries	–	0 to 1.5*
Ilzetzki, Mendoza and Vegh (2010)	VAR	1960 to 2007	44 countries (20 developed; 24 developing)	–	0 to 1.5*
Fair (2010)	SM	1960 to 2010	United States	1.0	2.0
CBO (2011)	SM	Indeterminate	United States	0.2 to 1.5	0.7 to 2.5
UNCTAD**	VAR	1980 to 2010	United States	0.71	1.87

   * Multipliers for overall fiscal policy, including changes in taxes and spending.
  ** UNCTAD secretariat calculations for this *Report*.

Box 3.2 (concluded)

The OECD *Economic Outlook* (OECD, 2009) reports fiscal multipliers based on the OECD global model that range from 0.9 (after one year) to 1.3 (after two years) for government expenditure, and from 0.6 to 1 for tax cuts (after one and two years, respectively). The study also reports data from several national models, and shows a higher multiplier for spending (1.1 on average, after one year) than for tax cuts: between 0.3 on average for corporate tax cuts and 0.5 for personal income or indirect tax cuts. The study's analysis also suggests that the size of the multiplier varies significantly from country to country. [b]

Fair (2010), using the Cowles Foundation model shows that for the United States in the period starting in 1960, multipliers for spending were at around 2, while those for cut taxes were half that size. These are essentially in the same range as the estimates presented by the Congressional Budget Office (CBO, 2011), which shows multipliers ranging from 0.7 (low estimate) to 2.5 (high estimate) for government purchases of goods and services – much higher than those resulting from temporary tax cuts for higher income brackets (0.2 to 0.6) or even income tax cuts for low- and medium-income levels (between 0.6 and 1.5). The CBO uses the estimates from the Macroeconomic Advisors and Global Insight private models, and the FRB-US model used by the United States Federal Reserve Board.

It is noteworthy that almost all the models suggest, as expected, that an expansionary fiscal policy has a positive effect on the level of economic activity. Further, the weight of the evidence indicates that spending multipliers tend to be larger than tax cut multipliers, and that tax cuts benefiting lower income households have a stronger effect than those benefiting high-income households.

---

[a] Reliable instruments are variables that are correlated to the endogenous explanatory variables, but not with the error term of the equation.
[b] These models cover Belgium, Canada, the euro area, France, Germany, Italy, Japan, Portugal, Spain, the United Kingdom and the United States.

---

fiscal expansion.[9] Such a regime would also reduce leakage of domestic demand to foreign markets. In other words, central bank policy, by managing not only the interest rate but also the exchange rate, is an essential element for expanding the fiscal space available to the public sector.

In this context, fiscal space tends to be smaller in countries that are more vulnerable to speculative capital flows. To the extent that volatile capital flows force these (typically developing) countries to maintain higher interest rates at home, fiscal policy may turn out to be less effective than in developed countries which can set interest rates with an eye on the domestic economy. However, as noted by Ocampo (2011), self-insurance measures against financial volatility, including but not limited to the accumulation of foreign reserves and capital controls, have created space for fiscal expansion in developing countries. This is

precisely because they have contributed to increasing the degree of monetary autonomy, thus allowing lower interest rates to support fiscal expansion. In this sense, it seems relevant to compare countries that managed to avoid significant real exchange rate appreciation before the Great Recession, and used monetary policy to accommodate fiscal expansion (e.g. Argentina, China), and those that were unable to do so (e.g. Greece, Ireland and Portugal). Further, in developed countries, where the bursting of the financial bubble was central to the unfolding of the Great Recession, the amount of resources utilized for rescuing financial institutions was much larger relative to the size of their economies than in developing countries (as noted in the previous chapter). It is therefore reasonable to assume that financial rescue packages, which might be important for preventing the collapse of financial markets, have a limited effect on the level of economic activity. Hence, financial conditions not only affect the size of the fiscal space; they may also influence the way it is used and its impact on economic recovery.

In sum, fiscal space depends not just on how fiscal policies are implemented, but also on how well those policies are supported by monetary policy and by the national and international financial environment. This is in addition to considerations of the political viability of the policy changes. If fiscal space is an issue in the design of countercyclical macroeconomic policies, this should be taken into account not when it has allegedly reached its limit, but at the outset (i.e. when decisions are taken on fiscal stimulus measures), because demand and fiscal feedback effects differ widely depending on which specific expenditures or taxes are changed. An optimal combination

An expansionary fiscal policy may be more likely to reduce the deficit and public debt ratio than a restrictive one.

of such changes would achieve a maximum expansionary effect, as there would be a minimum drain of demand in the income circulation process on savings and imports, and a maximum encouragement of additional private spending. As a result, there may be a debt paradox in the sense that the income effects of stimulus measures would lead to full compensation, or even overcompensation, of the initial deficit through additional tax incomes. Moreover, to the extent that it accelerates GDP growth, the debt-to-GDP ratio may fall. In other words, as a result of multiplier and accelerator effects on income, which increase the tax revenue at constant tax rates, a deficit can finance, and, under favourable conditions, even overfinance its own debt service, so that an expansionary fiscal policy may be more likely to reduce the deficit and the debt ratio than a restrictive one.

D. Dealing with public debt crises

Public debt crises are not a recent phenomenon. Sovereign lending dates as far back as the fourteenth century, and recurrent defaults show that such lending has always been risky (Cipolla, 1982; Kindleberger, 1996). However what constitutes a sovereign debt crisis is not at all clear. Crises have been occurring as a result of a lack of fiscal resources, but more frequently owing to problems associated with a lack of foreign exchange. The 1997 Asian crisis, for example, was due to the inability of a number of countries to stop a rapid devaluation of their currencies and to pay their foreign obligations. It was by no means a public debt crisis. In that sense, the Asian crisis differs from the Latin American debt crisis of the 1980s. In the case of Africa, public debt overhang problems plagued the region prior to the Heavily Indebted Poor Countries (HIPC) Initiative.

For decades African countries suffered from economic stagnation, while experiencing only sporadic balance-of-payments crises.

Two important distinctions are relevant when dealing with debt crises. First, there is a difference between private and sovereign borrowers. The latter may borrow in their own currency, which is legal tender and over which they have a monopoly of issuance. Second, there is a difference between public debt denominated in domestic currency and that denominated in foreign currencies. In the first case, the government can always monetize public debt by directly selling government bonds to the central bank, or the central bank can buy public debt in the secondary markets, thereby facilitating the financing of the government. The consequences of this kind of indebtedness differ from those resulting from foreign-currency-denominated debt, when the public sector is unable to service that debt. Thus, each of these debt situations requires different policies for preventing a crisis.

Additionally, there is the question of the law governing the issuance of debt and the ways in which it may be renegotiated. Debt issued under local legislation may be allowed flexibilities which differ from that issued under foreign legislation. And even in the latter case, rules will differ depending on the legislation which regulates the debt contract, such as the State of New York.

Finally, it should be emphasized that there are differing views about the causes of debt crises. While public debt crises can be caused by excessive fiscal spending for a given tax base, often the problem of financial crises lies with the system of international finance that provides liquidity to cash-starved agents in intermittent cycles, and with capital flows that vanish or even reverse exactly when they are needed the most. In fact, many crises are the consequence of an accumulation of private debt and mispricing in currency or other asset markets, encouraged by "push factors" (i.e. foreign entities seeking profitable investments). In other words, public debt crises may result from fiscal mismanagement and/or "financial fragility", to borrow Minsky's famous term. A better global monetary system (as discussed in chapter VI of this *Report*) that ensures more stable flows of capital and stricter regulation of its uses are the prescribed solutions, rather than fiscal adjustment.

> Credit in foreign currencies and sudden changes in capital flows and real exchange rates are a frequent cause of financial crises which often lead to public debt crises.

1. Preventing debt crises

Although public debt crises often do not have a fiscal origin, some are indeed caused by unsustainable fiscal policies, while others are caused by irresponsible lending for purposes that do not increase the overall productivity but amount to zero sum games over the medium term (see chapter IV of this *Report*). However, even when a debt crisis has a fiscal origin,

it may well be necessary to undertake expansionary fiscal policies to promote growth, which may lead to increasing public debt in the short run in order to forestall even worse consequences later.

Private domestic agents may borrow in an unsustainable way because they believe in infinite booms and bubbles, and suffer from a misconception that they can always obtain credit at very low interest rates. For sovereign borrowers that take loans on international markets, the same problems arise, since creditors have incentives to continue lending, while the debtors believe that fresh inflows at low interest will still be available. It is worth emphasizing in this context that, despite the risk of default by sovereign borrowers in international markets, more often than not lenders and bondholders benefit from their activities, since they can often charge higher interest to borrowing countries. This is why financial markets tend not to punish countries that cannot service their debts. For example, Lindert (1989) and Lindert and Morton (1989) show that investors in Latin American government bonds during the period 1850 to 1914 received an ex post annual premium that was 0.42 per cent over the interest payments received by holders of British consols (i.e. bonds), in spite of defaults. In a more contemporary study of the profitability of investing in developing countries' debt, it was calculated that, apart from the various crises, during the period 1970–2000 the average annual return on emerging markets' debt was 9 per cent (Klingen, Zettelmeyer and Weder, 2004).

These periods of financial euphoria are usually followed by financial crashes and may lead to widespread banking crises (Kindleberger, 1978; Reinhart and Rogoff, 2009). Since banking crises are often followed by sudden increases in public debt, associated with policy decisions to rescue financial institutions in distress, policies aimed at reducing the risk of debt crises need to include measures to keep in check private sector debt, both domestic and external. There are a number of useful instruments for limiting excessive risk-taking by the private sector, such as: tighter financial regulation, including guarantees that borrowers have income streams compatible with the accumulated debt; restrictions on certain types of predatory lending which misinform borrowers about payment conditions; caps on interest rates charged by certain types of credit lines; higher capital requirements for banks; and capital controls.

Debt denominated in foreign currencies which needs to be repaid with revenues earned in a national currency is another frequent cause of a financial crisis spilling over into a public debt crisis. Credit in foreign currencies has surged in increasingly deregulated international financial markets, such as in Hungary, Iceland and some other Eastern European countries. At the same time, these countries have been the targets of carry-trade speculation, leading to an appreciation of currencies in countries with high interest rates. This has contributed to long-lasting current-account deficits through currency appreciation, an import surge and increasing debt service. As a result, the countries concerned have become vulnerable to financial shocks in the global economy, such as sudden changes in capital flows or interest rate hikes in carry-trade funding countries such as Japan and Switzerland. After a reversal of capital inflows real depreciation is the only way to balance the external accounts in a debtor country (*TDR 2008*). However, when there is significant foreign-currency-denominated debt, a real depreciation will lead to a sudden jump in the debt-to-GDP ratio and in debt servicing payments in domestic currency. If, in the wake of a crisis, and under the influence of international lenders, the government tackles the external crisis with contractionary fiscal policies, seeking to restore the external balance by reducing domestic demand, it will make matters worse. In any case, debt sustainability is affected, possibly leading to a debt crisis and debt default. These are classical cases of a dual crisis: a balance-of-payments crisis, which leads to a fiscal crisis, either because the public sector has contracted a sizeable share of the foreign debt, or because it has assumed most of the burden of private debts.

The situation is even more complicated for countries that are members of a monetary union, have a currency board or are dollarized. In any of these cases, a real devaluation can only be achieved through wage cuts (sometimes referred to as internal devaluation). However, that may lead to deflation, which may have an even greater negative impact on debt sustainability because it would increase the real

> The response to a crisis should depend on the nature of that crisis ...

value of all liabilities, not only those denominated in foreign currency (Eichengreen, 2010). This in turn could result in debt deflation or a balance-sheet crisis, as discussed earlier.

Efforts to solve this problem have to start at the global level (discussed in chapter VI). At the national level, it should be recognized that during periods of economic boom, countries and their lenders sow the seeds of future crises.[10] During periods of global optimism, capital inflows flood developing countries, which are often unable to restrict the amounts, even if they can change the maturity profile of the inflows with capital controls. As mentioned before, this behaviour not only leads to a rapid accumulation of external debt, but often it also causes an appreciation of the real exchange rate and induces large external imbalances, which eventually provoke capital reversals, currency collapse, and, ultimately, a financial and real crisis.

Preventing a repetition of this familiar pattern requires a change of practices during good times, with less external debt, more reserves and a policy aimed at limiting currency appreciation. Development of domestic sources of finance and reducing foreign capital needs are therefore policies that should be encouraged during boom phases. These are precisely the policies which the largest emerging market economies have been pursuing since the late 1990s. As a change in the composition of public debt and a switch to domestic borrowing can reduce asymmetries and improve the trade-off discussed above, several developing countries are now retiring their external public debt and issuing domestic debt instead.

2. Responding to debt crises

Although debt crises do not always have a fiscal origin, the standard response to a sudden jump in public debt is often fiscal retrenchment. This appears to be a misguided policy, because the appropriate response should relate to the nature of the crisis. If a crisis originates from the bursting of an asset bubble, the response should be financial reform, and even quite the opposite of fiscal retrenchment, namely countercyclical policies to absorb private sector deleveraging so as to reduce the macroeconomic slump created by asset deflation (*TDR 2009*). If the crisis originates from excessive foreign currency lending and excessive real appreciation, the appropriate response at the national level might be to improve the debt structure and introduce policies aimed at avoiding misalignments of the real exchange rate as well as introducing controls on capital inflows.

Fiscal retrenchment as a response to a crisis not caused by irresponsible fiscal policies is problematic for several reasons. Fiscal adjustments tend to affect the most vulnerable groups of society, often with serious social consequences. Moreover, they may even be ineffective in reducing the debt-to-GDP ratio because they may amplify the recession, thus causing a decrease in the denominator of that ratio. As a result, fiscal contractions may cause painful adjustments in the short run and create costs in the long run. There is evidence that after recessions output growth tends to return to its previous trend, but the output loss is never recovered (Cerra and Saxena, 2008). Recessions therefore lead to a permanent output loss, and since contractionary fiscal policies amplify both the length and the depth of a recession they also increase this loss and weaken a country's overall ability to sustain a given level of public debt.

There is another important channel through which fiscal retrenchment may have a negative effect on long-term growth and thus reduce debt sustainability. Since current expenditure can be difficult to adjust (because it is composed mainly of wages and entitlement programmes), fiscal retrenchment usually leads to large cuts in public investment (Martner and Tromben, 2004; Easterly, Irwin and Servén, 2008). This reduction in growth-promoting public expenditure may lead to a fall in the present value of future government revenues that is larger than the fiscal savings obtained by the fiscal retrenchment. The outcome could be an improvement in the immediate cash flow of the government, but with negative consequences for long-term fiscal and debt sustainability. Fiscal policy should therefore explicitly consider how the fiscal adjustment will affect output growth and capital accumulation. It should also recognize that a deficit incurred in financing an investment project,

> ... If a crisis has not been caused by irresponsible fiscal policies, fiscal retrenchment is not an appropriate response.

and that some current spending, especially in areas such as health, education, nutrition, and sanitation, may result in an increase (and not a decrease) in the country's net wealth.

However, even sovereign borrowers that are targeting sound long-term fiscal indicators may lose access to credit in international markets and find themselves unable to finance their current cash deficits at a reasonable interest rate. This is where the international community should be able to step in and provide the needed financial support. It should be clear that provision of such support is not a bailout, but simply an intervention aimed at addressing a market failure. While Bagehot (1873) was right in saying that during crises the domestic lender of last resort should stand ready to lend freely at a penalty rate to solvent but illiquid banks, there are problems in applying Bagehot's suggestion of a penalty rate to the behaviour of an international lender of last resort. Bagehot's idea of lending at a penalty rate was aimed at avoiding moral hazard. However, it is doubtful that moral hazard is playing any significant role in international finance, and it is certainly not the main cause of sovereign debt crises.[11]

Therefore lending at a penalty rate would not generate any *ex ante* gain in terms of disciplining borrowers. On the contrary, by increasing the interest bill, it would contribute to debt accumulation and therefore aggravate the problem that emergency lending is trying to solve. The same line of reasoning holds even more for countries that are on the edge of insolvency. For these countries, high interest rates which are supposed to protect the resources of the lender of last resort can actually backfire and cause losses, as a lender of last resort that lends at a penalty rate may contribute to pushing the country towards insolvency.

3. Debt restructuring

When sovereign debt is denominated in domestic currency, default is unlikely since that debt can be repaid by issuing more money. But when debts are denominated in foreign currency, debt default and restructuring are bound to occur, even with the best possible international and domestic policies. However, this does not hold for private debt, since private agents are often rescued by domestic authorities. But from a purely legal point of view, a sovereign State cannot be declared insolvent. Further, the value of a country's assets (its land, its natural resources and the wealth of its citizens) is usually very large, and in any case cannot always be measured in terms of current values. Therefore, it is unthinkable for a country to be faced with a situation where its liabilities are larger than its assets (which for a firm would be considered as insolvency). In addition, creditors cannot unilaterally (or with the help of a court) take over a country's management (i.e. replace the country's government). In fact, the principle of sovereign immunity limits a creditor's ability to sue a sovereign entity, and even when that entity agrees to waive its immunity, verdicts remain difficult to enforce because assets that are located within the borders of the defaulting country cannot be confiscated.

Although sovereign States cannot be forced to repay their debts, sovereign defaults, beyond the foreign currency problem, remain very rare events. In most cases, States make considerable efforts and endure economic pain in order to service their debts, since policymakers seem to think that repaying is cheaper than defaulting. While it is easy to determine the cost of repaying (which is the value of the loan), it is harder to identify the costs associated with a sovereign default. This is far from being a purely academic question, because a better understanding of the costs of default is a necessary condition for devising policies that could reduce those costs as well as the prevalence of such defaults. It is worth pointing out that sovereign defaults have rarely been complete defaults; they are usually partial in nature, involving some amount of reduction/restructuring of the debt.

The economic literature has focused on the reputational and trade costs of defaults. Models that focus on reputational costs assume that default episodes reduce a country's ability to access international financial markets (Eaton and Gersovitz, 1981). Models that emphasize trade costs suggest that defaulters can be punished with trade sanctions (Bulow and Rogoff, 1989). Apart from some theoretical problems with these models (for a review, see Panizza, Sturzenegger and Zettelmeyer, 2009), the real issue is that their assumptions have no empirical basis. Reputational costs appear to be limited and short-lived (Borensztein and Panizza, 2010), and there is no evidence of trade sanctions (at least in recent times). A more recent class of theoretical models focuses attention on the domestic effects of a sovereign default (Cole and Kehoe, 1998). However, empirical evidence shows that the costs of a default seem to be limited, even in terms of its effects on GDP growth (Levy Yeyati and Panizza, 2011); and in any case, they have been smaller in countries that preemptively restructured their debts (De Paoli, Hoggarth and Saporta, 2006).

An outright debt default clearly undermines the general strategy of nurturing the confidence of financial markets as a key element for attracting foreign capital and spurring investment (referred to as the "confidence game"), and this may magnify the cost of a default by adding qualitative factors that are not visible in a quantitative, cost-advantage exercise. Thus a country's reputation would suffer less damage if a debt default appeared to be unavoidable (Grossman and Van Huyck, 1988). This may explain why some governments decide to assume a large cost in order to postpone a necessary default, thereby signalling to all interested parties that when the default eventually occurs, it is not a "strategic default" (Borensztein and Panizza, 2009; Levy Yeyati and Panizza, 2011).

> When defaults occur, debts need to be restructured.

When defaults do occur, debts need to be restructured, and the complexity of the restructuring process depends on the structure of the defaulted debt. Until the early 1990s most foreign debt of developing countries was either owed to official creditors (multilateral or bilateral) or to banks. When the Brady swaps of the 1990s transformed defaulted syndicated bank loans into tradable bonds, policymakers feared that the presence of a large number of dispersed and heterogeneous creditors could lead to long and costly debt renegotiations. There was also concern that vastly dispersed debt would provide strong incentives to individual creditors (possibly specialized vulture funds) to "hold out" from debt rescheduling and then litigate in the hope of collecting the full face value of their claims (Panizza, Sturzenegger and Zettelmeyer, 2009).

These preoccupations prompted several initiatives aimed at facilitating the debt restructuring process and, in the wake of the Argentinean crisis of 2001–2002, led to an IMF proposal for the creation of a sovereign debt restructuring mechanism (SDRM). This statutory approach to debt restructuring shared some of the features of an earlier UNCTAD proposal (*TDR 1981*), which in turn was based on Chapter 11 of the United States commercial code (i.e. the bankruptcy code for private agents). The SDRM was eventually rejected by the United States Treasury under pressure from financial groups involved in the emerging markets bond business. Instead it suggested that the hold-out problem could be solved using a contractual approach based on the introduction of collective action clauses (CAC) in debt contracts and the use of exit consent.[12] Countries that presented lower risks of requiring a future debt restructuring obtained more flexible terms than those that were more prone to debt problems. In some cases, however, creditors have prevented the use of "exit consents" in bond emissions, including CACs (Gelpern, 2003).

Furthermore, CACs do not solve other problems associated with the current non-system. As the current rules cannot enforce seniority (with the exception of the de facto seniority granted to multilateral organizations), it leads to too much lending in the run-up to a debt crisis (debt dilution) and too little lending during the restructuring process (lack of interim financing). Debt dilution occurs when new debt issuances can hurt existing creditors of a country that is approaching financial distress. It has been shown that debt dilution increases borrowing costs and may lead to risky levels of debt accumulation (Bolton and Olivier, 2007).[13] During the restructuring period, the defaulting country may need access to external funds to either support trade or to finance a primary current-account deficit, and lack of access to these funds may amplify the crisis and further reduce ability to pay. As the provision of such interim financing would require some sort of seniority with respect to existing claims, the defaulting country will not be able to obtain any credit from the private sector during the restructuring period. The second problem has to do with the fact that, while standard models of sovereign debt assume that countries have an incentive to default by too much

or too early, there is now evidence that policymakers are reluctant to default and do all they can to avoid it (Rogoff and Zettelmeyer, 2002). Delayed default may destroy the value of outstanding debt because a prolonged pre-default crisis may reduce both ability and willingness to pay.

It is for these reasons that, 10 years after the shelving of the original SDRM, there is still a debate on whether such a mechanism would be a valuable addition to the international financial architecture (Fernández-Arias, 2010). Those who oppose such a statutory approach argue that the current system is second best, because, in the case of non-enforceable contracts, willingness to pay is linked to the costs of default arising from an inefficient debt restructuring process (Dooley, 2000; Shleifer, 2003). Therefore, removing these inefficiencies would reduce the costs of default and increase borrowing costs. Those who support the statutory approach, argue that debt dilution, lack of interim financing and the presence of debt overhang lead to a loss of value for both debtors and creditors. The possibility that countries may delay necessary defaults in order to show that the eventual default was indeed unavoidable is an important consideration in the discussion on the desirability of international policies aimed at mitigating the costs of default. If a country's attempt to defend its reputation by suboptimally postponing a necessary default creates a deadweight loss, there are policies that can reduce the costs of default. In particular, the creation of an agency with the ability to certify necessary defaults, and thus protect the reputation of countries without forcing them to go through a painful and counterproductive postponing exercise, could reduce the costs of defaults while simultaneously increasing recovery values on defaulted debt. It would thereby facilitate access to credit and reduce the overall costs of borrowing. It is important to point out that postponement of a default is typically associated with contractionary measures that further reduce the ability to repay.

While it is impossible to directly test the hypothesis that the creation of a debt resolution mechanism would increase borrowing costs (because such a mechanism does not exist), it is possible to indirectly test this hypothesis by checking whether other mechanisms that facilitate sovereign debt

> A prolonged pre-default crisis may reduce both the ability and willingness to repay debt.

restructuring have an effect on borrowing costs. One candidate for such a test is CACs. When CACs were first introduced in New York bonds law, it was feared that by reducing the costs of default they would increase borrowing costs. However, there is now ample evidence that CACs have no impact whatsoever on borrowing costs. Proponents of the higher borrowing cost hypothesis often mention the possibility of some vaguely defined reputational cost. Again, these statements cannot be formally tested (and it is not clear why such a mechanism would affect reputation). However, reputational costs associated with sovereign defaults are either very small (Ozler, 1993; Benczur and Ilut, 2006) or short-lived (Borensztein and Panizza, 2009), or both small and short-lived (Flandreau and Zumer, 2004).

Summing up, debt restructuring may be part of a strategy to resolve a debt crisis, not just for the borrowing country but also for creditors, since the possibilities for renewed economic growth and the ability to repay increase. If debt renegotiation frees up resources for growth-enhancing activities it may allow a country to better finance its own reduced debt service. However, sovereign default or debt restructuring are no panacea, and their risks have to be weighed carefully against the risk of contagion, which is a major hazard in the European monetary union. There is also the possibility that domestic depositors will lose confidence in a government and flee the country – a risk that is particularly strong in a monetary union where people cannot be prevented from relocating their short-term deposits within the union.

E. Conclusions: growing out of debt

The above discussion suggests that the best strategy for reducing public debt is to promote growth-enhancing fiscal policies. Moreover, it would seem from the evidence that fiscal expansion tends to be more effective if spending takes precedence over tax cuts, if spending targets infrastructure and social transfers, and if tax cuts, in turn, target lower income groups, which generally have a higher propensity for spending. Fiscal expansion, by increasing the level of activity and income, as noted earlier, raises the revenue stream and reduces the debt-to-GDP ratio, in particular if interest rates are relatively low compared with GDP growth. In this sense, problems associated with the growth of public debt, particularly when that debt is not primarily related to fiscal problems, are best resolved by a strategy of fiscal expansion.

Further, if it is argued that, for economic and/ or political reasons there is little space for fiscal expansion, there is always the possibility to redirect spending and taxes to support more expansionary measures. Again, this suggests that spending should be given precedence over tax cuts, and that both measures should benefit low-income groups in particular. A more equitable distribution of income would make economic recovery more self-sustaining and improve the chances of achieving fiscal consolidation. In this sense, increasing real wages in line with productivity, and, especially in developing countries with large informal sectors, government transfers to the low-income segments of society, are important complements to fiscal expansion.

Beyond the notion that growth is the best solution to reduce public-debt-to-GDP ratios, it is important to emphasize that higher ratios of public debt per se, particularly in developed countries after the crisis, do not pose a threat to fiscal sustainability. The public debt today is much more sustainable than the private debt before the crisis. As long as interest rates are low and unused capacities exist, there is no crowding out of private investment, and the globally higher public debt ratios do not pose a problem for recovery. For the world as a whole, and for the big economies, the only strategy warranted is one of consolidation through growth. Growth, combined with low interest rates, will bring an increase in revenues and a fall in debt ratios over time. This implies that monetary policy should continue to maintain low interest rates in order to keep the burden of interest payments for the public sector bearable.

> The best strategy for reducing public debt is to promote growth-enhancing fiscal policies and low interest rates.

If inflation is perceived to be a serious threat to economic stability, and given that in most economies the pressures on prices have originated largely from the financialization of commodity markets, the subsequent, second round effects (such as a price-wage spiral) need to be dealt with by an incomes policy rather than by adopting restrictive macroeconomic measures. There are instances when an external constraint (e.g. when lack of competitiveness brings about current-account deficits) prevents fiscal expansion because it would aggravate the external imbalance. In such cases, priority should be given to resolving the balance-of-payments problem rather than introducing austerity measures. This is particularly important for countries that are members of a currency union. ∎

Notes

1   For instance, when the IMF provided large assistance packages to Argentina, Brazil, Indonesia, Mexico, the Republic of Korea, Thailand and Turkey, it was criticized for wasting taxpayers' money. But all these countries paid back, and the Fund (and thus the international taxpayer) even made a small profit. In fact, the Fund suffered a budget crisis when countries were no longer hit by crisis (which is not surprising as the business of the Fund is crisis management). Interestingly, the case of Argentina shows that even a failed rescue attempt ended up being profitable for the Fund.

2   Preferences for spending cuts over tax increases are also supported on the grounds that the tax burden is already high in developed economies, so that "there may be limited scope to raise tax without adverse effects on economic efficiency" (IMF, 2010c: 10).

3   The IMF (2010b) does not provide any empirical evidence of this alleged "typical" behaviour of central banks, which is fundamental to its policy recommendation of using spending cuts rather than tax increases. Neither does it provide convincing conceptual proof. It states that tax increases would raise prices in a way that would prevent central banks from reducing interest rates. However, it is not evident that direct taxes (that are not mentioned as a possibility) have any upward impact on prices, or even that higher rates of indirect taxes have more than a one-off impact on prices, which would justify a restrictive monetary stance. And if tax hikes effectively cause inflation, then real interest rates will fall, generating the economic stimulus without requiring central banks to cut nominal interest rates. Furthermore, the idea that fiscal tightening will reduce real exchange rates contradicts the view – also supported by the IMF – that lower fiscal deficits will improve confidence in financial markets and eventually attract capital inflows, which would then lead to currency appreciation.

4   Here, there is an implicit assumption that fiscal adjustment will reduce not only the fiscal deficit, but also the public-debt-to-GDP ratio. This is not guaranteed: even if fiscal tightening manages to improve the fiscal balance, this improvement may be insufficient to lower that ratio. For a debt reduction in absolute terms, a fiscal surplus would be needed.

5   For example, in 2005–2008 the average share of oil revenue in total fiscal revenue was over 80 per cent

in Angola, Bahrain, Brunei Darussalam, Congo, Equatorial Guinea, Libya, Nigeria, Oman, Saudi Arabia and Timor-Leste. Countries where this share was over 70 per cent include Algeria, Kuwait, United Arab Emirates and Yemen. A number of countries in the Commonwealth of Independent States (CIS), such as Azerbaijan, Kazakhstan and the Russian Federation, and Latin American countries such as the Bolivarian Republic of Venezuela, Bolivia and Ecuador, also exhibit a high degree of dependence on revenues from their hydrocarbons sector, although the share in total fiscal revenues is relatively lower than it is in the above-mentioned regions. The same applies to mineral-dependent countries such as Botswana, Chile, Guinea, Liberia, Mongolia, Namibia and Peru (Villafuerte, López-Murphy and Ossowski, 2010; IMF, 2011c).

6   For example, the Chilean Government increased the percentage of royalties to be paid by mining companies in order to help finance reconstruction following the 2010 earthquake. Similarly, the Government of Guinea is undertaking a review of its mining code in order to raise its stake in mining projects, and in South Africa a State mining company was recently launched and the Government is considering increasing royalties.

7   In this respect, it seems that the recent call for monetary tightening by the Bank for International Settlements (BIS, 2011) stems from an overly pessimistic view of the risks of inflationary acceleration.

8   Barro and Redlick (2011) argue that the evidence for the United States on the relative effects of government spending vis-à-vis tax cuts is unreliable. However, the evidence presented by Zandi (2008), suggests that government-spending programmes are more stimulating than tax cuts.

9   This concern is related to the conventional view that fiscal expansion increases interest rates, leading to capital inflows, and ultimately creating pressure for appreciation. However, Ilzetzki et al. (2010) do not find evidence of higher rates of interest being associated with fiscal expansion. This suggests that inflows might simply be the result of a growing economy, and that monetary accommodation is the main mechanism enabling managed exchange rate regimes to have larger fiscal multipliers. Indeed, there is ample evidence that capital flows to developing countries tend to be procyclical.

10 One way to deal with this problem and reduce the likelihood of debt crises would be to establish a set of principles on accountable sovereign lending and borrowing, which would include due diligence, fiduciary duty, proper approval, transparency and disclosure and consideration of the question of debt restructuring (UNCTAD, 2011b). These principles should apply to the private sector as well, since in several cases the public sector ends up paying for the excessive lending and borrowing of the private sector. Also, these principles in no way imply that borrowers should submit to the criteria selected by creditors on what constitutes appropriate rules of behaviour. Indeed, the legal effects of these principles would essentially depend on the State's views.

11 If there was a significant degree of moral hazard involved in international finance, spreads on lending to emerging markets should shrink to zero, creditors being absolutely sure that the IMF or some other actor would ensure full recovery of their lending (Lane and Phillips, 2002). For a sceptical view of the existence of moral hazard in international finance, see Kamin, 2002; for a more balanced view of the issue, see Corsetti, Guimarães and Roubini, 2003.

12 There are three main CACs: (i) majority action clauses, which allow a qualified majority of bondholders (usually bondholders representing 75 per cent of the principal of the outstanding bonds) to amend all the terms and conditions of the bonds, including the payment terms, and make those amendments binding on the remaining bondholders; (ii) representation clauses, allowing a single agent or group of agents to negotiate with debtors in the name of bondholders; and (iii) a distribution clause, under which any amounts received by any creditor would have to be distributed among all of them. Exit consent is a technique whereby a majority of bondholders can change the non-financial terms of a bond with the objective of reducing the secondary market value of the bond and thus increasing the incentive to accept an exchange offer.

13 In the corporate world, debt dilution is not a problem because courts can enforce seniority rules. However, it is a problem for sovereign debt, because after a sovereign default, all creditors, old and new, tend to receive the same haircut.

References

Admati A, DeMarzo P, Hellwig M and Pfleiderer P (2010). Fallacies, irrelevant facts, and myths in the discussion of capital regulation: Why bank equity is *not* expensive. Stanford GSB Research Paper No. 2063, Stanford University, Stanford, CA.

Angeriz A and Arestis P (2009). The consensus view on interest rates and fiscal policy: Reality or innocent fraud? *Journal of Post-Keynesian Economics,* 31(4): 567–568.

Arcand JL, Berles E and Panizza U (2011). Too much finance? Working paper, The Graduate Institute, Geneva.

Aschauer D (1989). Is public expenditure productive? *Journal of Monetary Economics*, 23(2):177–200.

Bagehot W (1873). *Lombard Street: A Description of the Money Market.* Available at: http://www.gutenberg.org/cache/epub/4359/pg4359.html.

Barba A and Pivetti M (2009). Rising household debt: Its causes and macroeconomic implications – a long-period analysis. *Cambridge Journal of Economics*, 33(1): 113–137.

Barro R (1974). Are government bonds net wealth? *Journal of Political Economy*, 82 (6): 1095–1117.

Barro R and Redlick C (2011). Macroeconomic effects from government purchases and taxes. *Quarterly Journal of Economics*, CXXVI(1): 51–102.

Benczur P and Ilut C (2006). Determinants of spreads on sovereign bank loans: The role of credit history. MNB Working Papers 2006/1, Magyar Nemzeti Bank (The Central Bank of Hungary), Budapest.

Berglund P and Vernengo M (2006). Fiscal policy reconsidered (introduction). In: Berglund P and Vernengo M, eds., *The Means to Prosperity: Fiscal Policy Reconsidered.* London, Routledge: 1–16.

Bernanke B and Reinhart V (2004). Conducting monetary policy at very low short-term interest rates. Lecture at the International Center for Monetary and Banking Studies, Geneva. Available at: http://www.federalreserve.gov/boarddocs/speeches/2004/200401033/default.htm.

BIS (2011). 81st Annual Report. Basel, 1 April 2010–31 March 2011.

Blanchard O, Dell'Ariccia G and Mauro P (2010). Rethinking macroeconomic policy. IMF Staff Position Note SPN/10/03, International Monetary Fund, Washington, DC.

Bolton P and Olivier J (2007). Structuring and restructuring sovereign debt: the role of a bankruptcy regime. IMF Working Paper 07/192, International Monetary Fund, Washington, DC.

Borensztein E and Panizza U (2009). The costs of default. IMF Staff Papers 56(4): 683–741, International Monetary Fund, Washington, DC.

Borensztein E and Panizza U (2010). Do sovereign defaults hurt exporters? *Open Economies Review*, 21(3): 393–412.

Bornhorst F, Budina N, Callegari G, ElGanainy A, Gomez Sirera R, Lemgruber A, Schaechter A and Beom Shin J (2010). A status update on fiscal exit strategies. IMF Working Paper WP/10/272, International Monetary Fund, Washington, DC.

Bulow J and Rogoff K (1989). A constant recontracting model of sovereign debt. *Journal of Political Economy*, 97(1): 155–178.

Cerra V and Saxena SC (2008). Growth dynamics: The myth of economic recovery. *American Economic Review,* 98(1):439–57.

Christiano L, Eichenbaum M and Rebelo S (2009). When is the government spending multiplier large? NBER Working Paper No. 15394, National Bureau of Economic Research, Cambridge, MA.

Cipolla C (1982). *The Monetary Policy of Fourteenth-Century Florence.* Berkeley, CA, University of California Press.

Cole HL and Kehoe PJ (1998). Models of sovereign debt: Partial versus general reputations. *International Economic Review,* 39(1): 55–70.

Congressional Budget Office (2011). Estimated Impact of the American recovery and Reinvestment Act on Employment and Economic Output from January 2001 through March 2011, Washington, DC, May. Available at http://www.cbo.gov/ftpdocs/121xx/doc12185/05-25-ARRA.pdf.

Corsetti G, Guimaraes B and Roubini N (2003). International lending of last resort and moral hazard: A model of IMF's catalytic finance. NBER Working Paper No. 10125, National Bureau of Economic Research, Cambridge, MA.

Corsetti G, Meier A and Müller G (2010). What determines government spending multipliers? Paper prepared for the project on International Dimensions of Fiscal Policy Transmission, sponsored by the Fondation Banque de France and the Center for Economic Policy Research. Available at: http://www.eui.eu/Personal/corsetti/research/multipliers.pdf.

De Paoli B, Hoggarth G and Saporta V (2006). Costs of sovereign default. Bank of England Financial Stability Paper 1, London.

Dooley M (2000). Can output losses following international financial crises be avoided? NBER Working Paper No. 7531, Cambridge, MA.

Dymski G (2003). The international debt crisis. In: Michie J, ed., *The Handbook of Globalization*. Cheltenham, Edward Elgar.

Easterly W, Irwin T and Servén L (2008). Walking up the down escalator: Public investment and fiscal stability. *World Bank Research Observer*, 23(1): 37–56, Oxford University Press.

Eaton J and Gersovitz M (1981). Debt with potential repudiation: Theoretical and empirical analysis. *Review of Economic Studies*, 48(2): 289–309.

Eichengreen B (2010). Ireland's rescue package: Disaster for Ireland, bad omen for the Eurozone. VOX EU, 3 December 2010. Available at: http://www.voxeu.org/index.php?q=node/5887.

Eisner R (1995). US national saving and budget deficits. In: Epstein GA and Gintis HM, eds., *Macroeconomic Policy after the Conservative Era: Studies in Investment, Saving and Finance*. Cambridge, New York and Melbourne, Cambridge University Press: 109–42.

Eisner R (2006). Budget deficits, unemployment and economic growth: a cross-section time-series analysis. In: Berglund P and Vernengo M, eds., *The Means to Prosperity: Fiscal Policy Reconsidered*. London and New York, Routledge: 202–220.

Fair R (2010). Possible macroeconomic consequences of large future federal government deficits. Cowles Foundation Discussion Paper 1727, Yale University, New Haven, CT.

Fernández-Arias E (2010). International lender of last resort and sovereign debt restructuring. In: Primo Braga CA and Vincelette GA, eds., *Sovereign Debt and the Financial Crisis: Will This Time be Different?*: 331–353. Washington, DC, World Bank.

Fisher I (1933). The debt-deflation theory of great depressions. *Econometrica*, 1(4): 337–357.

Flandreau M and Zumer F (2004). *The Making of Global Finance, 1880–1913*. Paris, Organisation for Economic Co-operation and Development.

Gale W and Orszag P (2003). Economic effects of sustained budget deficits. *National Tax Journal*, 56(3): 462–85.

Gelpern A (2003). How collective action is changing sovereign debt. *International Financial Law Review*, May: 19–23.

Grossman HI and Van Huyck JB (1988). Sovereign debt as a contingent claim: excusable default, repudiation, and reputation. *American Economic Review*, 78(5): 1088–1097.

Hall R (2009). By how much does GDP rise if the government buys more output? *Brookings Papers on Economic Activity*, (2):183–231. Washington, DC, Brookings Institution Press.

Heller SP (2005). Fiscal space: What it is and how to get it. *Finance and Development*: 42(2).

Hemming R, Kell M and Mahfouz S (2002). The effectiveness of fiscal policy in stimulating economic activity: A review of the literature. *IMF Working Paper 02/208*, International Monetary Fund, Washington, DC.

IMF (2003). Evaluation Report: Fiscal Adjustment in IMF-Supported Programmes. Washington, DC, Independent Evaluation Office.

IMF (2010a). *Fiscal Monitor*, Washington, DC, May.

IMF (2010b). *World Economic Outlook*. Washington, DC, October.

IMF (2010c). From stimulus to consolidation: Revenue and expenditure policies in advanced and emerging economies. Fiscal Affairs Department, Washington, DC.

IMF (2011a). *Fiscal Monitor*. Washington, DC, April.

IMF (2011b). *World Economic Outlook*. Washington, DC, April.

IMF (2011c). Revenue mobilization in developing countries. Washington, DC.

Ilzetzki E, Mendoza E and Vegh C (2010). How big (small?) are fiscal multipliers? NBER Working paper No. 16479, National Bureau of Economic Research, Cambridge, MA.

Institute of International Finance (2010). Interim report on the cumulative impact on the global economy of proposed changes in the banking regulatory framework. Washington, DC.

Kamin SB (2002). Identifying the role of moral hazard in international financial markets. Discussion Paper 736, Institute of International Finance. Washington, DC.

Kindleberger CP (1978). *Manias, panics and crashes. A history of financial crises*. The Macmillan Press Ltd, London and Basingstoke.

Kindleberger CP (1996). *World Economic Supremacies, 1500-1990*. Cambridge, MIT Press.

Klingen C, Zettelmeyer J and Weder B (2004). How private creditors fared in emerging debt markets, 1970-2000 IMF Working Papers, (04)13, International Monetary Fund, Washington, DC.

Koo R (2010). *Learning Wrong Lessons from the Crisis in Greece*. Nomura Securities Co Ltd, Japanese Equity Research - Flash Report, Tokyo, 15 June.

Lane T and Phillips S (2002). Moral Hazard; Does IMF Financing Encourage Imprudence by Borrowers and Lenders?, IMF Economic Issues No. 28, March.

Laubach T (2004). New evidence on the interest rate effects of budget deficits and debt, Board of Governors Federal Reserve System. Available at: http://www.crei.cat/activities/crei_seminar/04-05/laubach.pdf.

Levy Yeyati E and Panizza U (2011). The elusive costs of sovereign defaults. *Journal of Development Economics,* 94(1): 95–105, Elsevier.

Lindert P (1989). Response to debt crisis: What is different about the 1980s? In: Eichengreen B and Lindert P, eds., *The International Debt Crisis in Historical Perspective.* Chicago, University of Chicago Press.

Lindert P (2004). *Growing Public: Social Spending and Economic Growth Since the Eighteenth Century.* Cambridge, Cambridge University Press.

Lindert P and Morton P (1989). How sovereign debt has worked. In: Sachs J, ed., *Developing Country Debt and Economic Performance. Volume 1: The International Financial System.* Chicago, University of Chicago Press.

Marglin S (1990). Lessons of the golden age: An overview. In: Marglin S and Schor J, eds., *The Golden Age of Capitalism: Reinterpreting the Postwar Experience.* New York, Oxford University Press: 1–38.

Martner R and Tromben V (2004). Public debt indicators in Latin American countries: Snowball effect, currency mismatch and the original sin. In: Banca d'Italia, *Public Debt.* Perugia, Italy.

Nersisyan Y and Wray LR (2010). Deficit hysteria redux? Public Policy Brief 111, Levy Economics Institute of Bard College, Annandale-on-Hudson, NY.

NORAD (2009). Revenue Management: The Norwegian Fiscal Policy Framework, Norwegian Agency of Development Cooperation, Oslo.

Ocampo JA (2011). Global economic perspectives and the developing world. *Global Policy,* 2(1): 10–19.

OECD (2009). Economic Outlook Interim Report, March, Chapter 3: The effectiveness and scope of fiscal stimulus. Available at: www.oecd.org/dataoecd/3/62/42421337.pdf.

OECD (2010). *African Economic Outlook.* Paris, Organisation for Economic Co-operation and Development.

OECD (2011). *Restoring public finances. Journal on Budgeting,* 2. Paris, Organisation for Economic Co-operation and Development.

Ostry J, Ghosh A, Kim J and Qureshi M (2010). *Fiscal Space.* IMF Staff position Note, SPN/10/11, 1 September, International Monetary Fund, Washington, DC.

Özler S (1993). Have commercial banks ignored history? *American Economic Review,* 83(3): 608–620.

Panizza U, Sturzenegger F and Zettelmeyer J (2009). The economics and law of sovereign debt and default. *Journal of Economic Literature,* 47(3): 651–98.

Pasinetti L (1997). The social burden of high interest rates. In: Arestis P, Palma G, and Sawyer M, eds., *Capital Controversy, Post-Keynesian Economics and the History of Economic Thought.* Essays in Honour of Geoffrey Harcourt, vol. 1, London and New York, Routledge.

Reinhart C and Rogoff K (2009). *This Time is Different.* Princeton, Princeton University Press.

Reinhart C and Rogoff K (2010). Growth in a time of debt. *American Economic Review,* 100(2): 573–578.

Rogoff K and Zettelmeyer J (2002). Bankruptcy Procedures for Sovereigns: A History of Ideas, 1976–2001. IMF Staff Papers: (49)3.

Roubini N (2001). Debt Sustainability: How to assess whether a country is insolvent. New York University, New York. Available at: http://pages.stern.nyu.edu/~nroubini/papers/debtsustainability.pdf.

Shleifer A (2003). Will the sovereign debt market survive? *American Economic Review, Papers and Proceedings,* 93(2): 85–90.

Spilimbergo A, Symansky S, Blanchard O and Cottarelli C (2008). Fiscal policy for the crisis. IMF Staff Positions Note, (08)/01, International Monetary Fund, Washington, DC.

Torre ADL, Sinnott E and Nash J (2010). *Natural Resources in Latin America and the Caribbean: Beyond Booms and Busts?* Washington, DC, World Bank Publications.

UNCTAD (*TDR 1981*). *Trade and Development Report, 1981.* United Nations publications, Sales No. E. 81.II.D.9, New York and Geneva.

UNCTAD (*TDR 2005*). *Trade and Development Report, 2005. New features of global interdependence.* United Nations publications, Sales No. E. 05.II.D.13, New York and Geneva.

UNCTAD (*TDR 2008*). *Trade and Development Report, 2008. Commodity prices, capital flows and the financing of investment.* United Nations publications, Sales No. E. 08.II.D.21, New York and Geneva.

UNCTAD (*TDR 2009*). *Trade and Development Report, 2009. Responding to the global crisis: Climate change mitigation and development.* United Nations publications, Sales No. E. 09.II.D.16, New York and Geneva.

UNCTAD (*TDR 2010*). *Trade and Development Report, 2010. Employment, globalization and development.* United Nations publications, Sales No. E. 10.II.D.3, New York and Geneva.

UNCTAD (2011a). *Price Formation in Financialized Commodity Markets: The Role of Information.* New York and Geneva, United Nations, June.

UNCTAD (2011b). Draft Principles on Promoting Responsible Sovereign Lending and Borrowing. Working Document, Geneva, April.

Villafuerte M, López-Murphy P and Ossowski R (2010). Riding the roller coaster: Fiscal policies of non-renewable resources exporters in Latin America and the Caribbean. IMF Working Paper, no. 10/251, International Monetary Fund, Washington, DC.

Woodford M (2011). Simple analytics of the government
    spending multiplier. *American Economic Journal:
    Macroeconomics*, 3(1): 1–35.

Zandi M (2008). Assessing the macro economic impact
    of fiscal stimulus 2008. Moody's Economy.com.

Available at: http://www.economy.com/mark-zandi/
documents/Stimulus-Impact-2008.pdf.

Chapter IV

FINANCIAL RE-REGULATION AND RESTRUCTURING

A. Introduction

Financial markets are supposed to mobilize resources and allow their efficient allocation for productive investment. In addition, they are expected to facilitate transactions and reduce transaction costs, as well as reduce risk by providing insurance against low probability but high-cost events. Therefore, those markets are often seen as instrumental in promoting economic growth and broad social development. However, the hard reality is that they often serve as a means of speculation and financial accumulation without directly contributing to economic development and improving living standards, and throughout history they have been fraught with crises.

The development of financial markets in modern economies dates back to the thirteenth century, when they enabled the expansion of long-distance trade, the integration of domestic markets and the rise of manufacturing. Several financial innovations contributed to this expansion of the real economy, including bills of exchange, insurance of merchant trade, public debt, joint-stock companies and stock exchanges. However, financial crises also became relatively common, Tulipmania, the South Sea Bubble and the Mississippi Bubble being early examples of the havoc that financial markets could also cause.

Financial institutions developed in different historical contexts, and in the process they acquired a variety of specific characteristics. Two main types of financial systems can be distinguished: those based on capital markets, associated with the so-called "Anglo-Saxon" (i.e. British and American) tradition; and those based on credit, which reflected the continental European (mainly German) tradition (Zysman, 1983). In particular, continental European countries, being latecomers to the process of industrialization, relied on large banking institutions to promote initial investment and infrastructure development, from the late nineteenth century onwards (Gerschenkron, 1962).

In these latter countries, several major shareholders, usually banks, typically held a substantial share of total equity, whereas in the United Kingdom and the United States stock ownership was much more dispersed. For that reason, in the credit-based model there was a more stable relationship between banks and firms, compared with the Anglo-Saxon model, where firms relied more on internal sources of funds and on the stock market. In addition, the capital-market-based model was more prone to hostile takeovers and leveraged buyouts.

After the Great Crash of 1929 and the subsequent Great Depression, commercial banking was separated from investment banking mainly in the United States. At the same time, lender-of-last-resort functions were institutionalized, together with deposit insurance, which aimed at preventing bank runs. Moreover, in view of the destabilizing effects of speculation in financial markets, particularly in foreign exchange markets, capital controls were introduced in the Bretton Woods Agreement of 1944.

The establishment of the World Bank, regional and national development banks contributed to diversifying the financial market and strengthening those activities that focused on enhancing investment and social welfare. In this sense, financial markets during the so-called Golden Age of Capitalism could be seen as fundamentally promoting functional and social efficiency (Tobin, 1984; *TDR 2009*). This implies that a number of important financial institutions played a key role in supporting long-term economic growth.

By the 1970s the collapse of the Bretton Woods system of fixed but adjustable exchange rates, the two oil shocks and the consequent acceleration of inflation led to what has been called the "revenge of the rentier" (Pasinetti, 1997). Financial deregulation and higher interest rates, together with growing speculation in foreign exchange markets, shifted the balance of the financial sector from activities that were socially useful, and mainly linked to the real economy, to activities that increasingly resembled those of a casino.

The increasing financialization of the world economy (strongly driven by securitization) led to the growing dominance of capital-market financial systems over bank-based financial systems – a process that strengthened the political and economic power of the rentier class. There was also an explosion of financial trading, associated with a myriad of new financial instruments aimed at short-term private profit-making. However, such trading was increasingly disconnected from the original purpose of financial markets, that of allocating resources for long-term investment (Epstein, 2005). Moreover, the financial innovations not only demolished the walls between different financial institutions, they also generated increasingly uniform financial structures around the world. In international markets, this growing hegemony of the financial sector manifested itself both in widespread currency speculation and in the increasing participation of financial investors in commodity futures markets, creating imbalances that exacerbated the potential for financial crises (UNCTAD, 2009; see also chapters V and VI of this *Report*).

A major factor that led to an increase in the number of financial crises in both developed and developing countries was financial deregulation. Some of the most notorious crises in developed countries included the Savings and Loan Crisis, the dot-com bubble and the subprime bubble. In developing countries, notable examples of crises are the 1980s debt crisis, and the Tequila, Asian and Argentinean crises. There appears to be a consensus that deregulation was also one of the main factors behind the latest global financial and economic crisis, which began in 2007. Such deregulation was partly a response to pressure from competitive forces in the financial sector, but it was also part of a generalized trend towards the withdrawal of governments from intervention in the economy. But this ran counter to the generally accepted notion that financial markets are prone to market failures, herd behaviour and self-fulfilling prophecies.

The global financial and economic crisis has prompted a debate about re-regulation and restructuring of the financial sector so as to avoid crises in the future, or at least crises of such magnitude. To a large extent, the debate, both at national and international levels, has been about strengthening of financial regulations and improving supervision of their implementation. However, re-regulation alone will not be sufficient to prevent repeated financial crises and to cope with a highly concentrated and oversized financial sector that is dominated at the global level by a small number of gigantic institutions. In addition, it is not guaranteed that, even if the sector were to be better regulated and less prone to crisis, it would be able to drive growth and employment, particularly in low-income countries, or to make credit more easily available to small and medium-sized firms or to the population at large.

The remainder of the chapter is divided into three sections. Section B examines the malfunctioning of the financial market that led to the Great Recession. Section C analyses the issues that were left unresolved during the unfolding of the crisis, and examines the ongoing discussions on regulation of the financial sector. The final section discusses major proposals for reorganizing this sector, and emphasizes two reforms that are essential. First, public and cooperative banks need to play a more prominent role within the framework of a diversified banking sector, so that the sector caters more to the needs of the real economy in different countries around the world. Second, in order to curb the activities of the global financial casino, there needs to be a clear separation of the activities of commercial and investment banks.

B. What went wrong?

1. Creation of risk by the financial sector

Mainstream economic theory still suggests that liberalized financial markets can smoothly and automatically solve what it considers to be the most complex and enduring economic problem, namely the transformation of today's savings into tomorrow's investments. This assumes that, with efficient financial markets, people's savings and investment decisions pose no major problem to the economy as a whole even if those who invest face falling returns, as long as people save more (*TDR 2006*, annex 2 to chapter I). However, is the transformation of savings the only business of financial markets and do they function in the same way as the markets for goods and services? Is investment in fixed capital, intermediated by traditional banking and investment in purely financial markets, (through "investment banks", for example) a similar process? Why are the larger and more "sophisticated" financial markets more prone to failure, while investment and "sophistication" in the markets for goods and services do not pose major problems?

It is clear that investment in fixed capital is more profitable for the individual investor and beneficial to society as a whole if it increases the availability of goods and services. An innovation consisting of replacing an old machine with a new and more productive one, or replacing an old product with a new one of higher quality or with additional features is risky, because the investor cannot be sure that the new machine or the new product will meet the needs of the potential clients. If it does, the entrepreneur will gain a temporary monopoly rent until others copy the

innovation. Even if an innovation is quickly copied, this does not create a systemic problem; it may deprive the original innovator of parts of the entrepreneurial rent more quickly, but, for the economy as a whole, the rapid diffusion of an innovation is normally positive as it increases overall welfare and income. The more efficient the market is in diffusing knowledge, the higher is the increase in productivity, which could lead to a permanent rise in the standard of living, at least if the institutional setting allows for an equitable distribution of the income gains. This in turn could generate the demand that is needed to market the rising supply of products.

The accrual of rents through innovation in a financial market is of a fundamentally different character. Financial markets are mainly concerned with the effective use of informational advantages about existing assets, and not about technological advances. Temporary monopoly over certain information or correct guessing about an outcome in the market of a certain asset class provides a monopoly rent based on simple arbitrage. The more agents sense an arbitrage possibility and the quicker they are to make their transactions, the quicker the potential gain disappears. In this case, society is also better off, but in a one-off, static sense. Financial efficiency may have maximized the gains from the existing combination of factors of production and resources, but innovation in the financial sector has not shifted the productivity curve upwards; thus a new stream of income is not produced.

However, the serious flaw in financial innovation that leads to crises and to the collapse of the whole system occurs in a different way. Whenever herds of agents on the financial markets "discover" that reasonably stable price trends in different markets (which are originally driven by events and developments in the real sector) provide an opportunity for dynamic arbitrage, which involves investing in the probability of a continuation of the existing trend, the drama begins. If many agents (investors) disposing of large amounts of (frequently borrowed) money bet on the same plausible outcomes, such as rising prices of real estate, oil, stocks or currencies, they acquire the market power to move these prices in the direction that they favour. This is the process that drives prices in financialized markets far beyond sustainable levels; indeed, it produces false prices in a systematic manner. The instrument to achieve this is the generation of rather convincing information such as rising Chinese and Indian demand for oil and food. Even if such information points in the right direction its impact on the market cannot be quantified and yet it is used to justify prices that may diverge from the "fair price" by a wide margin. If this kind of information is factored into the decisions of many market participants, and is "confirmed" by analysts, researchers, the media and politicians, betting on ever-rising prices becomes riskless for a period, and can generate profits that are completely disconnected from the real economy.

Contrary to mainstream economic views, speculation or "investment" of this kind does not have a stabilizing effect on prices in the affected markets, but quite the opposite. As the equilibrium price or the "true" price simply cannot be known in an environment characterized by uncertainty, the crucial condition for stabilizing speculation, namely knowledge of the equilibrium price, is absent. Hence the majority of the market participants can only extrapolate the actual price trend as long as convincing arguments are presented to justify those trends. As a result, everybody goes long and nobody goes short. This happens despite the fact that economies growing at single-digit rates cannot meet the expectations of herds of financial

> Innovation and investment in the real economy normally increase productivity, welfare and income ...

> ... while in the financial sector, they frequently lead to destabilizing speculation, price distortions and misallocation of resources.

market participants. This type of behaviour ignores, at least temporarily, the lessons of the past (UNCTAD, 2009).

The bandwagon created by uniform, but wrong, expectations about long-term price trends will inevitably run into trouble, because funds have not been used for productive investment in a way that generate higher real income. Rather, what is created is the illusion of high returns and a "money-for-nothing" mentality in a zero sum game stretched over a long period of time. Sooner or later, consumers, producers or governments and central banks will be unable to meet the exaggerated expectations of the financial markets. For instance, soaring oil and food prices will cut deeply into the budgets of consumers, appreciating currencies will drive current-account balances into unsustainable deficit, or stock prices will be disconnected from any reasonable expectations of profit. Whatever the specific reasons or shocks that trigger the turnaround, at a certain point in time more and more market participants will begin to understand that, to quote United States presidential adviser, Herbert Stein, "if something cannot go on forever, it will stop". In this way, through herding and greed, financial markets themselves create most of the "fat-tail" risks (i.e. extreme, often severe and highly improbable events) that lead to their collapse.

That is why a reassessment of the management of financial risk has to start with the recognition that the financial system is fraught with uncertainty rather than quantifiable risk. Uncertainty is particularly high after a long period of investment, when the most important asset prices are driven far beyond their fair values by the herd behaviour of speculators or investors. The creation of risk by the financial sector is extremely costly for society at large, not only because of the bailout costs involved when crises erupt, but also because it produces price distortions and a misallocation of resources that are bigger than anything that was experienced in "normal" markets in the past (UNCTAD, 2009).

In sum, uncertainty on the asset side of a bank's balance sheet during bubbles can become so high that no capital requirement or liquidity buffer can absorb the subsequent shock. The question, then, is to what extent and under what conditions should governments step in – an issue that becomes even more serious in the case of large banks.

2. Deregulation and shadow banking

Over the past few decades, deregulation of financial markets has led to an increasing concentration of banking activities in a small number of very big institutions, as well as to the development of a largely unregulated "shadow banking system", particularly in developed countries. At the same time, commercial banks' assets and liabilities have experienced a complete transformation. The traditional form of commercial bank lending to well-known borrowers, relying on the safety of a deposit base for their financing, gave way to the financing of these institutions by capital markets, mostly on a short-term basis, which was a much less stable source of funding. On the assets side of their balance sheets, loans were packaged in funds to be sold in the financial market to third parties, with the banks themselves retaining only a very small proportion. This was the so-called "securitization" process, leading to the "originate and distribute" system. Additionally, and particularly in the case of the largest banks, trading became almost as important as lending, with their trading books becoming a significant part of their total assets. As a result, commercial banks became closer to playing the role of broker. It was therefore no surprise that the present crisis was characterized by a "creditors' run" rather than a "depositors' run", as the latter were largely protected by deposit insurance mechanisms.

Along with this transformation of the "regulated" system of institutions that is subject to some kinds of norms and supervised by official agencies, there emerged a large, unregulated financial system, particularly in the United States. This shadow banking system intermediated funds in ways that were very different from the traditional banking system (McCulley, 2007). The shadow banking system involves a complex chain of intermediaries specializing in different functions, ranging from originating loans, warehousing and issuing securities – normally asset-backed securities collateralized by packages of those loans – all the way up to funding operations in wholesale markets. At each step of the chain, different entities and forms of securitization intervene. The shadow banking system experienced explosive growth in the 1980s, greatly encouraged by the weakening of regulations that had prohibited banks from intervening in securities markets, and formalized in the United States with the repeal of large sections of the Glass-Steagall Act in 1999. As a result, by early 2008, the liabilities of the shadow banking system in the United States amounted to almost $20 trillion, while those of the traditional banking sector were less than $11 trillion (Pozsar et al., 2010).

These changes in legislation took account of the emergence of finance companies or money market funds that placed severe competitive pressures on traditional banks. As a result, banks sought to absorb many of those specialized entities or created their own – under the umbrella of bank holding companies. The traditional banking segment began to outsource a large share of its credit intermediation functions to these associated companies. In this way, banks multiplied the use of capital while preserving their access to public liquidity and credit support, and in turn providing lender-of-last-resort (LLR) support to the rest of the group. Large holding companies with activities in many jurisdictions also became involved in geographical arbitrage, searching for the most efficient location (normally in terms of capital savings) for their different activities. Generally, the volume of activity of these groups has always been backed by too little capital.

Shadow intermediation originated in the United States, but diversified banks in Europe and Japan also got involved in several of these operations. In particular, European banks and their offshore affiliates profited from the 1996 reform of the Basel-I regime by becoming important investors in AAA-rated asset-backed securities and collateralized debt obligations

> Weakening regulations resulted in the emergence of a large, deregulated and undercapitalized "shadow" banking system, intimately interlinked with the traditional one.

(CDOs) which had low capital requirements. Thus they entered a field in which they began to run into currency mismatches, funding United States dollar operations with euro resources and accessing LLR facilities only in euros. Hence, after the eruption of the latest financial and economic crisis, the United States Federal Reserve had to provide swap lines to central banks in Europe.

Another part of the shadow banking system that originated in the large investment bank holding companies is that of diversified broker dealers (DBDs). In the United States, the transformation of investment banks from partnerships into joint-stock companies was also a crucial element in the changing landscape of the financial sector. These companies have an advantage over the activities conducted by bank holding companies in that they can operate at much higher levels of leverage. As they do not own banks, their loans originate mainly from industrial loan companies and from subsidiaries of federal savings banks. Since they lack liquidity, they resort to large United States and European commercial banks that have vast deposit bases. Thus, again, the transformed banking sector has become intimately intertwined with the "shadow" one. The DBDs have been particularly important issuers of subprime and commercial mortgages. As bank holding companies, they can only seek financial assistance from the Federal Reserve and the Federal Deposit Insurance Corporation (FDIC) for their industrial loan companies and federal savings bank subsidiaries, but such support cannot be fully transferred to the rest of the group.

Another type of specialized credit intermediaries, mainly in the fields of automobile and equipment loans and other business lines, are heavily dependent on both DBDs and bank holding companies for access to bank credit and/or market access, which makes them particularly vulnerable. Finally, both bank holding companies and DBDs partly rely on private credit risk repositories, including insurance companies, for risk capital to enable them to qualify for triple-A ratings.

The major ultimate providers of finance for the shadow banking system are money market funds, which overtook the traditional sector in terms of the total value of funds under their management before the crisis – $7 trillion, compared with $6.2 trillion worth of bank deposits (Pozsar et al., 2010). The quality and stability of different sources of funding differ between the two systems. Banks have a privileged source of funding, due to the stability of bank deposits – resulting from a well-established deposit insurance mechanism – as well as their ability to access the discount window of central banks. The shadow banking system, on the other hand, depends on wholesale funding, which is extremely unstable and renders the system very fragile, as evidenced by the crisis. This is compounded by the fact that providers of credit lines and private credit risk repositories are very vulnerable in times of crisis.

> The shadow banking system depends on wholesale funding, which is extremely unstable and renders the system very fragile.

Indeed, the providers of wholesale funding constitute the weakest part of the system. In the same way as bank depositors, those providers expect to recover their resources at par, even though they are aware that there is hardly any capital buffer to protect them at times of asset losses. Therefore the question arises as to whether regulation will be extended to the shadow banking system and if it will allow that system to have access to LLR facilities and deposit insurance, or whether it will be banned altogether. The latter does not seem to be a realistic option. Moreover, it is likely that for each prohibition a new "shadow" entity will emerge. Therefore, what is needed is a reappraisal of the role of this financial segment and the creation of regulations based on function rather than on institutional form.

3. The role of lender of last resort at stake

The essence of a banking system is maturity transformation. A financial intermediary obtains its funds through short-term liabilities, such as deposits, money-market funds or commercial paper. It then invests these resources in assets of longer maturity, such as loans or different kinds of securities. Crises are associated with a shortage of liquidity (Morris and Shin, 2003). A rush for liquidity may arise from exogenous events or negative expectations in a context of asymmetric information between borrowers and lenders, as borrowers have more knowledge about their own situation than lenders, including the willingness and capacity to actually honour their debt. Indeed, in modern, securitized financial systems the initial provider of liquidity may be completely ignorant of the circumstances and the will of the ultimate borrower, as the chain leading from one to the other is extremely long and complex.

A shortage of liquidity is seldom limited to a single institution, which means that contagion can be widespread. On the liabilities side, this may take the form of a depositors' or a creditors' run, while on the assets side, the fall in the value of assets (due to forced sales in search of liquidity) affects the balance sheets of financial institutions or the value of the collateral that is backing those assets (e.g. real estate as collateral for mortgage lending). The system can then collapse, with extremely harmful consequences for the economy as a whole. In this context, State intervention may become the only recourse for stopping the process.

Thus an implicit accord has emerged over the past 150 years, whereby governments have played the role of lender of last resort in times of crises. And, given the recurrence of crises, governments and central banks have increasingly become involved in liquidity support, deposit insurance and, eventually, the provision of capital to prevent the collapse of individual institutions and the system at large. In return, the banks and financiers had to accept regulation of their activities. In an attempt to eliminate – or at least reduce – market failures, prudential regulation of financial activities and supervisory bodies for ensuring its application were introduced, generally at times of financial crises.

Last resort lending has been an important source of liquidity support for banks, in the United Kingdom since the nineteenth century. Deposit insurance was a response to the crisis in the 1930s, although among the industrialized countries it was initially limited only to the United States. This form of insurance for refunding depositors managed to curb, if not completely eliminate, the classical bank run. However, the development of the shadow banking system revived the risk of a depositors' (or creditors') run, since, in

principle, the entities involved had no access to this kind of insurance; moreover, they were not entitled to use the discount window of the central bank as lender of last resort.

Lender-of-last-resort actions and deposit insurance were normally subject to limits on the amount of liquidity support they could provide and other restrictions related to the solvency of the bank receiving the support. In principle, liquidity support should be granted only to solvent institutions against good-quality paper and at a "discouraging" rate of interest (Bagehot, 1873). However, those restrictions were often circumvented in times of crisis. For instance, deposit insurance, which in principle was to be limited to some modest amount, was frequently extended to cover all deposits. As a result, there was an increase in liquidity support as well as in the types of assets eligible as collateral. After some hesitation, in the United States support was extended to the shadow banking system during the global financial crisis and much riskier collateral became acceptable.

> While government regulation has weakened, its lender-of-last-resort support to the financial system has increased, and even extends to the shadow banking system.

The provision of capital by the government to banks under stress has been a less common phenomenon. The United States took the lead in the 1930s with the creation of the Reconstruction Finance Corporation. Since then, similar arrangements have been implemented in Asia, Latin America, Japan and the Scandinavian countries in response to the crises of the 1980s and 1990s, and again in a number of countries during the present crisis.

The past quarter-century has witnessed financial crises with increasing frequency in both developed and developing countries. At the same time, official support for the banking sector has become more common, increasing in amount and in the variety of instruments used. In spite of these developments, the trend of the past three decades has been to rely on the market, and consequently on deregulation. No doubt the hunger for ever rising profits and staff bonuses by banks and other financial intermediaries played a major role in such a development. However, governments also played an essential role in allowing it to happen.

Hence, regulation and LLR support have not evolved at the same pace, breaching the implicit accord between governments and the financial system. In fact, regulatory capacity has been weakened as a result of the emergence of a "shadow regulatory system". With a few exceptions, prudential regulations were removed from the public debate and were not subject to approval by parliamentary bodies. They were even made independent of executive powers. Supervisory agencies at the national level and informal committees of unelected officials from those same agencies at the international level led to a new

era of prudential – in fact, non-prudential – financial regulation. The framework approved by those international committees – which represented neither governments nor citizens' elected public bodies – was also adopted by developing countries that did not participate in those committees. Therefore, governments were no longer able to rein in the trend of ever-increasing risk-taking by the financial sector. To a large extent, financial markets were allowed to self-regulate, despite evident market failures.

C. Unresolved issues in financial regulation

Leveraged financial intermediaries are by nature prone to liquidity and solvency risks. Prudential regulation has therefore largely focused on this type of banking risk, which involves individual institutions. Regulation of the banking system – for instance the capital requirements established in different Basel agreements – has tried to deal with this dimension of risk, though not always successfully. However, a second type of banking risk, which is related to the systemic dimension of banking activities, is associated with the transfer of risks from one institution to another (i.e. risk contagion). It occurs especially when very large financial institutions are involved, and a chain reaction (a "run" in banking terminology) may affect the whole system, even those institutions that had individually made provisions to avoid risk. Another aspect of systemic risk is closely associated with developments at the macroeconomic level. This is mostly related to foreign exchange and balance-of-payments issues, as many financial crises have been triggered by currency crises, the so-called "twin crises" (Bordo et al., 2001).

> There is a paradox in deciding to regulate financial markets because of market failure, and then letting the market regulate itself.

1. Self-regulation and endogenous risk

There has been a notable absence of a strong regulatory framework to accompany the dramatic expansion of financial activities. Instead, there has been an increasing reliance on self-regulation of financial institutions. These institutions have tended to use similar risk models that do not address the nature of systemic financial risks.

In the past few decades, extremely sophisticated models have been developed to estimate risk, based on the widely held belief that risk could be accurately measured, and that such calculations could provide a solid basis for prudential regulation. However, these risk estimation models have serious shortcomings. First, they are not designed to capture those risks that materialize very rarely – the so-called "tail risks" produced mainly by herd behaviour in the financial markets themselves – but when they do occur the consequences are catastrophic (de Grauwe, 2007). In spite of their sophistication, the more commonly used risk models oversimplify the probability assumptions. For instance, the typical value-at-risk (VaR) models assume a normal distribution of risk events, which is symmetric with regard to potential gains and losses. This poses a serious problem, as the models do not take into account the occurrence of fat tails – the significant outlier events – which have proved to be a major problem in financial crises. Even more importantly, they do not provide an estimate of the level which the resulting losses could reach.[1]

An even greater cause for concern is the acquiescence of the regulatory authorities to the use of models that are only useful for estimating small, frequent events for individual firms, for also estimating the probability of large, infrequent events. In fact, the first set of events could be subject to back-testing over some reasonable period. However, the macro application of the models to large-scale events cannot be back-tested due to lack of a sample that covers a sufficiently long period. For a normal sample period of a few decades there have not been any truly extreme events, but only small, minor crises compared with the present one. In normal times, a drop in asset prices, or even a default, could be considered an independent event that does not have systemic implications. However, in crisis situations, supposedly uncorrelated events become highly correlated (Bank of England, 2007, box 4).

From a macroeconomic perspective, the Basel regulations have introduced a procyclical bias. These regulations place an emphasis on risk-sensitive models in which risk estimates are supposed to be based as much as possible on market developments (Persaud, 2008). However, the recurrence of financial crises is proof that financial markets do not function properly. Hence, financial institutions and rating agencies are bound to wrongly estimate risks if they use models that follow the market. In this context, there is a paradox in deciding to regulate financial markets because of market failure, and then letting the market regulate itself (Buiter, 2009). In particular, the use of risk models that rely on market prices and on mark-to-market accounting rules are not reliable instruments of financial regulation (Persaud, 2008). Moreover, as these models have tended to underestimate risks, they have led to lower bank capitalization than is necessary under the Basel framework, which bases capital requirements on risk-related weights (Danielsson, 2002; Danielsson et al., 2001).

It is essential for any prudential regulation to recognize that risk in the financial system is endogenous (i.e. it is created by the financial market itself), and that it has two dimensions: a cross-sectional and a time dimension. The first has to do with the interaction between the different financial institutions. In normal times, if the system is made up of numerous and heterogeneous institutions, their actions could approximately cancel each other out. However, experience has shown that over time different agents tend to become homogeneous and their portfolios highly correlated. This is the result of frequent herding and the rewards that herding is able to yield in the short to medium term. Diversity has been reduced because all types of financial firms tend to move towards the same high-yield activities, so that business strategies have come to be replicated across the financial sector (UNCTAD, 2009). The loss of diversity also makes the system more vulnerable to the second aspect of endogenous risk, which refers to the time dimension and procyclicality. Given the uniformity of the financial system, a macroeconomic shock will tend to affect all the agents at the same time in a similar way. Existing regulations, with their focus on market prices, are not curbing the tendency to assume more risk and to benefit from rising asset prices during booms, thereby accentuating the propensity for procyclicality.

> The loss of diversity of the financial system and uniformity of agents' behaviour increase the risk of a systemic crisis.

In assessing financial risk and its spread across institutions, the size of the institutions is a highly relevant factor: the contribution by large institutions to systemic risk is far out of proportion to their size (BIS, 2009). The rule of thumb that has been tested repeatedly is that 20 per cent of the (largest) members of a network are responsible for 80 per cent of the spread of contagion. Therefore, regulations should be built around an "un-level playing field" contrary to Basel I and II practice. In order to make the system more resilient, higher capital and other prudential requirements should be imposed on large institutions, and indeed, Basel III appears to be moving in this direction.

2. *Systemically important financial institutions*

A specific issue, which is closely related to systemic risk, concerns what have come to be labelled as systemically important financial institutions (SIFIs) that have been dubbed as too big to fail.[2] The concentration of banking activities in a small number of very big institutions is a relatively recent development. For example, in the United States between the 1930s and 1980s, the average size of commercial banks in relation to GDP remained largely constant, and over the subsequent 20 years their size increased threefold (BIS, 2008). At the global level, by 2008, 12 banks had liabilities exceeding $1 trillion and the ratio of liabilities to national GDP of 30 banks was larger than 50 per cent (Demirgüç-Kunt and Huizinga, 2011).

In terms of concentration, until the early 1990s the three largest banks in the United States held around 10 per cent of total assets of the commercial banking system, and between 1990 and 2007, that share had increased to 40 per cent. The share of the world's five largest banks in the assets of the world's 1,000 largest banks increased from around 8 per cent in 1998 to more than 16 per cent in 2009. Moreover, the size of the banking sector in the global economy remained almost constant since the beginning of the twentieth century until the 1970s. Thereafter, it began to increase in the 1980s. For example in the United Kingdom it increased tenfold to five times the value of the country's annual GDP (BIS, 2008).

> Banking activities are now concentrated in a small number of very big institutions, which tend to take greater risks than smaller ones.

In 2008, concentration in the banking sector was very high in most major developed countries; in Australia, Canada, France, Germany, Switzerland, the United Kingdom and the United States, between 2 and 6 institutions accounted for 65 per cent of those countries total bank assets (IMF 2010a). Moreover, "the vast majority of cross-border finance was [and still is] intermediated by a handful of the largest institutions with growing interconnections within and across borders" (IMF 2010a: 5). In order to lower costs, SIFIs switched from deposits to other funding sources, such as money market mutual funds, short-term commercial paper and repos. In the assets of these institutions, the trading book displaced loans as the most important asset group, thereby reducing the importance of net interest income and increasing the share of trading assets in total assets.

In parallel, banks' own lines of defence against negative shocks – liquidity and capital – have fallen dramatically. Since the beginning of the twentieth century, capital ratios in the United Kingdom and the United States have fallen by a factor of five. Liquidity ratios have fallen even faster since the 1950s, to reach almost zero, while bank profitability has shot up from a stable 10 per cent return on equity per annum to a volatile level of between 20 and 30 per cent per annum (Haldane, 2010).

In the years preceding the global financial crisis, SIFIs' financial leverage (i.e. the ratio of total assets to total common equity) grew considerably. Between 2004 and 2007, this ratio went from about 27 to 33 times in Europe, and from 15 to almost 18 times in Canada and the United States. At the same time, their liquidity ratios declined, as did the share of deposits in their total resources, which increased their vulnerability. In Canada and the United States, SIFIs' liquidity, as measured by the ratio of liquid assets to non-deposit liabilities, fell from 23 per cent in 2004 to about 20 per cent in 2007, while in Europe, it plummeted from 35 to 22 per cent over the same period. Similarly, their ratio of non-deposits to total liabilities increased from 62 to 67 per cent in Europe and from 50 to 54 per cent in Canada and the United States (IMF, 2010a, figure 1).

The problem with SIFIs is that they are "super spreaders" of crisis and of losses, as demonstrated during the recent global crisis when 18 of these large institutions accounted for half of the $1.8 trillion in losses reported by banks and insurance companies worldwide (IMF 2010a). Furthermore, the 145 banks with assets of over $100 billion in 2008 received 90 per cent of the total government support provided to financial institutions during the crisis starting in 2007 (Haldane, 2010). Thus, extreme concentration of the banking system implies that there are a number of institutions that pose the problem of being too big to fail, because their collapse risks bringing down the entire financial system.

Experience has shown that systemic risk is exacerbated by SIFIs, as they tend to take on risks that are far greater than those which any smaller institution would dare to take. This behaviour is based on the expectation that governments will not allow them to go under – an expectation that is also shared by credit-rating agencies. There is a significant gap (up to 4 basis points) – which has been observed to increase during crises – between ratings granted to SIFIs on a "stand-alone" basis and a "support" basis, the latter referring to potential government support. In a sample of global banks, the implicit average annual subsidy, calculated as the difference in the cost of obligations due to a better rating, reached almost $60 billion (IMF, 2010a: 5). The annual subsidy for the 18 largest banks in the United States is estimated to be over $34 billion (Baker and McArthur, 2009). When a crisis strikes, the sums involved can place a huge strain on government finances, particularly in countries where the size of the banking sector – and that of the large banks – in relation to GDP is very high.

Therefore, large banks survive against the logic of the market, profiting from a sizeable competitive advantage over the smaller banks. The repeated government support to these institutions in times of crisis, above and beyond what any other firm would receive, raises the question of the distribution of costs and benefits. It is a crucial issue because the public support to these financial institutions carries long-lasting consequences for public finances and for society as a whole.

3. Volatility of capital flows and the need for capital controls

Besides contagion, systemic risks are associated with macroeconomic shocks that affect all financial institutions simultaneously, particularly the largest ones. In the past few decades, major shocks of this kind, especially in developing and emerging market economies, have resulted from herding in currency speculation, leading to huge and volatile capital flows. These flows have driven exchange rates away from fundamentals for many years, and thus currency markets, left to their own devices, have systematically produced wrong prices with disastrous consequences for the economies involved (*TDR 2009*).

Arbitrary changes in exchange rates may strongly affect balance sheets of financial and non-financial agents due to currency mismatches. On the other hand, fixed exchange rate regimes that misleadingly appear to eliminate all exchange rate risks, attract short-term capital flows. These inflows, in turn, tend to generate an overaccumulation of foreign-currency-denominated liabilities, financial bubbles and real exchange rate appreciation, which eventually lead to crises. Thus, a better alternative is to adopt a managed floating exchange rate regime that avoids significant swings in exchange rates and allows the targeting of a desired level of the real exchange rate (see chapter VI).

> In developing and emerging market economies, volatile capital flows have been a major factor contributing to systemic risk, due to their strong impact on exchange rates and macroeconomic stability.

Under a managed floating exchange rate system, financial and monetary authorities should have the means to intervene in foreign exchange markets. In the absence of an international lender of last resort, and given that IMF assistance has not always been available in a timely manner, and in any case usually has undesirable conditionalities attached, countries have tried to rely on their own resources by accumulating international reserves.[3]

Several countries have also sought to tackle the root of the problem by setting barriers to destabilizing capital flows. For instance, until the 1980s most European economies had fairly strict capital controls, and even the United States had implemented measures to discourage capital outflows. Likewise, Switzerland granted lower interest rates on foreign-owned bank accounts in order to counter pressure for revaluation of its currency that could lead to an asset price bubble and adversely affect its export industries, including tourism.

In the 1990s, some developing countries that were integrating into the financially globalizing world introduced measures to reduce the instability of capital flows. These took the form of discouraging short-term capital inflows rather than raising barriers to capital outflows. For instance, Chile and Colombia introduced taxes and froze a proportion of the inflows going into unremunerated deposits. Other countries have used more direct barriers to capital movements. For instance, Malaysia in the 1990s and Argentina after the crisis of 2001–2002 introduced measures aimed at reducing the profitability of short-term flows and extending the time frame for foreign investments.

4. Liberalization of services and prudential regulation

For macroeconomic and prudential reasons there may be circumstances in which capital controls are a legitimate component of the policy response to surges in capital inflows (Ostry et al., 2010). The IMF (2011) has proposed the development of global rules relating to macroprudential policies, capital-account liberalization and reserve adequacy. Under those rules, countries would be allowed to introduce capital controls, but only under certain conditions; for example, if capital inflows are causing the exchange rate to be overvalued, thereby affecting economic activity, and if the country already has more than enough foreign exchange reserves so it does not need to use the capital inflows to add to those reserves. Furthermore, the IMF argues that since such controls are perceived to be always distorting, they should be used only temporarily, and should not substitute for macroeconomic policy instruments such as adjusting fiscal policy and the interest rate (even though these become much more difficult to control with mobile capital flows). In any case, only controls on inflows are considered acceptable, while controls on capital outflows are still frowned upon. (IMF, 2011).

In fact the possibility of imposing capital controls was already guaranteed under Article VI, Section 3, of the IMF's Articles of Agreement: "members may exercise such controls as are necessary to regulate capital movements …" Thus, what has been widely interpreted as a shift in the Fund's traditional opposition to capital controls, boils down to an attempt to

> Capital controls are a legitimate instrument for macroprudential regulation.

allow member countries to establish those controls only under certain conditions. However, if they are accepted only as an exceptional measure, to be taken as a last resort when the economy is already facing difficulties, capital controls would be of no use for macroprudential regulation – which is precisely what they are meant for.

In addition, the use of capital controls – as well as other financial reforms – may be severely circumscribed, if not banned, by bilateral or multi-lateral international agreements that countries have committed to in recent years or that are still under negotiation. The General Agreement on Trade in Services (GATS) of the World Trade Organization (WTO), many bilateral trade agreements and bilateral investment treaties (BITs) include provisions relating to payments, transfers and financial services that may severely limit not only the application of capital controls, but also other measures aimed at re-regulating or restructuring financial systems. Moreover, what could be construed as a violation of GATS obligations or specific commitments could lead to the imposition of trade sanctions. The following analysis focuses specifically on GATS,[4] although many of the issues raised also apply to most BITs with regard to their payment and transfer clauses.

Within GATS, some provisions seem to forbid, or at least severely limit, the use of capital controls by the countries that have signed the agreement. Among its general obligations and disciplines, a specific article on payments and transfers (Article XI) establishes that, unless a serious balance-of-payments situation can be claimed, no restrictions on international transfers or payments related to a country's specific commitments are permitted. Furthermore, Article XVI (Market Access), under specific commitments, stipulates that, once a commitment of market access has been made for a specific kind of service, capital movements that are "essentially part of" or "related to" the provision of that service are to be allowed as part of the commitment.

On the other hand, other dispositions apparently authorize the use of these controls. In particular, the paragraph on domestic regulation in the Annex on Financial Services states that a member "… shall not be prevented from taking measures for prudential reasons". This apparent contradiction creates scope for different interpretations, leading to uncertainties regarding how the WTO will eventually apply these rules. Therefore, it will be necessary to clarify certain wording that has not been tested in dispute settlement panels. For instance, the meaning of "prudential" is not clear. From one point of view, restrictions on capital inflows and outflows are clearly macroprudential in nature, but many governments and institutions, as well as well-versed GATS scholars, have argued that only Basel-type measures could be considered "prudential", which would exclude capital controls (Wallach and Tucker, 2010). Further, this concession to national autonomy is followed by the statement that, "where such measures do not conform with the provisions of the Agreement, they shall not be used as a means of avoiding the Member's commitments or obligations under the Agreement".

> Liberalization of services through GATS commitments may be an obstacle to re-regulating the financial system.

Thus, if countries have already made commitments to allow certain kinds of financial activities of foreign financial institutions, they cannot impose any prudential regulations that run counter to such commitments, even when they are necessary for the stability and viability of the system.

Different interpretations may also arise concerning the possibility of applying capital controls which are explicitly allowed by the IMF's Articles of Agreement. GATS Article XI states: "Nothing in this Agreement shall affect the rights and obligations of the members of the International Monetary Fund under the Articles of Agreement of the Fund". In principle, therefore, countries could resort to Article VI, section 3 of the Fund's Articles of Agreement to impose capital controls. However, the same GATS Article XI specifies that "a member shall not impose restrictions on any capital transactions inconsistently with its specific commitments regarding such transactions, except under Article XII [i.e. under balance-of-payments difficulties] or at the request of the Fund". Hence, on the one hand, as a member of the IMF a country is free to impose capital controls; and on the other hand, under GATS it can only resort to such a measure "provided" it is not inconsistent with its commitments made under GATS, or if it faces a balance-of-payments crisis (Siegel, 2002).

GATS may also be an obstacle for other sorts of regulations that are being proposed by several countries. For instance, the European Commission has realized that a tax on financial transactions that was greatly favoured by many of its member countries could be viewed as an indirect restriction on transfers and payments if it increases the cost of transactions, and as such would be a breach of GATS Article XI, as the EU had undertaken commitments relating to financial transactions even with third countries (Tucker, 2010). Furthermore, even the separation of commercial and investment banking, which many see as essential for coping with financial systemic risk, could be construed as a violation of Article XVI on Market Access, which, as noted earlier, places restrictions on limitations that could be imposed on the character of institutions. The GATS market access rules prohibit government policies that limit the size or total number of financial service suppliers in the "covered sectors" (i.e. those in which liberalization commitments have been made). Thus, if countries have already committed to certain kinds of deregulation, they cannot easily undo them, even with regard to critical issues such as bank size. Under the same rules, a country may not ban a highly risky financial service in a sector (i.e. banking, insurance or other financial services) once it has been committed under GATS rules.[5]

The situation is even more extreme for the 33 countries that in 1999 signed up to a further WTO "Understanding on Commitments in Financial Services", which states that "any conditions, limitations and qualifications to the commitments noted below shall be limited to existing non-conforming measures." These countries include almost all the OECD members, as well as a few developing countries such as Nigeria, Sri Lanka and Turkey. This Understanding established further deregulation-related commitments by specifying a "top-down" approach to financial liberalization, which means that a sector is, by default, fully covered by all of the GATS obligations and constraints unless a country specifically schedules limits to them. This effectively blocks further financial regulation of any kind. And there is no possibility of any kind of ban on specific financial products that are deemed to be too risky, such as certain derivatives, because every signatory to the Understanding has promised to ensure that foreign financial service suppliers are permitted "to offer in its territory any new financial service."

Summing up, the GATS multilateral framework for services (including financial services) was

negotiated at a time when most countries were convinced that financial deregulation was the best means to achieving financial development and stability. However, as a result of the crisis, many countries now favour re-regulation, but their GATS commitments may not allow this.

D. The unfinished reform agenda and policy recommendations

Proposals for financial reform have proliferated with the crisis. At the international level, in an effort to strengthen existing bodies in this field, the Basel Committee on Banking Supervision and the Financial Stability Board (FSB, formerly Financial Stability Forum) opened their membership to all G-20 countries. Following an ambitious examination of regulatory frameworks, they made some provisional proposals for change in 2009–2011.

In addition, some countries, particularly the United States, proceeded to draft new legislation on financial reform, and some changes were suggested and partially introduced in the United Kingdom and at the level of the EU. However, despite initial ambitious intentions for reform, official pronouncements have so far focused only on re-regulation aimed at strengthening some of the existing rules or incorporating some missing elements. Unlike proposals following the crisis of the 1930s, the recent proposals have paid little attention to a basic restructuring of the financial system.

This section discusses the limitations of the re-regulation efforts, and argues for a stronger re-structuring of the financial system to cope with its inherent proneness to crises. In this context, it proposes diversifying the institutional framework, giving a larger role to public, regional and community banks, and separating the activities of investment and commercial banks.

1. Re-regulation and endogenous risk

Financial regulations based on the Basel I and Basel II frameworks were focused on microprudential regulation. They failed to recognize the risks arising from the shadow banking system and the regulatory arbitrage pursued under that system, and completely overlooked endogenous and systemic risks. The global crisis highlighted the need for multinational and national regulatory authorities to examine these issues.

The crisis showed that the volume of transactions conducted under the shadow banking system exceeded that of the regular banking sector, that parts of this system (e.g. money market funds) were playing the same role as that of banks but without being subjected to virtually any of their regulations, and yet at the worst point of the crisis they had to be supported by central banks. Thus, in their case, the "contract" between financial intermediaries and the lender of last resort became one-sided. Proposals to fix this anomaly have varied, including bringing various parts of the shadow system into the "social contract". Of these, the most frequently mentioned candidates are the money market mutual funds but also the asset-backed securities market financed with repos, which is involved in large and risky maturity transformation. Another priority is the need to ring fence as much as possible the commercial banking system from what could remain of the unregulated system. For that purpose, and to improve understanding of how the "shadow" system works, there have been calls for more information about its operations (Tucker, 2010; Ricks, 2010; Adrian and Shin, 2009).

The Financial Stability Board, mandated by the G-20 summit in Seoul in November 2010, set up a task force on the shadow banking system that was supposed to present proposals by mid-2011. In the meantime, the FSB has produced a background note containing some initial proposals to cope with systemic risk and regulatory arbitrage. They fall into four categories: (i) indirect regulation via the regulated sector and its connections with the unregulated sector; (ii) direct regulation of shadow banking entities; (iii) regulation of activities, markets and instruments, rather than regulation of entities; and (iv) macroprudential measures to reduce risks of contagion (FSB, 2011).

Even though the Basel Committee remains focused mainly on microprudential regulation, it is also considering precautionary measures related to the systemic dimension of risk. For instance, it has introduced higher capital requirements for trading and derivatives as well as for complex securitizations. Additionally, some incentives are provided to use central counterparties for OTC derivatives, and the newly imposed liquidity requirements tend to curb wholesale funding. Thus, to some extent risks arising from individual exposures but with systemic consequences have been addressed (IMF 2010b; BIS, 2011). Furthermore, Basel III will incorporate the time dimension of endogenous risk – its procyclicality – through countercyclical capital buffers. However, such capital buffers may be insufficient to prevent excessive credit growth, and should be complemented by more direct regulations. Shin (2010) proposes limits on the liability side, specifically on non-deposit liabilities that have been the channel through which excessive credit growth funds itself. In addition, he suggests a leverage cap, with capital becoming a limit to excessive lending rather than a loss-absorbency tool in crisis situations.

Regarding the problem of SIFIs, international bodies have concentrated on improving regulation and supervision (rather than on restructuring), and on considering a special resolution procedure in case of crises which would not place a burden on government resources or be disruptive to the rest of the system. A policy framework for SIFIs would impose on them a higher loss absorbency capacity, improve the financial infrastructure to reduce the risk of contagion, and subject them to more intensive supervisory oversight. Higher loss-absorbency capacity – or limits to further expansion – could be achieved through higher capital requirements for SIFIs than for other institutions, as recently proposed by the Basel Committee. In order to improve the resilience of institutions, a range of alternatives have also been proposed by the FSB, including contingent capital instruments. Regarding improvements in infrastructure, the FSB recommends that derivatives should be standardized, and that they should be traded on exchanges or electronic platforms and cleared through central counterparties. Additionally, with regard to the global SIFIs, there has been a proposal for the establishment of international supervisory colleges and for negotiations and international cooperation on resolution mechanisms (FSB, 2010).

> The Basel Committee is now considering precautionary measures related to the systemic dimension of risk, including procyclicality and "too-big-to-fail" problems.

At the national level, in the United States the Dodd-Frank Wall Street Reform and Consumer Protection Act points to some progress in the treatment of SIFIs. According to the Act, all institutions with assets worth more than $50 billion are automatically considered to be SIFIs. They have to register with the Federal Reserve within 180 days, and are subject to enhanced supervision and prudential standards. The definition of an institution as a SIFI can also be decided by the Financial System Oversight Council set up by this Act. Moreover, regulators are empowered to force SIFIs to sell segments of their activities that are deemed to contribute to excessive systemic risk. In addition, mergers or takeovers that result in an institution surpassing more than 10 per cent of the total liabilities of the system will not be allowed; however, there will be no impediment to an institution exceeding that limit if it is the result of its own growth. The SIFIs are also required to produce and continuously update their own resolution regime in case a crisis erupts, and to keep regulators informed about it. The Federal Deposit Insurance Corporation (FDIC) will be responsible for any SIFI that goes

bankrupt. Outside the normal bankruptcy procedures, the FDIC will have the authority to take over
the institution, sell its assets, and impose losses on
shareholders and unsecured creditors. Additionally,
the sector as a whole will be forced to bear the costs
of this procedure.

In the United Kingdom, contrary to what was
widely expected, the Independent Commission on
Banking – the Vickers Committee – did not recom-
mend breaking up large institutions. Instead, its
interim report advocates that institutions planning to
operate in the retail banking market should establish a
subsidiary with increased capital requirements: 10 per
cent instead of the general rule of 7 per cent (ICB,
2011). Additionally, competition in this retail market will be imposed. This implies that Lloyds Bank,
which controls 85 per cent of the retail business, will
have to dispose of more than the 600 branches it was
already planning to shed. Overall, the Committee's
report is oriented more towards a change in the structure of the "industry" than to enhancing regulation
of the existing structure.

Indeed, the way to address the too-big-to-fail
problem should go beyond the additional capital
requirements or enhanced supervision recommendations coming out of international forums. For
instance, the five largest United States financial
institutions subject to Basel rules that either failed
or were forced into government-assisted mergers had
regulatory capital ratios ranging from 12.3 to 16.1 per
cent immediately before they were shut down. These
levels are comfortably above the required standards
(Goldstein and Véron, 2011).
Thus, while it is necessary to
increase capital requirements
and introduce liquidity standards, much more is needed.

The limitations of higher
capital requirements can be
overcome with four policy instruments. The first one, included in
the Dodd-Frank Act, is a require-
ment that financial institutions produce their own
wind-down plan when there is no sensible procedure
for shrinking them or reducing their complexity. The
second instrument – again part of the Dodd-Frank
Act – would be to grant special resolution authority
to avoid bankruptcy procedures that are too slow and
do not take into account externalities; that authority

should be able to intervene prior to a declaration of
insolvency. The third instrument would entail the
imposition of stern market discipline by removing
shareholders and management, paying off creditors
at an estimated fair value (and not at the nominal
value) and prohibiting the remaining institution
from being acquired by another large one. Finally,
the fourth instrument would be the introduction of
size caps, which may be absolute or relative to GDP.
Such caps are supported by empirical evidence that
shows that beyond $100 billion in assets there are no
economies of scale (Goldstein and Véron, 2011). An
additional proposal is to augment capital by issuing
"bail-in" debt that would automatically convert into
capital at times of crisis.

2. Beyond re-regulation: towards a restructuring of the banking system

The problem of negative externalities in financial markets has been evident during the latest global
crisis. This has been related mainly to the actions of
big banks, which generated huge costs for governments and the overall economy. The response to
this problem has been almost exclusively oriented
towards strengthening regulations to force banks to
add more capital and liquidity and, in the case of the
SIFIs, possibly adding an additional layer of requirements. However, in addition to better regulation, there
needs to be a new structure of the financial sector
that would not only reduce systemic risks but also
improve the sector's economic
and social utility.

> In addition to better regula-
> tion, the financial sector needs
> to be restructured in order to
> reduce the risk of systemic
> crises and to improve its eco-
> nomic and social utility.

One proposal for reform
revolves around three aspects:
modularity, robustness and
incentives. Modularity would
allow sections of the system to
operate independently of the
rest. With regard to robustness,
regulation should be simple and
adopt a strategy that would minimize the likelihood of
the worst outcome, focusing more on the system than
on behaviour inside the system. As for incentives, the
presence of endogeneity poses a serious problem for
regulators, which could be resolved by introducing
drastic changes to the structure of financial institutions and reducing their size (Haldane, 2010).

Therefore, a possible way to restructure the banking sector would be to promote a diverse set of banking institutions, ensuring that they serve growth as well as equality. A diversity of institutions, which would cushion the system from the vagaries of the international financial markets, along with regulatory simplicity, would create a more stable banking system. Moreover, inclusive development necessitates the involvement of a variety of institutions and a different role for central banks. Central banks should not only focus on fighting inflation; they should also be able to intervene in the provision of credit, as they did in many European countries for more than a century (Gerschenkron, 1962). The present system of private banks should be restructured to establish a clear separation between those that take deposits and those engaged in investment banking, bringing many of the legitimate activities now conducted by the shadow banking system within the scope of regulation. In this framework, government-owned banks would have a more important role, not only for development purposes but also as an element of diversity and stability. Additionally, a combination of postal savings facilities and community-based banks, similar to some local savings banks in parts of Europe, could also play a larger role in the functioning of the financial sector. All this would result in a much more diverse banking system, which will be more responsive to the needs of growth and of small communities, as advocated by Minsky et al. (1993).

> A more balanced and diversified banking system, which includes public and cooperative banks, will be more stable and effective in serving growth and equality.

3. The need for a more balanced banking sector: public and cooperative banks

The ongoing financial and economic crisis, which originated in private financial institutions, has significantly undermined many of the arguments repeatedly advanced over the past few decades against publicly-owned banks. In Europe and the United States, large private banks have been subsidized based on the belief that they are too big to fail. Indeed, when the crisis struck large banks were able to survive only because they received government funding and guarantees. Whereas during the boom period, private institutions and individuals enjoyed large profits and bonuses, during the bust, governments – or the "taxpayers" – had to bear the costs.

The criticism that only State-owned banks have the advantage of access to public resources is no longer valid. Governments generally have had full control of the operations of public banks throughout both boom and bust cycles, whereas private banks have retained their own management and control and have continued to pay themselves handsome bonuses, even when they have received large government bailouts. The allegation that State-owned banks are "loss-making machines" (Calomiris, 2011) is therefore more appropriately applicable to large private banks. With regard to the differences in efficiency between public and private banks, the crisis revealed that even the largest private banks failed to collect and assess information on borrowers and to estimate the risks involved in lending. The latter function was transferred to rating agencies instead.

Three beneficial aspects of State-owned banks have been highlighted recently. The first one relates to their proven resilience in a context of crisis and their role in compensating for the credit crunch originating from the crisis. A second beneficial aspect of publicly owned banks is that they support activities that bring much greater social benefits than the private banks and provide wider access to financial services. Finally, they may also help promote competition in situations of oligopolistic private banking structures (Allen, 2011).

From a regulatory point of view, information asymmetries could be overcome if the authorities had complete access to information, which, at present, is often retained as confidential by private banks. In addition, it has been argued that "if private banks are making significantly higher profits than public banks, this may provide a warning signal [to regulators] that they are taking too much risk or exploiting their monopoly power" (Allen, 2011).

In spite of large-scale privatizations during the 1990s, State-owned banks continue to play an important role in the banking systems of many developing countries. In 2003, these kinds of banks accounted for

80 per cent of total assets in South Asia, more than 30 per cent in the transition economies, more than 20 per cent in Africa and slightly less than 20 per cent in Latin America. But there were large variations within each region. In Argentina and Brazil, for instance, almost a third of the banking assets were held by State-owned banks (Clarke, Cull and Shirley, 2004).

Under certain circumstances, cooperative and community development banks might also be an important component of the restructuring of the banking sector. During the global financial crisis, small savings banks, such as the Sparkassen in Germany, did not have to resort to central bank or treasury support. Moreover, these institutions may give greater attention to small businesses and other agents that do not normally have access to banking credit.

4. Building a firewall between commercial and investment banking

In addition to stronger public banks, a restructuring of private banks would create a more balanced banking sector. As previously discussed, the loss of diversity of the banking system has been one of the major factors behind the latest crisis. Some responsibility for this development lies with the regulatory bodies, most specifically the Basel Committee in its misguided attempt to design a "level playing field" both within and across borders.

As barriers between different institutions fell, deposit-taking banks became involved in investment banking activities, and as a consequence, they were more fragile and exposed to contagion. Since these banks play a crucial role in the payments system, their higher exposure to systemic risk had the potential to make a greater adverse impact on the entire economy. This problem could be addressed in two ways. First, deposit-taking and payment systems should be separated from investment banking operations, as was done under the Glass-Steagall Act in the United States in 1933. In other words, commercial banks should not be allowed to gamble with other people's money. Second, and even more ambitious, large institutions should be dismantled, to overcome the too-big-to-fail or even, as coined by Reddy (2011: 10), the "too powerful to regulate" problem.

There are many possible ways to separate deposit-taking institutions from investment banks. Some authors advocate "narrow banking" (de Grauwe, 2008), whereby financial institutions should be forced to choose between becoming a commercial bank or an investment bank. The former would be allowed to take deposits from the public and other commercial banks, and place their funds in loans that carry a longer maturity while keeping them in their balance sheets. These banks would have access to a discount window at the central bank, lender-of-last-resort facilities and deposit insurance. However, their activities would also be subject to strict regulation and supervision. On the other hand, investment banks would be required to avoid maturity mismatches, and therefore would not be able to purchase illiquid assets financed by short-term lines of credit from commercial banks.

A recent proposal that would grant commercial banks more latitude is based on the concept of "allowable activities", along lines that also establish a separation between commercial and investment banks. Thus, deposit-taking institutions would be permitted to underwrite securities, and offer advice on mergers and acquisitions as well as on asset management. However, they would not be allowed to pursue broker-dealer activities, or undertake operations in derivatives and securities, either on their own account or on behalf of their customers. Neither would they be allowed to lend to other financial institutions or sponsor hedge funds and private equity funds (Hoenig and Morris, 2011). Separating the two activities could be an additional way to reduce the size of institutions, and would therefore address the too-big-to-fail problem. In this vein, the Governor of the Bank of England has proposed splitting banks into separate utility companies and risky ventures, based on the belief that it is "a delusion" to think that tougher regulation alone would prevent future financial crises (Sorkin, 2010).

> In order to reduce the risk of contagion, there needs to be a clear separation between the private banks that take deposits and those engaged in investment banking.

Notes

1   The inability for these models to assess the risk of a financial crisis is illustrated by the fact that during 2007, events that were 25 standard deviation moves took place for several days in a row. As explained by Haldane and Alessandri (2009), assuming normal distribution of events, a much smaller deviation of 7.26 moves could be expected to happen once every 13.7 billion years, approximately the age of the universe.

2   See Financial Stability Board, 2010 and 2011. The expression used by the IMF (2010a) is: large and complex financial institutions (LCFIs).

3   In addition, some countries' central banks have established swap lines with the United States Federal Reserve and/or the Swiss National Bank in order to meet the foreign currency needs of their domestic banks arising from their own obligations or those of their customers.

4   However, whether the GATS rules impose restrictions on regulatory policies is not totally clear and could be open to interpretation. Article 1 subparagraph 3(b) of the Agreement excludes "services supplied in the exercise of government authority" from the definition of services, and therefore from obligations under the Agreement, including activities conducted by a central bank or monetary authority. But, as argued by Tucker (2010), not any measure conducted by these authorities would be excluded from GATS, but only those that are directly related to monetary or exchange rate management.

5   The relevant case law provides some indication of how these rules might be interpreted in future. A WTO tribunal has already established a precedent of this rule's strict application in its ruling on the United States Internet gambling ban – which prohibited both United States and foreign gambling companies from offering online gambling to United States consumers. The ban was found to be a "zero quota", and thus in violation of GATS market access requirements. This ruling was made even though the United States Government pleaded that Internet gambling did not exist when the original commitment was made, and therefore could not have been formally excluded from the commitment list.

References

Adrian T and Shin HS (2009). The shadow banking system: implications for financial regulation, Staff Reports 382. Federal Reserve Bank of New York. July.

Allen F (2011). The AAF Virtual Debates: Franklin Allen on State-owned banks. World Bank, 2 February. Available at: http://blogs.worldbank.org/allaboutfinance/the-aaf-virtual-debates-franklin-allen-on-state-owned-banks.

Bagehot W (1873). *Lombard Street: A Description of Money Market*. London, Henry S. King and Co.

Baker D and McArthur T (2009). The value of the Too Big to Fail Big Bank Subsidy, Issue Brief, Center for Economic Policy Research, Washington, DC, September.

Bank of England (2007). *Financial Stability Report*, Issue 21, April.

BIS (Bank for International Settlements) (2008). *Annual Report*. Basel, June.

BIS (2009). *Annual Report*. Basel, June.

BIS (2011). *Annual Report*. Basel, June.

Bordo M, Eichengreen B, Klingebiel D and Martínez-Peria MS (2001). Is the crisis problem growing more severe? *Economic Policy*, 16(32): 51–82, April.

Buiter W (2009). Regulating the New Financial Sector, 9 March. Available at: http://www.voxeu.org/index.php?q=node/3232.

Calomiris C (2011). The AAF Virtual Debates: Charles Calomiris on State-owned banks. World Bank, 2 February. Available at: http://blogs.worldbank.org/allaboutfinance/the-aaf-virtual-debates-charles-calomiris-on-state-owned-banks.

Clarke G, Cull R and Shirley M (2004). *Empirical Studies of Bank Privatization: An Overview*. Washington, DC, World Bank, November. Available at: http://info.worldbank.org/etools/docs/library/156393/stateowned2004/pdf/cull.doc.

Danielsson J (2002). The emperor has no clothes: Limits to risk modelling. *Journal of Banking & Finance,* 26: 1273–1296, July.

Danielsson J (2008). Blame the models, *Voxeu.org*, 8 May. Available at: http://www.voxeu.com/index.php?q=node/1118.

Danielsson J and Shin HS (2002). Endogenous Risk, 21 September. Available at: http://www.ucd.ie/t4cms/DANIELSSON.pdf.

Danielsson J, Embrechts P, Goodhart C, Keating C, Muennich F, Renault O and Shin HS (2001). An academic response to Basel II. Financial Markets Group Special Paper No. 130, LSE Financial Markets Group and Economic & Social Research Council, London, May.

de Grauwe P (2007). The hard task of pricing liquidity risk. *EconoMonitor*, 17 December. Available at: http://www.economonitor.com/blog/2007/12/the-hard-task-of-pricing-liquidity-risk/.

de Grauwe P (2008). Returning to narrow banking. *Archive of European Integration*. Brussels, Centre for European Policy Studies, 14 November.

Demirgüç-Kunt A and Huizinga H (2011). Do we need big banks? 18 March. Available at: http://www.voxeu.org/index.php?q=node/6241.

Epstein G (2005). Introduction. In: Epstein G, ed., *Financialization and the World Economy,* Cheltenham, Edward Elgar, United Kingdom.

FSB (Financial Stability Board) (2010). Reducing the moral hazard posed by systemically important financial institutions; FSB recommendations and time lines, 20 October. Available at: http://www.financialstabilityboard.org/publications/r_101111a.pdf.

FSB (Financial Stability Board) (2011). Progress in the Implementation of the G20 Recommendations for Strengthening Financial Stability, Report of the Financial Stability Board to G20 Finance Ministers and Central Bank Governors, 10 April. Available at: http://www.financialstabilityboard.org/publications/r_110415a.pdf.

Gerschenkron A (1962). *Economic Backwardness in Historical Perspective – A Book of Essays*. Cambridge, MA, Belknap Press of Harvard University Press.

Goldstein M and Véron N (2011). Too big to fail: The transatlantic debate. Working Paper 11-2, Peterson Institute for International Economics, January.

Haldane AG (2010). The $100 billion question. Bank of England, March. Available at: http://www.bis.org/review/r100406d.pdf.

Haldane AG and Alessandri PG (2009). Banking on the State. Paper presented at the Federal Reserve Bank of Chicago Twelfth Annual International Banking Conference on The International Financial Crisis: Have the Rules of Finance Changed? Chicago, 25 September. Available at: http://www.bis.org/review/r091111e.pdf.

Hoenig T and Morris C (2011). Restructuring the banking system to improve safety and soundness. Federal Reserve Bank of Kansas, May. Available at: http://www.kansascityfed.org/publicat/speeches/Restructuring-the-Banking-System-05-24-11.pdf.

ICB (Independent Commission on Banking) (2011). Interim report: Consultation on reform options, April. Available at: http://media.ft.com/cms/bbf38fe0-640d-11e0-b171-00144feab49a.pdf.

IMF (2010a). Impact of regulatory reforms on large and complex financial institutions. IMF Staff Position Note SPN/10/16. Washington, DC, 3 November.

IMF (2010b). IMF-FSB Early Warning Exercise. Available at: http://www.imf.org/external/np/pp/eng/2010/090110.pdf.

IMF (2011). Recent experiences in managing capital inflows: Cross-cutting themes and possible policy framework. Washington, DC, 14 February. Available at: http://www.imf.org/external/np/pp/eng/2011/021411a.pdf.

McCulley P (2007). Teton reflections, PIMCO Global Central Bank Focus. Available at: http://easysite.commonwealth.com/EasySites/EasySite_Z3263Y/_uploads/Teton%20Reflections.pdf.

Minsky HP (1975). *John Maynard Keynes*. New York, Columbia University Press.

Minsky HP, Papadimitriou DB, Philips RJ and Wray LR (1993). Community development banking: A proposal to establish a nationwide system of community development banks. Public Policy Brief No. 3, Levy Economics Institute at Bard College, Annandale-on-Hudson, NY, January.

Morris S and Shin HS (2003). Liquidity black holes. Cowles Foundation Discussion Paper No.1434, Cowles Foundation for Research in Economics, Yale University, New Haven, CT, September.

Ostry JD, Ghosh AR, Habermeier K, Chamon M, Qureshi MS and Reinhardt DBS (2010). Capital inflows: The role of controls. IMF Staff Position Note SPN/10/04, International Monetary Fund, Washington, DC, 19 February.

Pasinetti L (1997). The social burden of high interest rates. In: Arestis P, Palma G and Sawyer M, eds., *Capital Controversy, Post-Keynesian Economics and History of Economics.* London and New York, Routledge: 511–514.

Persaud A (2008). How risk sensitivity led to the greatest financial crisis of modern times, 7 October. Available at: http://www.voxeu.org/index.php?q=node/2101.

Pozsar Z, Adrian T, Ashcraft A and Boesky H (2010). Shadow banking. Federal Reserve Bank of New York, Staff Report No. 458, July.

Reddy YV (2011). Financial crisis and financial intermediation: Asking different questions. Paper presented at the Conference on Macro and Growth Policies in the Wake of the Crisis. Washington, DC, 7–8 March. Available at: http://www.imf.org/external/np/seminars/eng/2011/res/pdf/yvrpresentation.pdf.

Reinhart C and Rogoff K (2008). Is the 2007 U.S. Sub-Prime Financial Crisis So Different? An International Historical Comparison. *American Economic Review,* 98(2): 339–344, April.

Ricks M (2010). Shadow banking and financial regulation. Columbia Law and Economics. Working Paper No. 370, 30 August.

Shin HS (2010). Procyclicality and Systemic Risk: What is the Connection? Available at: http://www.princeton.edu/~hsshin/www/ProcyclicalityandSystemRisk.pdf.

Siegel DE (2002). Legal Aspects of the IMF/WTO relationship: The Fund's Articles of Agreement and the WTO Agreements. *The American Journal of International Law,* 96(3): 561–599.

Sorkin A (2010). Big, in Banks, Is in the Eye of the Beholder. *The New York Times,* 18 January. Available at: http://www.nytimes.com/2010/01/19/business/19sorkin.html?ref=business.

Tobin J (1984). On the efficiency of the financial system. In: Jackson PM, ed., *Policies for Prosperity: Essays in a Keynesian Mode,* 282–295. Cambridge, MIT Press.

Tucker T (2010). The WTO conflict with financial transactions taxes and capital management techniques, and how to fix it. Memorandum, *Public Citizen,* Washington, DC, 9 July. Available at: http://www.citizen.org/documents/MemoonCapitalControls.pdf.

UNCTAD (*TDR 2006*). *Trade and Development Report, 2006. Global partnership and national policies for development.* United Nations publications, Sales No. E.06.II.D.6, New York and Geneva.

UNCTAD (*TDR 2009*). *Trade and Development Report, 2009. Responding to the global crisis: Climate change mitigation and development.* United Nations publications, Sales No. E.09.II.D.16, New York and Geneva.

UNCTAD (2009). *The Global Economic Crisis: Systemic Failures and Multilateral Remedies.* New York and Geneva, United Nations.

Wallach L and Tucker T (2010). Answering critical questions about conflicts between financial reregulation and WTO rules hitherto unaddressed by the WTO Secretariat and other official sources. Memorandum, *Public Citizen,* 22 June. Available at: http://www.citizen.org/documents/Memo%20-%20Unanswered%20questions%20memo%20for%20Geneva.pdf.

World Trade Organization (2010). Financial services, Background Note from the Secretariat, S/C/W/312, S/FIN/W/73. Available at: http://www.fiw.ac.at/uploads/media/JM_-_financial_serv_-_final-REV1_01.pdf.

Zysman J (1983). *Governments, Markets and Growth: Finance and the Politics of Industrial Change.* Ithaca, NY, Cornell University Press.

Chapter V

FINANCIALIZED COMMODITY MARKETS: RECENT DEVELOPMENTS AND POLICY ISSUES

A. Introduction

Recent developments in primary commodity prices have been exceptional in many ways. The price boom between 2002 and mid-2008 was the most pronounced in several decades – in magnitude, duration and breadth. The price decline following the eruption of the current global crisis in mid-2008 stands out both for its sharpness and for the number of commodities affected. Since mid-2009, and especially since the summer of 2010, global commodity prices have been rising again. While the oil price increases up to April 2011 were modest compared with the spike in 2007–2008, food prices reached an all-time high in February 2011.

Such wide fluctuations in the international prices of primary commodities can have adverse effects for both importing and exporting countries and firms. The economic and social impacts of price changes generally depend on the specific commodity, but typically, they tend to be stronger in developing than in developed countries at both macro- and microeconomic levels. Many developing countries depend heavily on primary commodities for a large share of their export revenues, while others are net importers of food and/or energy commodities.

Net commodity importing countries tend to experience a deterioration in their terms of trade and

current account balances as a result of global price hikes. These countries often spend a larger proportion of their foreign exchange earnings on the increased bill for essential commodity imports at the expense of other imported items, including capital and intermediate goods that are necessary inputs to enable diversification of their domestic economies. At the microeconomic level, surges in the prices of food and energy commodities have severe impacts on the most vulnerable households. Indeed, the high prices can be disastrous for the poor in developing countries who spend 60–80 per cent of their total income on food (FAO, 2008). This impact raises grave humanitarian concerns, but there are also longer term economic and social repercussions, as spending is switched to less nutritious foods and away from education and health.

Additionally, and this applies also to middle-income countries, significant increases in the import prices of essential primary commodities with a very low price elasticity of demand contribute to inflation and reduce the demand for domestically produced goods. If the negative impacts of commodity price movements on domestic producers and consumers are to be mitigated by fiscal measures – such as a reduction in taxes or import duties levied on food, or an increase in food subsidies – the budgetary costs will have to be met by cuts in other public spending. Such cuts are likely to have adverse effects on economic development. Alternatively, increased budgetary costs may require more government borrowing, which would heighten the public debt burden without strengthening the economic base for future tax receipts.

For primary commodity exporters, on the other hand, price hikes of those commodities imply revenue gains. However, depending on the specific commodity, the kind and degree of foreign control over production and distribution, and rent-sharing arrangements, a large proportion of those gains may not result in income gains for the exporting country, but may instead accrue to transnational corporations. This is often the case in the mining and hydrocarbon industries. Sharp increases in foreign exchange revenues as a result of surging export prices also pose problems for macroeconomic management in the exporting country. As expenditures on imports may not increase at the same pace as export earnings, the exchange rate will tend to appreciate, with attendant adverse effects on the competitiveness of domestic firms in markets where they compete with foreign suppliers – an effect often referred to as the "Dutch disease". At the same time, sharply rising domestic demand may generate additional inflationary pressure if domestic supply is unable to grow at the same pace. This pressure can be managed, as discussed in the next chapter, but it requires a proactive macroeconomic policy that may be challenging for several countries.

Sharply falling prices cause an immediate deterioration in the terms of trade, balance of payments and income growth of those countries that are heavily dependent on exports of primary commodities. Moreover, to the extent that government budgets depend on revenues from commodity exports, contractionary fiscal adjustments, or, if spending levels are to be maintained, greater debt financing may become necessary. Individual producers will often incur financial difficulties as a result of prices falling beyond the level required to cover their production costs.

The extent to which price developments at the global level are transmitted to the national level will depend on how deeply domestic markets are integrated with international markets, and on the effectiveness of domestic price support measures in dampening the impact of the international price movements on domestic prices.[1] During the 2007–2009 price hike and subsequent decline, there were fairly significant variations in the speed and degree to which world price movements of various products were felt in different regional and local markets. These differences can be explained by the diverse policy responses and degree of market openness, as well as by compensating exchange rate movements (see, for example, Robles and Torero, 2009; and Minot, 2010).

From a commodity-specific perspective, market structures have a considerable impact on the pass-through of international price changes, because in monopsonistic markets higher international prices do not always result in better prices for producers. This may explain why local producers might suffer more from higher prices of the commodities they use as inputs, such as fuel, than they gain from rising international prices of the commodities they produce themselves (see, for example, Bargawi, 2009).

Apart from adjustment problems resulting from strongly rising or falling prices, heightened price volatility can have serious economic repercussions. Excessive price fluctuations foster uncertainty and disrupt the forecasting abilities of the various economic actors. This uncertainty about the validity of the price signals emanating from international commodity markets adds to the lack of transparency of those markets. In such an environment, it becomes extremely difficult and risky to plan the quantity and composition of production, choose inputs and decide on investments in productive capacity. This is true particularly for agricultural activities where production cycles are long. Similar problems arise for producers who use primary commodities as production inputs.

The volatility of market prices has differed across commodity groups. Food commodities have experienced dramatic price hikes, and, probably due to their social implications, have often caused greater concern than the price gyrations of other commodity groups. However, market price volatility has been

> Excessive price fluctuations foster uncertainty about the validity of the price signals emanating from international commodity markets and add to the lack of transparency of those markets.

more pronounced for metal and energy commodities and for non-food agricultural commodities (see chart 1.4 in chapter I). Primary commodity markets have always exhibited greater price volatility than the markets for manufactures (*TDR 2008,* chap. II). Commodity-specific shocks, especially on the supply side of agricultural commodities, have generally played a key role in this respect. However, the frequent and wide price fluctuations that have been observed in the markets for many commodity groups since 2007, particularly in oil and agricultural markets, have been unprecedented, and in many instances they have had no obvious link to changes on the supply side.

The commodity price boom between 2002 and mid-2008 and the renewed price rise of many commodities since mid-2009 have coincided with major shifts in commodity market fundamentals. These shifts include rapid output growth and structural changes, both economic and social, in emerging-market economies, the increasing use of certain food crops in the production of biofuels and slower growth in the supply of agricultural commodities. However, these factors alone are insufficient to explain recent commodity price developments. Since commodity prices have moved largely in tandem across all major categories over the past decade, the question arises as to whether the very functioning of commodity markets has changed.

> The greater participation of financial investors may have caused commodity markets to follow more the logic of financial markets than that of a typical goods market.

Against this background, the French Presidency of the G-20 has made the issue of commodity price volatility a priority of the G-20 agenda for 2011, since excessive fluctuations in commodity prices undermine world growth and threaten the food security of populations around the world (G20-G8, 2011). These fluctuations are seen as being related to the functioning of financial markets and the regulation of commodity derivatives markets.[2] Indeed, a major new element in commodity markets over the past few years is the greater presence of financial investors, who consider commodity futures as an alternative to financial assets in their portfolio management decisions. While these market participants have no interest in the physical commodity, and do not trade on the basis of fundamental supply and demand

relationships, they may hold – individually or as a group – very large positions in commodity markets, and can thereby exert considerable influence on the functioning of those markets. This financialization of commodity markets has accelerated significantly since about 2002–2004, as reflected in the rising volumes of financial investments in commodity derivatives markets – both at exchanges and over the counter (OTC).

While the growing participation of investors in primary commodity markets is generally acknowledged, there has been considerable debate in recent years as to whether this has raised the level and volatility of commodity prices. Some authors consider broad-based changes in fundamental supply and demand relationships as the sole drivers of recent commodity price development, and argue that the greater participation of financial investors in commodity markets has actually moderated price swings (see, for example, Sanders and Irwin, 2010). Others argue that the financialization of commodity markets tends to drive commodity prices away from levels justified by market fundamentals, with negative effects both on producers and consumers (see, for example, Gilbert, 2010a; Tang and Xiong, 2010).

The issue of financialization of commodity markets was discussed by UNCTAD in its *Trade and Development Report 2008* (*TDR 2008*: 24–25), followed by a more detailed analysis in its Task Force Report (UNCTAD, 2009) and *TDR 2009*. These earlier discussions started from the observation that international commodity prices, equity prices and the exchange rates of currencies affected by carry-trade speculation had moved in parallel during much of the period of the commodity price hike in 2005–2008, during the subsequent sharp correction in the second half of 2008, and again during the rebound phase in the second quarter of 2009. *TDR 2009* concluded that a detailed empirical analysis of the link between speculation and commodity price developments was difficult due to the limited transparency and level of disaggregation of existing data. Nevertheless, that report provided some evidence that the activities of financial investors had substantially amplified commodity price movements. The strongest evidence was the high correlation between commodity prices and prices on other markets, such as equity markets and currency markets, where speculative activity played a major role.[3] As a result, commodity price risk hedging had become more complex and expensive, and often unaffordable for commercial users in developing countries. Moreover, the signals emanating from commodity exchanges had become less reliable as a basis for investment decisions and for supply and demand management by producers and consumers. At the time it was unclear whether financial investors would continue to consider commodities as an attractive asset class, given that the trading strategy of index investors had proved to be strongly dependent on specific conditions to be profitable. But it was expected that financial investors would move away from investing passively in indexes towards a more active trading behaviour, and that they would continue to amplify price movements (*TDR 2009: 79*). The report suggested that it would be desirable to broaden and strengthen the supervisory and regulatory powers of mandated commodity market regulators, who, in turn, would require more comprehensive trading data.

Meanwhile the debate has evolved. In reviewing recent developments in the functioning of commodity markets, this chapter pays particular attention to the crucial role of information flows in the trading decisions of financial investors that follow a more active strategy, compared with the relatively passive investment behaviour of traditional index investors which were the focus of *TDR 2009*. It also documents new empirical evidence regarding the impact of the behaviour of financial investors on international commodity price formation, complementing the evidence provided, for example, by UNCTAD (2011).

The chapter sets out to show that the trading decisions of market participants are determined not only by information on the fundamentals of a specific commodity market, but also by considerations relating to portfolio management and to profit opportunities that may arise from simply following a trend – factors totally unrelated to commodity market fundamentals. Under these circumstances it is difficult for market participants in commodity futures exchanges and OTC markets, but also for producers and consumers of the underlying physical commodity, to determine to what extent price developments accurately reflect information about fundamentals, which in any case is not always easy

to obtain or reliable. Trading decisions are thus taken in an environment of considerable uncertainty, where engaging in "herd behaviour" can be considered perfectly rational.

Thus, the greater participation of financial investors may have caused commodity markets to follow more the logic of financial markets than that of a typical goods market. In the latter, price discovery is based on information from a multitude of independent agents who act according to their own individual preferences. In typical goods markets, profit opportunities arise from individual, pioneering action based on the private, circumstantial information of market participants.

By contrast, in financial markets, especially those for assets which fall in the same broad risk category (such as equities, emerging-market currencies and, recently, commodities), price discovery is based on information related to a few commonly observable events, or even on mathematical models that mainly use past – rather than only current – information for making price forecasts. In such markets, the most profitable behaviour is often to follow the trend for some time and to disinvest just before the rest of the crowd does so. Acting against the majority, even if justified by accurate information about fundamentals, may result in large losses. A high correlation between returns on investment in commodities and those on other asset classes indicates that such behaviour has become widespread in commodity markets, thereby increasing the risk of commodity price bubbles. Perhaps most importantly, the fact that some countries have tightened monetary policy in reaction to price pressure stemming from commodity price hikes, which may well be speculative bubbles, indicates a worrisome aspect of financialization that has so far been underestimated, namely its potential to inflict damage on the real economy induced by sending the wrong signals for macroeconomic management.

Section B of this chapter discusses the recent evolution of the financialization of commodity markets. Section C investigates the trading behaviour of different types of commodity market participants and how their position-taking can cause asset prices to deviate from fundamental values. It argues that herd behaviour reduces the information content of prices, and increases the risk of commodity prices being subject to speculative bubbles and high volatility. Section D takes a closer look at the overall impact of financialized markets on commodity price developments. It finds that financial investors in commodities are increasingly motivated by the search for yield. As a result, they are likely to continue to treat commodities as an asset class for portfolio management purposes in spite of the decline in benefits from diversifying into investment in commodities, which gave them the initial impetus to engage in commodity markets. Section E discusses recommendations for regulatory and policy measures to contain the impact of the financialization of commodity markets and its negative economic and social repercussions.

B. Trends and developments in financialized commodity markets

The term "financialization of commodity trading" implies the increasing roles of financial motives, financial markets and financial actors in the operations of commodity markets. Financial investors have long been active on commodity markets,[4] but financialization of those markets gained increasing momentum following the bursting of the equity market bubble in 2000. This is because, based on empirical findings derived from data for the period 1959–2004, commodities as an asset class came to be considered as a quasi-natural hedge against positions in other asset markets. Commodity futures contracts exhibited the same average returns as investments in equities, while over the business cycle their returns were negatively correlated with those on equities (Gorton and Rouwenhorst, 2006). Financial innovation has played a facilitating role, as tracking commodity indexes, such as the Standard and Poor's Goldman Sachs Commodity Index (S&P GSCI), is a relatively new phenomenon. Commodity market deregulation, such as that enacted by the Commodity Futures Modernization Act (CFMA) of 2000, was a further facilitating factor, as discussed in *TDR 2009*.[5]

It is difficult to assess the size of the financialization of commodity trading due to the lack of comprehensive data. But it is reflected, for example, in the strong increase, starting around 2002–2004,

> The share of commodity assets under management in global GDP increased more than fourfold during the period 2008–2010.

in the number of futures and options contracts outstanding on commodity exchanges and in the amount of outstanding OTC commodity derivatives. The number of contracts outstanding on commodity exchanges has continued to increase since the collapse of commodity prices in mid-2008; it is now about 50 per cent higher than in the first half of 2008, when commodity prices peaked. In contrast, the notional amount of outstanding OTC derivatives[6] has dropped to about one third, which corresponds to roughly half of its 2005–2006 level, but also to about five times its 1999 level.[7]

A number of reasons could explain the recent sharp decline in the notional value of outstanding OTC commodity derivatives. The collapse of commodity prices between mid-2008 and early 2009 to about half their previous level clearly accounts for part of this decline. A second reason could be that the financial crisis led to a greater awareness of counterparty risk, making financial investors wary of exposure in bilateral OTC deals. Third, the recent fall in recorded OTC activity probably reflects a decline in the relative importance of broad-based passive index investments by financial investors in commodities, including the use of swaps on OTC markets, and an increase in the relative importance of more sophisticated active trading strategies that emphasize the use of futures contracts traded on organized exchanges.

Chart 5.1

FINANCIAL INVESTMENT IN COMMODITIES AND EQUITIES AS A SHARE OF GLOBAL GDP, 1998–2010

(Per cent)

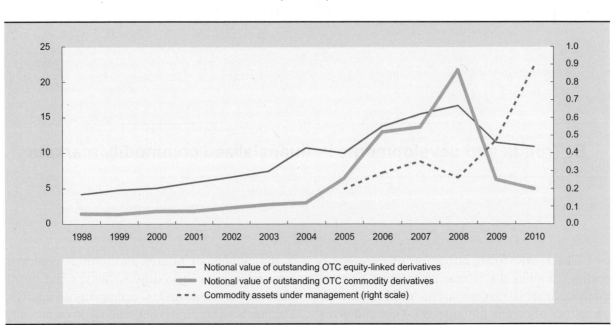

Source: UNCTAD secretariat calculations, based on Bank for International Settlements (BIS), *Derivatives Statistics*; Barclays Capital, *The Commodity Investor*, and *UNCTADstat*.

Evidence on the value of assets under management by financial investors in commodities (Barclays Capital, various issues) reveals two salient features. First, those investors have increased their involvement in commodities even more rapidly since mid-2010 than before the financial crisis when it was already growing fast. Judging from currently available data, commodity-related assets under their management recorded a historic high in March 2011, when they reached about $410 billion – about double the pre-crisis level of 2007. Second, while index investments accounted for 65–85 per cent of the total between 2005 and 2007, their relative importance has fallen to only about 45 per cent since 2008. This decline has occurred despite a roughly 50 per cent increase in the value of index investments between 2009 and the end of 2010 (UNCTAD, 2011: 16).

To put the size of financial investments in commodities in perspective, it is useful to consider how these have evolved relative to investments in equity markets, and relative to developments in the real economy. Between about 2002 and the outbreak of the financial crisis, the notional amount of outstanding OTC commodity derivatives increased considerably faster than comparable investments in equity-linked contracts. However, in 2008–2009 the value of commodity investments also declined considerably faster than that of equity-linked investments (chart 5.1). Perhaps more importantly, the share of the notional amount of outstanding OTC commodity derivatives in global gross domestic product (GDP) increased from 2–3 per cent in the early 2000s to more than 20 per cent in 2008, and, in spite of its subsequent rapid decline, this share has remained at about 5–6 per cent (i.e. roughly double its share about a decade ago). The evidence in chart 5.1 also reflects the differences in the evolution of commodity investments on exchanges and on OTC markets, noted above. It shows that the share of the value of commodity assets under management in global GDP increased more than fourfold during the period 2008–2010.

Chart 5.2

FINANCIAL INVESTMENT IN COMMODITIES AS A PROPORTION OF GLOBAL OIL PRODUCTION, 2001–2010

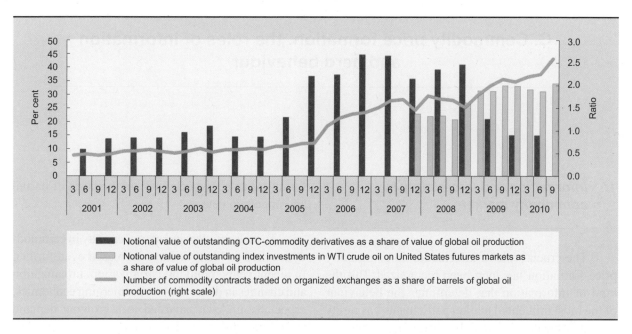

Source: UNCTAD secretariat calculations, based on BIS, *Derivatives Statistics*; Commodity Futures Trading Commission (CFTC), *Index Investment Data*; Energy Information Administration (EIA), *International Petroleum Monthly*; and *UNCTADstat*.

A comparison of the evolution of physical commodity production and financial investment in commodities sheds some further light on the size of the financialization of commodity markets. Concentrating on oil, which constitutes the largest share of total commodity production, reveals that the ratio of the notional value of total (i.e. not just oil for which no separate data are available) outstanding OTC-commodity derivatives to the value of global oil production increased about fourfold between the early 2000s and 2007–2008 when it reached 40–45 per cent (chart 5.2). A similar measure relating to financial investment in commodity futures exchanges shows that the ratio of the notional value of the outstanding index investments in West Texas Intermediate (WTI) crude oil on United States futures exchanges to the value of global oil production in 2010 was about 50 per cent higher than in 2007–2008 (chart 5.2). Given that WTI appears to have ceded part of its function as a benchmark for global crude oil prices to Brent, this increase may well be an underestimation. Indeed, the constant rise in the ratio of the number of commodity contracts traded on organized exchanges to global oil production (chart 5.2), is a clear indication that the financialization of commodity markets has been increasing unabated.

C. Commodity price formation: the roles of information and herd behaviour

1. Information and uncertainty in commodity markets

The crucial role of information in commodity price formation has long been recognized. But the kind of information that determines the behaviour of the most influential market participants has rarely been investigated. Is it mainly information about fundamental supply and demand relationships regarding a specific commodity? Or rather, is it information of a more general nature, including information about developments in the world economy and global equity and currency markets, or about long-term economic trends that would not have an immediate direct impact on the current supply and demand relationships in commodity markets?

The importance of information is closely related to the high degree of uncertainty on commodity markets. Indeed, uncertainty in decision-making has always been a defining characteristic of those markets. This is because: (i) medium- and longer-term commodity supply and demand conditions are subject to unknown factors, such as undetermined depletion rates of non-renewable resources and unknown effects of climate change on agricultural production; (ii) inventory data, which provide valuable signals for short-term price expectations, suffer from significant measurement errors (Gorton, Hayashi and Rouwenhorst, 2007; Khan, 2009); and (iii) data on current global commodity supply and demand conditions are published with long time lags and are frequently revised. Therefore, even well-informed traders must formulate price expectations on the basis of partial and uncertain data.

To make matters worse, uncertainty in commodity markets is likely to have increased even further. In recent years, rapid industrialization, urbanization and changes in dietary habits in emerging economies, especially in Asia, have led to a growing demand for commodities. And repeated news about these developments may well have signalled to market participants the beginning of a new commodity super cycle. On the other hand, it has been difficult to accurately assess the impact of these signals on the short-term evolution of supply and demand relationships. This is not only due to uncertainties about the stability of rapid economic growth in emerging economies, but also, especially, to the often wide gaps in the availability of data regarding these economies' commodity demand, supply and inventory situations.

These signals from the demand side have combined with growing doubts about the possibility of realizing technological breakthroughs any time soon, and the ability to promptly overcome emerging technological obstacles to a commensurate increase in commodity supply as had often been the case in the past. With regard to oil, for example, there has been a debate about whether the point of "peak oil" will be reached in the near future. With regard to agricultural commodities, news about slower growth of agricultural productivity has added to already growing concerns about land use, water shortages, and, more generally, the link between agricultural production and climate change. Moreover,

> The importance of information is closely related to the high degree of uncertainty on commodity markets.

first-generation biofuels, which are based on food stocks, seem to have greatly increased the relevance of information on energy for trading in agricultural commodities, and vice versa.

Low investment in production, infrastructure and research into ways of improving growth in commodity supply over the past few decades, when commodity prices were low, is identified as a major cause of these supply constraints. As a result, together with uncertainty about demand, a stream of information on the growing cost of profitable investment in sustained and resilient commodity supply growth has signalled to market participants that the probability of falling commodity prices is rather low. Consequently, information about fundamental supply and demand in commodity markets today has been supplemented by expectations that prices could rise any time soon, and for a long period of time.

In such a situation of enhanced price uncertainty, the traditional roles of commodity futures exchanges in price discovery and risk transfer have gained increasing importance. Commodity exchanges appropriately fulfil these roles if market participants, in addition to using publicly available information, trade on the basis of independent and individual information derived from an intimate knowledge of specific events relating to commodity markets and on their own plans to supply or demand commodities.

However, the financialization of commodity trading has increasingly jeopardized this function of commodity exchanges. Financial investors in commodity markets base their position-taking on risk and return considerations in which information about other asset markets and the overall economy plays a key role, as do financial motives more generally (see also box 5.1). Such trading behaviour, while relying on similar types of information, also anticipates the price impact of that information in similar ways. Taken together, the financialization of commodity trading poses the risk of herd behaviour and of self-fulfilling prophecy due to the pecuniary power of these market participants.

Even more worrying is the fact that herding fundamentally changes the behaviour of markets and the role that information plays in determining the right prices. As discussed in some detail in the following section, herd behaviour raises questions as to whether price determination is really based on the collection of vast amounts of independent and individual information about market-specific supply and demand relationships. It is also questionable whether market participants that are subject to herding actually bring liquidity to the market. A liquid market is one where many different participants with different sets of information and preferences are able to find counterparts who are willing to accept an offer to sell or buy because they have a different view of how a market is evolving. The textbook ideal of an atomistic goods market would be characterized by such conditions. By contrast, a market with a strong element of herding, which may be defined as the tendency of individuals to mimic the actions of a larger group rather than acting independently and on the basis of their own information, will not display those characteristics of differing views and dispositions.

2. Herd behaviour

Herd behaviour can take various forms (chart 5.3), and may be rooted in irrational behaviour, but it may also be fully rational. Early models of herd behaviour were based on assumed deviations from perfect rationality, or so-called "noise trading" (Shleifer and Summers, 1990). Investment by noise traders[8] is affected by pseudo-signals that convey no information about future returns in a specific asset market, or by changes in traders' beliefs and sentiments that are not justified by news on fundamentals. An example of pseudo-signals for positions in commodity markets is information related to other asset markets that triggers portfolio rebalancing, and hence leads to changes in investors' exposures to commodities.

> Herd behaviour may be rooted in irrational behaviour, but it may also be fully rational.

Changes in beliefs and sentiments may reflect investors' judgemental biases, such as overreacting to news or overoptimism.[9] It may also reflect the use of inflexible trading strategies, such as momentum investment or positive feedback strategies. Such strategies

Box 5.1

VIEWS OF COMMODITY MARKET PARTICIPANTS: RESULTS OF AN UNCTAD SURVEY

Interviewing commodity market participants is useful as it provides their perspectives on market developments, the process of price formation and trading strategies. It also gives an indication of how the presence of financial investors influences trading activities. Moreover, discussing regulatory issues with market participants helps in understanding potential compliance problems and unintended adverse effects of regulations on trading practices.

Between December 2010 and February 2011, the UNCTAD secretariat conducted interviews with commodity traders, financial institutions and other entities which are actively involved in the grain, cocoa, sugar and oil markets. Most of the interviewees were physical commodity traders and financial investors, such as bank and asset managers, located mainly in Geneva.[a]

Interviews with physical traders

The physical traders reported being subject to strict risk parameters set by the boards of directors of their companies. Therefore, they usually had only a marginal, if any, flat price exposure and tended to focus on spreads. The physical grain traders reported trading mainly on futures exchanges and only occasionally using OTC markets. Trading on OTC markets allowed very specific types of hedging, while the standardized specifications of futures contracts could result in mismatches with respect to desired trading patterns in terms of time and product quality. On the other hand, futures exchanges, being more liquid, made it easier to find a counterpart.

The interviews revealed that trading patterns for crude oil differ considerably from those for grains and soft commodities. Exchanges offer only a limited range of crude oil futures contracts and their specifications do not match the usual hedging requirements. Oil traders, in particular those who trade not only Brent and WTI but also a variety of other crude oils, therefore combine exchange-traded contracts (e.g. for WTI or Brent) with more specific OTC contracts to hedge their exposures. The OTC contracts they usually use are swaps (e.g. WTI against Dubai) for which the price is determined on the basis of quotations of a price reporting agency (e.g. Platts or Argus) that gathers information on market prices of different crude oil qualities in different locations on a daily basis.

Physical traders reported using a wide range of information from different sources, including: (i) publicly available statistics from official sources (such as the United States Department of Agriculture) and publicly available reports (both on "fundamentals" and financial markets); (ii) private information obtained from internal company sources; and (iii) communication with other market participants.

All the interviewed physical traders agreed that medium- to long-term price trends were driven by market fundamentals, and that this was the reason why they focused on fundamental supply and demand relationships in their market analyses. But they also mentioned the impact of the growing activities of financial players on trading in commodity markets, as evidenced by rising volumes of financial investments. Moreover, financial investors increasingly entered the physical markets by opening their own trading desks or devising physically backed exchange-traded funds (ETFs) or exchange-traded notes (ETNs). Banks were also reported to engage in commodity production.

There was a consensus that financial traders could not move prices in the long run, but they could cause substantial price volatility and distortions in the short run. Reasons cited for their strong short-term price effects were the enormous volumes of their trades, as well as the timing of their investments and withdrawals of funds. Further, most financial traders did not know the specifics of the respective commodity markets, but based their trading decisions on other considerations, algorithms (including high frequency trading) and/or their desired portfolio structure. The traders suggested that volatility made price discovery more difficult in all commodity markets and it also made hedging more difficult and expensive, as large price movements might trigger margin calls. Nevertheless, the overall assessment of financial players' presence in commodity markets was ambiguous. Most traders also saw benefits. They emphasized that speculators or financial investors provided liquidity which was indispensable for hedging.

The majority of traders agreed that further regulation was needed, particularly in Europe, in order to increase transparency. Adhering to reporting standards in Europe, such as those followed by the

Box 5.1 (concluded)

Commodity Futures Trading Commission (CFTC) for the United States, would be a big step forward. Nevertheless, they believed CFTC reporting was insufficient, with some flaws in its classification of traders. While most traders considered position limits to be necessary, they deemed them ineffective because they could easily be circumvented. For example, positions could be split between trading venues or between different subsidiaries of the same group, transactions could be carried out in the OTC market, and financial entities could acquire physical trading companies thereby obtaining exemptions from certain regulatory rules. While most of the respondents welcomed the Dodd-Frank Act, they regretted that similar regulatory reforms were not being extended to at least the other G-20 countries.

Interviews with financial traders

The financial traders interviewed were a less homogeneous group than the physical traders. While their experiences and views diverged significantly, most of them reported using all available financial instruments and trading both at exchanges and OTC, depending on the needs of their clients. They mentioned using official statistics about fundamentals most often, with a strong focus on crude oil. One banker at a large financial institution, focusing on the oil market, reported paying much more attention to financial markets than to fundamentals. For him, the most relevant information was the United States dollar exchange rate, "sentiments in equity and commodity markets" and CFTC data. He was mainly concerned with what the market was thinking. For the longer term, GDP growth, the Purchasing Managers Index (PMI), unemployment data and other economic indicators were other sources of information. He emphasized that financial investors tended to look at financial data, although they generally based their judgement on fundamentals.

Abundant liquidity due to the expansionary monetary policies adopted by many countries over the past two years and relatively low returns on other assets were mentioned as major reasons for recent investments in commodities. The respondents believed that the effects of financial investors' activities on prices were limited to the short term. One asset manager said that speculators could corner the market in the short run because of their strong financial power, but all interviewed financial traders were of the opinion that financial investors could not drive up commodity prices in the long run.

Regarding regulation, the interviewed financial traders agreed that more transparency was a key issue in commodity markets, and that position limits could easily be circumvented.

Interviews with brokers and consultants

The interviewed brokers and consultants operated close to the market, even though their business activities did not usually include position-taking. They observed that financial investors had come to play an increasingly important role in commodity markets, and that the recent emergence of ETFs caused commodities to be traded in the same way as equities. They noted that one consequence of financial investors' presence in commodity markets was increased volatility and divergences between the cash and the futures markets; another was the increasing short-run correlation between commodity and other financial markets.

Overall, the commodity market participants were in general agreement that: (i) due to their financial strength, financial investors could move prices in the short term, leading to increased volatility, which may harm markets and drive hedgers with an interest in the physical commodities away from commodity derivatives markets; (ii) in the medium to long term, commodity prices were determined by fundamental supply and demand relationships, even though the type of information used by market participants suggested that financial market information was much more important for trading decisions than was commonly acknowledged; (iii) market transparency needed to be increased, especially in Europe, where significant gaps existed, but also in the OTC market in the United States; and (iv) care should be taken with regard to introducing general bans (e.g. of high-frequency trading) and position limits, given that regulations were rather difficult to enforce.

---

[a] For detailed information about the methodology, choice of participants and questionnaires used, see UNCTAD, 2011.

Chart 5.3

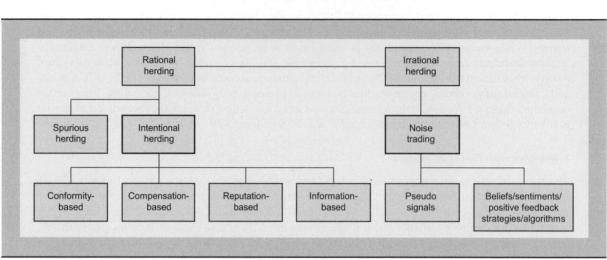

DIFFERENT TYPES OF HERD BEHAVIOUR

Source: UNCTAD secretariat, derived from Bikhchandani and Sharma, 2001; and Shleifer and Summers, 1990.

assume that past price developments carry information on future price movements, giving rise, for
example to trend chasing. This will result in buying
after prices rise and selling after prices fall, independently of any changes in fundamentals. Simple types
of positive feedback strategies are closely related to
technical analysis that utilizes past price and position data to assess patterns of activity that might be
helpful in making predictions. More sophisticated
trading techniques use computer-based algorithms
that strictly adhere to a predetermined set of rules.
Algorithms analyse market activity and produce
signals for trading strategies, established either on
the basis of past trading and price developments or
on the basis of the anticipated reactions by other
algorithmic traders to current market developments.[10]
Given that several positive-feedback and algorithmic
traders may use similar rules, they run the risk of collectively generating market movements that they then
individually identify and follow. Moreover, to the
extent that algorithms follow statistical strategies and
monitor market developments across different asset
markets, such rules will cause price signals to spill
over from, for example equity or currency markets
to commodity markets, even when there is no change
in the fundamentals on commodity markets.

Herd behaviour can also be fully rational. In
this context, "spurious herding" should be distinguished from "intentional herding" (Bikhchandani

and Sharma, 2001). Spurious herding describes
situations where agents facing similar decision-
making problems and information sets take similar
decisions. Given that this type of herding reflects
agents' common reaction to public information, it is
entirely compatible with the efficient market hypothesis (EMH), provided the information refers to the
fundamentals of the specific market.[11] Fundamentals-
driven spurious herding in commodity investment
can arise if, for example, a significant share of international supply is suddenly cut off, as occurred with
oil during the Gulf war in 1990–1991 and with rice
following the imposition of export bans by various
large exporting countries in 2008.

Intentional herding may be based on four
motives (Devenow and Welch, 1996; Bikhchandani
and Sharma, 2001). First, conformity-based herding
relates to an alleged intrinsic preference of individuals for conformity. Second, reputation-based herding
relates to imitation which arises when traders and
their employers are uncertain about the traders' abilities (Scharfstein and Stein, 1990). Traders who doubt
their own abilities will not take positions contrary to
those taken first by other traders, even if their own
information would lead them to do otherwise. Such
doubtful traders, by imitating others, will thus avoid
being considered low-skilled if taking positions
contrary to those taken by others turned out to be
loss-making. If the common decision turns out to be

loss-making, it will be attributed to a change in general market sentiment, rather than to poor individual judgement or performance.[12] Third, closely related to reputation-based herding is compensation-based herding. This refers to agents who invest on behalf of others and whose compensation schemes and terms of employment provide incentives that reward imitation. For example, risk-averse investors will align their positions with benchmark portfolios if their compensation increases when they do better than the benchmark but decreases when they underperform the benchmark. Compensation rules based on such relative performance measures can lead not only to herding but also to risk-loving investors taking excessively high risk.

> Information-based herding refers to imitation in situations where traders believe that they can glean information by observing the behaviour of other agents.

Fourth, information-based herding is perhaps the most important motive for intentional herding. It refers to imitation in situations where traders believe that they can glean information by observing the behaviour of other agents. In other words, investors converge in their behaviour because they ignore their private information signals (Hirshleifer and Teoh, 2003). As explained by Banerjee (1992), who calls this effect "herd externality", information-based herding exerts an external influence on decision-making processes and causes position-taking that is not in line with an agent's own information. Position-taking based only on other peoples' previous actions will lead to price changes without infusing any new information into the market. A sequence of such actions causes a so-called "informational cascade" (Bikhchandani, Hirshleifer and Welch, 1992) – a snowballing effect which will eventually lead to self-sustaining asset price bubbles.

> The speed at which opportunities for high return and incentives to engage in herding behaviour decline, and the extent to which herding affects prices, depend on the degree of uncertainty.

Informational cascades are most likely to occur when market participants are unequally informed and ignore the accuracy of other peoples' information. Market participants who judge their own information to be incomplete and approximate will tend to delay their decision-making, preferring to act only once they can make inferences on the basis of other, supposedly better informed and more experienced people's actions. This implies that position-taking by investors that make early decisions is likely to determine which way followers will decide to move, and it therefore has a disproportionate impact on price changes. This will be the case even if the assessments of the early movers are incorrect, based on overconfidence or on idiosyncratic motives (such as readjusting portfolio composition following price changes in other asset markets). It also implies that an increase in the number of market participants and in trading volume does not necessarily indicate that market transactions are based on more information.

Informational cascades are not limited to one market; they can spread across different asset markets if prices in those markets are correlated. Herding across markets can lead to excess correlation (i.e. a level of correlation between asset prices that exceeds the correlation between their fundamentals) (Cipriani and Guarino, 2008). Moreover, informational cascades and information-based herding can be altered or even reversed by a publicly observable shock or by the release of public information (Hirshleifer and Teoh, 2003). Both events add new information to the market. They also allow followers to assess the accuracy of the information on which they assumed precursors were acting, as they know that the newly released public information is more accurate than what they had inferred from the actions of the early position-takers. Such new public information may consist of easily observable events (such as extreme weather events that impact harvests) or well-researched findings by specialized agencies.[13] However, it may also consist of newsletter recommendations by investment banks or other analysts who base those recommendations on models that are proprietary knowledge.[14] This means that the methodologies that produce those findings are impossible to verify, and therefore their objectivity is open to question, which can lead to scepticism about the objectivity of such findings. Unless investment banks keep research and trading departments completely independent of one another, such predictions may well be an attempt to ignite a new informational cascade and be combined with the analysts' prior position-taking, the returns on which will increase through imitation by others.

If herd behaviour has an impact on price movements, early movers will benefit the most. Imitation by followers will gradually become less profitable the longer it is delayed, and the greater is the probability that newly arriving public information will alter the informational cascade. The speed at which opportunities for high return and incentives to engage in herding behaviour decline, and the extent to which herding affects prices, depend on the degree of uncertainty. When it is difficult to differentiate between uninformed traders, who are herding, and informed traders, market participants may believe, mistakenly, that most traders possess accurate information. The ensuing confusion allows uninformative herd behaviour to have dramatic effects on prices, and can lead to bubbles and excessive volatility (Avery and Zemsky, 1998). Such situations occur when the prevalence of uninformative noise trading is underestimated, either because of a lack of data on the relative importance of different trader categories, or because of the mistaken belief that trading from rational arbitrageurs will instantaneously balance any price effect from trading that is not based on fundamentals, as discussed below.

The persistence of price deviations from fundamental values caused by herding depends on the speed and efficiency of arbitrage. An arbitrage opportunity offers the possibility of earning a positive return at no risk. Such a possibility will arise if prices diverge from fundamental values or across markets on which identical assets are traded. According to the EMH, an arbitrageur will detect such an opportunity immediately, act upon it and thereby make such price divergences disappear. Given that all these actions are assumed to happen instantaneously, the notion of unlimited arbitrage implies the absence of any arbitrage opportunities. It also implies that irrational position-taking that drives prices away from fundamental values will not make profits, and hence be forced out of the market. Thus, from an EMH perspective, speculation must be stabilizing (Friedman, 1953).

> There are limits to arbitrage so that price deviations from fundamental values may persist.

However, there is widespread agreement that there are limits to arbitrage (for a recent survey, see Gromb and Vayanos, 2010). For example, rational arbitrageurs may not be able to correct mispricing, either because of risk aversion (de Long et al., 1990a) or because of capital constraints. Shleifer and Vishny (1997) argue that arbitrageurs may need to use other people's capital. In that case, if the market initially moves against the arbitrageurs, they will need to report intermediate losses. This will cause the arbitrageurs' client investors to withdraw part of their money, forcing the arbitrageurs to liquidate their positions at a loss. Given that arbitrageurs are aware of this possibility, they will exploit arbitrage possibilities only partially.

What is more, it may not even be optimal for rational arbitrageurs to counter the position-taking of irrational investors that follow positive feedback strategies. Instead, they may want to buy and push up the price following some initial good news, thereby providing an incentive for feedback traders to aggressively buy the asset. This reaction by feedback traders will allow the rational arbitrageurs to sell their positions at a profit. But in so doing, profitable arbitrage also contributes to the movement of prices away from fundamentals and feeds short-term price bubbles (de Long et al., 1990b).

> It may not be optimal for rational arbitrageurs to counter the position-taking of irrational investors that follow positive feedback strategies.

Bubbles may persist even over a substantial period of time. This can occur when a bubble bursts only once a sufficient mass of arbitrageurs have sold out and rational arbitrageurs know that there will always remain some agents that are overconfident or pursue momentum-trading strategies. Rational arbitrageurs who know perfectly well that the bubble will eventually burst then need to weigh the risk of overestimating the remaining number of irrational traders, which would imply losing all capital gains by getting out too late, against maximizing profits by riding the bubble as it continues to grow and exiting from the market just prior to the crash. New public information about market fundamentals would allow rational arbitrageurs to synchronize their exit strategies, and thus make the bubble burst earlier (Abreu and Brunnermeier, 2003). The same may be true for disclosure of data that indicate the true number of remaining "irrational traders".[15]

Taken together, the above discussion shows that financial investors have a variety of motives, either rational or irrational, for engaging in trend-following and momentum trading, as well as for engaging in arbitrage only to a limited extent. As a result, asset prices can deviate from fundamental values, at least for some time. The discussion also shows that herding can have sizeable detrimental effects since it reduces the information content of prices, and because, being based on only a little information, existing price levels become very sensitive to seemingly small shocks. Consequently, commodity prices risk being subject to speculative bubbles, moving far from fundamental values and displaying high volatility.

An empirical assessment of herd behaviour is notoriously difficult. It is particularly difficult to test models of informational herding where intentional herding must be distinguished from spurious herding (which reflects a common and simultaneous reaction to public announcements). Observing market transactions and prices cannot enable an identification of the factors that ultimately determine the decisions of market participants. This is because actions do not reveal the kind of private information or signals that agents receive and that motivate their position-taking. For commodity markets, this problem is exacerbated by the fact that data on market transactions are available only in aggregated form and at relatively long intervals, and it is often difficult to pinpoint what constitutes fundamentals and how they should be measured and quantified. This is the case especially when a variety of big events may change fundamentals gradually but permanently, such as climate-change-related events, peak-oil concerns, or increasing demand in emerging markets.

Nonetheless, despite these difficulties, a small number of studies have attempted to test for herd behaviour in commodity markets. In principle, trend-following and momentum trading in commodity markets can be examined by regressing speculative position-taking over price changes on previous days. In addition to the unresolved question as to which trader categories should be appropriately considered as "speculators", daily data on speculative position-taking are not publicly available. Therefore, using confidential position data from the CFTC, Irwin and Yoshimaru (1999), based on data for 1988–1989, and Irwin and Holt (2005), based on data for 1994, found evidence for the existence of trend-following or momentum trading strategies, but they also found that these had relatively low price effects. However, the data used in these studies are dated, and thus cannot reveal the effects of herding behaviour over the past few years.

> Herding can have sizeable detrimental effects, since it reduces the information content of prices, and because, being based on only a little information, existing price levels become very sensitive to seemingly small shocks.

A recent study by Gilbert (2010a) uses data for seven commodities (aluminium, copper, crude oil, maize, nickel, soybeans and wheat) and looks for evidence of trend-following behaviour in the pricing process itself. Using monthly data for the period 2000–2009, the study finds a single eight-month bubble for copper (February to October 2006), as well as one-month bubbles for aluminium (May 2006) and nickel (April 2007). Using daily data for the period 2006–2008 for crude oil and the three grains, and for the period 2000–2008 for the non-ferrous metals, the study finds clear evidence of price bubbles in copper trading (2004, 2006 and 2008), weak evidence for crude oil (first half of 2008), nickel (January–March 2007) and soybeans (early 2008), and clear evidence of the absence of any bubble for aluminium, maize and wheat.

In a further step, Gilbert (2010a) estimates the price impact of index-based investment by comparing the actual price developments with those that would have prevailed had there been no index investment. The evidence indicates that for crude oil, index investors accounted for about 3–10 per cent of the price increases in 2006–2007, but that their impact rose to 20–25 per cent in the first half of 2008. Their impact on grain prices is estimated to have been about half that for oil. Gilbert (2010a: 26, 28) concludes that during the first half of 2008 "index-based investment generated a bubble in commodity futures prices" and that overall "it would be incorrect to argue that high oil, metals and grains prices were driven by index-based investment but index investors do appear to have amplified fundamentally-driven price movements." However, Gilbert emphasizes that the results must be interpreted with caution because the identification of bubbles may be sensitive to the selection of the initial date for the sample,[16] and also because explosive price developments may indicate buoyant fundamentals (i.e. spurious herding) rather than speculative bubbles.

Phillips and Yu (2010), on examining the migration of price bubbles across equity, bond, currency and commodity markets (for cocoa, coffee, cotton, crude oil, heating oil, platinum and sugar) since the mid-1990s, find a sequence of price bubbles, each followed by a financial collapse. They show that

with the eruption of the subprime crisis in August 2007, financial investment transited from the United States housing and mortgage markets onto certain commodity and foreign-exchange markets. Growing awareness of the serious impact of the financial crisis on real economic activity, both in the United States and globally, caused the general collapse of asset prices in mid-2008. With respect to commodity prices, their results point to a price bubble in crude oil between March and July 2008, in heating oil between March and August 2008, and in platinum between January and July 2008, while no price bubbles are detected in cocoa, coffee, cotton and sugar. This supports the finding of Gilbert (2010a), whose product sample overlaps with that of Phillips and Yu (2010) only with respect to crude oil, for which he identifies a price bubble during the first half of 2008. Phillips and Yu (2010: 26) explain that early phases of speculative bubbles are characterized by only small price divergences from fundamental values, and are therefore statistically indistinguishable. This may explain why the estimated date for when the oil price bubble begun is somewhat later than the observed beginning of the rapid price increase.

D. Financialized markets: overall impact on commodity price developments

1. Trader positions and commodity prices

Several categories of market participants are active in commodity markets. These categories are usually distinguished on the basis of the reports on traders' positions published in anonymous and summary form by the CFTC, which is the institution mandated to regulate and oversee commodity futures trading in the United States.

The CFTC distinguishes three main trader categories.[17] One of them refers to market participants

with a commercial interest in commodities, and includes producers, merchants, processers and users. The other two categories refer to financial investors, and include "swap dealers", who may be considered a broad approximation of index traders,[18] and money managers. The money manager category includes a range of investors, such as hedge funds and institutional investors that adopt different trading strategies based on macroeconomic fundamentals, detailed commodity research, algorithmic trading or trend following, and general financial portfolio diversification considerations. Thus they are able to adjust their exposure in commodity markets according to changes in asset prices with a view to stabilizing the structure of their portfolios.

Scepticism is often expressed with regard to the link between financial investment and commodity price developments. The more theoretical aspects of this issue are addressed in box 5.2; the empirical evidence, comparing price developments and net financial positions of different trader categories, reveals a number of salient features (see chart 5.4A–C for maize, crude oil and copper).[19] First, market participants that have an interest in physical commodities (i.e. the category producers, merchants, processors, users (PPMU)) almost always take net short positions (i.e. they are net sellers of futures and options contracts). Second, financial investors almost always take net long positions (i.e. they are net buyers of futures and options contracts). Third, overall, the comparison provides only scant evidence of a *long-running* correlation between price changes, on the one hand, and index positions for cotton and maize or swap dealer positions for copper and crude oil, on the other. While there are clearly periods and commodities where positions and prices moved in tandem, especially during the price collapse in 2008 and occasionally during the previous price upturn, there are other times when positions did not increase during periods of rapid price appreciation. For example, in the wheat market, neither money managers nor index traders increased their positions during the price hike from mid-2007 to the end of the first quarter of 2008 (see *TDR, 2009*). By contrast, there appears to have been a positive correlation between market positions and maize prices during the same period (chart 5.4A). In the oil market, when oil prices rose almost continuously from the beginning of 2007 through the second quarter of 2008, money managers' positions exhibited strong volatility (chart 5.4B). Nevertheless, all graphs in chart 5.4 indicate some *short-term* correlation between index or swap positions and price changes, as peaks and turning points seem to have occurred at around the same time.

Fourth, there has been a fairly close correlation between money manager positions and prices of all the three commodities shown in chart 5.4. The occurrence of position peaks and troughs in the net positions taken by money managers closely mirrors those in prices – especially for copper and crude oil, but also for maize – even when seen over longer time periods.

Fifth, and perhaps most importantly, there has been an especially close correlation between changes in oil prices and in money managers' positions since about mid-2009 (chart 5.5), when commodity prices appear to have ended their downward overshooting and started to stabilize, followed by the onset of a price surge in mid-2010. This close correlation is reflected in a correlation coefficient as high as 0.82 for crude oil for the period July 2009–June 2011 (and even 0.87 for the period December 2010–June 2011). In the last week of February 2011, the ratio of long to short positions[20] taken by money managers more than doubled, followed by a rally in the oil price from about $99 per barrel to about $106 per barrel in the first week of March 2011. Similarly, in the first two weeks of May 2011, this ratio of money managers' positions almost halved, accompanied by a drop in oil prices from about $112 per barrel to about $97 per barrel.[21] While the sequence of events and the close correlation between changes in positions and prices are indicative of a price impact by money managers, a more formal testing of the direction of causality is not possible due to the shortness of the period during which these events occurred and the fact that position data are available only at weekly intervals.

> There has been a close correlation between changes in oil prices and in money managers' positions since about mid-2009.

Regarding copper, the long-standing correlation between money managers' net positions and prices, which can be observed for much of the period since mid-2009, appears to have broken down in late 2010–early 2011, when prices rose sharply before stabilizing at a high level while money managers' net positions remained relatively stable before dropping sharply in May 2011 (chart 5.4C). However, there is anecdotal evidence that this breakdown in the correlation is due to a new form of commodity investment by money managers, which involves holding physical copper inventories that remain unrecorded in official statistics.[22] Some of those copper inventories were stocked in European warehouses but unrecorded in the London Metal Exchange's official inventory data. A large number of these warehouses have come to

Box 5.2

THE INTERPLAY BETWEEN PHYSICAL AND FINANCIAL MARKETS[a]

Attempts to link financial investment and commodity price developments are often met with scepticism. Some critics suggest there are "logical inconsistencies" in the argument that financial investment can affect physical market prices on the grounds that financial investment only relates to futures market activity and does not concern spot market transactions.

Irwin, Sanders and Merrin (2009) and Sanders and Irwin (2010) have synthesized a number of arguments presented by the sceptics. The sceptics' main point is that financial investors are involved only in financial transactions in futures markets. Accordingly, any causal link between their position-taking and physical market prices would be complex and unclear. In particular, they argue that financial investors hold neither physical inventories nor futures contracts up to expiration and, therefore, do not participate in the delivery process where, the sceptics claim, price discovery takes place. However, as argued by Gilbert (2010b: 409), in many markets price discovery at delivery is often the mechanism of last resort, whereas the bulk of transactions are executed at futures prices with reference to the price of nearby futures contracts (i.e. contracts that are approaching maturity). For maize, soybeans and wheat, the empirical findings in Hernandez and Torero (2010) support earlier evidence by indicating that changes in futures prices lead changes in spot prices more often than not. Regarding crude oil, the International Energy Agency (IEA, 2009: 107) describes how common trading practices cause the futures market to determine the price at which physical delivery occurs. Moreover, financial investors may not hold physical inventories themselves, but their investments bid up the prices of futures contracts, which in turn provides an incentive for others to hold inventories.

The observation that no such accumulation of inventories occurred during the commodity price hike of 2006–2008 relates to a second argument introduced by Krugman (2008) with regard to oil prices. According to him, speculative activity that drives prices above fundamental equilibrium levels will cause market imbalances and excess supply, which eventually must result in inventory accumulation. This reasoning would suggest that, since reported oil inventories did not increase, speculation cannot have played a role in causing oil prices to rise in 2008. However, Khan (2009: 5) argues that data on oil inventories are notoriously poor. Data on oil inventories are not reported by most non-OECD countries, which account for almost half of the world demand for crude oil and include very large consumers such as China, and neither is the data on oil stored in tankers, thus underestimating the inventory data reported by OECD countries. Hence, no strong inferences can be drawn from such data. More fundamentally, Krugman's argument may take time to play out. As also argued by Gilbert (2010b: 408), rising demand for futures contracts tends to cause a price increase in long-dated futures contracts, which in turn will provide an incentive to accumulate inventories. But given the very low short-run price elasticity of commodity supply, the short-term inventory supply curve is close to vertical. As a result, only an increase in spot prices can meet the increase in demand. Over time, production and consumption will respond to

be owned by banks and trading companies. Since such inventories are either not at all or only partially reported in official inventories, it gives banks an informational advantage over other market participants regarding the "real" amount of inventories. Ownership of these warehouses also allows banks to occupy most of the suitable storage space, so that a shortage of storage facilities for owners of futures contracts makes it more difficult and expensive for

those owners to take delivery. As a result, they may prefer rolling over their contracts which they perhaps hold with the very bank that tightens the supply of suitable storage space.

There is similar anecdotal evidence which suggests that some financial institutions imported copper into China to stock in warehouses outside the reporting system. This copper was then purportedly

Box 5.2 (concluded)

the higher price, inventories will gradually accumulate and prices will decline. In the interim, however, a commodity price bubble may well occur.

Third, Irwin, Sanders and Merrin (2009) and Sanders and Irwin (2010) argue that even if financial investors had an impact on prices and drove a wedge between market prices and fundamental values, the resulting arbitrage opportunity would cause rational traders to trade against wrongly informed financial investors and bring market prices back to fundamental values. However, as mentioned earlier, there is widespread agreement that there are limits to arbitrage.

The possibility that even rational traders may feed short-term price bubbles also casts doubt on a fourth argument made by Irwin, Sanders and Merrin (2009) and Sanders and Irwin (2010), namely that there is no indication of excessive speculation. Estimating the appropriate level of speculation relative to hedging demands on the basis of positions taken by different trader categories, they argue that the level of speculation in commodity futures markets was within historical averages during the period 2006–2008. However, judging the appropriate level of speculation merely by the number of positions, rather than by the kind of information and expectations on the basis of which such positions are taken, ignores the possibility that fundamental values may not always be the only consideration, even for rational speculators. Moreover, even on the basis of such numerical comparisons, Büyüksahin and Robe (2010: 15) conclude that "[e]xcess speculation increased substantially, from about 11% in 2000 to about 40-50% in 2008."

Fifth, focusing on index investment, Irwin, Sanders and Merrin (2009) and Sanders and Irwin (2010) argue that, if index investors in futures markets had caused the commodity price hike, the prices of commodities not included in such indexes (such as iron ore, onions and rice) should not have risen. However, Tang and Xiong (2010) suggest that different mechanisms accounted for the price increases of these two groups of commodities, and that those commodities included in indexes were affected by financial investors.

Finally, Irwin, Sanders and Merrin (2009) and Sanders and Irwin (2010) argue that if index investment affects prices, its effect should be uniform across markets for the same relative position size, and they claim that this is not the case. However, the common effect of index investment occurs simultaneously with commodity-specific supply and demand shocks. These idiosyncratic shocks may counter or reinforce the common effect, depending on commodity-specific circumstances, and may do so in varying degrees. Moreover, the size of index trader positions in a specific market does not depend on the size or the liquidity of that market, but rather on the specific composition of the index that the trader follows.

---

[a]   This text is drawn from Mayer, 2011.

---

used as collateral to speculate in other markets, or to re-export to countries that host London Metal Exchange licensed warehouses, or, in the case of some Chinese enterprises, to finance corporate development. According to these sources, securing bank loans by borrowing against copper as collateral is cheaper than conventional borrowing because the monetary tightening measures taken by the Bank of China at that time only affected non-collateralized lending.[23] Tying up physical copper inventories in warehouse financing arrangements signals market tightness and supports prices, especially when those inventories are not entered into official inventory statistics. If this anecdotal evidence is accurate, it could also explain why China's copper imports remained high even during the run-up to the price peak in February 2011. Moreover, it would illustrate how schemes operated by financial investors can distort

Chart 5.4

PRICES AND NET LONG FINANCIAL POSITIONS, BY TRADER CATEGORY, SELECTED COMMODITIES, JUNE 2006–JUNE 2011

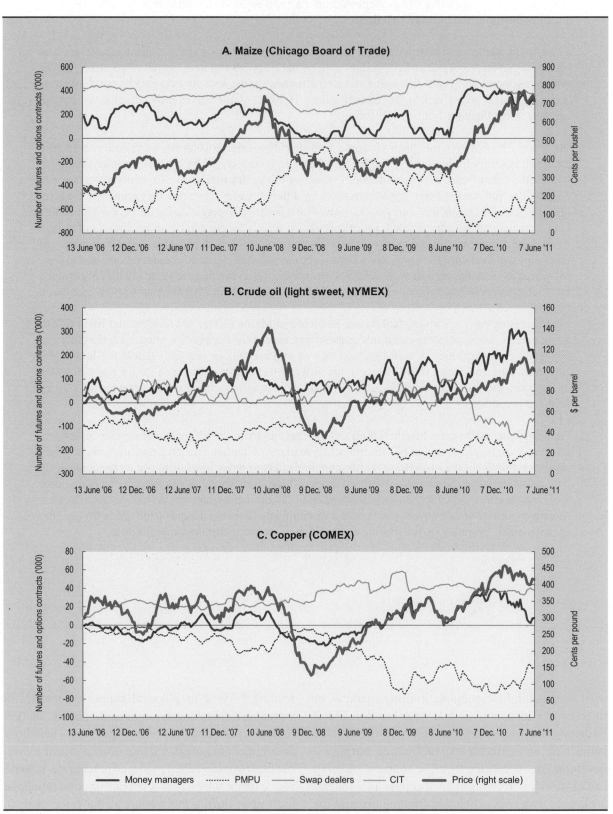

Source: UNCTAD secretariat calculations, based on CFTC, *Commitment of Traders*; and Bloomberg.
  Note: CIT = commodity index traders; PMPU = producers, merchants, processors, users.

Chart 5.5

MONEY MANAGER POSITIONS AND CRUDE OIL PRICES, JANUARY 2009–JUNE 2011

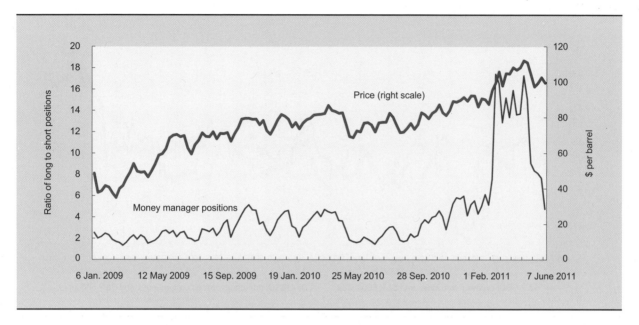

Source: UNCTAD secretariat calculations, based on CFTC, *Commitment of Traders*; and Bloomberg.

data which, in principle, are expected to reflect only market fundamentals. By doing so, such schemes further contribute to difficulties in disentangling the price effects of changes in market fundamentals and in financial investments.

2. Price effects of financial investors across different asset markets

As mentioned earlier, financial investors have sought to diversify their portfolios by investing in commodities as part of a broader strategy aimed at reducing their concentration on equities, bonds and currencies. This change in strategy is based on historical evidence which suggests that the broader portfolio composition improves risk-return performance. Using data for the period 1959–2004, Gorton and Rouwenhorst (2006: 1) argue that "the risk premium on commodity futures is essentially the same as equities, [whereas] commodity futures returns are negatively correlated with equity returns and bond returns. The negative correlation between commodity futures and the other asset classes is due,

in significant part, to different behavior over the business cycle."[24]

(a) Price developments on commodity and equity markets

Recent evidence suggests that adding commodity futures to their portfolios no longer helps investors hedge against equity market risk. The process of deleveraging that began with the onset of the current crisis in mid-2008 and affected all asset markets resulted in a strongly positive correlation between the returns on commodity futures and those on equity investments (chart 5.6).

From the evidence related to broad-based investment in commodities, reflected in chart 5.6, it would seem that this positive correlation emerged only in the run-up to the current financial crisis, and that it became accentuated only in its aftermath. However, it is well known that the greatest benefits from investing in commodity futures are derived from diversifying across not only different commodity categories but also individual commodities (Erb and Harvey, 2006; Basu and Gavin, 2011). Because the

Chart 5.6

CORRELATION BETWEEN COMMODITY AND EQUITY INDEXES, 1986–2011

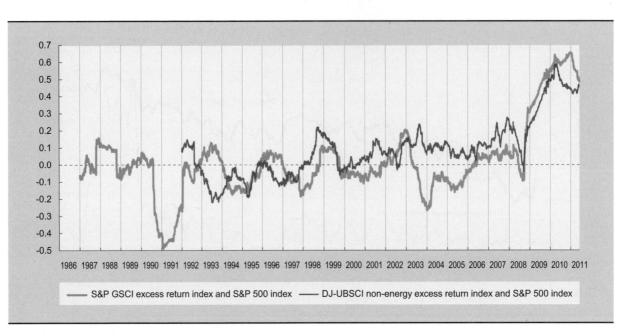

Source: UNCTAD secretariat calculations, based on Bloomberg.
  Note: The data reflect one-year rolling correlations of returns on the respective indexes on a daily basis.

S&P GSCI (chart 5.6), is heavily weighted in energy, it is possible that the evolution of this correlation during the early 2000s, and especially its strongly negative numbers in 2003, was strongly influenced by events in energy markets, and especially by the war in Iraq in 2003. Thus it is useful to examine the correlation between returns on non-energy commodity futures and equity investments. That correlation began to rise already in the early 2000s, well before the onset of the current crisis, as reflected in chart 5.6.[25] This evidence supports findings by Tang and Xiong (2010) that "the introduction of index trading led to a rise in the correlation among the individual commodities included in an index, thus reducing or even eliminating the gains to diversification within individual index funds" (Basu and Gavin, 2011: 46). But it also shows that the crisis-related deleveraging process implied a further shift, and gave rise to a strongly positive correlation between returns on commodity futures and equity investments.

> A tightening of monetary conditions is unlikely to eliminate the financialization of commodity markets.

The positive correlation between returns on investment in commodity futures and in equity reached a peak in late 2010–early 2011. This positive correlation is largely attributed to the second round of monetary easing initiated by the United States Federal Reserve in the third quarter of 2010.[26] Based on this perception, it is widely believed that a tightening of the United States monetary stance could go a long way towards increasing the cost of funding that underlies financial investments and that has led to an inflation of asset prices across financial markets. However, the fact that there have been two shifts, rather than just one, in the correlation between returns on commodity investment and equity investment (as shown in chart 5.6), indicates that monetary easing may only have accentuated cross-market correlations. By the same token, a tightening of monetary conditions would merely have eliminated the source of the second shift in the cross-market correlation, but it is unlikely to have eliminated the financialization of commodity markets altogether and brought cross-market correlations back to where they were at the end of the 1990s.

(b) Commodity markets and world business cycles

The most recent decline in world industrial output is known to have been by far the strongest of all downward cycles in the past 35 years. The sharp drop of 12 per cent from the peak makes other recessions seem like mild slowdowns in comparison (chart 5.7). However, in spite of the very low utilization of global industrial capacities at the beginning of 2009, the upward pressure on prices in commodity markets was much stronger when compared with similar positions of earlier business cycles – a development often overlooked by observers. Anticipation of recovery by the financial markets seems to have played a disproportionately significant role in this current bout of commodity price inflation.

The strong impact of financial investors on prices, which may be considered "the new normal of commodity price determination", affects the global business cycle in a profound way. Commodity price inflation inhibits a smooth recovery to the extent that it provokes a premature tightening of monetary policy. Indeed, it has played an important role in the tightening of Chinese and Indian monetary policies since early 2010, and in the first interest rate hike since the beginning of the crisis by the European Central Bank (ECB) in April 2011.

To illustrate this "new normal", it is useful to compare four global business cycles that have occurred since the mid-1970s.[27] Global economic activity may be assumed to be reflected in the monthly time series of world industrial production published by the Netherlands Bureau for Economic Policy Analysis (CPB).[28] The periods of recessionary troughs can be identified by applying the method proposed by Bry and Boschan (1971) in BUSY, the European Commission's software package. It shows four recessions for the period 1975–2010, with peaks in March 1980, October 1981, December 2000 and March 2008, and respective troughs in September 1980, December 1982, December 2001 and February 2009. To illustrate the cyclical response of financial markets, the series for industrial production were normalized by their respective troughs.

Chart 5.7

DYNAMICS OF WORLD INDUSTRIAL PRODUCTION AFTER THE PEAKS OF FOUR BUSINESS CYCLES

(Index numbers, peak = 100)

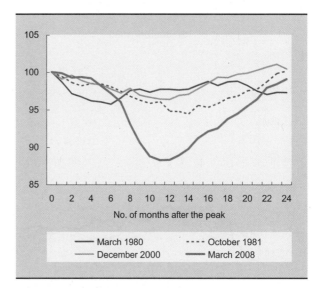

Source: UNCTAD secretariat calculations, based on data from the CPB Netherlands Bureau of Economic Policy Analysis; and OECD.

Note: The dates in the legend refer to the peak of each business cycle.

A comparison of the business cycles shows that commodity prices and equity prices moved in opposite directions during the previous identified business cycles (chart 5.8). In contrast, there has been a remarkable synchronization of equity price and commodity price movements in the most recent cycle.

This finding supports the results obtained by the International Monetary Fund (IMF, 2010: 31–33) in a similar exercise for developed economies. In interpreting the results, the IMF warns against considering the increased synchronization of commodity and equity prices as evidence of the financialization of commodity markets, and affirms that "increased co-movement, however, likely reflects the sensitivity of both markets to broader economic developments" (IMF, 2010: 33). However, such an interpretation neglects to take into account the low level of capacity utilization in the wake of the "Great Recession" of 2008 and 2009. Low capacity utilization, in principle, implies a low level of industrial use of commodities, and thus a low level of demand for commodities by their largest consumers. Under such circumstances,

Chart 5.8

EVOLUTION OF COMMODITY AND EQUITY PRICES BEFORE AND AFTER TROUGHS OF SELECTED BUSINESS CYCLES

(Index numbers; business cycle trough = 100)

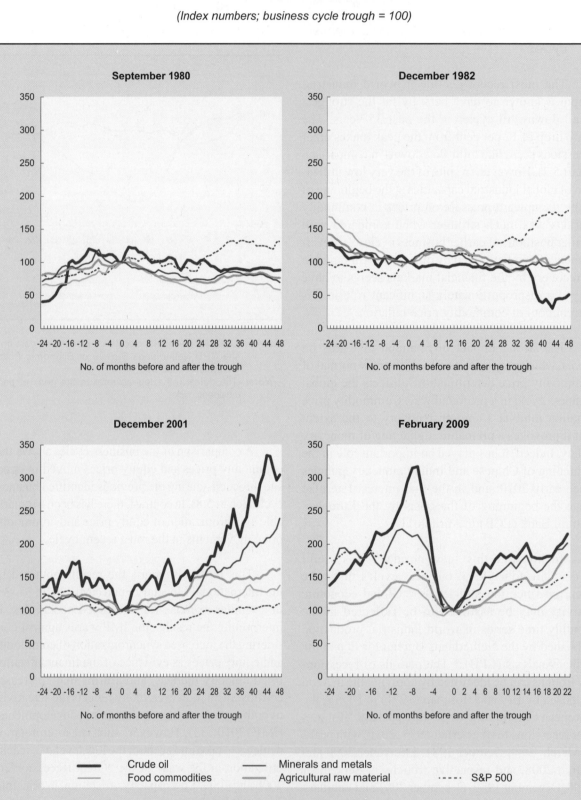

Source: UNCTAD secretariat calculations, based on Bloomberg; and *UNCTADstat.*
   Note: The dates refer to the corresponding troughs in the business cycle.

steadily rising prices of commodities, even ahead of the rebound of stock market indices, appear to be related more to an anticipation of a future revival of demand than to actually rising demand. The most plausible explanation for such price behaviour is financialization, which eventually, in 2008, led to an overshooting of commodity prices in both directions over their fundamental levels.

The fact that monetary policy reacts to price pressure stemming from rising commodity prices, rather than to bottlenecks in industrial production, points to a worrying aspect of the impact of financialization that has so far been underestimated, namely its capacity to inflict damage on the real economy as a result of sending the wrong signals for macroeconomic management.[29] This is an important reason why more effective regulation of commodity markets is necessary so as to restore an environment of sound price signals and efficient allocation of resources in today's modern market economies.

Monetary policy reacting to price pressure stemming from rising commodity prices points to a worrying aspect of the impact of financialization that has so far been underestimated ...

(c) Price developments on commodity and currency markets

The greater positive correlation between returns on commodity futures and investments in other asset classes is not limited to equity markets; it also appears to have emerged, perhaps even more strongly, with respect to currency markets.

It is common knowledge that dollar-denominated commodity prices often move in the opposite direction to the dollar exchange rate. This is because a lower value of the dollar makes commodities cheaper in non-dollar consuming areas, thereby increasing incentives to consume, while it reduces the revenues of producers in non-dollar areas, thereby decreasing incentives to produce (*TDR 2008*). This mechanism may well explain part of the increased negative correlation between returns on the S&P GSCI excess return index and the dollar exchange-rate index, which began in the early

... namely its capacity to inflict damage on the real economy as a result of sending the wrong signals for macroeconomic management.

2000s (chart 5.9). Indeed, this is consistent with the growing demand for commodities from emerging economies in a period of dollar depreciation, as noted by Tang and Xiong (2010: 11). However, the abrupt character and sizeable size of this shift, the fact that it occurred in 2002–2003 and that another similar shift occurred in the wake of the current crisis suggest that other factors have contributed to this development.

An additional factor is most probably the emergence of the dollar as a funding currency of carry-trade speculation.[30] In 2002–2004 (i.e. when the financialization of commodity trading began), there was a substantial change in the correlation between returns on commodity futures and the exchange rates of currency pairs that have been popular with carry-trade speculators (as shown in chart 5.9 for a number of selected currency pairs). This positive correlation clearly increased in the run-up to the peak in commodity prices in 2008, became fairly strong after the onset of the current crisis when there was a general process of deleveraging across different asset classes, and was further accentuated following the adoption of the second round of monetary easing by the United States Federal Reserve in the second half of 2010. However, since May 2011, when the Federal Reserve announced that it would not extend this second round beyond the month of June, these correlations have declined, returning to levels that existed prior to monetary easing. This evidence reinforces the point made above, that the effect of phasing out monetary easing in the United States on cross-market correlations of returns on financial investment merely led to a return to the situation that prevailed prior to the onset of the financial crisis but it is unlikely to have eliminated the price effects of the financialization of commodity trading altogether.

Taken together, the above evidence for the past two decades indicates that, relative to the historic importance of strategic portfolio diversification considerations, the search for higher yields has come to

Chart 5.9

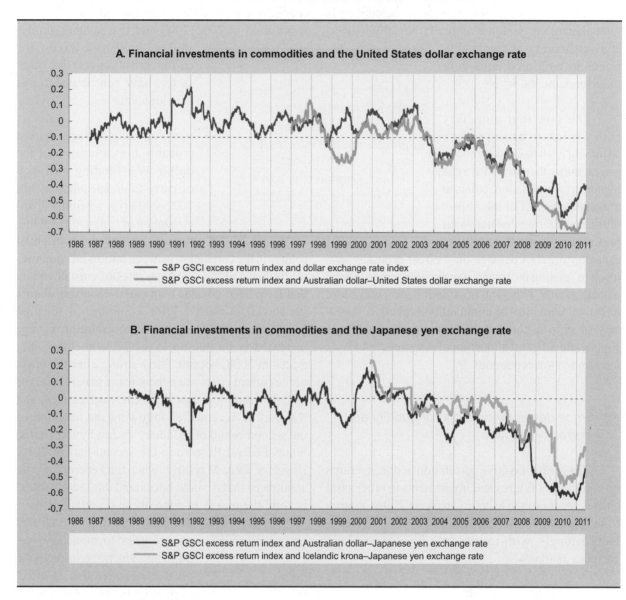

CORRELATION BETWEEN FINANCIAL INVESTMENTS IN COMMODITIES AND SELECTED EXCHANGE RATES, JANUARY 1986–JUNE 2011

A. Financial investments in commodities and the United States dollar exchange rate

S&P GSCI excess return index and dollar exchange rate index
S&P GSCI excess return index and Australian dollar–United States dollar exchange rate

B. Financial investments in commodities and the Japanese yen exchange rate

S&P GSCI excess return index and Australian dollar–Japanese yen exchange rate
S&P GSCI excess return index and Icelandic krona–Japanese yen exchange rate

Source: UNCTAD secretariat calculations, based on Bloomberg.
Note: The data reflect one-year rolling return correlations on a daily basis.

play an even greater role for financial investors in commodities. Given the historic diversification and hedging characteristics of financial investment in commodities, this search for higher yields through such investment may have been based on the illusion that it offered risk-free profit maximization. The recognition that the diversification benefit of commodity investment may have been overestimated could limit the amount of broad-based index investment in commodities. However, it could also increase the attractiveness of more targeted investment, such as through indexes limited to specific categories of commodities or even individual commodities. The recent increase in popularity of exchange-traded products, many of which are related to indexes that replicate the return on selected commodities, may indicate that financial investors are not yet ready to turn their back on commodities as an asset class.

E. Policy considerations and recommendations

Over the past decade or so, commodity price developments have been associated with marked shifts in supply-demand balances. For many commodities, demand has grown faster than supply resulting in declining stocks, especially of food commodities. In such a situation, any sudden increase in demand or major shortfall in supply – or both – rapidly leads to significant price increases. This is of particular significance for food commodities because of the immediate economic and social impacts of food price hikes on the most vulnerable populations. Hence, emergency food reserves need to be established or rebuilt to an adequate level in order to moderate the impact of temporary shortages, and be rapidly available to provide emergency food relief to the most vulnerable at times of food crisis.

Increased private and public investment aimed at higher production and productivity is a key element in any long-term solution to redressing the decline in commodity supply-demand balances. This will require the provision of more official development assistance to agriculture in developing countries. At the same time, it is necessary to provide incentives to increase production and productivity, particularly in food commodities in these countries. The incentives could include a reduction of trade barriers and domestic support measures in developed countries.

Apart from emergency measures designed to assist the most vulnerable and the long-term measures designed to tackle excessive commodity price volatility on the supply side, there is also a need to find ways of making commodity markets less prone to behavioural overshooting increasingly brought about by the financialization of those markets. For this, it is necessary to consider how the functioning of commodity futures exchanges and off-exchange OTC trading could be improved in a way that would enable those trading venues to better fulfil their role of providing reliable price signals to commodity producers and consumers, or at least prevent them from sending the wrong signals. Accordingly, the remainder of this section examines: (i) how information and transparency in physical commodity markets could be improved; (ii) how transparency in commodity futures exchanges and OTC markets could be improved; (iii) the need for tighter regulation of financial investors; and (iv) the need for broader policy measures, including schemes designed to avert or deflate speculative bubbles.

1. Improving transparency in physical commodity markets

Greater transparency in physical markets would enable the provision of more timely and accurate information about commodities, such as spare capacity and global stock holdings for oil, and for agricultural commodities, areas under plantation, expected harvests, stocks and short-term demand forecast. This would allow commercial market participants to more easily assess current and future fundamental supply and demand relationships. Insufficient availability of such information, at present, makes it difficult for commercial participants to determine whether a specific price signal relates to changes in fundamentals or to financial market events. This lacuna also facilitates the intentional introduction of misinformation, such as "research-based" price forecasts by big banks that have taken financial positions in commodity markets, and therefore could potentially reap financial benefits if those forecasts turned out to be accurate. Overall, the availability of high-quality and consolidated, timely information on fundamental supply and demand relationships in physical markets would reduce uncertainty, and thus the risk of market participants engaging in herd behaviour.

To achieve greater transparency in physical markets, there needs to be better producer-consumer dialogue and improved data collection, analysis and dissemination. Oil-market participants benefit from the JODI Oil World Database, which covers production, demand, refinery intake and output, imports, exports, closing stock levels and stock change (see also box 5.3). While this initiative has greatly improved transparency in the oil market, several gaps remain. For example, the data are published at monthly intervals and therefore do not provide adequate information about short-term events on which active financial investment strategies are based. Perhaps more importantly, the database does not include information on spare capacity. As pointed out by Kaufmann (2011), it was the lack of information on spare capacity in non-OPEC oil-producing countries that caused the sudden slowdown in the growth rate of non-OPEC crude oil supply after 2004, which caught market participants by surprise and ignited a sudden increase in oil prices. Also, the database does not include information on oil bunkered in cargo vessels, which is often owned by the private sector, so that associated information is commercially sensitive and remains undisclosed. Collecting and publishing this information in aggregate form in such a way that its proprietary character would not be jeopardized would be an important step towards greater transparency, and could help prevent sharp, short-term price changes.

There is even less transparency in the physical market for agricultural commodities. While information is available from various sources, the capacity of countries and international organizations to produce consistent, accurate and timely agricultural market data and analysis remains weak. Indeed, extreme weather events in both 2007–2008 and 2010 took the international community by surprise. The resulting increased uncertainty may well have induced misinformed, panic-driven price surges and triggered increased speculative investment that amplified the price increases.

Perhaps the major gap in transparency in the physical market for agriculture is the paucity of information on stocks. There are multiple reasons for this, a major one being that a significant proportion of stocks is now held privately, which makes such information commercially sensitive. As a result, stock data published by international organizations are an estimated residual of data on production, consumption and trade. Enhanced international cooperation could improve transparency by ensuring public availability of reliable information on global stocks. The JODI oil database could serve as a model for such an initiative, as outlined in the proposal to the Agricultural Market Information System (AMIS) put forward by the inter-agency report on agricultural price volatility prepared for the French Presidency of the G-20 (FAO et al., 2011).

2. Improving transparency in commodity futures exchanges and OTC markets

The ability of regulators to understand what is moving prices and to intervene effectively depends upon their ability to understand the market and to collect the required data. However, at present, comprehensive data are not available, particularly for off-exchange derivatives trading. While traders on OTC markets benefit from the information that traders on organized futures exchanges provide for price discovery, they do not provide comparable information of their own.

As expressed in paragraph 13 of the Leaders' Statement of the G-20 Summit in Pittsburgh in September 2009, as well as in the conclusions of the G-20 Task Force on Commodity Futures Markets

> Apart from emergency measures to assist the most vulnerable and long-term measures to increase investment ...

> ... there is also a need to improve market transparency, tighten regulation of financial investors and consider schemes designed to avert or deflate speculative bubbles.

Box 5.3

SOURCES OF INFORMATION ON COMMODITY MARKET FUNDAMENTALS[a]

Different types of commodity market information are available, including: (i) raw data from databases that cover prices, production, consumption, stocks and trade; (ii) processed data based on analyses of market trends and monitoring of the current situation; and (iii) forecasts or projections of the short- medium- and long-term evolution of market fundamentals. The frequency of such information varies widely, depending on the data source, and can range from daily to annual. However, most publicly available information from official sources is based on monthly data.

There is ample information on physical commodity markets, but it is not easy to obtain in a systematic way. A number of sources provide the same information, but in different formats. It therefore takes time and expertise to find out which are the most useful, relevant and reliable sources of information required for a specific commodity. Even from a single source the multiplicity of information can make it rather cumbersome to access the relevant information. The various sources of information include official sources, such as international organizations and study groups, organizations specializing in specific commodities or groups of commodities, and governments of countries which are key players in the commodity markets, such as Australia and the United States, as well as private sources. In many cases, even from official sources, information is not publicly available and can be accessed only against payment.

For agricultural commodities, the Food and Agriculture Organization of the United Nations (FAO) is the main international source for data, market analysis and monitoring of market fundamentals. The FAO publishes data at different frequencies for various agricultural commodities, most of which can be accessed on the Internet from its World Food Situation portal. Moreover, a national source, the United States Department of Agriculture (USDA), is among the most comprehensive sources of information on global agricultural markets. Its information is particularly important because the United States is a major producing country for a number of agricultural commodities such as cotton, maize, wheat and soybeans. Therefore, information about changes in estimations on crops in that country can have a strong impact on global markets. The Comité du Commerce des céréales, aliments du bétail, oléagineux, huile d'olive, huiles et graisses et agrofournitures (COCERAL) publishes forecasts for grain and oilseed crops for the countries of the European Union (EU).

Regarding crude oil, the most comprehensive source of data on production, demand, refinery intake and output, imports, exports, closing stock levels and stock changes is the Joint Organisations Data Initiative (JODI). This initiative comprises seven partner organizations: Asia-Pacific Economic Cooperation (APEC), EUROSTAT, the International Energy Agency (IEA), the International Energy Forum (IEF), the Latin American Energy Organization (OLADE), the Organization of the Petroleum Exporting Countries (OPEC) and the United Nations Statistics Division (UNSD). More than 90 countries, representing about 90 per cent of global oil supply and demand, participate in JODI. The JODI Oil World Database is freely accessible and is updated monthly. Information on the major energy-consuming countries is available through the *Oil Market Report* online service of the IEA, which provides a monthly assessment of supply, demand, stocks, prices and refinery activity. On the supply side, OPEC's *Monthly Oil Market Report* covers major issues affecting the world oil market, the outlook for crude oil market developments for the coming year, and a detailed analysis of key developments impacting oil market trends in world oil demand, supply and the oil market balance. At the national level, the United States Energy Information Administration provides a variety of data and analyses on the situation in United States and global energy markets, at different time frequencies. In the private sector, the widely used, publicly available annual *Statistical Review of World Energy* produced by British Petroleum provides objective data about world energy, markets and trends. In addition, Cambridge Energy Research Associates (IHS CERA) is a leading adviser to different clients, including international energy companies, governments, financial institutions and technology providers. It delivers critical knowledge and independent analyses on energy markets, geopolitics, industry trends and strategy.

Platts is a leading global provider of energy information, and among the foremost sources of benchmark price assessments in the physical energy markets. Argus publishes a full range of business intelligence reports, market assessments and special studies on all aspects of energy, transport and emissions markets. Commodity forecasts are also offered by companies specializing in market intelligence, such as the Economist Intelligence Unit, Business Monitor International and LMC International (agricultural commodities). In addition, the Working Group on Commodity Prices of the Association of European Business Cycle Institutes (AIECE) publishes a *World Commodity Prices* report twice a year, with price forecasts for two years.

This brief review shows that there is an abundance of data sources concerning the fundamentals of physical commodity markets. Nevertheless, a number of information gaps exist, and there are many areas in which the transparency of physical commodity markets could be improved, as mentioned in the main text.

---

[a]   This box is based on Fajarnes, 2011.

(IOSCO, 2010), transparency on OTC markets could be improved by registering contracts in a trade repository (see also the annex to this chapter).[31] This would be important especially for non-standardized, illiquid contracts where counterparty risk involves end-users of derivatives who hedge commercial risk in commodities. While such data would need to remain confidential, their availability to regulators would reduce the risk of market abuse. The rules proposed by the European Commission (EC, 2010), which, *inter alia,* envisage central clearing requirements for standardized contracts, including those involving index funds, would also help improve transparency and reduce counterparty risk. In order to capture contracts that are primarily used for speculation rather than for hedging commodity-related commercial risk, the requirements should exempt contracts relating to transactions that are intended to be physically settled.[32]

Significantly more information is available for trading on commodity futures exchanges, especially in the United States (as discussed in UNCTAD, 2011) where a substantial proportion of commodity futures trading is executed. However, on European exchanges, at present only very limited data are available for exchange trading. Therefore, transparency could be considerably improved if the European exchanges adopted reporting requirements and published aggregate position data similar to the weekly Commitment of Traders (COT) reports published by the CFTC. In addition to such aggregate data, detailed data should be made available to market authorities for transactions on exchanges, OTC markets and the related physical markets. Market authorities in different jurisdictions should cooperate and share such data.

3. Tighter regulation of financial investors

Regulation of commodity exchanges needs to find a reasonable balance between imposing overly restrictive limits on speculative position-holdings and having overly lax surveillance and regulation. Being too restrictive could impair the hedging and price discovery functions of commodity exchanges. On the other hand, if surveillance and regulation are not strict enough, prices could move away from levels warranted by fundamental supply and demand conditions, and would thus equally impair the basic

functions of the exchanges. However, finding such a compromise has become increasingly difficult. Financial investors are increasingly engaging in physical market transactions (such as by owning warehouse inventories or even agricultural land) and physical traders are also taking financial positions more frequently, so that the difference between these two types of traders is becoming blurred.

Tighter regulation of financial investors would make it easier for regulators to intervene when they detect irregularities. In addition, similar regulations should be adopted across commodity exchanges and across countries in order to avoid regulatory migration. In this sense, regulations relating to the major commodity exchanges in Europe need to catch up with those in the United States, but both need to be stricter. Tighter regulation could include four measures:

- One measure could be the imposition of limits on the positions taken by individual market participants and those taken by market participants in the same commodity but at different trading venues.[33] Exemptions from position limits should not be granted to hedge financial risk, as is currently the case in the United States, where swap dealer exemptions (which also apply to commodity index funds) are granted with regard to positions on some agricultural commodities. The issue of position limits is currently under discussion in both the EU (EC, 2010) and the United States (for details, see the annex to this chapter). Regulatory measures relating to positions for energy commodities, especially those taken by hedge funds, are equally relevant for agricultural commodities. This is because it has been shown that hedge funds drive the correlation between equity and commodity markets, and that food prices have become more closely tied to energy prices (Büyüksahin and Robe, 2010; Tang and Xiong, 2010). However, since the limited availability of data at present makes it difficult to determine what levels would be appropriate for position limits, the introduction of such limits may take a long time. As an interim step, the introduction of position points could be considered. A trader reaching a position point would be obliged to provide further data, on the basis of which regulators would decide whether or not action is needed (Chilton, 2011).

The imposition of position limits on commodity futures exchanges and OTC markets may facilitate the role of derivatives markets in price discovery. This is because they would not only limit the size of individual financial positions, but also reduce market concentration by ensuring broad-based market participation by diverse traders with supposedly different sources of information and different views on the market. As such, position limits would increase the informational content of trading.

Position limits would apply only to financial firms but not to so-called "bona fide hedgers" that are end-users of derivatives contracts or that offer those contracts as risk-management tools to customers that have a physical exposure to commodity prices in their business operations. Making this distinction requires defining how to separate bona fide hedgers from other market participants, which poses difficult problems.[34] It is also often argued that position limits are relatively easy to circumvent (see box 5.2).

Position limits would apply only to financial firms but not to end-users of derivatives contracts.

Perhaps the greatest shortcoming of position limits is that they are unlikely to be effective when traders engage in herd behaviour. In such a situation, the herding traders combined, but none of them individually, would be able to drive price bubbles. Thus, only position limits imposed on specific categories of market participants (such as money managers) could overcome this problem.

- A second measure could be the application of the Volcker rule (which prohibits banks from engaging in proprietary trading) to commodity markets. At present, banks that are involved in the hedging transactions of their clients have insider information about commercially based market sentiment. This amounts to a conflict of interest, as they can use this information to bet against their customers. Moreover, their position-taking may provide false signals to other market participants and, given the size of some of these banks, move prices away from levels normally determined by fundamentals, in addition to provoking price volatility.

- Third, a similar rule could be applied to physical traders, prohibiting them from taking financial positions and betting on outcomes that they are able to influence due to their strong economic position in the physical markets.[35]

- Fourth, a transaction tax or a requirement to hold positions for a minimum amount of time (say a few seconds) could be established to slow down financial investors' activities, especially those related to high-frequency trading (HFT).[36] Since market participants engaged in HFT usually close their positions by the end of a trading day, they are not a reliable counterparty to hedgers that seek to transfer risk. Moreover, given that they base their position-taking on the evolution of market prices, rather than on information on underlying fundamentals, their trading adds no information. It is therefore doubtful that HFT makes any contribution to commodity exchanges' traditional roles of price discovery and risk transfer, or, indeed, that it has any economic and social utility. HFT has attracted considerable attention following allegations that it caused the so-called "flash crash" on United States equity markets on 6 May 2010. Some observers have also blamed HFT trading for the increase in price volatility on sugar markets between November 2010 and February 2011.[37] A transaction tax or a requirement for cash deposits applied more broadly to all financial investors would make position-taking more expensive the more it is leveraged (i.e. debt-financed). It would thus have similar effects as position limits, but would also pose similar definitional problems.

4. Schemes for dealing with speculative bubbles

In the past, international commodity agreements that included provisions relating to internationally held buffer stocks and/or supply controls were often used to stabilize prices. It is commonly believed that these mechanisms were not very successful in reducing price volatility. They were more effective in moderating downward price movements than price surges. When there is a price surge, a buffer stock agency can only release to the market what it has previously bought, and once its stock is exhausted there are no further means to curb price increases. Mostly for these reasons, international buffer stock mechanisms either collapsed or were replaced by agreements whose main role was to provide market information (Gilbert, 2011).

A major problem for any price stabilization mechanism is that of being able to determine an equilibrium price and establish when market prices have moved away from their equilibrium. It is generally argued that, since a buffer stock agency cannot possibly have more and better information than market participants, there is a high risk of market interventions doing more harm than good (see, for example, Wright, 2009). The virtual reserve and intervention mechanism proposed by von Braun and Torero (2008) and Martins-Filho, Yao and Torero (2011) offers one possibility of circumventing this problem.[38] These authors propose an econometric model that would identify when observed price changes are abnormally high relative to a predefined parameter, such as a 5 per cent probability that a price change of such size will occur. The occurrence of such an event would signal abnormal market developments to traders and regulators. Therefore, this scheme would not need to define an equilibrium price. Traders may react to the signal itself, which would render an intervention by authorities unnecessary. The authors suggest that if traders would not react to restore price volatility to a more normal range, an autonomous technical committee could intervene by taking short positions in futures contracts (i.e. promises to sell the commodity at a specified price at a specified date) with a view to reducing extreme price volatility. The fact that these interventions would occur in the futures markets, rather than in the physical market, implies that the agency would not incur any significant storage costs.[39]

This proposed virtual intervention mechanism would require adoption of an additional, somewhat heavy technical apparatus, the functioning of which would not be materially different from margin calls that commodity exchanges impose on a fairly routine

basis.[40] At the Chicago Mercantile Exchange (CME), for example, the risk-management and compliance unit in charge of market surveillance determines margins according to quantitative factors, such as rising price volatility, and qualitative factors such as seasonality and relevant news events. Reliance on observable factors, such as price volatility exceeding predefined limits, makes changes in margin requirements largely predictable (i.e. the signals that margin calls emit to markets are similar to those implied by the virtual intervention mechanism). While margin requirements are designed to ensure that exchanges have sufficient capital to cover the expected losses caused by trader defaults, changing margin requirements can have significant impacts on position-taking and prices. For example, the series of increases in margin requirements for silver and oil most probably played an important role in the commodity price correction in early May 2011.

> International commodity agreements were not very successful in reducing price volatility.

One problem with margin calls is that the implied increase in trading costs can force small traders to close their positions, while larger traders may be better able to pay up and maintain at least some of their positions. Thus small commercial users may be disproportionally affected by margin calls. Another problem is that margin calls follow a microprudential regulatory perspective: they protect the respective exchange against default but do not take into account their impacts on positions and prices which may cause a wave of deleveraging and unintended ripple effects across asset markets.[41]

This problem could be resolved if market authorities in charge of surveillance were mandated to intervene directly in exchange trading on an *occasional* basis by buying or selling derivatives contracts with a view to deflating price bubbles.[42] Such intervention could be considered a measure of last resort to address the occurrence of speculative bubbles if reforms aimed at achieving greater market transparency and tighter market regulation, outlined above, were either not in place or proved ineffective (for example, because of definitional problems). It could also be deployed if a possible use of margin calls (which would need to be better coordinated across exchanges) to deal with price bubbles were judged as having strongly adverse impacts on the participation of small commercial users of commodity exchanges and as posing serious risks of unintended ripple effects. While most of the trigger mechanism could be rules-based, and therefore predictable, such intervention would necessarily have some judgemental components. This is because one source of commodity price bubbles is the increased impact on commodity markets of the evolution of other asset markets, which is due to the financialization of commodity trading, and because a speculative bubble may occur gradually rather than as a result of a sudden, abnormally high price hike. If this raises doubts about the ability of market authorities or government agencies to understand and follow the market, there is no reason for those doubts, because there is no reason why their understanding should be any different from that of other market participants; in markets

As a measure of last resort to avert or deflate speculative bubbles, market authorities in charge of surveillance could be mandated to intervene directly in exchange trading on an *occasional* basis by buying or selling derivatives contracts.

that are prone to herd behaviour, they all have access to similar information, as discussed in section C above. Contrary to the other market participants, such an intervening authority or agency would have no incentive to engage in any of the forms of intentional herd behaviour discussed in section C.2 above. Rather, it could break the informational cascades that underlie herd behaviour by announcing when, in its view, prices are far out of line with fundamentals.[43] Hence, as in the case of currency markets – and, recently, the bond markets – it should be possible for market authorities or another agency to undertake occasional targeted interventions in asset markets by acting as market maker or as the one institution that is able to shock the market once it becomes evident that it has gone into an overshooting mode. ∎

Notes

1. The degree of processing of final consumption goods also affects price transmission. A lack of domestic infrastructure and generally undeveloped or inefficient market structures can also significantly obstruct price transmission due to high transport and transactions costs.

2. Commodity derivatives include futures and options contracts traded on organized exchanges, as well as forward, options and swaps contracts traded on OTC markets. A derivative is a financial asset, generally a contract between two or more parties, whose value is dependent upon or derived from one or more underlying assets, such as a commodity futures contract or a commodity index.

3. These empirical findings went counter to those of, for example IMF (2008), Kilian and Hicks (2009), Irwin and Sanders (2010) and Sanders and Irwin (2010), but more recent academic papers and analysis are increasingly supporting the view that financial investors affect commodity prices (see, for example Büyüksahin and Robe, 2010; Gilbert, 2010a; Tang and Xiong, 2010; Kaufmann, 2011; and Singleton, 2011).

4. This is evidenced by the frequently quoted examples of commodity price bubbles created by financial investors, including the tulip mania in Holland in the 1630s, the Mississippi Bubble in France and the South Sea Bubble in England in the early 1700s (Garber, 1990).

5. For a detailed discussion on the evolution of position limit exemptions for commodity index traders, see United States Senate, 2011: 82–83.

6. Notional amount refers to the value of the underlying commodity. However, since traders in derivatives markets do not own or purchase the underlying

commodity, notional value is merely a reference point based on underlying prices.

7   For further discussion, see UNCTAD, 2011.

8   Noise traders may be defined as investors who take trading decisions without the use of fundamental data. They generally have poor timing, follow trends, and over-react to good and bad news.

9   Experimental evidence on persistent judgemental errors in decision-making abounds (see, for example, Ariely, 2010).

10 High-frequency trading (HFT) is a technologically advanced method of conducting algorithmic trading at ultra-high speed. Contrary to other types of algorithmic trading, which focus on price levels and maintain positions over a period of time, HFT traders attempt to benefit from price volatility and usually close out their positions by the end of a trading day. HFT has attracted considerable attention following allegations that it caused the so-called "flash crash" on United States equity markets on 6 May 2010. Some observers have also blamed algorithmic trading for the increase in price volatility on sugar markets since November 2010 ("High-speed trading blamed for sugar rises", *Financial Times*, 8 February 2011).

11 According to the EMH investment theory, it is impossible to "beat the market" because equity market efficiency causes existing equity prices to always incorporate and reflect all relevant information. The theory states that equities always trade at their fair value on stock exchanges, making it impossible for investors to either purchase undervalued equities or sell equities at inflated prices. As such, it should be impossible to outperform the overall market through expert equity selection or market timing, and the only way an investor could possibly obtain higher returns is by purchasing riskier investments.

12 Similar mechanisms apply when investors follow the advice of analysts who overweigh public information and underweigh their own private information in their messages. Conformity to other analysts' messages increases investment in the recommended asset and the associated return. This in turn improves the analysts' reputations.

13 Casual observation suggests that reports on livestock and agricultural crops by the United States Department of Agriculture (USDA) have significant price effects.

14 Price predictions can have a significant impact if they originate from a reputed source. For example, Arjun Murti, a Goldman Sachs analyst, gained considerable fame between 2004 and 2008 when his successive predictions of ever higher oil prices appeared to be vindicated by market developments. According to media reports, other investors questioned whether Goldman Sachs' own traders were benefiting from these predictions, but the bank's chief executive denied such accusations ("An oracle of oil predicts $200-a-barrel crude", *New York Times*, 21 May 2008).

15 While the "true number" is necessarily hypothetical, frequent disclosure of disaggregated data on positions taken by different trader categories in futures exchanges and OTC markets could be valuable in this context.

16 Phillips and Yu (2010) suggest that this problem can be solved by using an information criterion, rather than the beginning of the data series, to determine the date of the first observation.

17 Data on these categories have been available only since September 2009 when the CFTC started to publish *Disaggregated Commitment of Traders* (DCOT) reports. The discussion in this section ignores "non-reporting traders" (i.e. smaller traders who are not obliged to report their positions) as well as "other reporting traders" (i.e. every reporting trader that is not placed in one of the three categories mentioned in the text). Positions of the latter category are usually negligible but may at times become more important, such as in cocoa, cotton and soybeans in early 2011. For a further discussion of these trader categories and the evolution of position data reporting by the CFTC, see UNCTAD, 2011: 18–19.

18 This is a crude approximation. In fact, the index trader category of the *Supplementary Commodity Index Traders* (CIT) reports does not coincide with the swap dealer category in the *Disaggregated Commitment of Traders* (DCOT) reports. This is because the swap dealer category of the DCOT reports includes swap dealers who do not have commodity-index-related positions, and therefore are not included in the index trader category of the CIT reports. Also, the index trader category of the CIT reports includes pension and other investment funds that place their index investments directly into the futures markets rather than going through a swap dealer; these traders are classified as managed money or other reportables in the DCOT reports (see also Irwin and Sanders, 2010).

19 For the sake of simplicity, these charts show the net positions of only three trader categories. Both charts omit the category "other reporting traders". The chart for maize also omits the "swap dealer" category, whose positions correspond closely to those of the "commodity index traders" (CITs). Given that no data for CITs are available for crude oil, the respective graph shows only the swap dealer category. However, it should be noted that, contrary to agricultural commodities, for energy commodities such as crude oil, the positions taken by swap dealers and CITs may differ significantly. This is because swap dealers operating in agricultural markets undertake only a few transactions that are not related to index investments. On the other hand, swap dealers in energy markets conduct a substantial

amount of non-index-related transactions, which is the very reason why the CFTC has excluded energy commodities from its CIT reports. The CFTC (2008) estimates that in 2007–2008, less than half of the swap dealers' long positions in crude oil futures were linked to index fund positions. This may also explain why swap dealers' positions in crude oil have been significantly more volatile than those in agricultural commodities.

20 A high or increasing ratio of long to short positions may be considered an indication of herding by investors betting on rising prices, as it indicates that an increasing proportion of those investors are taking long positions. Since crude-oil markets were highly liquid over the period February–May 2011, the observed changes in position ratios cannot be attributed to statistical effects caused by low market participation.

21 The short-lived rebound in oil prices in the last week of May was preceded by a threefold increase in the ratio of long to short positions taken by money managers in the Intercontinental Exchange, which trades a similar WTI-contract as NYMEX but with a generally smaller market turnover.

22 For a good summary of this evidence, see "Bubble Trouble" on the BBC World Service, at: http://www.bbc.co.uk/programmes/p00gsmdd. Further anecdotal evidence is available in Thomson Reuters' *Metals Insider* of 27 April 2001, at: https://customers.reuters.com/community/newsletters/metals/MetalsInsider20110427.pdf, as well as in many blog entries on http://ftalphaville.ft.com.

23 The Chinese Government tightened the rules concerning such financial deals in April, resulting in declining copper inventories and prices, as discussed by Weiss, "China and copper – A dangerous carry trade", 16 May 2011, at: http://www.cnbc.com/id/43045324/China_and_Copper_A_Dangerous_Carry_Trade.

24 As discussed in more detail by Basu and Gavin (2011: 44–46) on the basis of additional empirical evidence, Gorton and Rouwenhorst (2006) found a statistically significant negative correlation between returns on equities and commodity futures only for longer periods, such as five years. For short periods it was nearly zero, and for periods up to one year it was negative but not statistically significant.

25 Statistical tests indicate that the shift in the mean of the correlation following the bursting of the equity market bubble in 2000 is strongly significant even if the post-crisis period is excluded. The evidence is qualitatively similar, though numerically less strong, if the S&P GSCI non-energy index is used instead of the non-energy index of the Dow Jones-UBS Commodity Index (DJ-UBSCI).

26 A recent econometric study (Anzuini, Lombardo and Pagano, 2010) on the impact of monetary conditions on commodity prices examined three direct channels (as opposed to indirect channels, such as global aggregate demand, expected inflation and a depreciation of the dollar) through which a decline in short-term interest rates could lead to higher commodity prices: (i) an increase in demand, given that lower interest rates reduce the opportunity costs of carrying inventories; (ii) a decrease in supply, given that low interest rates reduce the incentive to extract exhaustible resources; and (iii) an increase in financial investors' positions in commodity markets, given that lower interest rates reduce the carrying cost (caused, for example, by leveraging) of speculative positions. These authors found that "the impact of monetary policy on commodity prices is rather limited, though statistically significant" (Anzuini, Lombardo and Pagano, 2010: 5). They also found that among the three direct channels, financial positions had by far the largest price impact. However, these authors did not test for the price impact of unconventional monetary policy measures that were adopted in 2010–2011, especially by the United States Federal Reserve. These measures were characterized by the continuation of very low short-term interest rates and an easing of monetary and financial conditions. The latter was implemented by communicating the intention to maintain low policy interest rates and by purchasing financial assets on a large scale. These policies may have raised inflation expectations and lowered long-term interest rates. As a result, it is possible that the effect of the post-crisis monetary policy on commodity prices may have been somewhat stronger. However, to date no quantitative assessments of such potential effects are available. A study by Kawamoto et al. (2011) comes closest to such a quantitative assessment. On the assumption that unconventional monetary easing made financial investors relatively confident that no unexpected hike in interest rates would occur any time soon, these authors proxy the impact of unconventional monetary easing on commodity prices by an increase in financial investors' risk appetite, as measured by rising equity prices. In terms of policy implications, however, it would appear inappropriate to use monetary policy as an instrument to contain this "search for yield" by financial investors. Regulatory measures – and more targeted schemes such as those discussed in section E of this chapter – are perhaps more appropriate instruments to address potential asset price bubbles.

27 In the early 1990s, many countries in the world experienced recessions, but these recessions did not occur simultaneously. In Germany, for example, the boom after reunification delayed the cyclical downturn. For this reason no recession is identified for the world as a whole.

28 Given that these time series begin only in 1991, for the period 1975–1991 a proxy series was constructed

on the basis of the growth rates of the industrial production series of the Organisation for Economic Co-operation and Development (OECD) for all its member States. OECD industrial production and world industrial production show fairly similar dynamics in the early 1990s – that is, before the strong growth of the emerging economies unsettled this relationship.

29 It should be noted that even if such imported price pressure was based on fundamental factors, a tightening of monetary policy would not be the right policy response as it would imply reacting to a supply-side shock by a policy measure that addresses demand.

30 Carry-trade speculation is a strategy whereby an investor sells a currency that yields a relatively low interest rate (i.e. the so-called "funding currency") and uses those funds to purchase short-term assets denominated in a different currency that yields a higher interest rate.

31 For details on how planned rule-making in the United States is expected to deal with this issue, see Dodd-Frank Act 2010, sections 727 and 763, as well as Gensler, 2010.

32 Such exemptions are envisaged in the Dodd-Frank Act 2010, section 721.

33 The Stop Excessive Energy Speculation Act of 2008 that Senators Lieberman and Collins brought before the United States Senate on 25 July 2008 proposed that position limits on traders in energy derivatives markets be set in the aggregate, rather than on an exchange-by-exchange basis. However, the bill did not get a sufficient number of favourable votes for its supporters to invoke cloture (for details, see: http://ecip.loc.gov/cgi-bin/bdquery/ z?d110:SN03268:@@@L&summ2=m&). As explained by Greenberger (2009), aggregate position limits would apply to the "corporate control entity under which physical futures trading is done" and traders under that entity could operate within those limits at their discretion in any regulated or unregulated futures exchange or OTC market, so that the regulatory nature of the trading venue would become irrelevant.

34 Those opposed to position limits often argue that large institutional investors (such as pension funds that have traditionally taken passive broad-based index positions) that are not bona fide hedgers provide market liquidity, thereby reducing the dependence of bona fide hedgers on small-scale speculators as their counterparties which would make hedging more difficult and expensive. However, while it may be true, in principle, that the presence of more and larger traders makes it easier to find a counterparty, the price discovery function of derivatives markets requires positions to be taken on the basis of market fundamentals. This is not the case for institutional

investors who usually invest in commodities for portfolio diversification reasons.

35 For a recent example, see the Glencore case that was widely discussed in the media, such as by Blas and Farchy, 2011.

36 HFT is a technologically advanced method of conducting algorithmic trading at ultra-high speed.

37 See: *Financial Times,* "High-speed trading blamed for sugar rises", 8 February 2011.

38 Another proposal is for a multi-tier transaction tax system for commodity derivatives markets. Under this scheme, a transaction tax surcharge of increasing scale would be levied as soon as prices started to move beyond the price band defined on the basis of commodity market fundamentals (Nissanke, 2010).

39 The facility would nonetheless require funds to purchase the futures contracts. The authors propose that these funds be provided by the group of countries participating in the virtual reserve and intervention scheme.

40 Parts of this and the following paragraph draw on *The Wall Street Journal*, CORRECT: Margin increases didn't cause silver slide - CME Clearing Executive, 6 May 2011, available at: http://online.wsj.com/ article/BT-CO-20110506-714080.html; Pirrong C, No margin for error, 9 May 2011, available at: http:// streetwiseprofessor.com/?p=5114; and Leff J and Gibbons R, Analysis–Commodity price margins: Art, science or politics? 12 May 2011, available at: http:// www.reuters.com/article/2011/05/12/us-exchange-margin-idUSTRE74B0N320110512.

41 A further problem is that margin requirements are set by exchanges, which means that both the level of margin requirements and the timing of margin calls may differ across exchanges. This may create uncertainty among market participants.

42 The costs of such interventions could probably be easily funded from the proposed transaction tax on HFT, mentioned above. An alternative could be to apply additional capital requirements for financial investors, but this would again raise definitional problems as to how to distinguish purely commercial from financial market participants.

43 With regard to judging when such an occasional intervention should actually occur, it may be useful to draw another parallel with currency-market interventions. As expressed many years ago by Emminger (1982: 16–17), a former president of the Deutsche Bundesbank, who could hardly be considered as entertaining anti-market sentiments: "I wholeheartedly agree that the monetary authorities have no way of knowing exactly what is the 'right' exchange rate. But *in most cases one can recognize when an exchange rate is very much out of line, is destabilizing and distorting*, and is likely to turn round again" (emphasis in original).

References

Abreu D and Brunnermeier MK (2003). Bubbles and crashes. *Econometrica*, 71(1): 173–204.

Anzuini A, Lombardo MJ and Pagano O (2010). The impact of monetary policy shocks on commodity prices. Working Paper No. 1232, European Central Bank, Frankfurt, August.

Ariely D (2010). *Predictably Irrational*. New York and London, Harper Perennial.

Avery A and Zemsky P (1998). Multidimensional uncertainty and herd behaviour in financial markets. *American Economic Review*, 88(4): 724–748.

Banerjee A (1992). A simple model of herd behaviour. *Quarterly Journal of Economics*, 107(3): 797–818.

Barclays Capital (various issues). *The Commodity Investor*. Commodities Research, Barclays Bank PLC, London.

Bargawi H (2009). Assessing the impact of commodity prices on producers in low-income countries. *Development Viewpoint*, 36, March.

Basu P and Gavin WT (2011). What explains the growth in commodity derivatives? *Federal Reserve Bank of St. Louis Review*, 93(1): 37–48.

Bikhchandani S, Hirshleifer D and Welch I (1992). A theory of fads, fashion, custom and cultural change as informational cascades. *Journal of Political Economy*, 100(5): 992–1026.

Bikhchandani S and Sharma S (2001). Herd behaviour in financial markets. *IMF Staff Papers*, 47(3): 279–310, International Monetary Fund, Washington, DC.

Blas J and Farchy J (2011). Glencore reveals bet on grain price rise. *The Financial Times*, 24 April. Available at: http://www.ft.com/cms/s/0/aea76c56-6ea5-11e0-a13b-00144feabdc0.html#axzz1KtsjV7En.

Bry G and Boschan C (1971). Cyclical analysis of time series: Selected procedures and computer programs. NBER Technical Paper 20, National Bureau of Economic Research, Cambridge, MA.

Büyüksahin B and Robe MA (2010). Speculators, commodities and cross-market linkages (unpublished). Available at: http://papers.ssrn.com/sol3/papers.cfm?abstract_id=1707103.

CFTC (2008). Staff report on commodity swap dealers & index traders with Commission recommendations, Washington, DC. Available at: http://www.cftc.gov/stellent/groups/public/@newsroom/documents/file/cftcstaffreportonswapdealers09.pdf.

Chilton B (2011). Statement regarding position limits and interim position points, 4 January. Available at: http://www.cftc.gov/PressRoom/SpeechesTestimony/chiltonstatement010411.html.

Cipriani M and Guarino A (2008). Herd behaviour and contagion in financial markets. *The B.E. Journal of Theoretical Economics*, 8(1): Article 24.

De Long JB, Shleifer A, Summers LH and Waldmann RJ (1990a). Noise trader risk in financial markets. *Journal of Political Economy*, 98(4): 703–738.

De Long JB, Shleifer A, Summers LH and Waldmann RJ (1990b). Positive feedback investment strategies and destabilizing rational speculation. *Journal of Finance*, 65(2): 379–395.

Devenow A and Welch I (1996). Rational herding in financial economics. *European Economic Review*, 40(3–5): 603–615.

Emminger O (1982). Exchange rate policy reconsidered. Occasional Paper 10, Group of Thirty, New York, NY.

Erb CB and Harvey CR (2006). The strategic and tactical value of commodity futures. *Financial Analysts Journal*, 62(2): 69–97.

European Commission (2010). Proposal for a regulation of the European Parliament and of the Council on OTC derivatives, central counterparties and trade repositories. Document COM(2010) 484 final. Brussels, 15 September.

Fajarnes P (2011). An overview of major sources of data and analyses relating to physical fundamentals in international commodity markets. *UNCTAD Discussion Paper No. 202*, UNCTAD, Geneva, June.

FAO (2008). Crop prospects and food situation. Rome, April.

FAO et al. (2011). *Price Volatility in Food and Agricultural Markets: Policy Responses*. Policy report including contributions by FAO, IFAD, IMF, OECD, UNCTAD, WFP, the World Bank, the WTO, IFPRI and the UN HLTF. Available at: http://www.unctad.org/en/docs/2011_G20_FoodPriceVolatility_en.pdf.

Friedman M (1953). The case for flexible exchange rates. In: Friedman M, *Essays in Positive Economics*. Chicago, University of Chicago Press.

G20-G8 (2011). The Priorities of the French Presidency. Available at: http://www.g20-g8.com/g8-g20/g20/english/home.9.html.

Garber PM (1990). Famous first bubbles. *Journal of Economic Perspectives*, 4(2): 35–54.

Gensler G (2010). Remarks before the ISDA Regional Conference, 16 September. Available at: http://www.cftc.gov/PressRoom/SpeechesTestimony/opagensler-50.html.

Gilbert CL (2010a). Speculative influences on commodity futures prices 2006–2008. *UNCTAD Discussion Paper No. 197*, UNCTAD, Geneva, March.

Gilbert CL (2010b). How to understand high food prices. *Journal of Agricultural Economics*, 61(2): 398–425.

Gilbert CL (2011). An assessment of international commodity agreements for commodity price stabilization. In: Prakash A, ed., *Safeguarding Food Security in Volatile Markets*, Rome, FAO: 231–257.

Gorton G, Hayashi F and Rouwenhorst KG (2007). The fundamentals of commodity futures returns. NBER Working Paper No. 13249, National Bureau of Economic Research, Cambridge, MA, July.

Gorton G and Rouwenhorst KG (2006). Facts and fantasies about commodity futures. NBER Working Paper No. 10595, National Bureau of Economic Research, Cambridge, MA, March.

Greenberger M (2009). Testimony on behalf of the Americans for Financial Reform before the Commodity Futures Trading Commission on Excessive Speculation: Position Limits and Exemptions, 5 August. Available at: http://www.michaelgreenberger.com/files/CFTC_AFR_Sign_On_Testimony_August_3.pdf.

Gromb D and Vayanos D (2010). Limits of arbitrage. *Annual Review of Financial Economics*, 2: 251–275.

Hernandez M and Torero M (2010). Examining the dynamic relationship between spot and future prices of agricultural commodities. IFPRI Discussion Paper 00988, International Food Policy Research Institute, Washington, DC, June.

Hirshleifer D and Teoh SH (2003). Herd behaviour and cascading in capital markets; a review and synthesis. *European Financial Management*, 9(1): 25–66.

IEA (International Energy Agency) (2009). *Medium-Term Oil Market Report*. Paris, OECD/IEA.

IMF (2008). *Global Financial Stability Report*, Chapter I, Annex 1.2. Washington, DC.

IMF (2010) *World Economic Outlook*, April. Washington, DC.

IOSCO (2010). Report to the G-20. No. OR08/10. Task Force on Commodity Futures Markets, Technical Committee of the International Organization of Securities Commissions. Madrid, November.

Irwin SH and Holt BR (2005). The effect of large hedge fund and 2CTA trading on futures market volatility. In: Gregoriou GN, Karavas VN, Lhabitant FS and Rouah F, eds., *Commodity Trading Advisors: Risk, Performance Analysis and Selection*, Hoboken, NJ, Wiley.

Irwin SH and Sanders DR (2010). The impact of index and swap funds on commodity futures markets: Preliminary results. Working Paper No. 27, OECD Food, Agriculture and Fisheries, Paris.

Irwin SH, Sanders DR and Merrin RP (2009). Devil or angel? The role of speculation in the recent commodity boom (and bust). *Journal of Agricultural Applied Economics*, 41(2): 393–402.

Irwin SH and Yoshimaru S (1999). Managed futures, positive feedback trading, and futures price volatility. *The Journal of Futures Markets*, 19(7): 759–776.

Kaufmann RK (2011). The role of market fundamentals and speculation in recent price changes for crude oil. *Energy Policy*, 39(1): 105–115.

Kawamoto T, Kimura T, Morishita K and Higashi M (2011). What has caused the surge in global commodity prices and strengthened cross-market linkage? Working Paper No. 11-E-3, Bank of Japan, Tokyo, May.

Khan MS (2009). The 2008 oil price "bubble". Policy Brief 09/19, Peterson Institute for International Economics, Washington, DC, August.

Kilian L and Hicks B (2009). Did unexpectedly strong economic growth cause the oil price shock of 2003–2008? Discussion Paper No. 7265, Centre for Economic Policy Research, London, January.

Krugman PR (2008) The oil nonbubble. *New York Times*, 12 May.

Martins-Filho C, Yao F and Torero M (2011). High order conditional quantile estimation based on nonparametric models of regression (unpublished). University of Colorado. Available at: http://spot.colorado.edu/~martinsc/Research_files/martins-filho-et-al(2011).pdf.

Mayer J (2011). The growing financialization of commodity markets: an empirical investigation (unpublished). Geneva, UNCTAD, March.

Minot N (2010). Transmission of world food price changes to markets in sub-Saharan Africa. IFPRI Discussion Paper 1059, International Food Policy Research Institute, Washington, DC.

Nissanke M (2010). Mitigating commodity-dependence trap in LDCs through global facilities (unpublished). London, School of Oriental and African Studies, University of London.

Phillips PCB and Yu J (2010). Dating the timeline of financial bubbles during the subprime crisis. Cowles Foundation Discussion Paper No. 1770, Yale University, New Haven, CT, September.

Robles M and Torero M (2009). Understanding the impact of high food prices in Latin America. *Economía*, 10(2):117–164.

Sanders DR and Irwin SH (2010). A speculative bubble in commodity futures prices: cross-sectional evidence. *Agricultural Economics*, 41(1): 25–32.

Scharfstein D and Stein J (1990). Herd behaviour and investment. *American Economic Review*, 80(3): 465–479.

Shleifer A and Summers LH (1990). The noise trader approach to finance. *Journal of Economic Perspectives*, 4(2): 19–33.

Shleifer A and Vishny RW (1997). The limits of arbitrage. *Journal of Finance*, 52(2): 737–783.

Singleton K (2011). Investor flows and the 2008 boom/bust in oil prices (unpublished). Palo Alto, CA, Graduate School of Business, Stanford University. Available at: http://www.stanford.edu/~kenneths/.

Tang K and Xiong W (2010). Index investment and financialization of commodities. NBER Working Paper 16385, National Bureau of Economic Research, Cambridge, MA, September.

UNCTAD (*TDR 2008*). *Trade and Development Report, 2008. Commodity prices, capital flows and the financing of investment*. United Nations publications. Sales No. E.08.II.D.21, New York and Geneva.

UNCTAD (*TDR 2009*). *Trade and Development Report, 2009. Responding to the global crisis: Climate change mitigation and development*. United Nations publications, Sales No. E.09.II.D.16, New York and Geneva.

UNCTAD (2009). *The Global Economic Crisis: Systemic Failures and Multilateral Remedies*. New York and Geneva, United Nations.

UNCTAD (2011). *Price Formation in Financialized Commodity Markets: The Role of Information*. New York and Geneva, United Nations, June.

United States Senate (2011). Executive summary: Excessive speculation in the wheat market. Permanent Subcommittee on Investigations. Originally published on 24 June 2009, reprinted in Institute for Agriculture and Trade Policy ed. (2011), *Excessive Speculation in Agricultural Commodities – Selected Writings from 2008–2011*. Minneapolis, MN, Institute for Agriculture and Trade Policy.

von Braun J and Torero M (2008). Physical and virtual global food reserves to protect the poor and prevent market failure. Policy Brief 4, International Food Policy Research Institute, Washington, DC, June.

Wright B (2009). International grain reserves and other instruments to address volatility in grain markets. Policy Research Working Paper No. 5028, World Bank, Washington, DC, August.

REFORM OF COMMODITY DERIVATIVES MARKET REGULATIONS

The extreme commodity price movements that occurred around the outbreak of the financial crisis in 2007–2008 spurred an intense debate about the need for making appropriate changes in commodity market rules and their enforcement. In particular, the breadth of deleveraging that accompanied the commodity price collapse in 2008 illustrated the extent to which prices on global asset markets, including those for commodities, have become interlinked, as asset price fluctuations are an integral part of financial institutions' risk exposure.

Policymakers and regulatory authorities recognized that reform of commodity market regulations needs to be part of broader financial market reforms. The reforms aim at increasing transparency and the effectiveness of regulation in reducing financial risks, as well as ensuring greater harmonization of rules applied in different jurisdictions in order to avoid regulatory arbitrage (i.e. a shift of trading activities towards locations where regulation is perceived to be less restrictive).

This annex provides a brief overview of reform proposals elaborated by specifically mandated bodies at the international level, as well as by policymakers and regulators in the United States and the EU (i.e. where the major commodity futures markets are located). These proposals are based on the recognition that the use of complex derivative instruments in often opaque trading environments played a major role in triggering the crisis and its subsequent spread across asset markets. With respect to commodity markets, the three major areas for reform concern: (i) improving transparency in derivatives trading; (ii) extending regulation from exchange venues to OTC markets; and (iii) imposing limits on the size of positions held by market participants.

No attempt is made here to evaluate the various legislative proposals.[1] However, it is clear that their implementation and enforcement would involve substantial changes in commodity trading rules and practices. This would most probably help reduce the vulnerability of commodity price formation to undue impacts from financial investors' activities. It would also address more long-term concerns relating to market transparency, price volatility and contagion across asset markets resulting from financial investors' risk exposure. However, the time-consuming process of consultations with market participants to fully draft the rules, and the substantial funding required to finalize and implement the proposed regulatory reforms may explain why few, if any, of them have been enacted and implemented so far.

The international agenda

The international agenda for financial reform adopted a number of subjects directly focusing on financial markets in the aftermath of the Asian financial crisis in 1997–1998. Following the outbreak of the current financial crisis, this agenda has been broadened to cover other areas as well, including commodities. The G-8 Meeting of Finance Ministers in Osaka in June 2008 expressed concern over the functioning of certain commodity derivatives markets, and called for an examination of the functioning and regulation of those markets.[2] In response, in September 2008 the International Organization of Securities Commissions (IOSCO) established the Task Force on Commodity Futures Markets, jointly chaired by the CFTC and the United Kingdom's Financial Services Authority. The Task Force has given particular emphasis to oil, owing to the concern over price volatility in energy markets during 2008 expressed by the G-20 leaders at their meetings in Pittsburgh (United States) in September 2009 and Seoul (Republic of Korea) in November 2010.[3] The G-20 Pittsburgh Communiqué also called for all standardized OTC derivatives to be centrally cleared and, where appropriate, to be traded on exchanges or electronic trading platforms by the end of 2012. The G-20 Seoul Declaration requested the Task Force to report by April 2011 to the Financial Stability Board (FSB) and to provide recommendations to improve the transparency and overall functioning of commodity derivatives markets. The G-20 has also mandated the FSB to coordinate the design and implementation of the various facets of the international financial reform agenda, and to consider the appropriate next steps to be taken.[4]

In its first report, published in March 2009, the IOSCO Task Force: (i) reviewed existing studies on the issue of price volatility and financial investment in commodity markets and "saw no evidence to suggest that [financial investors in commodity futures markets] or any other particular class of investors'

activity alone were responsible for the volatility of commodity markets" (IOSCO, 2011: 6); (ii) recommended closer monitoring of commodity derivatives markets, as price discovery in these markets was of critical importance for the world economy; and (iii) recognizing the complexity and often opacity of factors that drive price discovery on commodity derivatives markets, called on governments to ensure greater transparency of commodity trading with a view to enabling "a more comprehensive understanding of the interaction between financial and non-financial participation in commodity derivatives and related physical commodity markets that affect price formation" (IOSCO, 2011: 8).

Subsequent reports to the G-20 summits in September 2009, and June and November 2010 surveyed the degree of compliance by Task Force members with the recommendations of the March 2009 report, and found a high degree of compliance. Its November 2010 report, which was considered at the G-20 summit in Seoul, also: (i) indicated its intention to work towards the creation of a trade repository for financial oil contracts;[5] (ii) requested an international energy markets agency to examine the impact of published cash market price assessments on related commodity futures; (iii) encouraged the International Swaps and Derivatives Association (ISDA) initiative to establish an OTC derivatives trade repository; and (iv) called for further disclosure of aggregated open interest information from exchange trading, as well as for greater availability of data from physical markets, including through a more detailed study on the impact of oil price reporting agencies.

In its April 2011 report, IOSCO (2011: 6) acknowledged "that commodity futures markets can experience periods of significant volatility and that improvements should be made to the functioning of these markets." It indicated an extension of its focus beyond oil derivatives markets to include agricultural derivatives markets. Its aim is to provide comprehensive policy recommendations, while keeping in mind commodity-specific issues, in order to improve the supervision of commodity derivatives markets. The emphasis will be on proposals to improve market transparency, oversight and surveillance of market abuse in all commodity markets, where necessary.

IOSCO (2011) encouraged other relevant organizations to work towards improving transparency in physical commodity markets. The Task Force also recommended that it be given the mandate to work on commodity derivatives markets on a permanent basis. It intends to finalize and submit a full set of recommendations to the meeting of G-20 Finance Ministers in October 2011.

Regulatory initiatives in the United States

The Dodd-Frank Wall Street Reform and Consumer Protection Act (Dodd-Frank Act for short), signed into law on 21 July 2010, is the regulatory response of the United States to the financial meltdown of 2008. The Act's overall objective is to improve market transparency and reduce the risk of systemic default. It extends regulation beyond futures exchanges to include swaps by generally requiring: (i) swaps to be subject to clearing and exchange-like trading; and (ii) dealers and major participants that trade swaps to be subject to capital and margin requirements (Greenberger, 2011: 152). Dodd-Frank is limited to swaps and its rules do not pertain to other derivatives, such as forward contracts or exchange-traded futures and options contracts.

The main part of Dodd-Frank that addresses commodities is Title VII, which deals with regulation of OTC derivatives. It stipulates four main requirements, that: (i) all "swap dealers" and "major swap participants" register with the appropriate regulators; (ii) all standardized swap transactions go through central clearinghouses; (iii) all cleared swaps be traded on an exchange venue or other regulated trading platforms; and (iv) all cleared and uncleared swap trading be reported in real time to a swap data repository or the CFTC in order for regulators to have information on the risk exposures of firms and counterparties. Before any proposed rule can be adopted and implemented, many of the terms used in the regulatory proposals require precise definitions (see Gensler 2010, for the

main ones). A crucial definition concerns the end-user exemption that will exempt eligible swap users from clearing requirements.[6] It is envisaged that in order to benefit from the exemption, swap users will not be financial entities, must use the swap to hedge or mitigate commercial risk and must notify the regulators as to how they plan to meet their financial obligations with respect to non-cleared swaps.[7]

In addition to these four items, Title VII also provides for the establishment of position limits on individual contracts and aggregate limits on positions on the same underlying commodity taken across different trading venues,[8] as well as the so-called "push-out rule" and the Volcker rule (Greenberger, 2011: 154–155). The push-out rule prohibits access to federal banking resources by any bank that operates as a swap dealer in commodity derivatives transactions. Thus it encourages banks to sell off their commodity-based swap divisions. The Volcker rule aims to limit banks' risk-taking, and prohibits banks from engaging in proprietary trading (i.e. trading for their own benefit, rather than on behalf of their customers) or acquiring or retaining an interest in hedge funds or private equity funds. Thus it encourages banks to move these activities to other smaller and less systemically risky entities.

The Dodd-Frank Act establishes a sequence of deadlines by which the new rules should be finalized with the overall objective of completing rule-making by July 2011. However, several deadlines have been missed due to the workload on CFTC staff caused by the immense number of rules to be drafted and comments on these drafts to be considered, as well as the difficulties in reaching consensus on a wide range of regulatory issues. At the time of writing (early June 2011) it was clear that the original timetable would not be met, and it was generally considered unlikely that the proposed Act would be implemented in its original form.

Regulatory initiatives in the European Union

In the EU, reform of the OTC derivatives market combines introducing the European Market Infrastructure Regulation (EMIR) with reviews of the Market Abuse Directive (MAD) and the Markets in Financial Instruments Directive (MiFID). The EU is also considering additional measures for commodity derivatives markets. The reform process has resulted in the creation of the European Securities and Markets Authority (ESMA) with a view to ensuring consistency of the technical rules and coordination in the implementation and enforcement of rules across EU member States.[9]

Given that regulators in the United States and the EU strive towards regulatory convergence in order to prevent regulatory arbitrage, the proposals put forward by the European Commission (EC) are very similar to those elaborated by the CFTC.[10] The EC's proposal for regulation of OTC derivatives trading (EC, 2010) requires all standardized swaps to be cleared by a central counterparty, except for swaps used by non-financial institutions whose derivative positions do not exceed a certain threshold. It also requires all cleared and non-cleared OTC derivatives contracts that exceed an "information threshold" to be reported to a trade repository. The thresholds are determined on the basis of the systemic relevance of the associated positions. The main objective of the MiFID review is to achieve greater transparency. It aims to achieve this by requiring derivatives to be traded on exchanges, when appropriate, and by exercising stronger oversight over positions, including through the potential introduction of position limits to combat market manipulation and excessive price volatility. As outlined by the EC (2010), an additional measure for commodity derivatives would require all commodity derivatives exchanges in the EU to report positions by trader categories. These additional reporting requirements would also cover OTC derivatives whose aggregate positions will already have been made publicly available by the trade repositories.[11] Taken together, Dodd-Frank and the EC proposals are similar in terms of establishing trade repositories that run common reporting frameworks, trading of standardized OTC derivatives on regulated trading venues, and centralized clearing of standardized OTC derivatives. They differ in that contrary to the rules outlined in Dodd-Frank, the EC's proposals do not include a push-out rule or the Volcker rule.[12]

The EC's proposals were discussed and amended by the Economic and Monetary Committee (ECON) of the European Parliament, which approved the draft regulation on 24 May 2011. However, a number of contentious issues remain unresolved (e.g. the treatment of pension schemes[13] and certain aspects of reporting retroactively that might be needed to apply clearing obligations). The draft regulation was to be submitted to the European Parliament for approval in July 2011 to enable negotiations to proceed with EU member States thereafter. The new rules are expected to enter into force in early 2013.

Taken together, the international agenda as well as the initiatives taken in the United States and the EU are largely a response to the fact that the financial crisis started in developed countries and to concerns relating to these countries' regulatory regimes. Developing countries have a stake in the success of the reforms undertaken by developed countries, as the cross-border impact of the financial crisis affected their levels of economic activity, asset prices and capital movements. However, the crisis and the subsequent regulatory response are also likely to have changed the general attitude towards the costs and benefits of regulation, and this could affect the design of financial policy and regulation in all countries, including developing countries. ∎

Notes

1   For an assessment of the United States' Dodd-Frank Act, see, for example, Adjemian and Plato, 2010; and for an assessment of the European Commission's Review of Markets in Financial Instruments Directive (MiFID review), see, for example, Suppan, 2011.

2   Statement of the G-8 Finance Ministers Meeting, Osaka (Japan), 14 June 2008, available at: http://www.mof.go.jp/english/international_policy/convention/summit/cy2008/su080614.htm.

3   The G-20 Pittsburgh Communiqué is available at: http://www.g20.org/Documents/pittsburgh_summit_leaders_statement_250909.pdf; the G-20 Seoul Declaration is available at: http://www.g20.org/Documents2010/11/seoulsummit_declaration.pdf.

4   The FSB was established in April 2009, following the G-20 summit in London, as an extension of the Financial Stability Forum (FSF). The latter was founded in 1999 by the G-7 Finance Ministers and Central Bank Governors. This extension involved, *inter alia*, an expansion of membership to include several developing countries (Argentina, Brazil China, India, Indonesia, Mexico, the Republic of Korea, the Russian Federation, Saudi Arabia, South Africa and Turkey). The FSB's mandate is to address vulnerabilities, and to develop and implement strong regulatory, supervisory and other policies in the interest of financial stability. Its secretariat is located in Basel, Switzerland, and hosted by the Bank for International Settlements. For further information, see the FSB's website at: financialstabilityboard.org.

5   Trade repositories create centralized databases and provide a structure for market participants to report transaction information in line with applicable regulatory requirements.

6   As pointed out by Greenberger (2009) in connection with rules for agricultural swaps, it is important to bear in mind that the Commodity Exchange Act (section 3) requires regulatory authorities to give priority to the price discovery needs and trading practices of bona fide hedgers over other commodity market participants. The term "bona fide hedgers" refers to market participants that have an interest in the physical commodity and use swap contracts to manage commercial risk, as opposed to those (such as index traders) that hedge financial risk.

7   In a sense, this would reverse the swap dealer exemption that had been introduced by the Commodity Futures Modernization Act of 2000, as discussed in *TDR 2009*: 76–77.

8   The CFTC's proposed rule was published on 26 January 2011, see *Federal Speculative Position Limits for Referenced Energy Contracts and Associated Regulations. Proposed Rule*. Federal Register, Vol. 76, No. 17, available at: http://www.cftc.gov/ucm/groups/public/@lrfederalregister/documents/file/2011-1154a.pdf.

9   ESMA was established on 24 November 2010 by regulation (EU) No 1095/2010 of the EP and the Council. (see: http://eur-lex.europa.eu/LexUriServ/LexUriServ.do?uri=OJ:L:2010:331:0084:0119:EN:PDF).

10 For an assessment of differences and possibilities for further convergence, see European Parliament, 2011.

11 See: http://ec.europa.eu/commission_2010-2014/barnier/headlines/speeches/2010/09/20100920_en.htm.

12 There is also some divergence in terms of the order in which the various rules are to be introduced, as explained by Gensler, 2010.

13 According to media reports, pension funds are to be granted a temporary reprieve and will not be required to have their OTC derivatives trading cleared through central clearing houses until at least 2015 (Ellen Kelleher, "Brussels hands EU pension funds OTC reprieve", *The Financial Times*, 6 June 2011).

References

Adjemian MK and Plato GE (2010). The Dodd-Frank Wall Street Reform and Consumer Protection Act. Changes to the Regulation of Derivatives and their Impact on Agribusiness. AIS-89. Economic Research Service, United States Department of Agriculture, Washington, DC, November.

European Commission (2010). Proposal for a Regulation of the European Parliament and of the Council on OTC derivatives, central counterparties and trade repositories. Document COM(2010) 484 final. Brussels, 15 September.

European Parliament (2011). Derivatives, central counterparties and trade repositories. Compilation of briefing notes. Document IP/A/ECON/NT/2010-14. Strasbourg. February. Available at: http://www.europarl.europa.eu/document/activities/cont/201103/20110324ATT16422/20110324ATT16422EN.pdf.

Gensler G (2010). Remarks before the ISDA Regional Conference, 16 September. Available at: http://www.cftc.gov/PressRoom/SpeechesTestimony/opagensler-50.html.

Greenberger M (2009). Testimony on behalf of the Americans for Financial Reform before the Commodity Futures Trading Commission on Excessive Speculation: Position Limits and Exemptions, 5 August. Available at: http://www.michaelgreenberger.com/files/CFTC_AFR_Sign_On_Testimony_August_3.pdf.

Greenberger M (2011). Overwhelming a financial regulatory black hole with legislative sunlight: Dodd-Frank's attack on systemic economic destabilization caused by unregulated multi-trillion dollar derivatives Market. *Journal of Business & Technology Law*, 6(1): 127–167.

IOSCO (2011). Report to the Financial Stability Board. Task Force on Commodity Futures Markets, Technical Committee of the International Organization of Securities Commissions (IOSCO), OR01/11, Madrid, April.

Suppan S (2011). Comment on "Review of the Markets in Financial Instruments Directive". In Institute for Agriculture and Trade Policy (2011) (*ed.*), *Excessive Speculation in Agricultural Commodities. Selected Writings from 2008–2011*. Minneapolis (Minnesota): Institute for Agriculture and Trade Policy.

UNCTAD (*TDR 2009*). *Trade and Development Report, 2009.* Responding to the global crisis: Climate change mitigation and development. United Nations publications, Sales No. E.09.II.D.16, New York and Geneva.

Chapter VI

THE GLOBAL MONETARY ORDER AND THE INTERNATIONAL TRADING SYSTEM

A. Introduction

One of the most intriguing discussions over the past few decades concerns competition among nations. There is a widespread notion that, with the accelerated pace of globalization, countries now have to compete in similar ways as companies. According to one view, the wealth of a nation depends on its ability to effectively adjust to the challenges created by open markets for goods and capital. Accordingly, it is believed that, as economies with low labour standards and inferior capital stocks are emerging as competitors, those with high welfare standards and sophisticated capital endowments are coming under increasing pressure to adjust to changing global market conditions. In particular, it argues that the emergence of a huge pool of idle labour in China, India and other large developing countries threatens to fundamentally reduce the capital/labour ratio for the world as a whole. This in turn would favour the remuneration of capital and have a strong equilibrating effect on labour in rich and poor countries alike, which could lead to a new global equilibrium somewhere in the middle of high and low wage extremes.

At first glance, this premise, derived from a neoclassical model of the global labour market, seems to be confirmed by developments during the past decade, as wages in many high-wage developed countries have come under pressure and the share of labour in total income has been falling. However, there are many reasons for this pressure on wages. A major reason is the occurrence of mass unemployment, the causes of which can vary. One explanation could be excessively high wages, while others could be too little demand or misguided economic policies. A serious problem with the global labour market model referred to is that it is based on an analogy of competition among companies, but such competition cannot apply to countries, particularly countries with independent currencies. In the dynamic setting of a market economy, market forces tend to equalize the prices of goods and services. Thus companies have to accept the exogenously set prices of capital and/ or intermediate goods as well as the going price for different labour skills. Therefore the success or failure of a company is determined by the specific value it can add to those goods and services and it competes mainly on the basis of differentiation of productivity.

While wages paid by individual companies tend to be uniform for similar qualifications and skills within a country, unit labour costs (i.e. the sum of wages paid to generate one unit of a product) can vary among companies. Thus, productivity enhancement in a firm through innovation and new products reduces unit labour costs and gives that firm a competitive advantage. These pioneers are therefore able to offer their goods at lower prices or make higher profits per unit of output at given prices. As long as the prices of labour and other intermediary products are given, competitors adjust by implementing the same or a similar technology, or they are forced to quit the race through bankruptcy.

By contrast, in a country, greater average productivity does not necessarily increase the competitiveness of all producers in that country against the rest of the world. This is because there is a tendency for national advantages in productivity to be matched by higher nominal (and real) wages, so that unit labour costs (or the growth of those costs) will remain largely unchanged. However, even a country where productivity is growing much faster than wages and unit labour costs will not automatically increase its competitiveness and that of all its enterprises. In a world of national currencies and national monetary policies, a country supplying its goods to the world market at much lower prices than others will temporarily gain market shares and accumulate huge trade and current-account surpluses, but sooner or later it will come under pressure to adjust wages and prices, as expressed in foreign currency. If adjustments are not made through wage increases in the domestic currency, a revaluation of the currency will be needed.

On the other hand, a country's competitiveness has often been distorted by an upward deviation of the flexible nominal exchange rate from what would be warranted by economic fundamentals. Such a currency appreciation often reflects the impact of private short-term capital inflows that are attracted by positive interest rate and inflation differentials vis-à-vis other countries, and thus by macroeconomic conditions that might otherwise warrant a depreciation of the exchange rate. When such an interest rate and inflation differential narrows or disappears completely, or in a situation of crisis, there typically follows an overshooting

> Overvaluation is typically caused by excessive short-term capital flows under flexible nominal exchange rates …

> … or by significant differences in unit labour costs in a context of fixed nominal exchange rates.

currency depreciation, which is again out of line with fundamentals, and thus compromises the efficiency of the international trading system.

While not all current-account disequilibria are the outcome of misaligned exchange rates, deviations of the real exchange rate from fundamentals, especially if persisting over long periods of time, have a major impact on the international competitiveness of producers, particularly manufacturers, and thus on the pattern of international trade and trade balances. The search for an appropriate system of exchange rate management that helps prevent trade distortions and instability in international financial relations is therefore central to the debate on the reform of global economic governance in the wake of the latest economic and financial crisis.

This chapter presents the rationale for a system of rules-based managed floating exchange rates against the background of recent experiences with the global imbalances that contributed to the build-up of the financial crisis. It also discusses problems for countries' international competitiveness arising from an overvalued exchange rate. The causes of overvaluation are typically either excessive short-term capital inflows that lead to an appreciation of a flexible nominal exchange rate, or significant differences in the evolution of unit labour costs in a context of fixed nominal exchange rates.

The chapter expands on an earlier treatment of this issue in *TDR 2009*, taking into account new developments, such as the crisis in the eurozone and the post-crisis surge of carry-trade flows to emerging market economies. It also discusses two alternative methodological approaches for the design of a currency regime based on rules that aim at achieving the following: (a) sufficient stability of the real exchange rate to enhance international trade and facilitate decision-making on fixed investment in the tradable sector; and (b) sufficient flexibility of the nominal exchange rate to accommodate differences in the development of interest rates across countries.

In principle, such a rules-based regime of managed floating can be regarded as a dynamic version of the Bretton Woods system, which was based on harmonized inflation targets and discretionary adjustment of exchange rates when a country could not meet the inflation target of the anchor country. Distinct from the Bretton Woods system, the concept of rules-based managed floating aims at a nominal exchange rate path related to either purchasing power parity (PPP) or uncovered interest rate parity (UIP).

As long as consumer prices or unit labour costs (in the first approach) rise at different rates across countries, or there are differences in interest rates (in the alternative approach), the nominal exchange rate will be adjusted accordingly. Unlike the Bretton Woods system, this alternative system aims at avoiding fundamental balance-of-payments disequilibria through continuous rules-based adjustments. It allows, if necessary, discrete adjustments of the nominal exchange rate whenever an exceptional shock occurs.

B. New thinking on global economic governance

Following the outbreak of the financial crisis in 2008, the G-20 developed and developing countries took the lead in designing a coordinated international policy response. The G-20 also highlighted the need to assess the persistently large global current-account imbalances and the measures necessary for rebalancing, with a focus on addressing the issues of internal structural balances, fiscal policy and currency alignment. This implies some new thinking on multilateralism and economic interdependence. Indeed, the issue of exchange rate management has gained considerable attention in this policy debate.

It is generally acknowledged that "leaving currencies to the market" entails considerable risks for both the global financial system and the multilateral trading system. There is an obvious contradiction between the belief that market forces lead to economically desirable outcomes and the experience of wide exchange rate fluctuations and frequent currency misalignments that ignore the fundamental determinants of competitiveness. This was revealed yet again in early 2011, when Brazil, a major emerging market economy with a current-account deficit and

> Leaving currencies entirely to market forces entails considerable risks for both the global financial system and the multilateral trading system.

relatively high (albeit historically low) inflation rates, had to fend off huge capital inflows that were causing an unsustainable appreciation of its currency.

Trade imbalances resulting from exchange rate misalignments are not a new phenomenon. In 1985, the market's inability to resolve long-standing trade imbalances between Germany, Japan and the United States was finally resolved by the historic Plaza Accord. After all other approaches had failed, coordinated intervention by the members of the G-5 led to a huge devaluation of the dollar. Today, there is an even greater need for coordination, but achieving it is more difficult, since, as a result of globalization, a much larger number of economies are involved, and therefore the magnitude of trade and capital flows is also much larger. In order to monitor global trade imbalances and progress towards achieving external sustainability as part of a mutual assessment process, the G-20 is proposing the development of technical guidelines to indicate when the overall scale of imbalances is moving away from what is deemed to be a sustainable position. Finding "a mechanism to facilitate timely identification of large imbalances that require preventive and corrective action" (G-20 Communiqué, 2010) is indeed crucial for world trade. Trade cannot work effectively to foster growth and reduce poverty if the global community fails to find such a mechanism. One suggestion has been to focus on the size of a country's current-account deficit or surplus, as a percentage of gross domestic product. Other viewpoints favour looking at a range of indicators that contribute to imbalances, and identifying inconsistent fiscal, monetary and exchange rate policies. This renewed focus on multilateral cooperation to resolve long-standing imbalances, and concrete proposals for mechanisms to reduce global monetary and financial volatility, are timely. But it would be a mistake to use the current account as the indicator of choice for measuring the "sustainability" of large imbalances without considering the specific causes of those imbalances.

Furthermore, focusing on current-account imbalances alone requires consideration of all the circumstances under which exceptions might be tolerated. There are many reasons why the current account of a specific country may be in deficit or surplus at any given point in time. One reason is that the domestic economy may be growing faster than that of its main trading partners, causing imports to rise faster than exports (e.g. the United States during the 1990s). Or a country may be a major importer of a commodity, the price of which tends to rise repeatedly, thereby increasing the import bill without there being a parallel increase in export earnings (e.g. the group of low-income, food deficit countries). A third reason could be where a country experiences large increases in commodity export earnings but has a low absorptive capacity (e.g. Saudi Arabia). Finally, a country may serve as a hub for foreign firms to produce manufactures on a large scale, but, overall, its population may not have the earning capacity to consume a sufficient quantity of imports to equilibrate its exports (e.g. China). In all such cases, a short-term buffer of net capital inflows or outflows is needed to enable the smooth functioning of the international trading system. In other words, current-account imbalances per se are not indicative of a systemic problem that needs coordinated intervention. Rather, it is a loss of competitiveness at the national level which causes an unsustainable current-account deficit.

> Current-account imbalances per se are not indicative of a systemic problem that needs coordinated intervention ...

An empirical analysis of the factors that have influenced current-account reversals in the past supports the contention that exchange rates play a central role in the rebalancing process. In *TDR 2008* it was shown that, rather than being driven by autonomous savings and investment decisions of domestic and foreign agents, current-account reversals tend to be driven by external shocks on goods markets and financial markets. In particular, improvements in the current account have usually been accompanied by positive terms-of-trade shocks, a real exchange rate depreciation, or panic in the international capital markets followed by sudden stops in capital flows.

> ... rather, it is a loss of competitiveness at the national level, which causes an unsustainable current-account deficit.

The following two sections discuss current exchange rate problems and the case for a system of rules-based managed floating from two angles. They point to the need for a comprehensive macroeconomic approach that focuses on the real exchange rate and its determinants, namely the key macroeconomic prices of nominal exchange rates, wages and interest rates. Section C illustrates the curse of undesired capital flows, with reference to the recent new surge of carry-trade flows to emerging markets. Section D then discusses the problems that arise when unit labour costs start drifting apart in a regime of inflexible nominal exchange rates, with special reference to the difficulties being experienced in the eurozone, which is an example of an extreme case of exchange rate fixing.

C. Destabilizing private capital flows: back to business as usual

1. Appetite for risk and carry-trade speculation

There has been a strong rally in private capital flows to emerging markets in 2010 following their sharp drop during the financial crisis and the global recession. These flows, driven mainly by private portfolio investments, have increased particularly rapidly in Asia, Central and Eastern Europe, Latin America and sub-Saharan Africa following their initial downturn when the financial crisis erupted. Such movements are attributed to international investors' increased appetite for risk as the global economic recovery – and especially that of emerging markets – progresses. But what is meant by appetite for risk? Moreover, are short-term investments in emerging markets riskier than those in developed economies, and if so, why? A closer look at the movements of short-term capital and the economic incentives that are driving them reveals that there is a deeper reason why investors are eager for a quick comeback.

Developing and emerging market economies expect international financial markets to channel steady and reliable capital flows to their economies, for investment in fixed capital and to finance temporary shortages of financial resources. However, what they get instead are volatile and unreliable inflows that are often harmful to their sustained economic development and hamper their ability to catch up with the more developed economies. Neither a flood of capital inflows at one point in time, nor a reversal of such flows at another reflect the real needs of countries to import capital or the true state of their macroeconomic fundamentals. This is why countries' central banks have increasingly tried to shelter their economies as much as possible against the negative

impacts of such undesired and volatile capital flows. Direct intervention has become the most appropriate instrument to dampen the negative effects of this volatility. The huge stocks of foreign reserves that some major emerging countries have been piling up in the aftermath of the Asian crisis indicate that their currencies are under permanent pressure to appreciate. An appreciation would, of course, endanger their competitiveness on the world market and compromise whatever welfare effects a liberal multilateral trading system may generate.

The "appreciation wind" (IMF, 2010) that has become a common threat to many emerging market economies is driven by the more attractive rates of return on short-term financial assets in these economies.[1] There have been huge differentials in short-term nominal interest rates between emerging economies and developed economies for most of the time since the mid-1990s (chart 6.1).

Particularly remarkable has been the size and persistence of the interest rate differential between Japan and most emerging markets over the past 15 years. Interest rates in most Asian emerging markets fell significantly after the Asian financial crisis, and remained below 5 per cent and very close to those of the major developed economies. In the Latin American and Caribbean countries, particularly in Brazil, interest rates also fell, but were consistently higher than the Asian rates, at between 5 and 10 per cent.

With the aggressive monetary expansion in the United States after 2008, dollar interest rates fell to the level of Japan's. This has changed the relationship of the United States financial market with developing-country and emerging markets compared with the

Chart 6.1

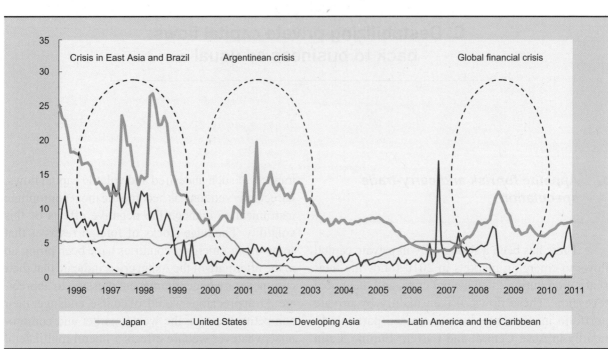

SHORT-TERM INTEREST RATE DEVELOPMENTS, JANUARY 1996–FEBRUARY 2011

(Per cent)

Source: UNCTAD secretariat calculations, based on IMF, *International Financial Statistics* database.
Note: Regional interest rate aggregates are PPP-based GDP weighted using current PPP weights.

years before the crisis. In the past, the bulk of the carry trades, which exploit the differences in short-term interest rates, used the low-yielding Japanese yen as a funding currency, while the Swiss franc was used for targets in Eastern Europe. International operators, for example a hedge fund located in the United States or in a Caribbean State, would borrow money in Japan and deposit it in Brazil, South Africa, Turkey, or, before 2008, in Iceland. The widening interest rate differential between the United States and emerging market economies has induced a switch in the funding currencies from the yen to the dollar. It is worth noting that the United States Federal Reserve's attempt to put pressure on long-term rates (i.e. quantitative easing) is likely to have played a smaller role in this context, since carry-trade returns are essentially calculated on the basis of differentials in short-term interest rates.

According to traditional theory, the market determines exchange rates according to uncovered interest rate parity (UIP), whereby high interest rates are compensated for by an expectation of a currency depreciation, or according to purchasing power parity (PPP), whereby high inflation rates are associated with an expectation of a compensating currency depreciation. However, while observed interest rates have been closely associated with inflation rates (chart 6.2) and show significant differentials between countries, there is no evidence that exchange rates adjusted to these differentials in line with theoretical considerations.

The persistence of interest rate differentials also points to the absence of an endogenous mechanism for ensuring a convergence of interest rates across national money markets. Huge inflows of short-term money do not cause a fall in the domestic interest rate in the country receiving such inflows, and neither do they cause that rate to rise in the country from where they originate. This stability of short-term rates reflects monetary policy decisions by central banks to set and to hold the short-term interest rate at a level conducive to achieving national economic objectives.

Chart 6.2

INFLATION AND SHORT-TERM INTEREST RATES IN EMERGING MARKET AND TRANSITION ECONOMIES, JANUARY 1996–FEBRUARY 2011

(Per cent)

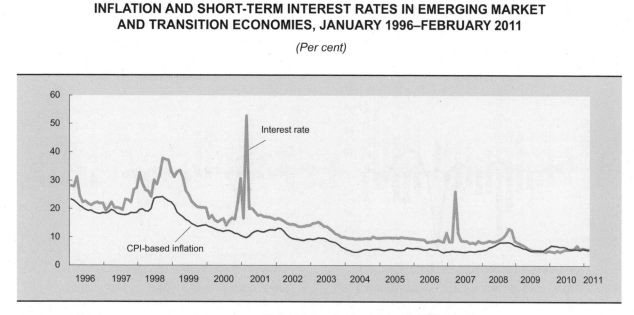

Source: UNCTAD secretariat calculations, based on IMF, *International Financial Statistics* database.

Note: Emerging market and transition economies include Brazil, Chile, Colombia, the Czech Republic, Hungary, India, Indonesia, Malaysia, Mexico, the Philippines, Poland, Romania, Singapore, South Africa, Thailand and Turkey. Emerging market averages are PPP-based GDP weighted using 2005 weights.

In order for monetary policies to successfully support national economic objectives while avoiding external disequilibrium, an effective external adjustment mechanism is needed to help central banks cope with external shocks. At present, central banks try to deal with this problem unilaterally, through intervention in the foreign exchange market, leading to accumulation of reserves, or they may impose certain restrictions on private capital inflows or outflows.

Currency market intervention and reserve accumulation have been used systematically to counter the effects of volatile capital flows (chart 6.3). In the second quarter of 2007, for example, Brazil's central bank purchased dollars, corresponding in amount to almost the entire inflow of portfolio investments and other inflows during that period. South Africa's central bank intervened similarly when the rand started to appreciate sharply in late 2009 and early 2010.

Normally, central banks are not willing to reduce short-term interest rates aggressively to discourage these inflows. As a result, capital flows of the carry-trade type are resilient, and intervention in the foreign exchange market can soon become an uphill struggle. However, there would be less need to maintain high interest rates if other instruments of macroeconomic policy, especially an incomes policy, were employed more broadly, as discussed in *TDR 2010*. Indeed adopting such instruments would enlarge the macroeconomic policy space in general, and would avoid the risk of attracting large, destabilizing short-term capital flows each time inflationary pressures occurred.

The amounts involved in carry trade have been huge in recent years, and they have dominated most of the other determinants of overall capital flows. There may be statistical limitations to establishing the full amount of such movements, but their existence and domination is the only logical explanation for the fact that, despite massive interventions, exchange rates have been moved against the fundamentals repeatedly, with interruptions only during financial crises.

Carry trade is a classical example of trading behaviour that feeds on itself. In addition to the interest rate differential, investors are also gaining from the exchange rate appreciation they themselves generate, and this further fuels carry-trade speculation. The resulting overshooting of exchange rates, as experienced over the past decade in many emerging

Chart 6.3

CHANGES IN EXCHANGE RATES AND RESERVES, AND NET PORTFOLIO INVESTMENTS, THIRD QUARTER 2005–THIRD QUARTER 2010

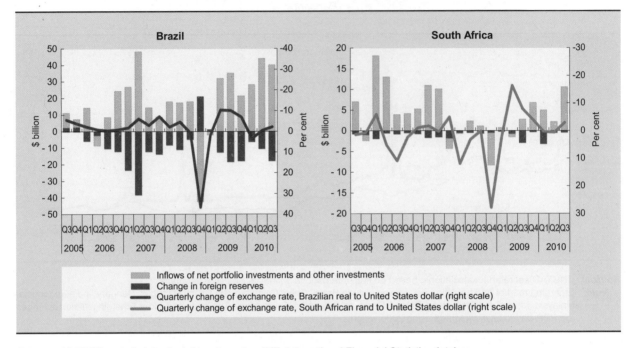

Source: UNCTAD secretariat calculations, based on IMF, *International Financial Statistics* database.

Note: A negative value of reserves means an increase in reserves (capital outflow). A positive value of the exchange rate change represents a depreciation of the currency.

Chart 6.4

NET PRIVATE FINANCIAL FLOWS (EXCLUDING FDI): EMERGING MARKET AND DEVELOPING ECONOMIES, 1990–2010

(Billions of dollars)

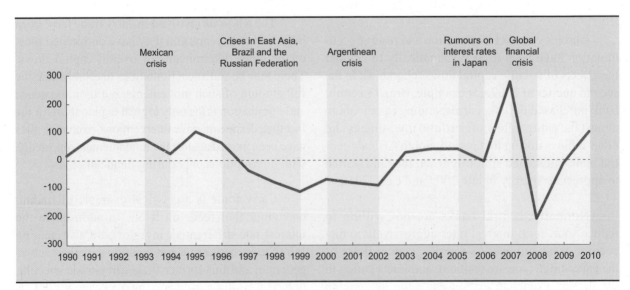

Source: UNCTAD secretariat calculations, based on IMF, *World Economic Outlook* database.

markets, is likely to have distorted trade much more than trade policy measures. It has also destabilized investment in fixed capital that is so imperative for sustained development.

With large, unstable flows in the short and medium term pointing to unsustainable outcomes in the long term, the occurrence of major shocks is just a matter of time. Over the past two decades, there have been five big shocks, with clear consequences for capital flows (chart 6.4). The first was the Mexican crisis in 1994, followed by the Asian, Russian and Brazilian crises of 1997, 1998 and 1999 respectively, and the Argentinean crisis in 2001. And in 2006, a minor crisis affected capital flows to emerging market economies as a result of rumours that Japan would increase its interest rate. Finally, the latest global crisis, sometimes referred to as the Great Recession, led to the biggest drop ever in capital flows to emerging market economies.

These shocks result in very volatile capital flows, because, in an environment where the exchange rate is moving against the fundamentals (the inflation rate or the interest rate), market participants are particularly exposed to the tail risk of their strategy. In such an environment, different events might provoke sudden reversals of flows, which are intensified by herd behaviour in the financial markets. Therefore, carry trade or investment in currencies is considered to be as risky as investment in other asset classes such as equities or commodity derivates. Whenever the evidence mounts that the bubble could soon burst, a small event suffices to start the stampede.

2. The Japanese yen and the United States dollar as funding currencies

Evidence of carry-trade activity in the spot markets is difficult to track, since detailed data on individual investors' positions and on funds that have been borrowed and deposited simply do not exist. However, in some futures markets, such as the one in the United States, market participants have to report their daily positions at the end of the trading day. This provides some indication of the net positions of non-commercial traders (pure financial traders) in currency futures markets in the United States (chart 6.5). In the chart, since data on direct

Australian dollar-Japanese yen currency futures are not available, both currencies are considered vis-à-vis the United States dollar. The bars show the number of contracts in the market, while net long positions represent the difference between long and short positions of the respective currencies vis-à-vis the United States dollar. Thus, a net long position in Australian dollars has a positive value, while a net short position has a negative value.

Overall, the data from this futures market in the United States provide clear evidence of massive yen-funded carry-trade activity from January 2005 to July 2007, a yen-funded carry-trade reversal as the global crisis unfolded from September 2008 to February 2009, and three alternating periods of net long positions in both funding and target currencies from November 2007 onwards. These periods of build-up and reversal of carry-trade positions add to the findings presented in *TDR 2008* and *TDR 2009*.

Additionally, since the third quarter of 2007 there have been net long positions in both funding and target currencies and increasing use of the United States dollar as a funding currency for carry-trade activities. This is confirmed by investors' expectations as reflected in the so-called carry-to-risk ratio, a popular *ex-ante* measure of carry-trade profitability. This ratio reflects the gains stemming from the interest rate differential adjusted by the risk of future exchange rate movements.[2] The higher the ratio, the higher is the *ex-ante* profitability of the carry-trade strategy. Until April 2008, the expected profitability of yen-funded carry trades was much higher than that of United States dollar-funded carry trades, and the carry-to-risk ratios diverged consistently (chart 6.6). However, as the financial crisis unfolded and the United States interest rate declined, the carry-to-risk ratios converged and carry trades funded in United States dollars were even perceived as being slightly more profitable than yen-funded carry trades.

This switch in the funding currencies of carry trade in futures markets shows that investors' carry-trade strategies in currency markets are driven mainly by their expectations of interest rate movements. It also suggests that the reduction of the short-term interest rates in the United States immediately after the beginning of the crisis was a much greater push factor for funding short-term capital flows in the United States than the two subsequent rounds of quantitative easing. However, the fact that more flows

Chart 6.5

NET POSITIONS OF NON-COMMERCIAL TRADERS ON AUSTRALIAN DOLLAR AND JAPANESE YEN FUTURES, JANUARY 2005–APRIL 2011

(Number of contracts, thousands)

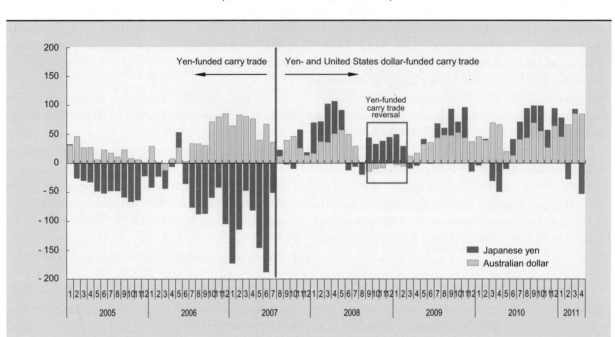

Source: UNCTAD secretariat calculations, based on Bloomberg; and United States Commodity Trading Futures Commission database.

Chart 6.6

CARRY-TO-RISK RATIO, 2005–2010

(Percentage points)

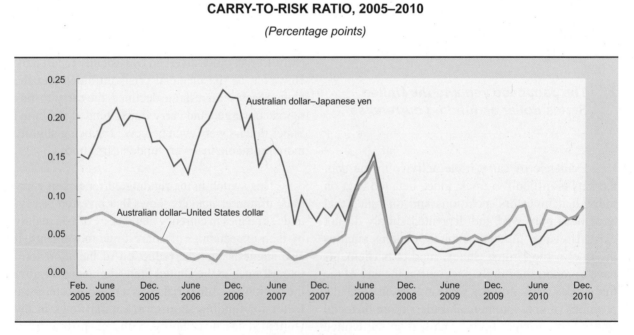

Source: UNCTAD secretariat calculations, based on Bloomberg database.

Chart 6.7

INFLATION DIFFERENTIAL AND NOMINAL AND REAL EXCHANGE RATES IN BRAZIL, JANUARY 1996–FEBRUARY 2011

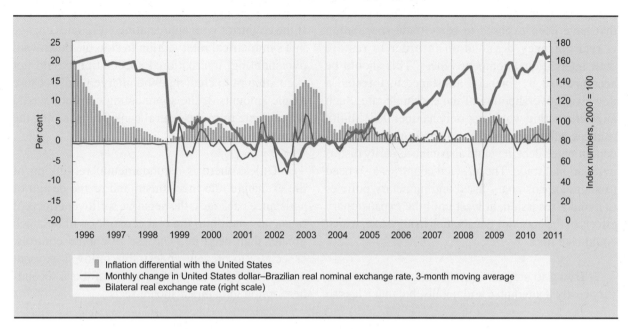

Source: UNCTAD secretariat calculations, based on IMF, *International Financial Statistics* database.

not only originated in the United States but were also financed there, rather than originating there and being raised in Japan, have not changed the fundamental logic and the consequences of carry trade in currency markets.

3. The cost of leaning against the wind of appreciation

The cost of destabilizing capital flows can be devastating. During a period when carry-trade flows are building up in developing and emerging economies, the consequent currency appreciation in those countries places an enormous burden on their external trade. For example, during most of the period between August 2005 and August 2008, the Brazilian real appreciated in nominal terms (as indicated in chart 6.3, whenever the percentage change is above zero). This amounted to a cumulative appreciation (in nominal terms) vis-à-vis the dollar of more than 45 per cent. Considering that Brazil had higher inflation rates than the United States, during that entire period, the real exchange

rate between Brazil and the United States appreciated by even more than 50 per cent (chart 6.7).

Once a crisis hits and there is a reversal of inflows, central banks try to defend the exchange rate of their currency against downward overshooting by applying restrictive monetary and fiscal policies. However such tightening – reminiscent of the procyclical policy response to the Asian crisis – has the effect of deepening the crisis or delaying economic recovery. During the Asian and Latin American crises, many countries experienced dramatic interest rate hikes. By contrast, in the United States, interest rates were cut to close to zero immediately after the dot-com crisis began in 2001 and again after the outbreak of the Great Recession in 2008 in order to stimulate the domestic economy (see chart 6.1 above).

IMF assistance, at times combined with swap agreements or direct financial assistance from the EU and the United States, has helped to ease the immediate pressure on the currencies and banking systems of troubled countries. But when the origin of the problem is speculation of the carry-trade type, the traditional IMF approach is inadequate.

Traditional assistance packages, combined with cuts in government spending, are unnecessary and tend to be counterproductive, while raising interest rates to avoid further devaluation is like the tail wagging the dog. Instead, what is needed for countries that have been exposed to carry-trade speculation is real currency devaluation in order to restore their international competitiveness. This should be accompanied by financial assistance to forestall a downward overshooting of the exchange rate. Such an overshooting would not only hamper their ability to check inflation and increase their foreign-currency-denominated debt, it would also unnecessarily distort international trade. The affected countries also need to adopt expansionary fiscal and monetary policies to avoid a recession, at least until the expansionary effects of the currency devaluation materialize, which could take time.

Trying to stop an overshooting devaluation is very costly if attempted unilaterally, but much less so if countries under pressure to devalue join forces with countries facing revaluation. Countries that are struggling to stem the tide of devaluation are in a weak position, as they have to intervene by mobilizing their foreign exchange reserves, which are always limited. If the countries with appreciating currencies engage in a symmetrical intervention to stop the downward overshooting, international speculation would not even attempt to challenge the intervention, because ample amounts of the appreciating currency would be available from the central bank that is issuing the currency.

Unless there is a fundamental rethinking of the exchange rate mechanism and of the design of assistance packages, the negative spillover effects of financial crises into the real economy will be much greater than need be. The use of capital controls, especially to prevent undesirable inflows, may not address the problem at its source, but it is a second-best option to dampen such effects.

D. Real exchange rate misalignment in the European Economic and Monetary Union

The previous section has discussed the problems arising from destabilizing capital flows, especially of the carry-trade type, in a system of flexible exchange rates and free mobility of capital. But there are other problems associated with insufficiently flexible nominal exchange rates in situations where they would need to be adjusted to reflect deviations in the development of macroeconomic fundamentals across countries. This is very clearly demonstrated by the ongoing crisis in the eurozone, where countries have adopted a common currency (i.e. the most extreme case of exchange rate fixing). In the past, other countries that maintained an inflexible exchange rate peg for too long experienced problems similar to those encountered by some eurozone countries today. However, when the real exchange rate had appreciated so much that a payments crisis occurred, those countries still had the possibility to adjust, albeit painfully, through a sharp devaluation of their nominal exchange rates – a possibility that eurozone countries do not have.

In a world of absolutely fixed exchange rates, or in a single currency area, a lasting deviation of changes in prices and unit labour costs in one country from those of its main trading partners creates unsustainable external deficits and threatens the survival of the currency arrangement. From this perspective, the crisis in the common European currency was foreseeable. Since the end of the 1990s, Germany, the largest economy of the eurozone and the main trading partner of its other members, has engaged in a vigorous

Chart 6.8

UNIT LABOUR COSTS AND GDP DEFLATOR IN EMU, 1999–2010

(Index numbers, 1999 = 100)

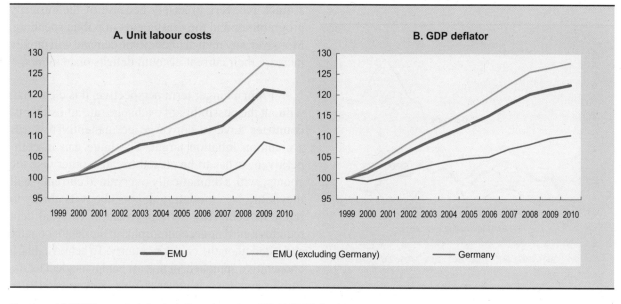

Source: UNCTAD secretariat calculations, based on *EC-AMECO* database.

Note: EMU comprises: Austria, Belgium, Finland, France, Germany, Greece, Ireland, Italy, Luxembourg, the Netherlands, Portugal and Spain.

attempt to tackle its persistently high unemployment. Traditionally, nominal wage increases in Germany had been moderate, and in line with the objective of maintaining a low but positive inflation rate of about 2 per cent. But real wages (nominal wages divided by inflation) had risen mostly in line with productivity (GDP divided by the number of hours worked). The new approach – inspired by neoclassical employment theory – sought to reduce unemployment by keeping unit labour costs from rising. This policy shift in Germany coincided with the start of the European Economic and Monetary Union (EMU). German unit labour costs – the most important determinant of prices and competitiveness – barely rose after the start of EMU (chart 6.8), resulting in a dramatic divergence of movements in unit labour costs among EMU members.

In most of the eurozone countries of Southern Europe, nominal wage growth exceeded national productivity growth and the commonly agreed inflation target of 2 per cent by a rather stable margin. France remained in the middle, with nominal wages growing perfectly in line with the national productivity

path and the inflation target of 2 per cent. However, the dynamics of such a "small" annual divergence become dramatic when it is repeated every year for over 10 years or more. Thus, at the end of the first decade of EMU the cost and price gap between Germany and the Southern European eurozone members amounted to about 25 per cent, and between Germany and France to 15 per cent. In other words, Germany's real exchange rate had depreciated quite significantly despite the absence of national currencies.

The divergent growth of unit labour costs was reflected in similar price differentials. Whereas the EMU as a whole achieved its inflation target of 2 per cent almost perfectly, there were wide variations among the member countries (chart 6.8). Again, France was by far the best performer, aligning its inflation rate perfectly with the European target, whereas Germany undershot and the eurozone countries of Southern Europe overshot the target by a wide margin. Therefore, the expectation that the European Single Market would lead to an equalization of prices through the free movement of goods, capital and labour has not been fulfilled. The accumulated gaps

Chart 6.9

CURRENT-ACCOUNT BALANCES IN EMU, 1991–2010

(Per cent of GDP)

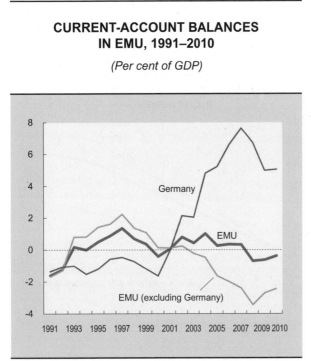

Source: UNCTAD secretariat calculations, based on *EC-AMECO* database.

Note: For member countries in EMU, see note to chart 6.8.

give Germany a significant absolute advantage in international trade and an absolute disadvantage to the other countries. A comparable product, which in 1999 was sold at the same price in the European and global markets, could be sold by Germany in 2010, on average – compared with the other countries in EMU – at a price 25 per cent lower than a decade before, without affecting the profit margin.

The significance of the huge price and cost difference accumulated over the past decade is shown by the fact that it had an enormous and cumulative impact on trade flows. With Germany undercutting the other countries by an increasing margin, its exports flourished and its imports slowed down. Meanwhile, France and the eurozone countries of Southern Europe developed widening trade and current-account deficits. While trade was reasonably balanced over many years up to the start of the currency union, the latter marks the beginning of a sustained period of rising imbalances (chart 6.9). Even after the shock of the financial crisis and its devastating effects on global trade, this trend remains unchanged: Germany's current-account surplus rose again in 2010 and is heading for a new record in 2011.

The deep recession following the crisis and the austerity programmes subsequently introduced by the deficit countries tend to reduce the deficits. However, unless these countries are able to improve their overall competitiveness, there is a rather low probability of a quick recovery precisely because of the austerity programmes and the drastic cuts in public spending. Moreover, any revival of domestic demand will rapidly increase their current-account deficits once more.

From a longer term perspective, it is clear that, without the possibility of exchange rate adjustments, countries have to converge permanently towards a common inflation target. The huge gap in competitiveness has to be closed because otherwise the country with a dramatically overvalued currency will inevitably face mounting doubts about its ability to repay its debt. Any net repayment of external debt requires a current-account surplus in the debtor country and a deficit on the creditor country. To achieve this, a cooperative approach, or at least benign neglect by the surplus countries, is indispensable (Keynes, 1919).

Countries with an unsustainable external deficit and external debt cannot go bankrupt or disappear like failed companies; they have to find ways to cope with a situation where nearly all their companies are at an absolute disadvantage against their competitors in other countries. The least costly solution would be to reduce the cost of production (i.e. mainly nominal wages) exclusively in those parts of the economy that are exposed to international competition. But this is not possible when no distinction is made in wage setting between exporting and non-exporting firms, and when most firms produce for export as well as for the domestic market. Only a depreciation of the currency would reduce wages – expressed in foreign currency – when it is needed. In this way, domestic demand would be hit less than if there was a general fall in wages, but imports would become more expensive and would tend to be replaced by domestically produced goods, while exports would become cheaper on the external market.[3]

Therefore, in EMU and similar arrangements where it is not possible to make adjustments in the nominal exchange rate, the situation is particularly complicated, because a deficit country does not have the option to devalue its nominal exchange rate. The only solution is a devaluation of the real exchange rate through a wage reduction by the country concerned relative to the wages in the competing countries that have undervalued real exchange rates. If this process has to rely exclusively on an overall wage reduction in the deficit countries it will have major negative effects on domestic demand. For example, if the eurozone countries of Southern Europe try to regain their competitiveness vis-à-vis Germany inside the EMU, their unit labour costs will have to undercut the inflation target of the union for quite some time or to a large extent. The effect for the EMU as a whole would clearly be deflationary and pose a threat to recovery, in particular if such policies are implemented in an environment where demand remains weak (see also chapter I). The process of labour cost convergence could be facilitated, and undesirable deflationary effects for the EMU as a whole avoided, if Germany's unit labour costs were to rise faster than the EMU inflation target during the period of adjustment.

The EMU experience offers lessons not only for countries within the union, but also for other countries, especially developing and emerging market economies. It shows that in order to avoid misalignments of the real exchange rate, which would have a number of negative effects, including on the international competitiveness of producers, on domestic investment in productive capacity, and thus on the entire process of industrial diversification and upgrading, it may be advisable for these countries to avoid excessively rigid exchange rate arrangements. At the same time, they should not leave the determination of their nominal exchange rate to market forces, which are frequently dominated by speculative capital movements that can generate excessive volatility.

E. Rules-based managed floating as a possible solution[4]

1. Flexibility of the nominal exchange rate

The current financial crisis has amply demonstrated the vulnerability of developing and emerging market economies that are exposed to sudden reversals of capital inflows. What is needed to contain such speculative flows and reduce their damaging impact on global economic stability is strengthened international cooperation in macroeconomic and financial policies as well as a new framework for exchange rate management. As discussed in *TDR 2009*, a system that helps prevent large movements and misalignments of the real exchange rates would promote greater stability of the conditions under which international trade is conducted and decisions on investments in real productive capacity are taken. Rules-based managed floating targeting a stable real exchange rate would serve this purpose and at the same time reduce the incentives for carry-trade speculation.

Unlike the Bretton Woods system and the similar pre-euro European Monetary System (EMS), the proposed system should be designed to prevent the build-up of large imbalances instead of correcting them after they have emerged. Both Bretton Woods and EMS were based on the idea that the member countries, in principle, would be able to achieve similar inflation targets, and that exchange rate changes would be necessary only in exceptional circumstances. By contrast, an approach aimed at stable real exchange rates while allowing for, and under certain circumstances requiring, changes in the nominal exchange rate, would not assume that countries pursue the same objectives in terms of inflation. Each country could decide autonomously on the acceptable or desirable level of inflation, but in order to prevent undesirable effects of inflation differentials on international trade and current-account balances, any emerging price and cost differentials would immediately be compensated by commensurate adjustments of the nominal exchange rate.

The exchange rate is a key variable in the conduct of both international trade and international financial transactions. Thus a system of rules-based managed floating could be built on either of the two following principles: adjustments of nominal exchange rates according to changes in purchasing power parity (PPP); or adjustments of nominal exchange rates according to uncovered interest rate parity (UIP). In the first case, the real exchange rate would be maintained by adjusting nominal exchange rates to inflation (or unit labour cost) differentials. The effect on the real exchange rate of higher inflation in one country would then be offset by a devaluation of the nominal exchange rate. In the second case, adjustments would follow the emergence of interest rate differentials between countries. As a result, the incentive for speculative capital flows in the form of significant differences between short-term interest rates, and the impact of such flows on the nominal exchange rate, would largely disappear. The real exchange rate would remain stable in both cases if inflation differentials were reflected exactly in the interest rate differentials. The first principle addresses more directly the need to avoid imbalances in trade flows, while the second is more directly related to avoiding imbalances in financial flows. However, both approaches tend to lead to a similar outcome, since differentials in official interest rates largely reflect differences in the rate of inflation, which itself is very closely correlated to changes in unit labour costs.

At least three important technical problems need to be addressed in order to implement either scheme. One is the determination of the level and range of nominal exchange rates as a starting point of this mechanism. Determining the appropriate "initial equilibrium exchange rate" will require a detailed investigation into the absolute purchasing power of all currencies. The second problem is the choice of the right indicator to measure the relevant exchange rate. In some cases there may be large differences between price and cost indicators. The third problem is the way the rules would be implemented by central banks. While the first problem is not tackled here, the following sections discuss possible solutions to the second and third problems.

> Rules-based managed floating targeting a stable real exchange rate would help create stable conditions for international trade ...

2. Towards greater stability of the real exchange rate

If the domestic prices increase, for whatever reason, the real exchange rate will appreciate because domestic goods become more expensive than foreign goods. Since a country trades not only with one but many trading partners, the real *effective* exchange rate (REER) may be the more relevant variable, since it measures the price levels of all the main trading partners, and is calculated by using the weighted average of a basket of currencies. The REER measures the overall competitiveness of a country vis-à-vis these trading partners, and a real effective appreciation implies a loss of competitiveness of the country.[5]

There can be significant differences in the measurement of the REER, depending on whether it is calculated on the basis of changes in the consumer price index (CPI) or on changes in unit labour costs (ULC). Over the longer term, ULCs (i.e. the sum of wages paid to generate one unit of a product) are the main domestic determinant of the rate of inflation (Flassbeck and Spiecker, 2007: 66–70). Chart 6.10 shows these two indicators for the four largest economies using 1995 (a year with low trade imbalances among the G-20) as the base year for the PPP path. On both counts, the REERs of Japan and Germany indicate a significant increase in competitiveness compared with the base year. Despite the persistent surpluses of these two economies and the recent nominal appreciation of the Japanese yen, their real exchange rates did not significantly appreciate in the subsequent years. On the other hand, the dollar appreciated sharply in real terms between 1995 and 2001, together with high and further rising current-account deficits. Although competitiveness in the United States has been steadily recovering since then, the 1995 level of the REER was again reached only in 2008. For all three countries the two measures move more or less in tandem, indicating that urgent policy action is required to reduce imbalances by realigning nominal exchange rates with domestic costs.

By contrast, in China the CPI-based REER has remained reasonably constant since the end of the

Chart 6.10

EVOLUTION OF CPI- AND ULC-BASED REAL EFFECTIVE EXCHANGE RATES, SELECTED COUNTRIES, 1991–2010

(Index numbers, 1995 = 100)

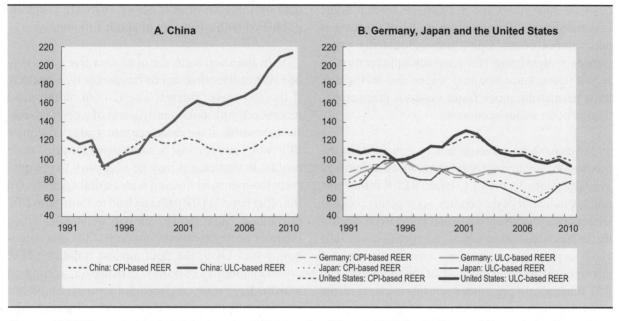

A. China

B. Germany, Japan and the United States

- - - - China: CPI-based REER ———— China: ULC-based REER

— — Germany: CPI-based REER ———— Germany: ULC-based REER
· · · · Japan: CPI-based REER ———— Japan: ULC-based REER
- - - - United States: CPI-based REER ———— United States: ULC-based REER

Source: UNCTAD secretariat calculations, based on IMF, *International Financial Statistics* database; and Economist Intelligence Unit.

1990s, but the ULC-based REER has appreciated sharply since 1994. It rose consistently and strongly between 2000 and 2010, indicating an overall loss of competitiveness of this economy by about 40 per cent during this period. While the data used for this exercise do not cover the entire Chinese labour force, there are strong indications that wages in the Chinese economy have risen rapidly in recent years (ILO, 2010). An important indication of this trend of strongly rising nominal and real wages is the booming private domestic consumption.

Thus, on the basis of the ULC-based REER over several years, a rise in China's current account has coincided with a loss of international competitiveness of its producers. This can be explained by the particularities of China's economic development over the past two decades: China is the only large economy where foreign enterprises dominate exports and imports. Affiliates of foreign firms account for more than

> … It would also facilitate decisions on investments in real productive capacity and reduce the incentives for carry-trade speculation.

60 per cent of all Chinese exports, and most of them use advanced technologies, incorporating high labour productivity and combining it with low absolute wages. This combination results in extraordinarily high profit margins and allows companies to conquer global markets by means of lower costs and prices.

Even if nominal and real wages and the ULC have been rising strongly in China over the past 10 years, the profit margins remain large enough for foreign producers to keep prices low in order to preserve market shares. This advantage of foreign investors will recede only slowly, as the process of catching up will take many years, or even decades, given the original low level of wages and low domestic capital stock in China compared with the most developed economies.

Contrary to what has been suggested by a number of prominent economists (see, for example, Bergsten, 2010), China cannot be accused of unfair behaviour in international trade on the grounds that it has been keeping its nominal exchange rate fixed. What matters for competition in international trade is not the nominal exchange rate, but the REER and how it changes, because it is the latter measure that should be used to estimate the impact of domestic costs on trade flows and imbalances. Even if some uncertainty concerning the accuracy of the data is taken into account, China has undoubtedly experienced a significant real currency appreciation in recent years, since nominal wages and real wages have been rising much faster vis-à-vis productivity than in other major economies.

Since China serves as a hub of manufacturing production, employing the most advanced technology available globally, the ULC-based REER is the most reliable indicator of the country's competitiveness. If labour costs increase sharply in relation to productivity, as has occurred in China, competitiveness falls vis-à-vis producers in countries where the increase in labour costs has been lower. If, at the same time, the REER based on a price index remains unchanged, the economic situation of producers nevertheless deteriorates, because they accept falling profit margins to maintain their trade volumes. In this case, the ULC-based REER indicates the true outcome, whereas the CPI-based REER is misleading.

3. Exchange rate adjustment according to uncovered interest rate parity

Instead of targeting the real exchange rate by referring to a PPP path, rules-based managed floating could also refer to the size of an interest rate differential also referred to as the UIP. Under this approach the nominal exchange rate would be regularly adjusted according to the difference between the domestic interest rate and the interest rate of a reference currency.

In order to prevent short-term speculative carry trade, the UIP should be based on the short-term money market rate (ideally for one month, as it is more stable than the overnight rate), which is typically closely linked to the policy rate determined by central banks. From a technical perspective, a UIP rule is easier to implement than a PPP rule. Data on interest rates are available on a daily basis, whereas data on inflation or unit labour costs are normally published with a time lag of about a month.

In the short term the outcomes from applying one rule or the other can differ markedly, especially if the short-term interest rate is used as the main macroeconomic policy instrument of a central bank. In other words, if the exchange rate is targeted along a PPP path, there can still be some scope for carry-trade profits. In that case it may be necessary to complement the managed floating with capital controls. On the other hand, a UIP path can lead to short-term PPP deviations. Such deviations will be smaller when incomes policy measures are part of the macroeconomic tool kit in the fight against inflation (*TDR 2010*, chapter V, section C). However, compared with the large short- and medium-term exchange rate swings under the current regime of flexible exchange rates, any temporary deviations of this kind would appear to be of relatively minor importance.[6]

In principle, the UIP rule may be regarded as an implicit PPP rule. However, in cases where domestic inflation, and thus the domestic policy rate, is very high, devaluation resulting from managed floating following the UIP rule would lead to a rapid rise in import prices, and thus additionally fuel inflation. In this case, applying the PPP rule based on the unit labour cost might be the more appropriate solution.

For the euro-dollar exchange rate over the past 12 years, the differences are almost negligible (chart 6.11A). For other currencies, especially those of emerging markets, the differences are larger. The choice should therefore depend on the specific circumstances of each country. Nevertheless, for a country like Brazil the application of both rules would have avoided the sharp, unjustified real appreciation (chart 6.11B).

Chart 6.11

EXCHANGE RATES OF SELECTED CURRENCIES:
ACTUAL VALUES AND SIMULATED PPP AND UIP PATHS

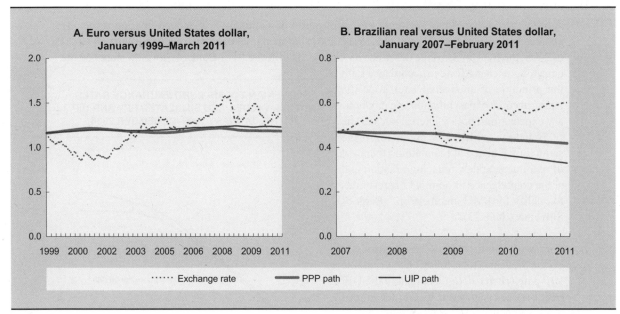

A. Euro versus United States dollar,
January 1999–March 2011

B. Brazilian real versus United States dollar,
January 2007–February 2011

······ Exchange rate   ——— PPP path   ——— UIP path

Source: UNCTAD calculations, based on Bloomberg; and IMF, *International Financial Statistics* database.

F. Limitations and effectiveness of managed floating

1. Effectiveness of intervention in foreign exchange markets

Either approach to rules-based managed floating as outlined in the previous section implies regular intervention by central banks in the foreign exchange market. An important question, therefore, is whether such intervention is feasible in view of the huge amount of transactions on today's currency markets. It has been argued that foreign exchange market interventions are not effective, and that targeting the exchange rate is not possible. This is because of the high mobility of capital and because attempts at sterilization may prove futile in view of the huge size of international capital flows. A central bank attempting to target the exchange rate through

intervention in the foreign exchange market would, sooner or later, lose control over the domestic money supply (Lee, 1997: 3).

The assertion that foreign exchange market interventions are ineffective suffers from a major methodological weakness, namely proving the counterfactual, which would require a generally accepted theory of exchange rate determination in a regime of fully flexible rates. But such a theory is simply not available. Moreover, the concrete objectives of central banks are not announced publicly and are likely to change over time, which makes it difficult to assess empirically whether interventions have delivered on the intended goal. Ineffectiveness would imply that major additional sales or purchases of an asset have no effects on its market price. This would only

Box 6.1

SLOVENIA – A CASE OF SUCCESSFUL MANAGED FLOATING

A little known example of the successful application of a strategy of managed floating is the one adopted by Slovenia (see Bohnec and Košak, 2007) before it joined the euro area. In its annual report of 2003, the Bank of Slovenia described its strategy as follows: "The Bank of Slovenia managed the euro/tolar exchange rate in accordance with the principle of uncovered interest parity, taking account of past inflation and inflationary expectations, policy interest rates of the ECB and the implicit risk premium. At the same time it aimed at maintaining the level of real interest rates, reducing inflation and at the convergence of nominal interest rates to qualify for EMU membership" (Bank of Slovenia, 2003: 23).

For many years the euro exchange rate vis-à-vis the Slovenian tolar followed a very stable UIP path (chart), being identical to the UIP path between January 1999 and the end of 2001. Thereafter, it followed a slightly flatter, but still very stable trend. From January 2004 onwards, a stable exchange rate vis-à-vis the euro was targeted, as the tolar became a member of the European Exchange Rate Mechanism II.

SLOVENIAN TOLAR–EURO EXCHANGE RATE: ACTUAL VALUES AND SIMULATED PPP AND UIP PATHS, JANUARY 1999–DECEMBER 2006

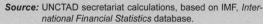

Source: UNCTAD secretariat calculations, based on IMF, *International Financial Statistics* database.

be plausible if central bank intervention triggered a change in the demand or supply of that asset by other market participants, by an amount that would exactly offset the sales or purchases by the central bank. But as central bank interventions are normally carried out secretly, systematic compensating responses by market participants are impossible.

The potential for effective interventions depends on their direction: a central bank trying to stop a depreciation of its currency is much less likely to succeed than one that is trying to stop an appreciation. To counter a depreciation tendency, a central bank has to buy its own currency on the foreign exchange market by selling foreign currency. In the present system, the scope for an intervention of this kind is limited by the amount of foreign exchange reserves accumulated over the past. Financial market participants are of course aware of this constraint, and thus may often speculate successfully against the central bank. By contrast, a central bank which aims at preventing an

appreciation of its currency buys foreign currency by selling domestic currency. As there are no limits to the supply of domestic currency, there are no quantitative barriers to such intervention, so that market participants will be discouraged from speculating persistently against this form of intervention.[7] Hence, developing and emerging market economies should target real exchange rates in a way that prevents overvaluation (see box 6.1).

2. The scope and cost of sterilization of foreign exchange market intervention

Another argument against a policy of foreign exchange market intervention concerns the potential cost of sterilization (Lee 1997:5; Bénassy-Quéré and Pisani-Ferry 2011: 30). Under normal conditions, the largest positions on the asset side of a central

Box 6.2

STERILIZED INTERVENTION AND THE BALANCE SHEET OF THE CHINESE CENTRAL BANK

The balance sheet of the People's Bank of China reflects a situation in which the central bank aims at sterilizing the liquidity effect of foreign exchange market intervention on the domestic banking system by attracting bank deposits and by issuing sterilization bonds.

SIMPLIFIED BALANCE SHEET OF THE PEOPLE'S BANK OF CHINA, DECEMBER 2010
(Billions of yuan)

Assets		Liabilities	
Foreign assets	21 542	Short-term bonds	4 050
Claims on other depository corporations	949	Monetary base	18 531
Other domestic assets	3 437	Other liabilities	3 347
Total	**25 928**	**Total**	**25 928**

Source: Balance sheet of the Monetary Authority of the People's Bank of China, Survey and Statistical database, available at: http://www.pbc.gov.cn/publish/html/2010s04.htm.

On the assets side, foreign exchange reserves account for 83 per cent of the total, while credits to depository institutions constitute only 4 per cent of the central bank's assets. On the liabilities side, 16 per cent of total liabilities are bonds. China's central bank relies heavily on minimum reserve requirements for the sterilization of foreign exchange market intervention, which explains the high share of the monetary base in total assets. Since April 2011, a record minimum reserve rate of 20 per cent is required. From the perspective of the central bank, sterilization through minimum reserves may have the advantage of avoiding interest payments to the banks. However, non-interest-bearing minimum reserves constitute an implicit tax on credit intermediation via banks, which creates a strong incentive to channel funds outside the regular banking system. This can be avoided if, as in China and a number of other countries, minimum reserves are interest-bearing (for China, see Geiger, 2008).

bank's balance sheet are refinancing credits for the domestic banking system and domestic government bonds. A central bank that buys foreign assets for a given amount has to reduce these refinancing credits by the same amount if it wants to avoid an impact of the intervention on the monetary base. On the other hand, refinancing credits for the domestic banking system are short term and can be easily adjusted, and the stock of domestic government bonds held by the central bank can be reduced at very short notice through open-market sales.

Even if upward pressure on the exchange rate is so strong that it requires a scale of intervention that exceeds the sum of refinancing credits and other domestic assets held by the central bank, the bank could still continue sterilizing the liquidity effect of foreign exchange market intervention by issuing short-term notes. Alternatively, it could offer banks the possibility to deposit the excess liquidity in an interest-bearing central bank account. In principle, both instruments could be applied without quantitative limits. The domestic banking system would thereby switch from a net-debtor to a net-creditor position vis-à-vis the central bank (see the example of the central bank of China in box 6.2). As a result, the policy rate with which the central bank controls the domestic money market rate would no longer be the rate for its refinancing operations; it would be the rate for the deposit facility or the yield that it offers for its short-term notes.

The costs of sterilized interventions are determined by interest costs and the valuation losses or gains from a central bank's foreign exchange reserves. The interest-related costs are determined by the reduced revenue from interest as a result of lower refinancing credits, plus eventual interest payments to be made by the central bank for a deposit facility or for sterilization bonds, minus interest revenue that is generated by the foreign assets acquired by the intervention. If the domestic policy rate is higher than the foreign short-term rate, the central bank indeed incurs an interest rate loss from the sterilized intervention. However, the total costs of sterilized interventions are also determined by the value of the net foreign assets. If the exchange rate is targeted along a UIP or PPP path and the domestic interest rate is higher than the foreign rate, the value of the foreign assets increases with the appreciation of the foreign currency. Thus the interest-related costs of sterilized intervention for the central bank are offset by a revaluation gain.

Assuming that the central bank had no foreign assets before the sterilized intervention, and that, consequently, the exchange rate is adjusted in line with the uncovered interest rate parity, the revaluation gains of the foreign assets compensate for the losses stemming from the difference between the interest earned on foreign exchange holdings and the cost of interest payments to domestic banks on sterilization instruments. However, there may be some costs for the economy as a whole, because, as with the value of the central bank's foreign assets, the domestic currency value of the private and public foreign debt of the country will also increase. The net effect then depends on whether the economy as whole is a net foreign debtor or a net foreign creditor. As long as a country has a high net foreign debt, it might therefore be more cautious about pursuing this strategy.

In any case, even if there are some costs involved in applying a system of managed floating based on PPP/UIP rules, these are likely to be largely outweighed by the macroeconomic gains from greater stability and predictability of the exchange rate obtained as a result of greater international competitiveness of domestic producers, more stable conditions for investment in real productive capacity, and thus faster GDP growth.

G. International cooperation on exchange rate management

Rules-based managed floating can be practiced as a unilateral exchange rate strategy, or, with much larger scope for intervention, through bilateral agreements or as a key element of regional monetary cooperation. However, the greatest benefit for international financial stability would result if the rules for managed floating were applied at the multilateral level, as part of global financial governance.

When adopted as a unilateral approach, the strategy of managed floating offers individual countries protection against the threat of carry-trade in situations where the domestic interest rate is higher than the interest rate of the country of the reference currency. This is because it considerably reduces or completely removes the risk-free profit potential of carry-trades. Thus an appreciation of the nominal and real exchange rates and its negative effects on the competiveness of the tradable sector of an economy can be avoided. It also removes the incentive for domestic debtors to incur their debt in foreign currency, when this is not indispensable for lack of foreign exchange from export earnings. The Asian crisis, but also the experiences of Iceland and some East European countries over the past decade, show the high risks associated with household and enterprise debt that is denominated in foreign currency. However, unilateral rules-based managed floating faces the constraint of limited foreign exchange reserves if pressure for depreciation arises, as discussed above. This constraint can only be overcome by cooperation between central banks. If two central banks involved in a bilateral exchange rate determination are willing to cooperate, one of them is always in a stronger position than the other because it is able to intervene with its own currency.

Bilaterally managed floating allows two countries almost perfect control over their bilateral exchange rate. As revaluation pressure on one currency is always mirrored by depreciation pressure on the other, the two countries are able to defend their bilateral parity without the reserve-related limitation of the unilateral case (symmetrical intervention). In other words, the two countries would no longer fall prey to a speculative attack against their bilateral parity. Clearly, for such a bilateral solution to work without friction, the countries should pursue relatively similar macroeconomic policies.

In a regional approach to managed floating, a group of countries could agree on a common exchange rate policy based on the rules for managed floating discussed in this chapter. They could agree on a matrix of bilateral exchange rate parities, which would be modified continuously according to PPP and/or UIP rules. The European Monetary System preceding the introduction of the euro could be considered a de facto managed floating system where the adjustments were made in a discrete way, with the German central bank intervening in favour of weaker currencies in the system, and where ample short-term intervention credits were available. A similar rules-based managed floating system could be a central component of regional monetary cooperation in parts of Asia and Latin America.

An international approach to managed floating could be established in the form of a multiple hub and spoke system. Major currencies (i.e. the dollar, euro, renminbi, yen, pound sterling) could form a mutual network of bilateral exchange rate paths based on PPP and/or UIP with a commitment to bilateral intervention when necessary. The remaining countries could choose one of the hubs as the reference currency and organize, in collaboration with the central bank of a "hub" currency country, a bilateral nominal exchange rate path. This would, of course, require a commitment by the central banks of the "hub" currency country to intervene in favour of the weaker currency countries in case of a strong devaluation pressure on the latter.

> If a currency appreciation due to speculative capital flows could be prevented, it would significantly reduce the risk of a speculative attack that could lead to depreciation pressure.

In any case, if the system could prevent a currency appreciation due to speculative capital flows, the risk of a speculative attack that could subsequently lead to depreciation pressure would be much smaller. This would also reduce the need for central banks to accumulate foreign exchange reserves as a precautionary measure as well as the need for symmetrical intervention. Nevertheless, should a depreciation pressure arise, the use of capital controls as a supplementary measure is another line of defense. Predictable exchange rates are at least as important for the functioning of the international trading system as abiding by multilaterally agreed rules for trade policy.

H. Economic policy and the role of intervention

It is clear from what has been discussed in this chapter that it is possible to create a rules-based global monetary system. Such a system would:

- Be conducive to a fair international trading system,

- Create a level playing field for companies,

- Avoid the adverse effects of competition among countries,

- Enlarge policy space for national monetary policies, and

- Minimize the frictions stemming from short-term capital flows.

A system grounded in consistent intervention by the monetary authorities based on internationally agreed rules would help sovereign States open up their economies and mutually benefit from a greater exchange of goods and services.

A well-functioning currency system is crucial because it is the valve that regulates the pressure in all parts of the system, preventing any increase in pressure in certain parts that would endanger the survival of the whole system. There is ample proof that, left to its own devices, the market is unable to set exchange rates that reflect the fundamentals of the countries wishing to exchange goods and services. International economic policy-making has often assumed that it is mainly real shocks that need to be absorbed by the international system. However, after several decades of experience, it has become abundantly clear that monetary shocks, in particular in a system of flexible exchange rates, are much more important and could be dangerous if not managed collectively. The divergence of nominal values between economies has become a much more frequent feature of the globalized economy than real divergence.

Sovereign States, some with independent central banks, may not easily be convinced to agree to the necessary monetary cooperation. This is why the main and urgent task of the international community is to find a non-partisan rule that defines the values of currencies against each other. In the current non-system, individual countries can find only temporary and pragmatic solutions to their problems of over- or undervaluation. One of them is intervention – even on a daily basis – in the currency markets; another is capital controls or taxing inflows of hot money. These measures are perfectly justified when the prevailing belief continues to be that the market is able to set the right exchange rates. However, they do not solve the most urgent issue, that of applying the "categorical imperative" of international exchange, which would require finding the international value of the currency of one country that all its trading partners could accept.

In this chapter two rules are recommended for that purpose, which are somewhat complementary. The PPP rule, based on inflation differentials, aims at ensuring a level playing field for international trade and the prevention of shocks due to the loss of competitiveness for a country as a whole. The UIP rule aims at preventing interest rate differentials and thereby minimizing short-term capital flows that use these differentials to speculate with currencies and that often have the effect of driving the value of the currency in the wrong direction (i.e. away from fundamentals) over prolonged periods of time. Whereas PPP could be called the "categorical imperative" because it directly neutralizes nominal shocks arising from inflation differentials and creates a level playing field on the monetary side of the economy, UIP is more pragmatic and can be applied for much shorter periods of time. The latter is of some significance in a world of high frequency financial trading, where market participants act in seconds to exploit price differences. In such a situation, with the UIP approach central banks can apply computer programs to steer the exchange rate with similar rapidity as the market participants so as to remove the incentive for this kind of destabilizing speculation. The PPP approach, where the fundamental data (the inflation differentials) are normally available only on a monthly basis, can be considered as the overarching medium-term rule that has to be re-established if the exchange rates based on UIP go astray due to extraordinary monetary policy actions.

While the concrete terms for such a scheme need to be discussed further, agreement could be reached on the principle. Those who reject it, for instance on the grounds that governments cannot know the correct value of a currency better than the markets, should consider the performance of financial markets and acknowledge that these markets have failed. The reason for this failure is easy to understand. Acknowledging it does not undermine the idea of the superiority of the market in finding prices in individual markets in general, but there is an important difference between financial markets and normal markets for goods and services. This difference is about information (as discussed in chapter V). Prices on goods markets are determined on the basis of bits of information that are individually available to many independent producers and consumers (for example, the atomistic market of Hayek (1949)). In financial markets there is not much individual information based on preferences; rather those markets are characterized by permanent guessing about the behaviour of all the other market participants. All market participants have more or less the same set of general information about the overall economy or a special market, but as a result,

the market is very much determined by expectations of what others will do. Such herd behaviour is a general and persistent feature of these markets, and does exactly the opposite of what is expected from an atomistic market as described by Hayek. The processing of independent individual information is replaced by guessing and eventually betting on the most probable market outcome based on the generally shared and always incomplete information about future developments. There is no reason to believe that governments or central banks cannot play this game as successfully as market participants.

As far as the currency market is concerned, governments and their respective central banks generate the most important information themselves, namely about inflation rates and interest rates. As short-term interest rates are directly set by central banks with the aim of achieving a given inflation target, it would be absurd to argue that the market knows better than two central banks what the right relative price is between their two currencies. In the same efficient way as they can set national targets and use their instruments to achieve them, the central banks can also determine the price between the two currencies. Clearly, the price they could regularly agree upon will be the UIP- or the PPP-based price.

Hence, intervention by governments and central banks in financial markets should not be seen as an exception to the rule of free markets, but rather, as a means of making the market function more efficiently. Experience has shown that by leaving the most important macroeconomic prices (e.g. the exchange rate, the interest rate and the wage rate) entirely to market forces, there is a high probability of strong destabilizing effects, which will eventually require even more far-reaching government intervention. ∎

> Intervention by governments and central banks in financial markets should not be seen as an exception to the rule of free markets, but as a means of making the markets function more efficiently.

Notes

1 Many developing countries are not receiving such short-term flows, and are therefore less susceptible to appreciation pressure, despite their higher interest rates. This is because, given the high transaction costs in these countries, there would have to be a very large interest rate differential to make the transaction profitable. Those high costs are due to the lack of an adequate financial infrastructure that enables or facilitates short-term financial placements, or because market participants may be concerned about the safety of such investments in some of the countries.

2 The ratio is defined as the three-month interest rate differential between the target and funding currency divided by the one-month implied volatility of the bilateral exchange rate.

3 In any case, real wages fall across the board in the depreciating country to the extent that inflation tends to rise with higher import prices.

4 This section benefits from a background paper by Bofinger, 2011.

5 In this analysis, references to real exchange rates refer to real effective exchange rates.

6 Over the medium term, the difference between the two approaches is not significant. Taking the case of two countries, for the sake of simplicity, it can be assumed that in both countries the policy interest rate (i) is determined according to the following Taylor rule: $i = r + \pi + 0.5\,(\pi - \pi^T) + 0.5\,y$. If both countries use the same rule, and assuming that over the medium term the output gap (y) and the inflation gap (i.e. the difference between the actual inflation rate (π) and the inflation target (π^T)) are zero, and that the real interest rate (r) is identical, the differences between the nominal interest rates and the inflation rates are identical.

7 As the central bank can create the liabilities with which it acquires foreign reserves *ex nihilo*, it is not correct to say that sterilized interventions "divert savings that could be harnessed for more productive uses" (Bénassy-Quéré and Pisani-Ferry, 2011: 31; see also *TDR 2009*, chapter IV, box 4.2).

References

Bank of Slovenia (2003). Annual Report 2003. Ljubljana, Slovenia. Available at: http://www.bsi.si/iskalniki/letna_porocila_en.asp?MapaId=711.

Bénassy-Quéré A and Pisani-Ferry J (2011). What international monetary system for a fast-changing world economy? Bruegel Working Paper No. 06, April Brussels.

Bergsten CF (2010). Correcting the Chinese exchange rate. Testimony before the Hearing on China's Exchange Rate Policy, Committee on Ways and Means, United States House of Representatives, 15 September. Available at: http://www.iie.com/publications/testimony/bergsten20100915.pdf.

Bofinger P (2011). The scope for foreign exchange market interventions. Mimeo. Background paper prepared for UNCTAD's *Trade and Development Report, 2011.*

Bohnec D and Košak M (2007). Central Bank Sterilization Policy: The Experiences of Slovenia and Lessons for Countries in Southeastern Europe. In: Proceedings of OeNB Workshops. Oesterreichische Nationalbank, Workshop No. 12, March. Available at: http://www.oenb.at/de/img/workshop_12_tcm14-65927.pdf.

Flassbeck H and Spiecker F (2007). Das Ende der Massenarbeitslosigkeit, Mit richtiger Wirtschaftspolitik die Zukunft gewinnen. Frankfurt, Westend.

G-20 Communiqué (2010). Meeting of Finance Ministers and Central Bank Governors, Gyeongju, Republic of Korea, 23 October 2010. Available at: www.g20.utoronto.ca/2010/g20finance101023.pdf.

Geiger M (2008). Instruments of Monetary Policy in China and their Effectiveness: 1994–2006. UNCTAD Discussion Paper No. 187, February, United Nations Conference on Trade and Development, Geneva.

Hayek FA (1949). *Individualism and Economic Order.* London, Routledge and Kegan Paul.

ILO (International Labour Office) (2010). Global Wage Report 2010/11: Wage Policies in Times of Crisis. Geneva.

IMF (2010). Regional Economic Outlook, Western Hemisphere, October, Washington, DC.

Keynes M (1919). The Economic Consequences of the Peace, In: Johnson E and Moggridge D, eds. (1971), *The Collected Writings of John Maynard Keynes*, vol.II. London and Basingstoke, Macmillan.

Lee JY (1997). Sterilizing capital inflows. *Economic Issues* No. 7. Washington, DC, International Monetary Fund.

UNCTAD (*TDR 2008*). *Trade and Development Report, 2008. Commodity prices, capital flows and the financing of investment.* United Nations publications, Sales No. E. 08.II.D.21, New York and Geneva.

UNCTAD (*TDR 2009*). *Trade and Development Report, 2009. Responding to the global crisis: Climate change mitigation and development.* United Nations publications, Sales No. E. 09.II.D.16, New York and Geneva.

UNCTAD (*TDR 2010*). *Trade and Development Report, 2010. Employment, globalization and development.* United Nations publications, Sales No. E. 10.II.D.3, New York and Geneva.

**UNITED NATIONS CONFERENCE
ON TRADE AND DEVELOPMENT**

Palais des Nations
CH-1211 GENEVA 10
Switzerland
(www.unctad.org)

Selected UNCTAD Publications

Trade and Development Report, 2010   United Nations publication, sales no. E.10.II.D.3
Employment, globalization and development   ISBN 978-92-1-112807-9

Chapter   I   After the Global Crisis: An Uneven and Fragile Recovery

                Annex: Credit Default Swaps

Chapter   II   Potential Employment Effects of a Global Rebalancing

                Annex: Simulation of the Trade and Employment Effects of Global Rebalancing:
                          A Technical Note

Chapter III Macroeconomic Aspects of Job Creation and Unemployment

Chapter IV Structural Change and Employment Creation in Developing Countries

Chapter   V   Revising the Policy Framework for Sustained Growth, Employment Creation and
               Poverty Reduction

Trade and Development Report, 2009   United Nations publication, sales no. E.09.II.D.16
Responding to the global crisis   ISBN 978-92-1-112776-8
Climate change mitigation and development

Chapter   I   The Impact of the Global Crisis and the Short-term Policy Response

                Annex: The Global Recession Compounds the Food Crisis

Chapter   II   The Financialization of Commodity Markets

Chapter III Learning from the Crisis: Policies for Safer and Sounder Financial Systems

Chapter IV Reform of the International Monetary and Financial System

Chapter   V   Climate Change Mitigation and Development

Trade and Development Report, 2008   United Nations publication, sales no. E.08.II.D.21
Commodity prices, capital flows and the financing of investment   ISBN 978-92-1-112752-2

Chapter   I   Current Trends and Issues in the World Economy
                Annex table to chapter I

Chapter   II   Commodity Price Hikes and Instability

Chapter III   International Capital Flows, Current-Account Balances and Development Finance
                Annex: Econometric Analyses of Determinants of Expansionary and Contractionary
                          Current-account Reversals

Chapter   IV   Domestic Sources of Finance and Investment in Productive Capacity

Chapter   V   Official Development Assistance for the MDGs and Economic Growth
                Annex: Details on Econometric Studies

Chapter   VI   Current Issues Related to the External Debt of Developing Countries

Trade and Development Report, 2007   United Nations publication, sales no. E.07.II.D.11
Regional cooperation for development   ISBN 978-92-1-112721-8

Chapter   I   Current Issues in the World Economy
                Statistical annex to chapter I

Chapter   II   Globalization, Regionalization and the Development Challenge

Chapter III   The "New Regionalism" and North-South Trade Agreements

Chapter   IV   Regional Cooperation and Trade Integration Among Developing Countries

Chapter   V   Regional Financial and Monetary Cooperation
                Annex 1   The Southern African Development Community
                Annex 2   The Gulf Cooperation Council

Chapter   VI   Regional Cooperation in Trade Logistics, Energy and Industrial Policy

Trade and Development Report, 2006   United Nations publication, sales no. E.06.II.D.6
Global partnership and national policies for development   ISBN 92-1-112698-3

Chapter   I   Global Imbalances as a Systemic Problem
                Annex 1: Commodity Prices and Terms of Trade
                Annex 2: The Theoretical Background to the Saving/Investment Debate

Chapter   II   Evolving Development Strategies – Beyond the Monterrey Consensus

Chapter III   Changes and Trends in the External Environment for Development
                Annex tables to chapter III

Chapter   IV   Macroeconomic Policy under Globalization

Chapter   V   National Policies in Support of Productive Dynamism

Chapter   VI   Institutional and Governance Arrangements Supportive of Economic Development

Trade and Development Report, 2005   United Nations publication, sales no. E.05.II.D.13
New features of global interdependence   ISBN 92-1-112673-8

Chapter   I   Current Issues in the World Economy

Chapter   II   Income Growth and Shifting Trade Patterns in Asia

Chapter III   Evolution in the Terms of Trade and its Impact on Developing Countries
                Annex: Distribution of Oil and Mining Rent: Some Evidence from Latin America, 1999–2004

Chapter   IV   Towards a New Form of Global Interdependence

The Global Economic Crisis:
Systemic Failures and Multilateral Remedies
Report by the UNCTAD Secretariat Task Force
on Systemic Issues and Economic Cooperation

United Nations publication, sales no. E.09.II.D.4
ISBN 978-92-1-112765-2

Chapter   I   A crisis foretold

Chapter   II   Financial regulation: fighting today's crisis today

Chapter   III   Managing the financialization of commodity futures trading

Chapter   IV   Exchange rate regimes and monetary cooperation

Chapter   V   Towards a coherent effort to overcome the systemic crisis

* * * * * *

The Financial and Economic Crisis of 2008-2009
and Developing Countries
Edited by Sebastian Dullien, Detlef J. Kotte,
Alejandro Márquez and Jan Priewe

United Nations publication, sales no. E.11.II.D.11
ISBN 978-92-1-112818-5

Introduction

The Crisis – Transmission, Impact and Special Features

Jan Priewe
What Went Wrong? Alternative Interpretations of the Global Financial Crisis

Daniela Magalhães Prates and Marcos Antonio Macedo Cintra
The Emerging-market Economies in the Face of the Global Financial Crisis

Jörg Mayer
The Financialization of Commodity Markets and Commodity Price Volatility

Sebastian Dullien
Risk Factors in International Financial Crises: Early Lessons from the 2008-2009 Turmoil

The Crisis – Country and Regional Studies

Laike Yang and Cornelius Huizenga
China's Economy in the Global Economic Crisis: Impact and Policy Responses

Abhijit Sen Gupta
Sustaining Growth in a Period of Global Downturn: The Case of India

André Nassif
Brazil and India in the Global Economic Crisis: Immediate Impacts and Economic Policy Responses

Patrick N. Osakwe
Africa and the Global Financial and Economic Crisis: Impacts, Responses and Opportunities

Looking Forward – Policy Agenda

Alejandro Márquez
The Report of the Stiglitz Commission: A Summary and Comment

Ricardo Ffrench-Davis
Reforming Macroeconomic Policies in Emerging Economies: From Procyclical to Countercyclical Approaches

Jürgen Zattler
A Possible New Role for Special Drawing Rights In and Beyond the Global Monetary System

Detlef J. Kotte
The Financial and Economic Crisis and Global Economic Governance

* * * * * *

These publications may be obtained from bookstores and distributors throughout the world. Consult your bookstore or write to United Nations Publications/Sales Section, Palais des Nations, CH-1211 Geneva 10, Switzerland, fax: +41-22-917.0027, e-mail: unpubli@un.org; or United Nations Publications, Two UN Plaza, DC2-853, New York, NY 10017, USA, telephone +1-212-963.8302 or +1-800-253.9646, fax: +1-212-963.3489, e-mail: publications@un.org. Internet: http://www.un.org/publications.

Regional Monetary Cooperation and Growth-enhancing Policies:
The new challenges for Latin America and the Caribbean
United Nations publication, UNCTAD/GDS/2010/1

Chapter   I   What Went Wrong? An Analysis of Growth and Macroeconomic Prices in Latin America

Chapter   II   Regional Monetary Cooperation for Growth-enhancing Policies

Chapter   III   Regional Payment Systems and the SUCRE Initiative

Chapter   IV   Policy Conclusions

* * * * * *

Price Formation in Financialized Commodity Markets: The role of information
United Nations publication, UNCTAD/GDS/2011/1

1.   Motivation of this Study

2.   Price Formation in Commodity Markets

3.   Recent Evolution of Prices and Fundamentals

4.   Financialization of Commodity Price Formation

5.   Field Survey

6.   Policy Considerations and Recommendations

7.   Conclusions

* * * * * *

These publications are available on the website at: www.unctad.org. Copies may be obtained from the Publications Assistant, Macroeconomic and Development Policies Branch, Division on Globalization and Development Strategies, United Nations Conference on Trade and Development (UNCTAD), Palais des Nations, CH-1211 Geneva 10, Switzerland; fax +41-22-917-0274.

UNCTAD Discussion Papers

No. 202	June 2011	Pilar FAJARNES	An overview of major sources of data and analyses relating to physical fundamentals in international commodity markets
No. 201	Feb. 2011	Ulrich HOFFMANN	Assuring food security in developing countries under the challenges of climate change: Key trade and development issues of a fundamental transformation of agriculture
No. 200	Sep. 2010	Jörg MAYER	Global rebalancing: Effects on trade flows and employment
No. 199	June 2010	Ugo PANIZZA, Federico STURZENEGGER and Jeromin ZETTELMEYER	International government debt
No. 198	April 2010	Lee C. BUCHHEIT G. MITU GULATI	Responsible sovereign lending and borrowing
No. 197	March 2010	Christopher L. GILBERT	Speculative influences on commodity futures prices 2006–2008
No. 196	Nov. 2009	Michael HERRMANN	Food security and agricultural development in times of high commodity prices
No. 195	Oct. 2009	Jörg MAYER	The growing interdependence between financial and commodity markets
No. 194	June 2009	Andrew CORNFORD	Statistics for international trade in banking services: Requirements, availability and prospects
No. 193	Jan. 2009	Sebastian DULLIEN	Central banking, financial institutions and credit creation in developing countries
No. 192	Nov. 2008	Enrique COSIO-PASCAL	The emerging of a multilateral forum for debt restructuring: The Paris Club
No. 191	Oct. 2008	Jörg MAYER	Policy space: What, for what, and where?
No. 190	Oct. 2008	Martin KNOLL	Budget support: A reformed approach or old wine in new skins?
No. 189	Sep. 2008	Martina METZGER	Regional cooperation and integration in sub-Saharan Africa
No. 188	March 2008	Ugo PANIZZA	Domestic and external public debt in developing countries
No. 187	Feb. 2008	Michael GEIGER	Instruments of monetary policy in China and their effectiveness: 1994–2006
No. 186	Jan. 2008	Marwan ELKHOURY	Credit rating agencies and their potential impact on developing countries
No. 185	July 2007	Robert HOWSE	The concept of odious debt in public international law
No. 184	May 2007	André NASSIF	National innovation system and macroeconomic policies: Brazil and India in comparative perspective
No. 183	April 2007	Irfan ul HAQUE	Rethinking industrial policy
No. 182	Oct. 2006	Robert ROWTHORN	The renaissance of China and India: Implications for the advanced economies

* * * * * *

UNCTAD Discussion Papers are available on the website at: www.unctad.org. Copies of *UNCTAD Discussion Papers* may be obtained from the Publications Assistant, Macroeconomic and Development Policies Branch, Division on Globalization and Development Strategies, United Nations Conference on Trade and Development (UNCTAD), Palais des Nations, CH-1211 Geneva 10, Switzerland; fax +41-22-917-0274.

G-24 Discussion Paper Series

Research papers for the Intergovernmental Group of Twenty-Four
on International Monetary Affairs and Development

No. 59	June 2010	Andrew CORNFORD	Revising Basel 2: The Impact of the Financial Crisis and Implications for Developing Countries
No. 58	May 2010	Kevin P. GALLAGHER	Policy Space to Prevent and Mitigate Financial Crises in Trade and Investment Agreements
No. 57	December 2009	Frank ACKERMAN	Financing the Climate Mitigation and Adaptation Measures in Developing Countries
No. 56	June 2009	Anuradha MITTAL	The 2008 Food Price Crisis: Rethinking Food Security Policies
No. 55	April 2009	Eric HELLEINER	The Contemporary Reform of Global Financial Governance: Implications of and Lessons from the Past
No. 54	February 2009	Gerald EPSTEIN	Post-war Experiences with Developmental Central Banks: The Good, the Bad and the Hopeful
No. 53	December 2008	Frank ACKERMAN	Carbon Markets and Beyond: The Limited Role of Prices and Taxes in Climate and Development Policy
No. 52	November 2008	C.P. CHANDRASEKHAR	Global Liquidity and Financial Flows to Developing Countries: New Trends in Emerging Markets and their Implications
No. 51	September 2008	Ugo PANIZZA	The External Debt Contentious Six Years after the Monterrey Consensus
No. 50	July 2008	Stephany GRIFFITH-JONES with David GRIFFITH-JONES and Dagmar HERTOVA	Enhancing the Role of Regional Development Banks
No. 49	December 2007	David WOODWARD	IMF Voting Reform: Need, Opportunity and Options
No. 48	November 2007	Sam LAIRD	Aid for Trade: Cool Aid or Kool-Aid
No. 47	October 2007	Jan KREGEL	IMF Contingency Financing for Middle-Income Countries with Access to Private Capital Markets: An Assessment of the Proposal to Create a Reserve Augmentation Line
No. 46	September 2007	José María FANELLI	Regional Arrangements to Support Growth and Macro-Policy Coordination in MERCOSUR
No. 45	April 2007	Sheila PAGE	The Potential Impact of the Aid for Trade Initiative
No. 44	March 2007	Injoo SOHN	East Asia's Counterweight Strategy: Asian Financial Cooperation and Evolving International Monetary Order
No. 43	February 2007	Devesh KAPUR and Richard WEBB	Beyond the IMF
No. 42	November 2006	Mushtaq H. KHAN	Governance and Anti-Corruption Reforms in Developing Countries: Policies, Evidence and Ways Forward
No. 41	October 2006	Fernando LORENZO and Nelson NOYA	IMF Policies for Financial Crises Prevention in Emerging Markets
No. 40	May 2006	Lucio SIMPSON	The Role of the IMF in Debt Restructurings: Lending Into Arrears, Moral Hazard and Sustainability Concerns
No. 39	February 2006	Ricardo GOTTSCHALK and Daniela PRATES	East Asia's Growing Demand for Primary Commodities – Macroeconomic Challenges for Latin America

* * * * * *

G-24 Discussion Paper Series are available on the website at: www.unctad.org. Copies of *G-24 Discussion Paper Series* may be obtained from the Publications Assistant, Macroeconomic and Development Policies Branch, Division on Globalization and Development Strategies, United Nations Conference on Trade and Development (UNCTAD), Palais des Nations, CH-1211 Geneva 10, Switzerland; fax +41-22-917-0274.

QUESTIONNAIRE

Trade and Development Report, 2011

In order to improve the quality and relevance of the Trade and Development Report, the UNCTAD secretariat would greatly appreciate your views on this publication. Please complete the following questionnaire and return it to:

Readership Survey
Division on Globalization and Development Strategies
UNCTAD
Palais des Nations, Room E.10009
CH-1211 Geneva 10, Switzerland
Fax: (+41) (0)22 917 0274
E-mail: tdr@unctad.org

Thank you very much for your kind cooperation.

1. What is your assessment of this publication?

	Excellent	*Good*	*Adequate*	*Poor*
Overall	☐	☐	☐	☐
Relevance of issues	☐	☐	☐	☐
Analytical quality	☐	☐	☐	☐
Policy conclusions	☐	☐	☐	☐
Presentation	☐	☐	☐	☐

2. What do you consider the strong points of this publication?

_____
_____
_____

3. What do you consider the weak points of this publication?

_____
_____
_____

4. For what main purposes do you use this publication?

Analysis and research	☐	Education and training	☐
Policy formulation and management	☐	Other (*specify*) _____	

5. Which of the following best describes your area of work?

Government	☐	Public enterprise	☐
Non-governmental organization	☐	Academic or research	☐
International organization	☐	Media	☐
Private enterprise institution	☐	Other (*specify*) _____	

6. Name and address of respondent (*optional*):

_____
_____
_____

7. Do you have any further comments?

_____
_____
_____